CADOGANguides

take the kids
Short breaks
from London

JOSEPH FULLMAN

About the series

take the kids guides are written specifically for parents, grandparents and carers.
In fact, they're the perfect companion for anyone who cares for or about children.
Each guide not only draws on what is of particular interest to kids, but also takes into
account the realities of childcare – from tired legs to low boredom thresholds –
enabling both grown-ups and their charges to have a great day out or a fabulous holiday.

Cadogan Guides
Network House, 1 Ariel Way, London W12 7SL
cadoganguides@morrispub.co.uk
www.cadoganguides.com

The Globe Pequot Press
PO Box 480, Guilford,
Connecticut 06437–0480

Copyright © Cadogan Guides
Maps © Cadogan Guides,
Maps based on Ordnance Survey mapping with the
kind permission of the Controller of Her Majesty's
Stationery Office, and drawn by Map Creation Ltd

Art direction: Sarah Rianhard-Gardner
Cover design: Kicca Tommasi
Series design: Andrew Barker
Snapshots of southern England: Tracey Ridgewell
Original Photography: Travel Pictures
www.travelpictures.co.uk

Editorial Director: Vicki Ingle
Series Editor: Melanie Dakin
Series Consultant: Helen Truszkowski
Author: Joseph Fullman
Series Assistant: Tori Perrot

Proofreading: Vanessa Raison
Indexing: Isobel McLean
Production: Book Production Services
Printed and bound in Italy by Legoprint.
A catalogue record for this book is available
from the British Library
ISBN 1-86011-8763

The author and publishers have made every effort
to ensure the accuracy of the information in this
book at the time of going to press. However, they
cannot accept any responsibility for any loss, injury
or inconvenience resulting from the use of information contained in the guide.

Please help us to keep this guide up to date.
We have done our best to ensure that information
is correct at the time of printing, but places and
facilities are constantly changing, and standards and
prices fluctuate. We will be delighted to receive your
comments concerning existing entries or omissions.
Authors of the best letters will receive a copy of the
Cadogan Guide of their choice.

About the authors

Joseph Fullman

Joseph Fullman is a professional travel writer who has lived in London all his life and cherishes happy childhood memories of traipsing around the country with his determinedly enthusiastic mum and dad. He is the author of Cadogan's *take the kids England*, Navigator Guides: *Britain's Top Tourist Attractions* and co-author of *take the kids Paris & Disneyland® Resort Paris*, as well as guides to Britain's steam railways and London's markets. He has also contributed various articles to newspapers, websites and WAP guides.

Series consultant

Helen Truszkowski is series consultant of Cadogan's *take the kids* series, and author of *take the kids Travelling* and of *take the kids Paris & Disneyland® Resort Paris*. Helen is an established travel writer and photographer. Over the past decade her journeys have taken her around the globe, including six months working in South Africa. She contributes to a range of magazines worldwide, and is a former travel editor of *Executive Woman* magazine. Helen's seven-year-old son, George, has accompanied her on her travels since he was a few weeks old.

Series editor

Melanie Dakin is series editor of Cadogan's *take the kids* series, having previously acted as consultant editor on the Time Out *London for Children* guide and editor of *Kids Out* magazine. As a mother of two and with family both north and south of the capital, Melanie has spent a great deal of time on trains and other modes of transport with children, pushchairs, toys and luggage. To date only a couple of baby bottles and a small coolbag have been left behind.

Contents

Snapshots
of southern England

Festival fun

There's loads to see and do throughout the year in southern England. At Easter, egg hunts and trails take place between the end of March and beginning of April, often in the beautiful grounds of National Trust and English Heritage properties. Air shows, outdoor concerts, fairs and festivals are numerous in summer, which is also the time to enjoy the seaside and outdoor swimming pools. Museums and other attractions put on extra kids' entertainment to coincide with all the major holidays, so you'll never be stuck for something to do, even if it rains. As the nights draw in, you can make the dark hours count by paying a visit to a spooky location for a Hallowe'en party. November brings us Guy Fawkes night with bonfires galore in most local towns, some with the added fun of fireworks, lantern parades or a fairground. And to round the year off, there's a host of Christmas spectacles too, with Christmas lights and Santa's grottoes in every town and shopping centre and the *Santa Express* on many a steam railway. All in all, we think you'll agree, its a very entertaining timetable.

All events listed below are detailed under the relevant counties.

Babel Project, Bath – All Year

Babel is a literature and visual arts festival aimed at older children, aged from about 13 upwards. It's a fairly new event that encourages children to get involved in writing, drama, dance, film and art through year-round projects and live events.

Bath International Music Festival – May

Bath has hosted a music festival since the 1950s. Originally focusing on classical, it now embraces most forms of music including Jazz, World and Contemporary.

Brighton Festival – May

England's largest mixed arts festival is a three week long extravaganza. There's an awful lot to see and do and there are many events specifically aimed at kids, such as the young circus troupe, costumed children's parade and festival of family fun.

Windsor Horse Show – May

During World War II, a couple of highly motivated citizens, Count Robert Orssich and Geoffrey Cross, organised a horse and dog show to raise funds for the war effort.

The turnout was impressive and included the Royal Family. The dogs, however, didn't last long as a permanent fixture in the show. Apparently, the Count's mischievous pooch stole a chicken leg from the King's plate. As a result, dogs were banned from the event, which may seem a bit harsh on the rest of the canine population. It is now a prestigious equestrian event, combining entertainment with fierce competition.

Stilton Rolling – May

Sadly, real blocks of Stilton are not used in this race. Instead, far more practical wooden 'cheeses' are rolled through the streets of Stilton guided by enthusiastic teams. Started in the 1960s to help revive the town's fortunes, the cheesy event now draws quite a crowd. Incidentally, Stilton cheese has never been made in Stilton. It was brought from Leicestershire to the town by a local innkeeper

who loaded it on to coaches bound for London. As its popularity grew, it became Stilton cheese by association.

Biggin Hill Air Fair – June

Flying displays have been a taking place on Biggin Hill since the 1920s and the RAF base here played a key part in air battles in both world wars. World War I aircraft, World War II fighter and bomber planes through to modern planes are all on display, as well as collections of aviatory memorabilia. The Red Arrows usually put in an acrobatic appearance, demonstrating their considerable aeronautical skills.

Blenheim Palace Fireworks – June

This stunning palace was the birthplace of Winston Churchill in 1874 and hosts a fantastic annual firework display.

Broadstairs Dickens Festival – June

Dickens spent time visiting Broadstairs and wrote a large chunk of one of his most famous novels, *David Copperfield*, there. The custom of turning back the clock to the Victorian era for nine days every June dates back to 1937, the centenary of Dickens' first visit to the town. There are concerts, craft markets, plays, fairs and Punch and Judy shows, plus the spectacle of the townspeople in full Victorian garb. You're welcome to join them, or you can just stick to your jeans and T-shirts.

Royal Norfolk Show – June

The UK's largest annual agricultural show has numerous craft stands, exhibitions, displays of farm machinery and, of course, animals. A junior farm, sheep shearing competitions and dog shows will keep the kids amused, and even the boldest will be awed by the enormous Shire horses.

Glastonbury Children's Festival – July

This 4-day event features a whole host of activities for kids. There are puppet shows, clowns, jugglers and trampolinists, storytellers, workshops and talent shows. Just be sure to have lots of fun.

Henley Royal Regatta – July

The Regatta's been going since 1839 and the 'royal' title was bestowed in 1852 when Prince Albert became the Regatta's first royal patron. Originally more of a fair, Henley is now a key date in competitive amateur rowing.

7

Chichester Festivities – July

Back in 1975, Chichester Cathedral held a lavish party to celebrate its 900-year centenary. What was meant to be a one-off event proved so popular that it's still going strong and gets bigger and bigger every year. There are concerts, street art exhibitions, parades, firework displays, circus shows and even breakdancing workshops.

Bristol Balloon Fiesta – August

The Fiesta started in 1978 and is now the largest hot air balloon festival in Europe. The Special Shapes Fiesta will delight kids, who'll have great fun spotting giant inflatable versions of Thomas the Tank Engine, Bertie Bassett the Liquorice All-Sorts Man and the infamous Coca-Cola bottle.

Rye Medieval Festival – August

Return to life in the Middle Ages at this weekend event. Knights, maidens and minstrels wander the streets, while market stalls serve up traditional crafts and spit-roast pig. It may seem a slightly eccentric idea, but it certainly is a big hit with the kids. You might even want to dress up too.

Leeds Castle Balloon and Vintage Car Weekend – September

The grounds of Leeds Castle make a great setting for this event. Alongside the assortment of regular and novelty shaped balloons, there are aerial performances from a parachute formation display team, show cars and ballooning demonstrations. The vintage cars then speed off to rescue the balloonists from wherever they've landed.

Morris Dancing – September

One of the most bizarre dances you're ever likely to see. Why a group of men decided to dress in white, cover themselves in bells and jig around waving sticks and hankies, no one is quite sure. Morris Dancing is known to date back to at least the 15th century and is associated with the Cotswold area; Stow-on-the-Wold hosts an annual celebration. It's probably a fertility ritual, but with different theories flying around, it's easier just to sit back and watch the (baffling) fun.

Cheltenham Literature Festival – October

This long-running celebration of literature began in 1949 as a small gathering of writers organised by author John Moore. It now attracts an audience of over 40,000; not bad for something that started out as a gathering for a few friends. The kids' events come under the title 'Book It!' and include meetings with popular children's authors and characters from books, as well as play readings and storytelling sessions.

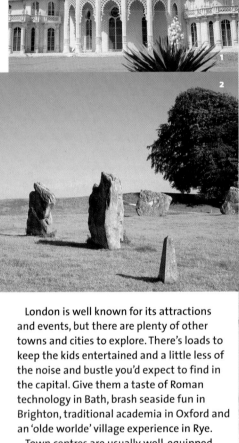

London is well known for its attractions and events, but there are plenty of other towns and cities to explore. There's loads to keep the kids entertained and a little less of the noise and bustle you'd expect to find in the capital. Give them a taste of Roman technology in Bath, brash seaside fun in Brighton, traditional academia in Oxford and an 'olde worlde' village experience in Rye.

Town centres are usually well-equipped with shopping facilities, places to eat, cinemas and sports centres. Parks and public gardens are another common feature, which are great if you're feeling in need of a bit of nature without straying too deep into the surrounding countryside.

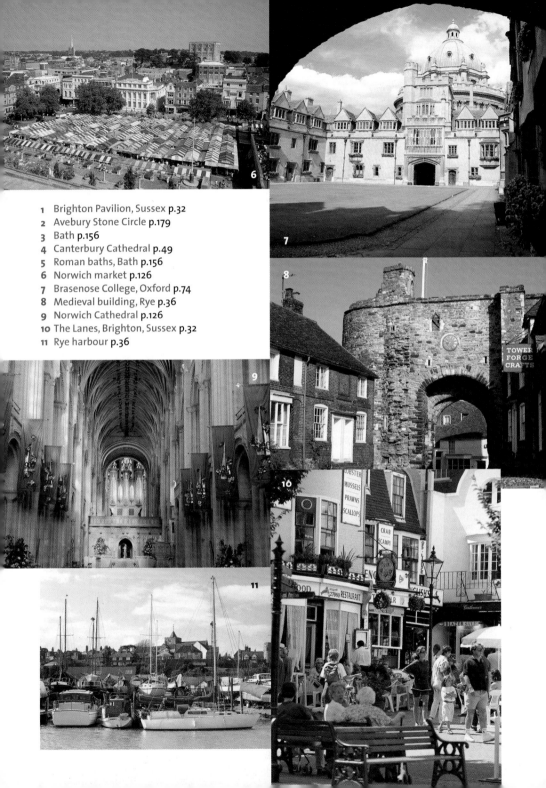

Sporty kids

On a hot summer's day most major towns have a sports centre or swimming pool for kids to cool off in. Ice-rinks and bowling alleys are never hard to track down either. If these seem a bit tame, a laser quest or paintballing session is sure to sort the men from the boys, and a go-kart track or velodrome will certainly quench many a youngsters' thirst for speed.

If you feel you need to head outdoors, there are dozens of activities to have a go at: such as boating on the Norfolk Broads, cycling in the New Forest and watersports off Calshot Spit. If your kids are happy enough to go without all this high-tech gadgetry, however, there are some beautiful spots to go to for a quiet country walk. You can have an interesting day out in Bluebell Woods and Hellfire Caves in the Chilterns, take a nature trail through the Forest of Dean, or play Poohsticks on the original Poohsticks bridge in Ashdown forest.

Bricks and mortar

Nothing brings history alive for kids quite like seeing a proper castle complete with moat, drawbridge, battlements and shining suits of armour. Inside, castles can often seem a little stuffy and covered in 'do not touch' signs, but many have realised that kids need a bit more to do and so provide children's trails and guides. These usually contain lists of interesting things to spot, stories and intriguing facts. All of which adds up to a livelier experience for young visitors.

Castle grounds can often be the highlight of the outing. Large stretches of lawn are the perfect place to let the energetic wear themselves out, whilst grottoes and mazes are always fun to explore. Attractions such as aviaries, butterfly houses and play-grounds are not uncommon either, and there are often lakes and woodland in the castle grounds to wander round.

Buckets and spades

The merest gleam of sunshine at the weekend and half the population heads for the beach. The traditional English seaside experience still retains a strong appeal, particularly for children who delight in the tackiest of beachfronts, amusement arcades and fish and chip shops. Thankfully the best seaside towns usually have a lot more to offer than just the beach itself, such as sealife centres, museums and shops. This is a godsend when that promisingly sunny morning turns into a miserable wet afternoon. There are some genuinely attractive, clean, safe beaches to be found, for example at Bognor Regis, Bournemouth and Poole. And if enthusiasm for building sandcastles or pouring the sea into a hole starts to wane, there is usually plenty to do on the pier, in the sea or along the sands – from donkey rides and bouncy castles to pedalloes and Punch and Judy shows.

Fun parks

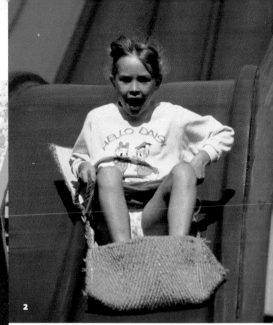

Rollercoasters, log flumes, ghost trains bumper boats, water slides, go-karts... the list goes on and on, as does the battle for the most extreme ride. Theme Parks are, in theory, dedicated to fun, although long queues and high prices may make parents' hearts sink. But if there's one in your area, you'll be unlikely to be able to avoid a visit as kids just love them.

There's usually a good combination of rides ranging from adrenaline junkie treats such as Chessington's 'Samurai' to the gentler 'Tiny Tots Town' at Paulton's Park. So no matter how much your charges (or you) can take, a trip to a theme park is a safe bet You'll need to set aside a whole day to explore the larger parks such as Legoland, Thorpe Park and Chessington, which will allow you to get the most out of them (and the entrance fee). Many of the theme parks are combined with zoos, which may make a welcome relief from all that hurtling around and these areas are usually less crowded than the rides.

There's also an increasing number of more ingeniously themed sites such as the Look Out Discovery Centre and Wyld Court Rainforest which should prove equally entertaining and a little more thought-provoking.

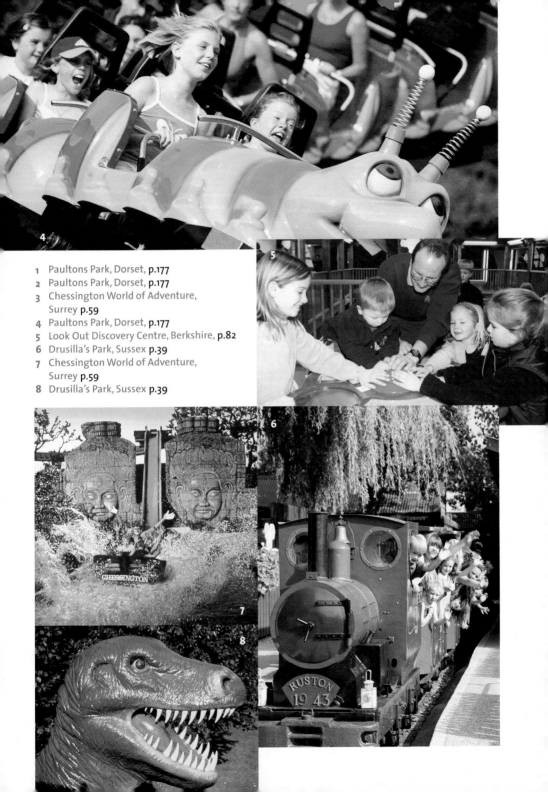

Nature lovers

'Hands-on' is one of the buzz words in children's entertainment and many wildlife attractions have begun to take this on board. You'll be hard pushed to find a farm these days where kids can't get close to the animals, whether it's stroking rabbits, feeding goats or even milking cows. The era of gaping at animals in cages has long gone as zoos try hard to make their animal enclosures as close to a natural habitat as possible. Conservation and understanding of the animals is also a key concern and this has resulted in some really imaginative wildlife centres that truly involve and fascinate children. There are some excellent aquariums as well, displaying the underwater kingdom in an equally inventive fashion. Submerged walkways, frequent feeding times and petting tanks bring kids as close to the sea as possible, which is exactly what they want.

Trains, planes and automobiles

Miniature railways, racing cars, fighter planes, steam engines – they're all a world away from the daily grind of commuting that we usually associate with transport. There's certainly no shortage of attractions to cater for a child's fascination with big shiny vehicles. Aircraft museums offer the thrill of sitting at the controls of a jet fighter and airshows reveal planes in their natural habitat – the sky. Classic car collections at Brooklands and Beaulieu Palace range from the grand, vintage Rolls Royces to the speed demons of Formula 1. And for kids who can't get enough of a certain blue Tank Engine, many of the local steam-powered railways have special 'Thomas' days, which may well be the highlight of their holiday.

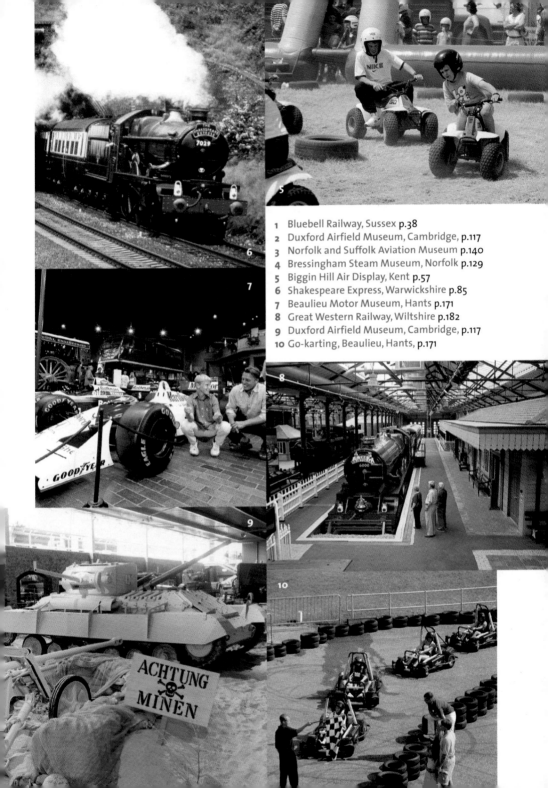

Photo acknowledgements

Cover
Girl on beach © Melanie Dakin; Hot air balloons © Leeds Castle Enterprises Ltd.; Cows © Travel Pictures; Dover Castle © English Heritage Photographic Library; Nowton Park © St Edmundsbury Borough Council; Swimming pool © Spectrum Leisure Centre; Cambridge Children's Festival © Brendan Kelly

Festival highlights
1, 3 © Bath International Music Festival; 2, © Dickens Festival; 4 © Leeds Castle Enterprises Ltd; 5 © Terry R Duffell 6 © Blenheim Palace; 7 © National Trust Photographic Library/Rob Cousins; 8 © National Trust Photographic Library/Chris King

Top towns
1–10 © Travel pictures

Sporty kids
1, 4 © Spectrum Leisure Centre; 2 © Calshot Activity Centre; 3 © Kit Houghton; 5 © Xscape; 6, 7, 8 © Trax Leisure Ltd.

Bricks and mortar
1–5, 7 8 © Travel Pictures; 6, © Skyscan Balloon Photography/English Heritage; 9 © Mountfitchet Castle

Buckets and spades
1, 3, 5, 8 © Travel Pictures; 2, 6 © Chris Parker; 4 © Southend-on-Sea Borough Council; 7 © Margate

Fun parks
1, 2, 4 © Paultons Park; 3, 7 © Chessington World of Adventure; 5 © Look Out Discovery Centre; 6, 8 © Drusilla's Park

Nature lovers
1 © David Lawson/Whipsnade; 2 © Drusilla's Park; 6 © Odds Farm; 4, 5, 8 © The Living Rainforest; 3, 7, 10 © Travel Pictures; 9 © J.R. Day/Whipsnade

Trains, planes and automobiles
1 © Travel Pictures; 2, 9 © Duxford Imperial War Museum; 3 © Ian J. E. Hancock/Norfolk and Suffolk Aviation Museum; 4 © Bressingham Steam Museum Trust; 5 © Air Displays International; 6 © Shakespeare Express; 7 © Beaulieu; 8 © STEAM Museum of the Great Western Railway; 10 © Beaulieu

This page © Travel Pictures

Introduction

INTRODUCTION

Take the kids? *Please* take the kids! When the charms of the familiar and everyday begin to dwindle it becomes not only a good idea but a virtual necessity, both for you and the kids, to get on out. Even a day spent somewhere new can make all the difference, both to their boredom thresholds and your sanity. But what to do? Where to go? How to get there?

This guide is bubbling over with ideas, 250 to be exact, of great day trips and weekend breaks, all of which are within 100 miles or so of London.

Yet despite this easy proximity, it's extraordinary how little many of us, with kids or otherwise, venture out to the many fantastic attractions on our own doorstep. We all probably know of a handful of good places close by to take the kids to, and have perhaps even been to one or two. But how many of us have played Poohsticks from the very bridge where the game was invented in Ashdown Forest, or entered a crab-catching competition in Suffolk, looked round a secret nuclear bunker in Essex or gone in search of the rare red squirrel on Brownsea Island in Dorset?

Not many probably.

These kinds of days out, cheap, fun and simple are mixed in with the low-down on the big, brand name attractions such as Legoland and Thorpe Park which most kids clamour to visit. So whether you're after giving the kids a special treat or just getting out of the house for a day to do something a little different, you need only flick through this book to see what's on offer.

For starters, there are more seaside resorts than you can shake a bucket and spade at. There's Brighton, of course, cosmopolitan and upwardly mobile. And Southend-on-Sea, the favourite of London's Eastenders. But there's also Broadstairs, one-time spiritual home of Charles Dickens, with its crescent-shaped bay and sleepy 1950s ice-cream parlours. Or Whitstable, where you can grab a plate of chips from the pub and scoff them on the beach.

Nearby towns and cities also make good day-trip destinations. Oxford and Cambridge, with their dreamy spires and gently-flowing rivers, world-class museums and bustling city-centres, have plenty to offer. As do smaller towns like Rye, once a seaside town and now two miles inland, or Stratford-upon-Avon, where Will Shakespeare first picked up a quill and began his famous scribbling.

Sometimes, of course, a day simply won't be enough. Bath's many charms can easily devour 48

Foot and Mouth disease

In early 2001 Britain's farmers endured a severe outbreak of Foot and Mouth disease. The disease, which principally affects sheep and cattle, is not a danger to humans, but poses a serious threat to any country's farming and food and livestock markets. In order to prevent its spread, much of the countryside was closed. Fortunately, rural England has now been given the all clear and is welcoming visitors once again. Even so, many attractions, particularly those run by the National Trust, ask visitors to take special care to protect the countryside from further outbreaks of foot-and-mouth disease by following this code:

▶ Don't go on farmland if you have handled farm animals in the last 7 days
▶ Avoid contact with farm animals and keep dogs on a lead where they are present
▶ If you step in dung, remove it from your boots before you leave that field.
▶ Don't go on paths displaying a local authority 'closed' notice.

hours, which is why we've included a section on where to stay. Some of these hotels, such as the Woolley Grange or the Cliveden, are destinations in their own right and you may wish to go straight to the accommodation section, decide which hotel you like the sound of and plan a weekend around what's close by.

In short, there's no need to be bored or at a loss for ideas when it comes to finding things for you and the kids to do. The local park, again? The shops, again? The nearby swimming pool, again? Possibly. Or, flicking through the manuscript of this book at random, a visit to Mountfitchet Castle and Norman Village to see what life was like in medieval times? It is, as they say, a no brainer.

The following games are probably the sort of tactics your parents used on you. They have proved successful and, what is more, there is no need for pricey technical equipment. Use these to jog your memory.

Fun & games

Just in case the kids have time to be bored which we very much doubt, here are a few ways to keep them occupied.

Pub cricket

Pubs in England have names like the Dog & Duck and The Red Lion. You can play a game called pub cricket in which you score runs according to the number of legs a pub has, i.e The Dog & Duck scores six runs (a dog having four legs and a duck two). Just as in cricket, the object of the game is to score as many runs as possible. If you spot a pub with no legs, such as The Crown, then you lose a wicket. Ten wickets and you're out and it is someone else's turn to score a few runs. The game can get a little more complicated with a pub such as the Horse & Hounds – decide for yourself just how many hounds are to be counted or use the picture on the pub sign as a guide.

Quick draw

You will need:
a pocket-sized pad of plain paper
a pen that glides easily across the page
This really is the simplest game imaginable. Rest the pad on your knee and lightly poise the pen over it. As the vehicle you are in moves around the pen will jump leaving a crazy pattern on the paper. Kids can either take turns making the patterns or trying to figure out what the drawings looks like. They could even spend time colouring in the shapes should you experience a long delay to your journey.

What am I?

Think of a person or object. Everyone must take it in turns to guess what or who this is by asking no more than 20 questions, which can only be answered with a simple 'yes' or 'no'. A variation on this game is Who am I? in which players take it in turns to be a famous person or What animal am I? – which is a particularly good choice when visiting to a zoo or wildlife park. Everybody else has to guess who or what you are by asking questions, like do you have four legs? Or do you have fur?

Can you see it?

Do a squiggly doodle on piece of paper and see if someone else can turn it into a picture in 20 seconds. There may be time to colour in your masterpiece as well.

Charades

A good game for all the family to enjoy of an evening. One person selects a book, film, TV programme, play or character to act out. The other players take turns to guess who or what this is. The player miming can prompt ideas by acting out associated themes. The player who guesses correctly gets the next turn.

> ### *How this guide is organized*
> We've divided this guide into four main areas which roughly correspond to north, south, east and west of London. Each area has then been divided up by county or, when appropriate, counties. Within each of these subsections the guide follows a regular pattern. Each section begins with the top towns and cities, and contains all the information on what to see and do there as well as cinemas and theatres and local leisure centres and activities of note. Then come the 'Special trips'. These are the kind of places that are day-trip destinations in their own right, such as Hampton Court or Whipsnade Wild Animal Park. After 'Special trips' comes 'Around and about' which is further subdivided into 'Bricks and mortar' (which includes palaces, castles, stately homes etc), 'Buckets and spades' (the seaside, obviously), 'Nature lovers' (which includes walks in the country, visits to wildlife parks and assorted natural phenomena), 'Look at this!' (containing the best of the region's out-of-town child-friendly museums, science centres etc) and, finally, 'Steam power' (which includes train trips and railway museums). Each area section is then rounded off with 'Eating out' where you'll find detailed listings of family-friendly dining, ranging from pubs with beer gardens to fully-fledged nosh-ups. The guide then has an in-depth section on accommodation including a list of recommended hotels and sources for obtaining further information and a short 'Practicalities A-Z' section with details on getting out of London by a variety of means and general info on medical matters, discount passes, opening hours etc. Finally, we've included not one but two indexes. The first is a general alphabetical index. The second is thematic and lists all the attractions and destinations by kind. Looking for a castle, a theme park, a zoo? Try here first.

Toys and books

Anything that can keep children amused is worth bringing along, though the loss of a favourite toy away from home is hard to forget. Even though there is plenty to do indoors and out, it is still a good idea to bring a few well-chosen games from home to pass the time.

Toys to take

▶ Any large, snap-together plastic construction bricks, such as stickle bricks, Duplo or Mega Bloks. Losing one or two won't be a great tragedy.
▶ Hand puppets for their outstanding versatility. They are always a mood lifter.
▶ Non-stain, washable colouring pens.
▶ A disposable, automatic camera for a kid's eye view of the trip. (Boots make a Photo Bug throw-away. Fisher Price make a kid's first 35mm.)
▶ The classic travel toys, Etch a Sketch and Magna Doodle. Pocket versions are now available too.

For the baby

Plenty of toys especially designed to captivate your baby will allow you to concentrate on the task at hand. You can buy all sorts of mobile, fold-away diversions that are ideal for keeping your baby amused and helping develop their motor skills at the same time. Inflatables are particularly versatile.

One early favourite consists of eye-catching cards which you slot into transparent pockets and attach by velcro to the back of your travel seat. On one side are bold black and white geometric patterns to encourage your baby's focusing ability. On the reverse are basic patterns of sharply contrasting colours intended to engage older babies. This theme is now being used on all sorts of soft toys.

Wrist and sock rattles are an ideal distraction for babies still finding their hands and feet. Colourful, multi-sensory play mats and activity centres, too, combine all sorts of noises and textures to enhance your baby's sensory awareness. Board books and cloth books with velcro attachments to go on pushchairs are great while you're on the go and equally good to wind down with at the end of the day.

Shopping centres

Though these huge monuments to retail can be a little soulless – and certainly don't have the charm or character of some local streets – they do at least offer the convenience of having everything (shops, restaurants, leisure facilities etc) under one roof. They also have crèches, thereby allowing you a couple of hours of tantrum-free retail therapy.

Bluewater
Greenhithe, Kent
t 08456 021021
www.bluewater.co.uk
⇌ Greenhithe
Open Mon–Fri 10am–9pm, Sat 9am–8pm, Sun 11am–5pm

Still the big daddy of shopping centres, the massive Bluewater not only offers some 320 shops, dozens of fast-food outlets and chain restaurants, a multiplex cinema and the Academy Crèche (which takes children up to the age of 12), but also has facilities for a range of activities, including a fishing lake, a Wintergarden, an outdoor play area, a boating lake and cycle paths. Of particular note to health-conscious parents, the centre pumps fresh air in and is non-smoking throughout.

Lakeside Thurrock
West Thurrock, Essex
t (01708) 869933
⇌ Lakeside
Open Mon–Fri 10am–10pm, Sat 9am–7.30pm, Sun 11am–5pm

Over 300 shops and food outlets, market stalls, cinema and a Stay 'n' Play Crèche for 2–7-year-olds.

Xscape
602 Marlborough Gate, Milton Keynes
t (01908) 200020
www.xscape.co.uk
⇌ Milton Keynes
Open From 9am, closing times vary

Retail and leisure centre with shops, a cinema, a bowling alley, indoor climbing walls and a fitness club. The real treat here is the Snozone, the country's largest 'real' snow slope. You'll find none of that funny dry netting stuff here; Snozone uses snow-cannons and keeps the temperature at a constantly chilly −2°C, making it suitable for proper skiing and snowboarding. Lessons are offered.

Down South

Sussex · Kent · Surrey

02

Down South

Highlights

Beach fun, Broadstairs p.55
Castle fun, Bodiam, p.41
Cute animal fun, Drusilla's Park, p.39
Historical site, Battle Abbey, p.40
Most baffling maze, Hampton Court, p.59
Rural history, Weald and Downland Open Air
Museum, p.36
Steam train ride, Bluebell Railway, p.38
Theme park, Chessington World of Adventures,
p.59 and Thorpe Park, p.61
Top town, Brighton p.32
Walking the South Downs, p.46

When it comes to taking the kids on a day trip or weekend break, a Londoner's natural inclination is to head down south. There's seaside aplenty of course, whether it be Brighton with its trendy lanes, pebbly beach and chirpy pier, or the simpler fun of a Punch and Judy show and a donkey ride on Broadstairs' crescent-shaped beach. The whole region, but especially Kent, is peppered with castles. From these, children can learn something about England's turbulent past, while in Surrey, for years the playground of royalty, they can see how the other half lived at Hampton Court Palace, once home to Henry VIII. As well as Brighton, there are some wonderful towns to visit. There's historic

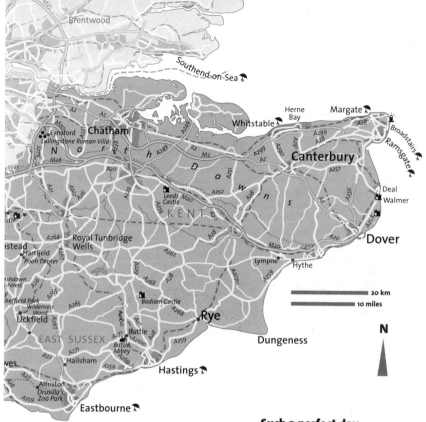

Chichester, founded by the Romans in the 1st century AD; Rye, with its higgledy-piggledly streets and quaint shops; and the cathedral city of Canterbury which gave its name to Chaucer's famous poem, *The Canterbury Tales*, and witnessed the violent end of the Christian martyr Thomas à Becket in 1170. Nature lovers may be tempted by a walk along the shady paths of Ashdown Forest (once home to the winsome Pooh Bear), or by a visit to Drusila's Park to stroke the cuddly animals. And if that sounds a bit tame, thrill seekers could do a lot worse than take the controls of a JCB at Diggerland or cling on for dear life as they sample the new trio of blood-thumping rides dreamt up by the pleasure-heads at Thorpe Park.

Such a perfect day

Morning: Battle Abbey – take a tour of the battle-field where King Harold was slain by William's conquering army (p.40).

Lunch: At the nearby Copper Kettle – be sure to check out the scale model of the town just outside (p.67).

Afternoon: Train to Hastings (10 minutes) to play on the beach, explore the Smugglers' Adventure or Underwater World (p.44) before riding the West Hill Railway up the cliff face.

Special events

May
Brighton Festival **t** (01273) 292589/599
June
July
Chichester Festival **t** (01243) 775888
August
Rye Medieval Festival **t** (01797) 226696
September
Leeds Castle: Hot Air Balloon and Vintage Car weekend **t** 0870 6008880
November
London–Brighton Car Rally

BRIGHTON

Getting there By road: The A23 links Brighton directly with London. Alternatively, take the M23 part of the way, rejoin the A23, then follow the signs. The journey should take little over an hour. By rail: A regular train service runs from London Victoria (30 departures a day). The journey takes around 50 min. Trains also run from London Bridge and King's Cross. National Express coaches and Southdown bus services arrive at Pool Valley bus station on Old Steine, not far from the seafront. If your kids are aged 5 or over, it's a good idea to travel to Brighton by train. The seafront is an easy 10-minute downhill walk from the station (making the station a slightly harder 15-minute uphill walk from the seafront) giving your kids plenty of time to get excited about the prospect of seeing the sea. It comes into a view about halfway down – see who can spot it first

Tourist office 10 Bartholomew Square **t** (01273) 292589/599 **www.**brighton.co.uk/tourist

Britain's seaside resorts tend to have largely similar characteristics. They are cheery and cosy and somewhat old-fashioned – the final bastions of olde worlde music hall entertainment – and, outside the summer season, they're often rather sleepy and quiet. Brighton, however, is different. It's brash and loud and determinedly modern and remains so all year round. 'London's south coast outpost' is a fitting description for this briney metropolis. It has always been the resort of choice for fashionable city dwellers; George IV, that most style-conscious of monarchs, kickstarted the Brighton phenomenon in the late 18th century when he began making regular weekend visits here in the company of his mistress. Such was his fondness for the place that he had a palace, the weirdly wonderful Royal Pavilion, built here in the 1810s. Ever since, Brighton has acted as a magnet for London's 'in crowd', an attraction that will no doubt be reinforced by the resort's recent elevation to city status.

The great thing about Brighton is that it manages to be both fashionable, with its clubs and designer stores, and yet extremely family-orientated with lots of child-friendly attractions. There's the pier, of course, with its funfair, arcades and inexhaustible supply of giant teddy bears, the Marina, with its arcades and bowling alleys, the Sea Life Centre and, last but not least, the beach itself. Brighton boasts a mighty eight miles of seafront, made up of pebbles rather than sand, so bring your sturdiest pair of sandals.

Things to see

Booth Museum of Natural History
194 Dyke Road **t** (01273) 292777
Open Mon–Wed and Fri–Sat 10–5, Sun 2–5
Free
Gift shop, mother and baby room, guided tours, wheelchair access

Based on the collection of the Victorian naturalist and Brighton resident, Edward Thomas Booth, this holds a fascinating display of insects, butterflies, fossils and animal skeletons. Events for children are organized during the school holidays when kids can turn their hand to fossil collecting, butterfly mounting or even taxidermy.

Brighton Palace Pier
Off Madeira Drive **t** (01273) 609361
Open Summer 9am–2am, winter 10am–12 midnight
Adm Free, rides are individually charged
Three bars, various fast food outlets, wheelchair access, disabled toilets

After the beach, this should probably be your first port of call. Vaguely reminiscent of an ocean liner on stilts, this beautiful snow-white pier stretches a mighty 1,722ft out to sea and is lined with snack bars, stalls and child-friendly attractions. About halfway down you'll find an amusement arcade full of all the latest video games, a few fairground-style stalls plus a couple of old-fashioned and rather neglected one-armed bandits. Next door stands a 250-seat fish and chip restaurant while, beyond this, right at the end of the pier, is a funfair with several gentle carousel-type rides, a small go-kart track, a helter-skelter, a log flume and a rollercoaster 'The Crazy Mouse'.

Did you know?
That Brighton is over 1,000 years old and that the Lanes are its oldest part. The town is even mentioned in the Domesday Book, the catalogue of the country which William the Conqueror had compiled shortly after becoming king – although back then Brighton was known as Brithelmstone, much more of a mouthful.

The pier was constructed in the 1890s after the original 'chain' pier was destroyed in a storm and, had you visited it back then, you would have found a very different type of attraction. In Victorian times, piers were regarded simply as over-sea walkways, platforms designed to give people the sensation of being at sea without the bother (or potential seasickness) of a boat trip. Nobody thought of building any attractions on the pier until the 1930s when a rather small ferris wheel was erected. By this time it was understood that visitors wanted more from their day at the seaside than just the prospect of a bracing walk. Ever since, the number and size of the pier's attractions have increased year on year. Nonetheless, the simple pleasure of walking on a platform out over the sea is one which still appeals to children and they will probably get as much enjoyment from peering through the gaps in the wooden slats at the breaking waves below as they will hurtling down the helter-skelter (well, almost as much).

Royal Pavilion

North Street **t** (01273) 290900
www.brighton.co.uk/tourist
Open Oct–May 10–5; June–Sept 10–6
Adm Adult £4.50, child £2.75
Queen Adelaide Tearoom, gift shop, children's quiz sheets, mother and baby room, guided tours, many disabled facilities

The Pavilion is, without a doubt, Britain's most over-the-top Royal Palace. Designed by John Nash in the 1810s on the orders of the Prince Regent, it's usually described as being 'in the Indian style with a Chinese interior'; in other words, it's a bit of a mishmash. Neither Nash nor his patron were great believers in the maxim 'less is more' and together they produced a glorious icing sugar concoction of domes, turrets and cast iron palm trees.
It has had its critics over the years – the famously austere Queen Victoria absolutely hated the place and refused to go anywhere near it – but, today, following extensive restoration work, it's difficult not to be seduced by the sheer extravagance of it all. Kids, in particular, usually respond favourably to its fairytale-like exuberance. Forget notions of taste and style, just come and enjoy the excess: the flouncy soft furnishings, vast crystal chandeliers, the lashings of gilt, the hand-knitted carpets and bizarre trompe l'oeil décor.

Can you spot?
The silver dragon which holds up the 1-ton chandelier in the Banqueting Room. Note its bright red forked tongue and the fire shooting from its nostrils.

Sea Life Centre

Marine Parade **t** (01273) 604234
www.sealife.co.uk
Open Daily 10–6
Adm Adults £5.95, under-15s £3.95, under-4s **free** (ticket valid for unlimited visits throughout the day)
Shop, restaurant, mother and baby room, disabled facilities

It's the world's oldest aquarium and, although it looks it in places, it is still a great place to while away an afternoon. The centrepiece is the transparent tunnel running through the middle of a huge tank where you can pretend to be walking along the ocean floor while various exotic sea creatures, from sharks to seahorses, swim and glide overhead. Elsewhere you'll find floor to ceiling tanks where freshwater and tropical fish swim through model wrecks and caves (many have bubble windows giving you the sensation of being in the tank with them). There is also a touch pool full of friendly rays and lots of interactive displays designed to keep kids informed as they gawp. Children are well catered for with various themed areas including 'Adventures at 20,000 leagues' where they can hear about the adventures of Jules Verne's *Nautilus* while perched on the edge of a mock-up submarine, a Victorian marine display, complete with waxworks in period costume, and a soft play area for the under-5s. Feeding time for most fish takes place twice a day (for sharks it is once every two days). In truth, the layout and presentation of information is a bit uninspired in places, although this is likely to bother parents much more than children who'll simply be thrilled at the chance to see a shark close up.

Tip If visiting in the winter months, wrap children up very warmly as the aquarium tends to be quite cold and damp.

Vintage Penny Arcade

On the beach, 50 yards west of the Palace Pier
Open Easter–Oct weekends and school hols 12 noon–late

A collection of original Edwardian penny slot machines (strength testers, fortune-tellers, 'what the butler saw' gizmos, etc.) that will probably prove just as popular as the more modern whizz-bang stuff on offer at the pier. Buy a collection of old pennies at the entrance to feed into the machines.

Things to do

Brighton Marina
Brighton **t** (01273) 693636
www.brighton-marina.co.uk
Open Daily 10–6

Quite a way east of the town centre, the Marina is still well worth a visit. It's a nice place to eat (try one of the various cafés and restaurants that line the water's edge) and there's a large entertainment complex with a cinema, an arcade, tenpin bowling and pool. Boat cruises around the harbour, to the pier and out to sea are also offered. The best way to reach the Marina is aboard the Volk's Railway, Britain's oldest electric railway, built in 1883.

Note *The journey, which starts at the Palace Pier, takes in views of the local nudist beach – which should, at least, give you something to talk about.*

Bus tours
The South Downs, which make up some of England's most beautiful countryside, start a few miles inland from Brighton. The no.77 open-top sightseeing bus makes eight trips a day during high summer from the Palace Pier to the Devil's Dyke (p.46), one of the Downs' most famous beauty spots. Its elevated position has proved popular with both hang-gliders and kite flyers. If you fancy joining in (with the kite-flying, that is) you can pick up a suitable stunter in Brighton at Air Born Kites, 42 Gardner Street.
Devil's Dyke tour information t (01273) 886200 (Brighton and Hove Buses) www.buses.co.uk
Stops North Street, Palace Pier, Brighton Station
Tour times 8 times daily between 9.30–4.30 mid July-early Sept
Fares Adult £2.60, child **free**

Take home a souvenir
Just back from the seafront are the Lanes, the heart of 'designer' Brighton, a maze of narrow alleyways and pedestrianized streets, full of antique shops, jewellers, designer clothes stores and restaurants. Look out for the Cat Shop, 21 Prince Albert Street, with its fascinating display of cat models and sculptures, the Teddy Bear Hospital, 131/2 Prince Albert Street, and The Lanes

Armoury, which holds a collection of military weapons and uniforms every bit as good as a museum.

Cinemas
Duke of York's Cinema
Preston Circus **t** (01273) 602503
Look out for the legs! Art house cinema with children's films on Saturday mornings.
The Odeon
Kingswest Centre, West Street **t** (0870) 50 50 007
Multiplex. Handy for the cafés on West Street.
Virgin 8 Screen
Marina Village **t** (0541) 555145
A little tricky to reach without a car; take the no. 7 bus or hop on the Volks Railway.

Theatres
Komedia
Gardner Street, **t** (01273) 647100
Puts on a range of shows from cabaret to comedy with a number of special shows for children (phone for details).
Sallis Benney Theatre
Grand Parade **t** (01273) 643010
Brighton University's showcase venue.
Theatre Royal
New Road **t** (01273) 328488
One of Brighton's grander theatres; the place to come for the big names during the panto season.

Activities
Bowlplex Brighton
Marina Way, Brighton Marina **t** (01273) 818180
Open Daily 9.30am–12 midnight (later on weekends)
26 bowling lanes, pool tables and video games.
Hove Lagoon Watersports
Kingsway, Hove **t** (01273) 424842
Adm Call for details of times and prices
Watersports for kids and adults.
Neilson
120 St Georges Road, Brighton **t** (01273) 626284
Adm Call for details of times and prices
Sailing courses at Brighton Marina for all ages and abilities.

CHICHESTER

Getting there By road: Chichester is 60 miles southwest of London. Take the A3 then the A286. By rail: the station is on South Street. There is a regular service from London Victoria. By bus/coach: National Express Coastline buses run from Brighton and Portsmouth, National Express services leave daily from London; the bus station is next door to the train station
Tourist office 29a South Street **t** (01243) 775888
www.chichester.gov.uk

Chichester is a quiet, attractive market town with lots of handsome architecture and a reserved, slightly stuffy atmosphere. Founded by the Romans in the 1st century AD, the roads still follow the Roman grid layout although most of the architecture is Georgian, the principal exceptions being the very grand Norman cathedral and the 16th-century market cross which marks the centre of town – you can't miss it, it looks a bit like an enormous stone crown. Radiating out from this are the town's four main streets (North, South, East and West Street) which are pleasant and pedestrianized and lined with shops, tearooms and the sort of pubs which have large, curved glass windows jutting out into the street. In July, thousands of tourists flock here for the Chichester Festival, a two-week celebration of theatre, dance and music (the choice of works on offer is famously traditional with nothing too racy or experimental allowed) which usually kicks off with a carnival and firework display.

Although the town itself boasts few out and out tourist sites (of most interest to children will be the Mechanical Music and Doll Museum on Church Road and the Chichester Canal, where you can hire canoes and rowboats and take narrowboat trips), it is within easy reach of a number of excellent attractions: the South Downs are just to the north (p.46), as is Goodwood Racetrack and the Weald and Downland Open Air Museum (p.36).

South of the town is Chichester Harbour, a popular sailing marina where you can hire boats and take sightseeing trips along the coast. Three miles east of Chichester is the Tangmere Military Aviation Museum while, two miles west, is Fishbourne Roman Palace, the largest Roman building in the country.

Things to see

Fishbourne Roman Palace

Salthill Road, Fishbourne, nr Chichester
t (01243) 785859
Open Mar–July and Oct daily 10–5; Aug daily 10–6; Nov–Dec daily 10–4; Jan Sat and Sun 10–4
Adm Adults £4.40, under-15s £2.30, under-5s **free**, family £11.50
Café, gift and book shop, on-site parking

Although little of the actual building remains there are four beautifully preserved mosaics, including a very famous one depicting Cupid riding a dolphin, and there's an audiovisual presentation to give you some idea of what the complex must have looked like in Roman times. During the school holidays kids can try their hand at a range of Roman activities including pottery and, of course, mosaic-making.

Goodwood Racetrack

Goodwood **t** (01243) 755055 **www**.goodwood.co.uk
Getting there It's a few miles north of Chichester off the A286
Open Call in advance
Adm Call in advance
Café, shop, disabled access

On its event days you can watch sports cars whizzing around a track and helicopters and planes landing and taking off.

Mechanical Music and Doll Museum

Church Road **t** (01243) 785421
Open Easter–Sept Sun–Fri 1–5; Oct–Easter Sun 1–5
Adm Adult £2, child 75p
Gift shop, guided tours, disabled access, on-site parking

Collection of barrel organs, polyphons and Victorian wax and china dolls.

Tangmere Military Aviation Museum

Tangmere, nr Chichester **t** (01243) 775223
www.wealddown.co.uk

'Glorious Goodwood'

Goodwood Week, 'Glorious Goodwood' to its friends, is held each year in late July. Next to Ascot, it's the most important race meeting in the country. Even if you can't make this famous meet, there are plenty of other race meetings throughout the summer. Phone **t** (01243) 774107 for details.

Open Mar–Oct daily 10–5.30; Feb–Nov daily 10–4.30 (last adm 1 hr before closing)
Adm Adult £3, child £1.50
Gift shop, café, guided tours, disabled access, on-site parking

An RAF airfield during the Second World War, Tangmere is now one of the country's most important military aviation museums. There's lots of fearsome looking hardware on display, including a Meteor, a Hunter, a Hurricane and, of course, a Spitfire, the most famous fighter plane of them all. There is even a Battle of Britain flight simulator.

Weald and Downland Open Air Museum

Singleton, nr Chichester **t** (01243) 811348
www.wealddown.co.uk
Getting there It's about 6 miles north of Chichester off the A286
Open Mar–Oct daily 10.30–6; Nov–Feb Wed, Sat and Sun 10.30–4
Adm Adults £6, under-16s £3, under-5s **free**, family £15
Gift shop

Combining the best elements of a day in the country and a trip to a museum, the Weald and Downland Centre provides a fascinating (and highly accessible) insight into traditional rural life. The vast, 50-acre site contains over 40 historic rural buildings recovered from all over southeast England and lovingly reassembled here by a team of volunteers. There are shepherds' huts, cottages, a blacksmith's forge, a 17th-century watermill, a Tudor farmstead, a charcoal burners' camp and even an old Victorian village school. You can sit at a school desk, lie down on one of the tiny beds or try to figure out how the archaic toilet system might have worked. You can also see demonstrations of rural crafts such as woodturning, spinning and candle-making and children can even have a go at bricklaying, roof-pegging, willow-hurdle-making or grinding flour at the watermill.

Things to do

Centurion Way Cycle Hire

Bicycles can be hired from City Cycles, 44 Bognor Road **t** (01243) 539992

Centurion Way is a cycle and pedestrian path running around the west side of Chichester decorated with sculptures designed by local school children.

Chichester Canal Society

Canal Basin, Canal Wharf **t** (01243) 771363

The society hires out rowboats and canoes and organizes narrowboat canal trips and guided towpath walks.

Chichester Harbour Conservancy

The Harbour Office, Itchenor **t** (01243) 512301

Organizes guided walks (stream walks, bird walks, wildflower walks, cream tea walks, etc.) and activities (pond dipping, butterfly collecting, etc.) around Chichester Harbour.

Chichester Harbour Water Tours

9 Cawley Road **t** (01243) 786418
Open Mar–Oct
Fares Adult £5, child £2

One and a half hour tours of Chichester Harbour from Itchenor.

Cinemas

New Park Film Centre, New Park Road **t** (01243) 786650

Theatres

Chichester Festival Theatre and **Minerva Theatre**, Oaklands Park **t** (01243) 781312

Built in 1962 the Chichester Festival Theatre has a strong youth wing and does a good line in theatrical summer schools for children. Ring for details.

Activities

Westgate Leisure Centre

Cathedral Way, Chichester **t** (01243) 785651
Open Mon–Sat 9am–10.30pm, Sun 9am–9.30pm
Adm Adult £2.90, child £1.70

Three swimming-pools including a toddlers' pool, a 50m covered waterslide, squash, badminton, table-tennis, short tennis, a crèche and a café.

RYE

Getting there By road: Rye is 62 miles southeast of London off the A259 and A268. By rail: Trains run daily from London (Charing Cross), Ashford, Hastings and Dover. By bus/coach: Services link Rye with Hastings, Dover and Brighton.
Tourist office The Heritage Centre, Strand Quay **t** (01797) 226696 **www.rye.org.uk/heritage**

Did you know...

Though mechanical instruments originated in the Middle Ages, full-size mechanical music makers became truly popular at the turn of the 20th century, especially in bars and cafés. The instruments varied in complexity and quality from machines like the Player Piano which produced only piano tunes through to monsters such as the Orchestrion which contained a piano, xylophone, 68 pipes (with piccolo, flute and clarinet effects), a bass drum, snare drum, timpani, cymbal, triangle and, for that Latin flourish, castanets.

It has been called the most beautiful village in England and it certainly conforms to many people's expectations of an idealized English town, full of narrow, cobbled streets, half-timber buildings and quaint tearooms. In truth, there's something rather theme-park-like about Rye. Wonderfully preserved it may be, but look closely and you'll see a subtle commercialization at work. This is not a town cut off from the modern world but rather a sort of outdoor museum, a vision of an ideal England preserved in aspic.

Nonetheless, it's a very pleasant place, especially if you manage to avoid the August crowds, and, despite the overwhelming picturesqueness, surprisingly child-friendly. The kids will certainly like the Rye Town Model Sound and Light Show, an audiovisual introduction to Rye using a large-scale model of the town, and the Rye Treasury of Mechanical Music where you can see demonstrations of old music machines, such as phonographs and pianolas (which were the forerunners of modern jukeboxes). The town museum is also well worth a visit. Housed in the Ypres Tower, the town's small castle, it contains a fascinating display on smuggling. Every summer the town hosts a medieval weekend when costumed characters (Lords and Ladies, Knights and jesters, etc.) parade through the streets, and on Bonfire Night there's a torchlit procession.

Should you tire of the town's attractions, Camber Sands, Battle and the rest of the regions 1066 sites are all close by. At New Romney, just north of Rye, you can go for a ride on the Romney, Hythe and Dymchurch steam railway (see p.58) and visit the Romney Toy and Model Museum which has one of the largest model railways in the country.

If you had visited Rye in the Middle Ages, you could have gone for a swim. Unfortunately, the sea retreated several hundred years ago and Rye is now a coastal town without a coast, although it does still have a small harbour.

Things to see and do

Rye Castle Museum

Rye Castle, Gungarden **t** (01797) 226728
Open Easter–Oct daily 10.30–5.30; Nov–Easter Sat and Sun 10.30–5.30
Adm Adult £1.50, child 50p
Gift shop, guided tours

Rye Town Model Sound and Light Show

Rye Heritage Centre, The Strand Quay
t (01797) 226696
Open Daily 10–5
Adm Adult £2, child £1, family £5

Rye Treasury of Mechanical Music

20 Cinque Ports Street **t** (01797) 223345
Open Mar–Oct Wed–Mon 10–5
Adm £3

Tell me a story: Cinque or swim

Being so close to Europe (France is only 22 miles away from Dover) Kent's coast has long been important both in terms of trade and defence. So much so that in 1278 the five ports of Hastings, New Romney, Hythe, Sandwich and Dover were given a special charter under Edward I and were named the Cinque Ports (cinq means five in French). In return for special trading privileges, these ports had to guarantee that they would provide help to the monarch (by transporting troops) during times of war. Later Rye and Winchelsea joined the group as well as several other ports along the coast and the confederation continued until Henry VIII formed a professional Royal Navy and the need for the Cinque Ports vanished. The trading privileges were officially abolished in 1855 and though some of the ports, such as Rye, are not even by the sea any more thanks to severe silting, the Cinque Ports live on, in name at least. One of the present Queen Mother's honorary titles is Lord Warden of the Cinque Ports.

SPECIAL TRIPS

Ashdown Forest

Getting there It's just to the southeast of East Grinstead off the A22

Tourist information East Grinstead Tourism Initiative, The Library, West Street, East Grinstead **t** (01342) 410121

Children who have grown up knowing only the Disney version of Winnie-the-Pooh and his chums may be surprised to learn that the forgetful bear is an English creation. This great swathe of West Sussex forest and heathland provided the inspiration for AA Milne's tales of the famous bear, Christopher Robin and their various furry friends. The village of Hartfield is the centre of Pooh country from where you can visit the 'Hundred-Acre' Wood where most of the Pooh stories were set and even have a game of Poohsticks off the original Poohsticks bridge.

Poohsticks Bridge is a must for all fans of Winnie-the-Pooh. About a mile through the woods from 'Poohsticks Car Park', you come to the bridge on which, according to legend, Christopher Robin first played Poohsticks with his nanny. Be sure to pick up a few sticks before you reach the bridge as they become harder to find the closer you get. The game of Poohsticks, in which competitors toss a stick over one side of the bridge then rush to the other side to see which stick emerges first, was immortalised in *The House at Pooh Corner* when Winnie-the-Pooh first played the game. Today the bridge has become a veritable shrine and the river is in danger of being blocked altogether thanks to the massive number of Poohsticks already tossed over the side!

Other places which have became familiar through AA Milne's stories such as the Enchanted Place, North Pole and Roo's Sandypit are all within easy reach of Gill's Lap car park which can be found just off the B2026. Otherwise, Ashdown is serious walkers' territory with lots of nature trails and sandy tracks.

Fancy a souvenir?

Visit the pretty village of Hartfield for 'Pooh Corner', a 17th-century house that contains the world's largest collection of 'Pooh-phernalia'. Christopher Robin and his nanny used to come to this tiny 300-year-old shop for sweets and today

the store has thousands of items and souvenirs and seemingly similar numbers of tourists crowding in for mementos.

Pooh Corner

High Street, Hartfield **t** (01892) 770453
www.poohcorner.co.uk

Bluebell Railway

Sheffield Park station, nr Uckfield **t** (01825) 723777
Talking Timetable **t** (01825) 722370
www.visitweb.com/bluebell
Getting there Sheffield Park station is 8 miles south of East Grinstead on the A275, 2 miles north of the A272 junction. You can book direct to the Bluebell Railway from London Victoria and intermediate stations on Connex South Central's East Grinstead line. There is also a special bus service from East Grinstead station
Operating times Weekends throughout the year; daily Easter–Sept and school hols; special events during Dec
Fares Adult £7.80, child £3.90, family £21
Restaurant, real ale bar, gift shop, wheelchair access, adapted toilets

There is something distinctly pleasing about old-style railway travel. Kids, in particular, love the experience of riding a proper puffing train, à la Thomas the Tank Engine. The Bluebell, perhaps the country's most famous 'proper' railway, wends its way through fields and meadows between Sheffield Park (p.46) and Kingscote in Sussex. A ten-mile round trip aboard one of the stylishly restored 1930s carriages takes about one and a half hours. Every last detail of the railway has been meticulously restored from the elegant fittings in the sumptuous Pullman dining cars to the period advertisements that adorn the station walls.

Kids love the sheer noise and puff of these mighty beasts and the banging and slamming of doors, the conductor's whistle and the anticipation as the train jolts into motion, only serve to build up the excitement.

The stations are as much a part of the fun as the trains themselves. Sheffield Park Station has been lovingly restored to look as it would have at the turn of the 20th century and also has a collection of railway memorabilia while Horsted Keynes (just 15 minutes down the line) has all the appearance of a busy 1930s railway station with piles of leather suitcases and trunks. Horsted Keynes also includes a period buffet (all the stations have some sort of refreshment stand, while drinks and snacks are generally sold in transit). If the weather is nice, you can bring your own picnic as the stations along the line have their own picnic spot. In spring, the trains zip along past the fields of bluebells which give the line its name. Get off at Horsted Keynes for a walk in the bluebell-packed woods.

Fancy a souvenir?

The gift shop at Sheffield Park has plenty to appeal to children who have been fired up by the thrill of steam. If the kids want anything apart from train sets, train models or train books they are likely to be disappointed though.

Drusilla's Park

Alfriston t (01323) 870234 www.drusillas.co.uk
Getting there It's 7 miles northeast of Eastbourne off the A27
Open April–Sept 10–6; Oct–Mar 10–5
Adm Adult £7.60, child £6.50, under-3s **free**
'Explorers' restaurant, gift shop, mother and baby facilities, disabled access, on-site parking

There are no tigers, elephants or giraffes here, no animals your kids will simply stand and point at because of their sheer size or fearsomeness. At Drusilla's the watchword is small. As one of the country's most child-orientated zoos, it understands that the best way to get kids to appreciate animals is by providing them with as much access as possible to the animals own world – which isn't really a feasible option with a tiger. Here, animals are displayed in new and different ways and from imaginative viewpoints. Children can watch meerkats running and frolicking from inside a plastic dome within the meerkat enclosure. They can walk through a bat house as the bats fly over and around their heads and look at penguins cavorting under the water from a special viewing area. The zoo tries to encourage as much participation as possible and organizes lots of activities and games to help kids understand the zoo's inhabitants better – they can hang upside down like a monkey or a bat on a climbing frame, try to run as fast as a llama on a treadmill or get up close and personal with an owl, a snake or a monkey at one of the animal encounters sessions.

The zoo even provides kids with their very own guide book which they can consult as they make their way round. The guide is packed with 'Did you knows?' (did you know that some poison frogs can produce enough poison to kill fifty people or that porcupines can have as many as 30,000 pointy quills when fully grown?) as well as word games, puzzles, fun facts and a route planner.

There are art competitions, talks by the keepers and numerous themed weekends (Reptile Weekend, Primate Weekend, etc.); everything, in fact, for a perfect day at the zoo. And, should the animals lose their appeal, you could always climb aboard one of the two miniature trains which give tours of the park in summer or head to the park's play area where you'll find swings, slides, a tractor and even an old fire engine as well as a soft play area for toddlers.

Fancy a souvenir?

Drusilla's hasn't missed a trick as far as purchasing opportunities go and three gift shops (not to mention a doughnut factory) mean that children should have no difficulty in finding a little something to take home to show their classmates.

Become a zoo keeper for the day

Older children (min age 10) might like to try out a bit of work experience by becoming a zoo keeper for the day. It's not cheap (£60) but the day includes a tour of the zoo to explain the role of zoo keepers and aims to offer a 'typical day's work' at the zoo. Though Drusilla's can't guarantee what kids will get up to (this is a zoo after all) they should get the chance to take part in a range of core activities including feeding the penguins, cleaning and feeding the bats and grooming the donkeys and ponies. Phone the zoo for an application form.

AROUND AND ABOUT

Bricks and mortar

Arundel Castle

Arundel **t** (01903) 882173

Getting there Arundel is 4 miles north of Littlehampton, 8 miles east of Chichester off the A27 and A284

Open April–Oct Sun–Fri 12 noon–5

Adm Adult £6.70, child £4.20, family £18

Café, gift shop, on-site parking

Arundel was first acquired by the Duke of Norfolk some 700 years ago and has remained in the family ever since. Unlike many other stately home-style castles, which are often more stately home than castle, this has all the requisite features befitting a fairytale fortress. Parents and kids can tick them off together: moat (check), drawbridge (check), portcullis (check), battlements (check), suits of armour (check). Although there are many roped off areas and plenty of 'do not touch' signs, this is still a pretty accessible place, although it's probably best toured in the company of a young person's guide (available at the museum shop) which will point out all the most interesting features, as well as providing activities (such as pictures to colour in) and interesting facts. In particular, look out for Mary Queen of Scots' prayer book and the keep – it's 120 steps to the top from where there are fantastic views out over the coast towards the Isle of Wight (p.164). Do also check out the Arundel Toy and Military Museum in the town, a fascinating collection of old toys, games, dolls and teddy bears housed in a Georgian cottage.

Battle Abbey

High Street, Battle **t** (01424) 773792

Getting there Battle is about 6 miles northwest of Hastings on the A2100 and A271. It's about a 10-min train ride

Open April–Sept daily 10–6; Oct daily 10–5; Nov–Mar daily 10–4

Adm Adult £4, child £2, family £10

Gift shop, disabled access

The Battle of Hastings, the most famous battle in British history, actually took place here, a few

---

Tell me a story: The Battle of Hastings

Who?

Harold, King of England and William, Duke of Normandy (and their respective armies of course). Interestingly, although we tend to think of the Normans as French, they could equally well be described as Viking. William and his army were the descendants of Viking raiders who had seized part of northern France in the 10th century. The name Norman is a corruption of 'Norse Man'.

When?

1066, of course, the most famous date in English history.

Why?

The battle was really an argument over who should be king of England. William said that Edward the Confessor, who had been king before Harold, had promised the crown to him. Harold disagreed and, upon Edward's death, seized the crown for himself.

What happened?

Harold had prepared a large fleet for William's invasion but in September was forced to speed northwards with his army to suppress his own rebellious brother Tostig. Meanwhile the wind, which had not favoured William, turned – and the Normans set sail for England. William invaded in October 1066 with several thousand troops and set up camp in Hastings. Hearing of William's arrival, Harold was forced to march his army back down south where they arrived exhausted three days later. They took up position on the high ground of Battle and waited for William to make his move. William's forces made several unsuccessful attempts to gain control of the high ground but were repelled by Harold's troops. William then pretended to retreat, whereupon Harold's army charged down the hill, only for William's troops to turn round and engulf the English in a hail of arrows. Harold was shot in the eye and, as he tried to pull the arrow out, was cut to pieces by Norman soldiers. Upon hearing that their king was dead, the English army's morale collapsed and William marched on London, the new king of England.

Before the battle had commenced, William made a promise that if he should win he would build an abbey on the spot where Harold fell as a way of atoning for the bloodshed. Being a king, he kept his word and Battle Abbey was built in 1070.

miles inland from the seaside resort. William I had an abbey erected as penance for the number of men slain during the fighting, although most of the buildings you see date from the later medieval and Tudor periods. Visitors to the site today are taken on a virtual journey through the bloody conflict beginning with an exhibition on the background history, a video on the battle as well as a look at the changes the Norman invasion brought to the country – in the years after 1066, around half the land in England became the property of just 30 or so individuals, none of whom spoke English. Afterwards, you get to take an audio tour of the battlefield itself (you can hear the story of the battle retold from various viewpoints – a Saxon soldier, a Norman knight etc.) and can stand on the very spot where Harold fell after having been shot in the eye by a Norman arrow. Activity sheets and quizzes are provided and there's also a themed play area for very young children. Dazzling battle re-enactments take place every weekend in summer.

Housed in a barn near the abbey is Buckley's Yesterday's World which holds a collection of recreated shop and house interiors from the 1850s to 1950s as well as a children's village of huts to explore, a penny arcade, a miniature golf course and a toddlers' activity area.

Buckley's Yesterday's World
80–90 Battle High Street, Battle t (01424) 775378
www.yesterdaysworld.co.uk
Open Daily 10–6
Adm Adult £4.50, child £3, under-4s free
Café, gift shop, mother and baby room

Bodiam Castle
Bodiam, Robertsbridge t (01580) 830436
Getting there Bodiam is 10 miles north of Hastings off the B2244. In summer there are river cruises to Bodiam from Newenden. The Kent and East Sussex Steam Railway also makes trips from Bodiam to the nearby town of Tenterden, see p.48.
Open Mid Feb–Oct daily 10–6; Nov–mid Feb Tues–Sun 10–4
Adm Adult £3.50, child £1.75, family £8.75
Café–restaurant, gift shop, picnic areas, mother and baby facilities, some disabled access, on-site parking

When children try to draw a castle, they nearly always come up with something that looks like Bodiam. Bodiam is a proper storybook castle with round turrets on each corner, crinkly battlements,

arrow-slit windows, and a portcullis, and is surrounded by a deep moat. It has been uninhabited since the Civil War and much of the interior is open to the elements which means that, unlike many other castles where you have to stop your children bumping into precious relics and monuments, here kids can run about to their heart's content. And they do – they climb the narrow spiral staircases, peer though the high windows at imaginary invaders and hunt for ducks and carp in the moat. If you can get them to sit still for long enough, they'll probably enjoy the 15-minute audiovisual presentation showing what life was like in a medieval castle (pretty grim in truth). After that, however, it's probably best just to let them off the leash to explore. See if they can find the castle's medieval toilets which emptied straight into the moat (those poor ducks).

The inside of the castle, most of which is covered in grass, makes a perfect spot for a picnic and there are numerous family events organized throughout the year, including treasure hunts, donkey rides and open air theatre performances. In summer there are boat trips from Bodiam up and down the river to Newenden and back (it's a 90-minute round-trip) and you can also take a ride aboard The East Sussex Steam Railway which runs between here and the nearby town of Tenterden.

Buckets and spades

Bognor Regis
Getting there Bognor is on the south coast 5 miles east of Chichester and 6 miles west of Littlehampton on the A259. There are regular train services from London (Victoria) and Brighton
Tourist information Belmont Street t (01243) 823140

In truth, there is nothing particularly regal about it. Bognor Regis these days (it is the site of a Butlins Holiday Camp, after all, the epitome of simple knees-up entertainment), although the town itself is pleasant enough and, what's more (and I bet you didn't know this), officially the sunniest place in England. According to the Met Office it enjoyed more sun on average per day in the 1990s than anywhere else, including such traditional hotspots as the Isle of Wight and the English Riviera. And, if that isn't reason enough to come, there's always the beach, one of the cleanest and best maintained on the south coast. Wide, sandy and over eight miles long, it's lined along its entire length with ice cream kiosks, snack bars and pubs. Donkey rides are offered in summer and a dog ban is in operation between May and September. The best place to head to on the Blue Flag beach is east of the pier where, at low tide, shingle gives way to sand. The bathing is safe and the foreshore station includes a first aid and a lost children centre.

Butlins

Gloucester Road **t** (01243) 822445
www.butlins.co.uk
Open April–Oct 9.30–11 (last entry 5)
Adm Adult £12, child £9, family £36
Fast food outlets, cafés

Founded by South African-born William 'Billy' Butlin, who began his career as a fairground entertainer before virtually inventing the British holiday camp, this Butlins site has the best of both, with circus acts, splash pools, rollercoasters, puppet shows, jugglers, singers, costumed characters, go-kart tracks, indoor and outdoor adventure playgrounds. It's loud, it's garish and it's unashamedly tacky and it's exactly what your kids will want.

Did you know?
The Regis suffix was awarded to Bognor by George V, a frequent and appreciative visitor in the early part of the 20th century. Indeed, such was his fondness for the place that on his deathbed his aides suggested he might like to pay it one final visit. His last words were reputedly 'Bugger Bognor'.

Eastbourne

Getting there Eastbourne is on the south coast 21 miles east of Brighton, 18 miles west of Hastings on the A259, just south of the A27. There are regular train services from London (Victoria) and Brighton.
Tourist information 3 Cornfield Road, Eastbourne **t** (01323) 411400 **www.**eastbourne.org

Part owned by the Duke of Devonshire, Eastbourne has a cultured, almost dignified air to it. Indeed for a popular British tourist resort, there's a distinct lack of the normal tourist tat. There are no souvenir shops or candyfloss sellers along the seafront, just elegant Victorian homes and a few hotels and restaurants. Nothing is allowed to disturb the resort's relaxed and (some might say) slightly stuffy atmosphere. Perhaps unsurprisingly, this haven of south coast tranquillity has become a popular retirement home with all the benefits (peace and quiet) and problems (too much peace and quiet) that this implies. Nonetheless, the authorities haven't managed to stamp out all the fun just yet. Despite its polished veneer, Eastbourne actually has a good deal to offer in terms of family entertainment. There's the pier, one of the best and most visited in the country, an adventure playground 'Treasure Island', a children's adventure fun park 'Fort Fun', a leisure complex 'The Sovereign Centre' and, of course, the beach, a long stretch of sand and shingle with numerous rockpools (lifeguards patrol in summer). The seafront is framed by two old towers, the Redoubt Fortress, where classical concerts and firework displays are held in summer, and the Wish Tower, which holds a collection of puppets.

Every summer, in early June, Eastbourne plays host to a prestigious women's tennis tournament which attracts many of the top players hoping to get in some grass court practice before Wimbledon at the end of the month.

There is no need to restrict your holidaying to the town itself. Eastbourne makes a good base for exploring the South Downs Way which starts a couple of miles west at Beachy Head and continues all the way to the Sussex–Hampshire border (p.46). The Head itself is well worth visiting for its spectacular 575ft high cliff overlooking a crashing sea and interactive countryside centre. The Seven Sisters Sheep Centre is four miles west (p.46), Drusilla's Park 7 miles northeast (p.39), while the

Herstmonceux Science Centre, one of the best science museums in the country (p.47) is nine miles north in Hailsham.

Beachy Head Countryside Centre

Beachy Head Road **t** (01323) 737273
Open Mar–Sept daily 10–5.30; Oct daily 10–4; Nov–Feb Sat and Sun 11–4
Free
Disabled access
  Hands-on exhibits, play areas and guided walks along the clifftops.

Fort Fun

Royal Parade **t** (01323) 642833
Open Easter–May and Sept–Oct Sat and Sun 10–6; June–Aug 10–8
Free, rides are charged individually
Café–restaurant, some disabled access
  Boasts a rollercoaster, a giant slide, go-karts, a miniature railway and 'the largest indoor soft play area in Sussex'.

How We Lived Then Museum of Shops and Social History

20 Cornfield Terrace **t** (01323) 737143
Open Daily 10–5.30
Adm Adult £3, child £2
Gift shop
  You can wander through four floors of authentic shop and house interiors including a grocer's, a chemist's, a wartime living room, a seafarer's inn and, for the kids, a toy shop.

The Pier

t (01323) 410466
Open 8am–2pm
Free (also **free** deckchairs)
Restaurants, cafés, fast food, souvenirs, disabled access
  Lined with arcades and restaurants, speedboat rides are offered from the tip.

The Sovereign Centre

Royal Parade, Langney Point **t** (01323) 738822
Open Daily 9–7
Adm Adult £4.20, child £3.20, family £14.30
Café–restaurant
  There's an indoor splash pool and wave-machine, a tenpin bowling alley and go-karts. Horse-riding, tennis and windsurfing are also offered.

Treasure Island

Royal Parade **t** (01323) 411077

Open Daily April–Oct 10–6
Adm Child £2.85, accompanying adult £1.75
Café
  Well-equipped adventure playground.

Wish Tower Puppet Museum

King Edward's Parade **t** (01323) 417776
www.puppets.co.uk
Open Easter–June and Sept–Oct Sat and Sun 11–5; July–Aug daily 11–5
Adm Adult £1.80, child £1.25, under-2s **free**
Café
  Explores the history of puppetry.

Cinemas

Curzon, Langney Road **t** (01323) 738845

Activities
Knockhatch Adventure Park

Hempstead Lane, Hailsham **t** (01323) 442051
Getting there It's 9 miles north of Eastbourne off the A22
Open April–Sept Sat and Sun and school hols 10–5.30
Adm Adult £5.25, child £4.25, family £16.95
Café, gift shop, mother and baby room, disabled access, adapted toilets, on-site parking
  Knockhatch has a vast 2,000sq ft indoor play area, an adventure playground, free-fall slides, go-karts, a laser shooting-range, a boating lake, a bird of prey centre and a children's farm.

Lloyds Lanes and Laserquest Centre

Broadwater Way, Eastbourne **t** (01323) 509999
Open Bowling daily 10–late, Laserquest daily 4–late
Adm Bowling £3.25 per game (shoe hire £1 per person), Laserquest £3.25 per game
Fast food outlets
  20 bowling lanes, a laserquest arena, pool tables and video games.

Trax Indoor Karting Centre

46 Brampton Road, Hampden Park Industrial Estate, Eastbourne **t** (01323) 521133
www.traxkart.freeserve.co.uk
Open Daily 10–8
Adm £10 per person
  Minimum age 9 years, minimum height 4ft 10in.

Look out for...

The Stade, a traditional working fishing beach in East Hastings, just below the old town, where fishermen still haul their boats on to the beach. It's a fascinating place. Look out, in particular, for the net shops, three-storey wood and tar sheds where fishermen hang their nets out to dry. In the mid 19th century, the town council attempted to get the fishermen to move off the beach by increasing ground rents – these constructions were the fishermen's response.

Hastings

Getting there Hastings is on the south coast 18 miles northeast of Eastbourne on the A259. There are frequent train services from London (Victoria and Charing Cross), Gatwick, Brighton, Eastbourne, Portsmouth and Rye. National Express coaches arrive from London; South Coast buses from Brighton and Dover
Tourist information Queen's Square **t** (01424) 781111 www.hastings.gov.uk

As every school child knows, Hastings is where William conquered in 1066 when his Normans beat the English army and poor old Harold was shot through the eye with an arrow. In fact, despite its name, the Battle of Hastings actually took place at Battle, 7 miles inland (and so should really have been called the Battle of Battle). Still, the Hastings tourist industry has always made the most of the connection and the town does boast a castle erected on the orders of William himself where you can see the 1066 Story, an audiovisual presentation on the battle in a mock-up siege tent.

Hastings has had its problems in recent years and parts of it are rather run down, however, the old town is still very pleasant with its rickety old 15th-century timber-framed buildings and 13th-century church of St Clements, and there are two rather jaunty Victorian funicular railways (the West Hill Railway which ascends Hastings cliff face is the most fun).

Down by the seafront there's a very good Sea Life Centre with a walkthrough sea-bed tunnel and, jutting out from the wide sandy beach, a pier lined with arcade games and candyfloss stalls. Perhaps the most fun attraction the town has to offer, apart from the beach, is the Smugglers' Adventure, a labyrinth of deep caves and passageways used by 18th-century duty-dodgers and now inhabited by life-size waxworks arranged in a variety of nefarious tableaux (with the obligatory spooky lighting and sound effects). The 240ft Hastings Embroidery, inspired by the famous Bayeux Tapestry and depicting scenes from British history, can be seen in the White Rock Theatre.

Hastings Embroidery
White Rock Theatre **t** (01424) 781000
Open Daily 11–4
Adm Adult £2, child £1
Café, gift shop, disabled access

Smugglers Adventure
St Clement's Caves, West Hill **t** (01424) 422964
Open Easter–Sept daily 10–5.30; Oct–Easter daily 11–4.30
Adm Adult £4.50, child £2.95
Gift shop

1066 Story in Hastings Castle
Castle Hill Road, West Hill **t** (01424) 781111
Open Easter–Sept daily 10–5; Oct–Easter daily 11–3.30
Adm Adult £3, child £2
Gift shop, disabled access

Underwater World
Rock-A-Nore Road **t** (01424) 718776
www.underwaterworld-hastings.co.uk
Open Daily 10–6
Adm Adult £4.95, child £3.50
Café, gift shop, mother and baby room, disabled access

Cinemas
Odeon, Queens Road **t** (01424) 431180

Littlehampton

Getting there Littlehampton is on the south coast, 6 miles east of Bognor, 14 miles west of Brighton off the A259
Tourist information Windmill Complex, Coastguard Road **t** (01903) 713480

Come to Littlehampton to experience the archetypal British seaside weekend – making sandcastles, collecting seashells and hunting for crabs in pools. Littlehampton's charms are as familiar and timeless as the sea itself. The beach is clean and well maintained with a a Kidzone safety scheme, which splits the seafront into colour-coded sections (kids are issued with matching wristbands) and a modern first-aid and lost children unit nearby. The seafront is lined with fish and chip restaurants, seaside rock emporiums and shops selling plastic buckets and spades, beach balls and other such seaside essentials and there's a small road train offering trips up and down the front. Low tide exposes a vast expanse of sand and the gentle slope of the beach means that the sea remains shallow many metres from the shore making it perfect for paddling. The River Arundel meets the sea at the western end of the beach and sightseeing boat trips are offered up the river to Arundel where you can visit the famous castle (p.40) as well as around the harbour and along the coast. Beyond the river is an extensive area of unspoilt sand dunes. The only downside of a trip to Littlehampton will be the crowds, which in summer can be pretty intense, although still nothing compared with the hordes that descend on Brighton during the holiday season.

Look out for Harbour Park on the seafront, a small, very seasidey children's fun park with a soft play area, a ball pond, an assault course, a 'giant' (relatively speaking) helter-skelter and that evergreen seaside favourite, a crazy golf course.

It may come as a surprise to some, that this little seaside town is home to the Body Shop's visitor centre. Here, visitors can see how the ethical cosmetics company, founded by Anita Roddick who opened her first store in Brighton in 1976, became a worldwide network of shops which (so it is estimated) sold a product every 0.4 seconds in 1997/8.

During the 80-minute tour you can see how the Body Shop makes its products, learn more about the principles which made the company such a success and, of course, sample some of the sweet-smelling cosmetics, soaps and bubble-baths.

The Caribbean-style visitor centre also has a branch of the Body Shop where you can buy the full range of products and pick up a few bargains at trade prices. Tours are available by appointment only.

The Body Shop Visitor Centre

Watersmead **t** (0800) 096 0809
Tours available Mon–Sat 10.20am–3.40
Cost Adult £4.50 child £3.50 family £14.00
Cafe, car park

Harbour Park

Seafront **t** (01903) 716663 **www**.harbourpark.co.uk
Open Daily 10–late
Adm Adult £4.15, child £4.50
Fast food outlets

Nature lovers

Ashdown Forest

For further information *see* p.38.

Bentley Wildfowl and Motor Museum

Harveys Lane, Halland, Lewes **t** (01825) 840573
Getting there It's 14 miles northwest of Eastbourne off the A22
Open April–Oct daily 10.30–4.30
Adm Adult £4.80, child £3, under-4s **free**, family £14.50
Café, gift shop, guided tours, disabled access, on-site parking

It's a slightly odd combination of attractions but definitely well worth a visit. Start at the museum which is full of bright, gleaming sportscars from throughout the history of motoring – Ferraris, Aston Martins. Kids will be attracted to all the shiny metal but may find the lack of interaction rather frustrating. Visitors are not even allowed to touch these speed machines (much less climb inside, which is what they really want to do). The grounds, however, offer much more scope for kids to get their hands dirty with woodland trails and a miniature steam train offering rides in summer. The main attraction, however, is the birds. Pick up an identification chart and a bag of seed at the entrance and see what you can find. There are well over a thousand birds living on the park's collection of ponds and enclosures with three marked routes taking you past all the assorted ducks, geese and swans who will rush up to meet you as soon as they hear the first faint rustle of seed.

Drusilla's Park

For further information *see* p.39.

Fishers Farm Park

Newpound Lane, Wisborough Green, nr Billingshurst **t** (01403) 700063
www.fishersfarmpark.co.uk
Getting there It's 7 miles south east of Horsham off the A272
Open Daily 10–6
Adm Adult £5, child £4.50, family £17
Café, gift shop, mother and baby facilities, on-site parking

Your day begins at the animal barns by the entrance where you can meet the farm's resident cows, pigs, goats and sheep and, in early summer,

The South Downs

The South Downs are a great rolling ridge of chalk hills running along the southern half of Sussex and Hampshire. They contain numerous areas of outstanding natural beauty, and are traversed by the South Downs Way, one of the country's great walks, which stretches for 106 miles from Eastbourne all the way to Winchester.

Cissbury Ring

(3 miles north of Worthing off the A24)

Huge Iron-Age rampart offering good views out over the coast towards the Isle of Wight.

Devil's Dyke

(4 miles northeast of Brighton off A23), Estate Office, Saddlescombe Farm, Brighton **t** (01273) 857712

One of the Downs' most famous beauty spots (and a favourite jumping-off point for hang-gliders), Devil's Dyke can provide wonderful views of Brighton and the coast.

Ditchling Beacon

(6 miles north of Brighton off the B2116)

Great views and a sweet country village.

Wilmington

(4 miles northeast of Eastbourne off the A27).

Huge chalk figure 'The Long Man' cut into the hillside. No one knows when or why.

Riding the Downs
Freewheelin's Trekking

Northcommon Farm, Golf Links Lane, Selsey **t** (01243) 602725

Open All year, rides must be booked in advance

Horse-trekking on the South Downs. Half-hour lessons for beginners.

Southdown Llama Trekking

Muddleswood Farm, Brighton Road, Newtimber **t** (01273) 835656

Open April–Oct Wed and Sat (11am start)

Accompanied llama treks on the South Downs. Suitable for children aged 10+.

Willowbrook Riding Centre

Hambrook Hill South, Hambrook, nr Chichester **t** (01243) 572683

Open All year round, call in advance

Horse-riding on the South Downs for all ages.

goat kids and lambs – children may even be allowed to get inside the lamb enclosure for a quick cuddle. Then, after a brief inspection of the games in the indoor play barn, it's off to the farm's open-air section where you can enjoy tractor and pony rides (and, even, combine-harvester rides), go for a spin on a 1950s carousel, take the wheel of a go-kart, climb over the equipment at the adventure playground and, if you've still got any energy left, perhaps visit the cows and sheep in their paddocks.

Leonardslee Gardens

Lower Beeding, Horsham **t** (01403) 891212

Getting there It's 8 miles west of Haywards Heath, just off the A281

Open April–Oct daily 9.30–6

Adm Adult £6, child £2.50

Refreshments, gift shop, on-site parking

Set in a 240-acre valley on the edge of the ancient St Leonard's Forest, these grand, sweeping gardens – full of rhododendrons, magnolias and conifers – contain no fewer than seven lakes, as well as a rock garden, a Japanese garden and wallaby and deer enclosures. And as if this wasn't enough, there are plants for sale and there's an exhibition of Victorian motorcars which date from 1895–1900.

Seven Sisters Sheep Centre

The Fridays, East Dean, Eastbourne **t** (01323) 423207

Getting there It's just west of Beachy Head off the A259

Open May–Sept Mon–Fri 2–5 Sat and Sun 11–5

Adm Adult £3, child £2

Café, gift shop, guided tours, on-site parking

As well as meeting the woolly favourites them-selves (there are over 45 breeds), you can watch demonstrations of sheep-shearing, wool-spinning, milking and cheese-making at this family-run farm. In spring–early summer, there are baby lambs to cuddle and bottle-feed and tractor rides to enjoy. The Seven Sisters Country Park, on the South Downs Way, is a few miles to the west.

Sheffield Park Garden

Sheffield Park, Uckfield **t** (01825) 790231

Getting there It's between East Grinstead and Lewes, just northwest of Uckfield off the A275

Open Mar–Oct Tues–Sun 10.30–6 (or dusk); Nov–Dec Tues–Sun 10–4; Jan–Feb Sat and Sun 10.30–4

Adm Adult £4.20, child £2.10, family £10.50

Café, picnic areas, shop, guided tours, disabled access, on-site parking

It doesn't really matter what time of year you visit this huge 120-acre Capability Brown-land-scaped park with no fewer than five lakes lined by cascades and waterfalls. In spring the grass is carpeted with daffodils and bluebells; in summer it's likewise filled with flowers – rhododendrons, azaleas etc; even in autumn the gardens are ablaze with colour. Family events such as Teddy Bear Picnics and nature walks (to look for bats, fungi, birds) are organized in summer. The Bluebell, probably the country's most famous steam railway, departs for trips through the local countryside from Sheffield Park Station (p.38).

Look at this!

Amberley Industrial Museum

Amberley, near Arundel **t** (01798) 831370
www.amberleymuseum.co.uk
Getting there Amberley is 4 miles north of Arundel, 8 miles north of Littlehampton, 12 miles northeast of Chichester off the B2139
Open Mar–Oct Wed–Sun 10–6, daily during school hols
Adm Adult £6.25, child £3.25, under-5s **free**, family £17
Café, gift shop, disabled access, on-site parking

Dedicated to the industrial history of southeast England, the Amberley Industrial Museum is a busy, bustling and surprisingly child-friendly place. A former chalk quarry, this 36-acre site is now home to over 20 recreated workshops where you can see skilled craftsmen demonstrating tradi-tional rural crafts like pottery, printing and boat building. If all the noise gets a bit much, you can always take some time out to enjoy the beautiful South Downs setting aboard the open-top 1920s bus which tours the site, or take a ride through the woods on a workman's steam train to the small railway museum.

Bear Museum

38 Dragon Street, Petersfield **t** (01730) 265108
Getting there Petersfield is 14 miles northwest of Chichester on the A3
Open Tues–Sat 10–5
Free

Refreshments, souvenirs, mother and baby facilities

Petersfield is home to the world's first Teddy Bear Museum. Vintage bears are displayed sitting at a Teddy Bears Picnic and in a Victorian nursery and there are plenty of modern bears on hand for chil-dren to cuddle.

Bentley Wildfowl and Motor Museum

For further information *see p.45.*

Diggerland

Whitehall Road, Strood **t** (01634) 291290
www.diggerland.com
Getting there From M2, take J11 and follow A289 into Medway City Estate
Open Weekends and bank holidays 10–5
Adm £2.50 (but see below)
Refreshments, gift shop, on-site parking

Mud-loving kids could do worse than head for Diggerland, a construction-style theme park, where there are pedal-powered diggers, and full-size JCB diggers and dumpers to ride in. Older kids can have a go in a JCB at £1 extra a pop (an £18 wristband allows unlimited rides and drives for an entire day) while younger children will probably head for the sandpit and bouncy castle.

Herstmonceux Science Centre

Herstmonceux, Hailsham **t** (01323) 832731
www.science.project.org
Getting there It's about 9 miles north of Eastbourne off the A271
Open April–Oct daily 10–6
Adm Adult £4.50, child £3.30, under-5s **free**, family £13
Café, shop, picnic areas, on-site parking

Excellent science centre set between five enor-mous telescope domes with over 70 hands-on exhibits. You can look at yourself in a 'real' mirror which reverses your image so that you can see yourself as others see you (not a pretty sight), examine tiny objects through a TV microscope and find out how lasers work. There's also an exhibition on astronomy and a recently opened outdoor Discovery Park with many more hands-on exhibits and experiments.

Tangmere Military Aviation Museum

Tangmere, near Chichester **t** (01243) 775223
www.wealddown.co.uk
Open March–Oct daily 10–5.30; Feb–Nov daily 10–4.30 (last adm 1 hr before closing)
Adm Adult £3, child £1.50

The Battle of Britain began in August 1940 when Herman Goering's Luftwaffe began an all-out attack on British ports, airfields, and, finally, on London. Germany's aim was to crush British morale and destroy the RAF in preparation for Operation Sea Lion, an invasion of England. Thanks to planes like the Spitfire and the Hurricane, and aided by RADAR, the outnumbered RAF were able to inflict heavy casualties on the Luftwaffe. Midway through the campaign, Goering berated his generals for their poor performance. The German fighter ace, Adolf Galland, replied that what the Luftwaffe needed was not rebukes but Spitfires. In the end, the Luftwaffe were unable to sustain such heavy losses and Operation Sea Lion was suspended indefinitely. Prime Minister Winston Churchill was in no way exaggerating in his famous remark about the RAF pilots: 'Never has so much been owed by so many to so few.'

Shop, café, tours, disabled access, on-site parking
An RAF airfield during the Second World War, Tangmere is now one of the country's most important military aviation museums. There's lots of fearsome looking hardware on display, including a Meteor, a Hunter, a Hurricane and, of course, a Spitfire, the most famous fighter plane of them all. There is even a Battle of Britain flight simulator.

The first full-size light railway in the world when it opened in 1900, the Kent and East Sussex Railway has been carefully restored in recent years by a team of dedicated volunteers. Its puffing engines and beautiful 'blood and custard' carriages (the nickname of the red and yellow colour scheme) now transport passengers on a scenic journey through seven miles of Kentish countryside from Tenterden, where there is a small museum of railway memorabilia and an adventure playground, to Bodiam, site of the famous castle (p.41), passing streams, lily ponds and acres of hop farmland on the way.

Steam power

Bluebell Railway
For further information *see* p.38.

Kent and East Sussex Railway
Tenterden Town Station, Tenterden **t** (01580) 765155
Talking Timetable **t** (01580) 762943
www.seetb.org.uk/kesr
Getting there It's 7 miles northeast of Bodiam off the A28
Operating hours Suns in Mar; weekends and bank holidays from April to Oct; June and Sept Tues–Thurs; daily in July and Aug; Santa Specials in Dec
Refreshments, wheelchair access, adapted toilets, on-site parking

CANTERBURY

Getting there By road: Canterbury is linked to London via the A2/M2 and to Ashford via the A28. The city centre is largely pedestrianized, but there's a good park and ride system in operation. By rail: There are two train stations, Canterbury East (northwest of the town centre) which receives services from London Victoria, and Canterbury West (south) which receives services from London Charing Cross and Waterloo; both are a 10-minute walk from the city centre. By bus/coach: National Express services arrive daily from London. The bus station is on St George's Lane

Tourist office 34 St Margaret's Street
t (01227) 766567 **www.canterbury.co.uk**

This was where the seeds of English Christianity were first sown when, way back in AD 597, the Pope sent his emissary Augustine here to convert the population to Christianity. Throughout the Middle Ages it was the country's most important pilgrimage centre and, even today, it's still England's second most visited city (after London). If possible, you should try to avoid coming in high summer when its narrow streets will be thronged with people.

Do also be aware that, though well worth visiting, the city's attractions are principally religious and/or historical and thus may prove a little dry for very young children. This is certainly true of the city's prime site, the imposing Christ Church Cathedral, the ecclesiastical and theological headquarters of the English Church. Christ Church – along with the remains of the abbey founded by St Augustine, and St Martin's, the oldest parish church still in constant use – has been designated a World Heritage Site by Unesco. All three are linked by a marked walk. Nonetheless, there's plenty here for families to enjoy. Many of the city's

---

Tell me a story: Thomas à Becket

'Who will rid me of this turbulent priest?' These fateful words, spoken by Henry II in 1170, sealed the fate of Thomas à Becket, the then Archbishop of Canterbury. During his reign, Henry was in almost constant disagreement with the Pope in Rome – who at that time was still the head of the English church – over religious policy. Henry didn't like the idea of a foreign leader having so much influence over his church and so appointed his close friend and advisor, Thomas à Becket, as Archbishop of Canterbury (the English church's top job) thinking that Thomas would let him run the church the way he wanted. Unfortunately, for Henry, Thomas proved much more devout and loyal to Rome than he had expected. Previously known for his fondness for fine living, upon assuming the archbishopric, Thomas immediately renounced his old hedonistic ways (and his friendship with Henry) and devoted himself to matters of the church (i.e. the Pope's) law. Over the succeeding years, Henry and Thomas had numerous arguments and run-ins resulting, at one stage, with Thomas being banished from the country. Though they did manage to patch things up, and Thomas did return from exile, it proved to be a short-lived peace. The two men soon fell out again, this time so seriously that Henry was prompted to make his fateful request.

Upon hearing his words, four knights rushed to Canterbury and on 29 December 1170 they found Thomas preparing for evensong in the cathedral and slew him where he stood. When he heard the news, Henry was mortified. He claimed that he had only been speaking out loud, not issuing orders. Racked with guilt, he later decided to pay penance by walking barefoot from Hambledon to the cathedral at Canterbury where he allowed himself to be flogged as punishment for his sins.

Thomas, meanwhile, achieved even greater fame in death than he had in life. He was declared a Saint and his tomb in Canterbury Cathedral became the country's most popular and important site of pilgrimage. Indeed, catering for the needs of pilgrims became the principal activity of most of the town's inns and taverns. In the *Canterbury Tales* (*see also* p.50), Chaucer describes how the streets of medieval Canterbury were lined with tradesmen trying to sell souvenirs to visitors – not much changes.

Unfortunately for Thomas, in the 16th century, Henry VIII, like Henry II before him, began to distance himself from the Pope. This particular argument, however, proved terminal. Henry removed the English church from the Pope's control, abolished the country's monasteries and had all the saints' shrines, including Thomas' at Canterbury, destroyed.

museums and exhibitions – including the Canterbury Tales, the Heritage Museum and the Roman Museum – are presented in a lively, hands-on way.

Need to sit down?

There are pleasant riverside gardens (notably the West Gate Gardens with its summer floral displays) and boat trips on the River Stour to enjoy.

The city centre itself, which is pedestrianized and filled with picturesque medieval buildings (particularly on Palace Street, Burgate and St Peter's Street), is fun to explore with lots of good shopping although, thanks to some hefty wartime bombing, it does have its uglier parts. Furthermore, Canterbury is only a short distance from the resort of Whitstable on the Kent coast (see p.55).

Things to see

Canterbury Cathedral

Cathedral House, The Precincts **t** (01227) 762862
Open April–Sept Mon–Sat 8.45–7, Sun 12.30–2.30 and 4.30–5.30; Oct–Mar Mon–Sat 8.45–5, Sun 12.30–2.30
Adm Adult £3, child £2, under-5s **free**, guided tours £3 per person (minimum charge £30)
Shop, Welcome Information Centre; audiovisual presentations on the 'Story of the Cathedral', advance notice of wheelchair visits needed

The multi-pinnacled Canterbury Cathedral is a grand, imposing and highly evocative building – it looks particularly magical at night when spotlights pick out the detail in the exterior carving. Most of what you see was constructed in the 15th century although parts, including the crypt and some of the stained glass (among the very oldest in Britain), date back to the 12th century. Look out for the Martyrdom in the northwest transept, the spot where Thomas à Becket was murdered in 1170 at the wish, if not the order, of Henry II (see p.49). Becket's shrine attracted thousands of pilgrims in the Middle Ages following his elevation to the sainthood, but was destroyed in the 16th century in the wake of the English church's breach with Rome and replaced by the Trinity Chapel – you can still see the deep grooves worn into the steps by countless pairs of devotional knees. See if you can also find the stained-glass images of Becket's murder and the saint performing miracles.

During the Second World War, Canterbury was targeted for bombing by Germany as part of its Baedecker Campaign – an attempt to break Britain's will by destroying its most precious religious and cultural landmarks (picked out of a Baedecker guide). Miraculously, however, the Cathedral and its beautiful stained glass managed to survive the war unscathed.

Pick up an audio guide or a children's 'Explorer' guide at the entrance which will point out all the places of interest and fill you in on all the background stories and legends that, for children, will help bring the place alive.

Canterbury Heritage Museum

Stour Street **t** (01227) 452747
Open Mon–Sat and Sun 10.30–5
Adm Adults £2.30, under-18s £1.15, under-5s **free**, family £5.15
Guided tours, disabled access

Housed in a former Poor Priests' Hospital, the museum provides an overview of the major events from the city's 2000-year history – the coming of the Romans, the murder of Thomas à Becket, the burning of 40 heretics at the stake during the reign of Mary I, the bombing of the city during the Second World War and, of course, the adventures of Rupert the Bear, the lovable soft toy with the bright checked trousers (created by local artist Mary Tourtel) who gets a whole devoted gallery. It's much better presented than most local museums with state-of-the-art video, computer and even hologram displays and well worth an hour or two of your time.

Canterbury Roman Museum

Butchery Lane, Longmarket **t** (01227) 785575
Open Mon–Sat 10–5
Adm Adults £2.30, under-18s £1.15, under-5s **free**, family £5.15
Gift shop, guided tours, disabled access

Come and see what's left of Durovernum Contiacorum, the Roman town that preceded modern Canterbury in this spirited underground museum. There are reconstructions of Roman house interiors and market stalls to explore, interactive computer displays and a special 'hands-on' area where children can handle some genuine Roman artefacts.

Canterbury Tales

St Margaret's Street **t** (01227) 454888
Open Daily 9.30–5.30
Adm Adults £.5.50, under-16s £4.60, under-5s **free**, family £17.50

Gift shop, café, guided tours, disabled access

An exuberant, albeit slightly cheesy retelling of Geoffrey Chaucer's literary masterpiece using jerky animatronic models enlivened by sound, lighting and even smelly effects. You can listen to the tales retold through a headset as you wander around. It's particularly good for kids though its more for fun that education – they arrange ghost tours and organize children's events for the school holidays.

West Gate Museum

St Peter's Street **t** (01227) 452747
Open Mon–Sat 11–12.30 and 1.30–3.30
Adm Adult £1, child 50p

The medieval city of Canterbury was enclosed behind a thick stone wall lined with a number of gatehouses where soldiers would have been stationed to watch for potential invaders. The West Gate is the last remaining gatehouse, and you can tour the battlements for views out over the city, or repel imaginary foe through the murder holes where invaders were welcomed with a quick dousing of boiling oil. Less grisly kids can do brass rubbings and try on replica suits of armour.

Things to do

Canterbury Guild of Guides

Arnett House, Hawks Lane **t** (01227) 459779
Daily walks from the Canterbury Visitor Information Centre 1 April–28 Oct at 2 (and 1 July–31 Aug and Bank Hols at 11.30 and 2)
Prices Adult £3.50, child £3, family £8.50

Canterbury Historic River Tours

Weavers Garden, St Peter's Street **t** 07790 534744
Open April–Oct daily
Half-hour sightseeing trips along the River Stour. Punts can also be hired from near the West Gate **t** (0585) 318301.

Downland Cycle Hire

Canterbury West Station **t** (01227) 479643
Price £10/day's hire+£50 returnable deposit
Hires out bikes for tours along the famous 'Crab & Winkle' route between Canterbury and Whitstable.

Cinemas
ABC

43–45 St Georges Place **t** (01227) 770829

Theatres
The Marlowe

The Friars **t** (01227) 787787

SPECIAL TRIPS

World Naval Base – Chatham Historic Dockyard

Chatham **t** (01634) 823800
www.worldnavalbase.org.uk
Getting there Chatham is on the north Kent Coast between Rochester and Gillingham on the A229 (J3 from M2)
Open April–Oct daily 10–5; Nov and Feb–Mar Wed and Sat–Sun 10–4; closed Dec–Jan
Adm Adult £6.20, child £4, under-5s **free**, family £16.40
Café, gift shop, disabled access

Founded by Henry VIII and once the HQ of the Royal Navy, Chatham's docks have been turned into one of the country's best maritime museums with lots to see and do. Pick up a site plan at the entrance as the scale of the place, with its vast shipbuilding sheds and warehouses, is awe-inspiring. Check out the Rope-Making Room – officially the largest room in the country – where great, thick quarter-mile long ropes are laid out on the floor and regular demonstrations of rope-making are held.

As well as containing lots of straightforward historical exhibits such as Wooden Walls – a series of waxwork animatronic tableaux designed to illustrate the construction of an 18th-century warship – the museum also provides plenty of opportunity for kids to clamber in and around the exhibits with no less than 15 historic lifeboats to explore – kids can run over the decks, pop their heads through the portholes and pretend to steer the ship sitting in the captain's chair. The undoubted highlight of the museum, however, is Battle Ships!, a display of three very different fighting vessels: *HMS Cavalier*, Britain's last remaining Second World War destroyer, *HMS Ocelot*, a 1960s spy submarine, and the *Gannet*, the last Victorian fighting sloop (a, small, extremely manouverable sailing warship mounted with about 20 guns). When the weather is good, trips are offered from the pier aboard a paddle steamer that was made in the dockyard.

The town of Chatham is also home to Fort Amherst, a well-preserved 18th-century fort surrounded by 18 acres of parkland, with a network of secret tunnels to explore and a battery of guns to pretend to fire.

AROUND AND ABOUT

Bricks and mortar

Deal Castle

Victoria Road, Deal **t** (01304) 372762
www.english-heritage.co.uk
Getting there Deal is on the east Kent coast, 7 miles north of Dover on the A258
Open April–Oct 10–6; Nov–Mar Wed–Sun 10–4
Adm Adult £3, child £1.50
Gift shop, some disabled access

A few miles north of Dover, Deal supposedly marks the spot where Julius Caesar and his Roman troops first set foot on British soil. Some 1,600 years later Henry VIII ordered the construction of this peculiarly shaped castle (from above it resembles a Tudor Rose) in order to prevent anyone else on the continent from getting a similar idea. With its towering views of the coast and long, dark passageways to explore, Deal Castle provides an excellent afternoon's entertainment. Call in advance for details of any family events that might be coming up, which might include battle re-enactments, puppet-making workshops, Tudor printing workshops and special child-friendly guided tours.

Dover Castle

Dover **t** (01304) 211067
www.english-heritage.org.uk
Getting there By road: From London take the M20 then the A20. By rail: Dover Priory train station is half a mile northwest of the town centre and is served by London (Victoria and Charing Cross) and Canterbury.
Open April–Oct daily 10–6; Nov–Mar daily 10–4
Adm Adult £6.90, child £3.50, family £17.30
Gift and book shop, café, mother and baby facilities, disabled access, on-site parking

The castle is very child-friendly with lots of interactive exhibits, a children's activity centre and an audiovisual presentation on what life would have been like during a 13th-century siege. A range of family events is put on throughout the year including archery tournaments, battle re-enactments and storytellings by costumed characters. Within its walls are the remains of a Pharos or lighthouse erected by the Romans in AD 50 (making it Britain's oldest standing building), while, beneath the castle, is a network of subterranean passageways known as the 'Secret Wartime Tunnels' dug during the Napoleonic wars and extended in the Second World War. Spooky guided tours are offered every 20 minutes when you are also shown a short film on Operation Dynamo – the evacuation of Dunkirk. The views from the castle's battlements are stupendous.

Cinemas

Silver Screen Cinema, White Cliffs Experience **t** (01304) 228000

Hever Castle

Hever, near Edenbridge **t** (01732) 865224
www.hevercastle.co.uk
Getting there Hever is about 8 miles west of Tonbridge off the B2027
Open Mar–Nov daily 11–6
Adm Adult £7.80, child £4.20, under-5s **free**, family £19.80
Café, gift shop, guided tours, mother and baby facilities, disabled access, on-site parking

It may look similar, with its turrets, battlements and moat, but Hever is very much the antithesis of the rough and ready Bodiam; its interior is sumptuously decorated with antiques, fine tapestries and suits of armour – although many of the more interesting areas are (frustratingly) roped off. There are, however, a few nooks and crannies worth exploring, as well as costumed waxworks of Henry VIII and his six wives (this was where Anne Boleyn, his second wife, lived as a child), a display of dolls' houses and the castle's picnic-perfect grounds. Here you'll find a yew maze, a lake and an Italian garden with a lakeside theatre where a renowned season of plays, musicals and opera performances takes place each summer. There's also a water maze (from April to Oct), lined with water jets that spray visitors every time they take a wrong turning.

Leeds Castle

Maidstone **t** 0870 6008880
www.leeds-castle.co.uk
Getting there Leeds Castle is 40 miles southeast of London near Maidstone off the M20 and B2163. There are direct services from London Victoria to Bearsted, the nearest train station, from where there's a regular shuttle bus to the castle. Eurostar

services from London Waterloo stop at Ashford International, 20 minutes away
Open Castle: Mar–Oct 11–5.30; Nov–Feb 10.15–3.30; park and gardens: Mar–Oct 10–5; Nov–Feb 10–3
Adm Adult £9.30, child £6, under-5s **free**, family £25
Gift shops, restaurant, guided tours, some wheelchair access

Leeds Castle looks like a castle should look – dramatic, romantic and mysterious. Set on two islands in the middle of a lake in 500 acres of beautifully sculpted Kent countryside, this was the famously hard to please Henry VIII's favourite castle. He spent a fortune on it during his lifetime as seen in his fabulously opulent Banqueting Hall with its ebony wood floors and carved oak ceiling. Architecturally, it's a bit of a hotch potch – the cellar dates from the 11th century, the Gatehouse from the 12th (it contains a rare collection of dog collars, some over 400 years old), the Maiden's Tower is Tudor, while the main residential quarters were built in the last century – but it all hangs together perfectly and is an undeniably beautiful place. Unfortunately, beauty doesn't always cut it with children. The trouble with Leeds, as far as kids are concerned, is that, inside, it's a bit starchy and formal. The interior is stuffed full of precious paintings and furniture but the rarefied 'don't touch' atmosphere means that kids can't really interact with the space as much as they would like. A suit of armour quickly loses its appeal if you're not allowed to take it apart and get inside. It's a different story, however, in the castle grounds. With a maze, an underground grotto, an aviary and lots of wide grassy spaces to run around on, the grounds provide a wonderful opportunity for kids to let off steam. What's more, family entertainments are put on in the grounds throughout the year. These include Easter celebrations with face-painting, Punch and Judy shows, circus workshops, Half-Term Fun, when a range of impromptu mazes are constructed in the castle grounds and, of course, the famous Balloon Festival in September, when the sky around the castle becomes filled with dozens of weird and wonderfully shaped hot air balloons.

Walmer Castle
Kingsdown Road, Walmer, Deal **t** (01304) 364288
www.english-heritage.org.uk
Getting there Walmer Castle is in Deal on the east Kent coast, 7 miles north of Dover on the A258

Open April–Sept daily 10–6; Oct daily 10–5; Nov–Dec and Mar Wed–Sun 10–4; closed Jan–Feb
Adm Adult £4.50, child £2.30
Café, gift shop, disabled access, on-site parking

Built at the same time as nearby Deal Castle, Walmer has likewise been designed to look like a Tudor Rose (when viewed from above) and can offer equally splendid views of the Kent coastline, although it's perhaps slightly less child-friendly. Unlike many other castles, Walmer is still used by the Royal Family, albeit only for ceremonial occasions. It is the official seat of the Lord Warden of the Cinque Ports, the military official who, in centuries past, was charged with overseeing Kent's coastal defenses. In the mid 19th century this role was fulfilled by the Duke of Wellington, Napoleon's conqueror, and the castle contains an exhibition on his life and times featuring a pair of his famous waterproof boots. These days, however, it's a purely honorary title currently held by Her Majesty the Queen Mother, a frequent visitor to the castle. A garden was created in the castle grounds in honour of her 95th birthday. Garden tours, Easter Egg hunts and fairytale re-enactments are just some of the family events put on at the castle throughout the season.

Buckets and spades

Margate
Getting there Margate is on the Isle of Thanet at the northeastern tip of Kent, 14 miles northeast of Canterbury, 4 miles northwest of Broadstairs. Train services run regularly from London (Victoria), Chatham, Canterbury West and Dover.
Tourist office 22 High Street **t** (01843) 220241

It's not St Tropez. Neither, for that matter, is it Yalta, the swanky Black Sea resort with which it is twinned. Nevertheless, London's holidaymakers have been giving it the thumbs up for over two centuries now and, for many, Margate represents the very essence of the traditional British seaside experience; the sort of place where you can still occasionally spot sunburnt heads sporting knotted hankies.

There are four principal attractions: the beach, which is sandy and small; the Shell Grotto, an underground shell 'temple' discovered by children

Smuggling

In the 13th century Edward I became the first English monarch to introduce duty tax on exported and imported goods with the result that his subjects soon became the country's first smugglers. Throughout the Middle Ages duty-dodging thrived right along England's coast helped, in no small part, by the tolerant attitude of the general population who welcomed the cheap goods (typically small, easily portable luxury items such as tea, tobacco, silks, spices and spirits) that this illicit trade provided. Measures introduced to curb smuggling in the 17th century had little effect. Customs officials were usually severely underpaid and, thus, easy to bribe. Nonetheless, smugglers would often go to extreme lengths to keep their activities hidden from the authorities. Rather than secreting their goods in cliff-face caves in the traditional manner, by the 18th century some smugglers had entire coastal villages at their disposal with each house linked to the other via a network of secret passageways. The best smugglers even had getaway vehicles. Small galleys, powered by oarsmen rather than sails, were their vessels of choice as they were not only highly manoeuverable but very fast (especially over short distances) and could easily outrun the lumbering craft of the customs officials.

Though the age of mass smuggling came to an end in the late-19th century when Britain began to adopt free-trade policies, it's a problem that has never fully died out. So long as the duty paid on alcohol and cigarettes on the continent remains lower than it is in England, there'll always be people willing to take the risk.

in 1835 and made up of no less than 185sq m of passageways decorated with intricate shell mosaics (nobody knows who built it or, more importantly, why); the Margate Caves, a network of large, spooky caverns, and Dreamland, a very Margate sort of theme park, full of reasonably scary rides, including a rollercoaster built in 1863 (which is perhaps scary for the wrong reasons).

Dreamland

Marine Terrace **t** (01843) 227011
Open Easter–Oct daily 10–6 (till 10 in Aug)
Adm Adult £12, child £8
Cafés, fast food, mother and baby room, some disabled access, adapted toilets, on-site parking

The Shell Grotto

Grotto Hill **t** (01843) 220008
Open April–Oct daily 10–4
Adm Adult £1.80, child 90p
Gift shop

Cinemas
Dreamlan d Triple Cinema

Marine Terrace **t** (01843) 227822

Activities
AMF Bowling Centre

51 Addington Street, Margate **t** (01843) 291010
Open Daily 10–late
Adm Adult £1.85 (daytime) £2.90 (eves and weekends) + 80p shoe hire, child £1.45 (daytime) £2.50 (eves and weekends) + 55p shoe hire
Baby changing facilities, wheelchair access
24-lane bowling alley.

Ramsgate and Broadstairs

Getting there Ramsgate and Broadstairs lie about 4 miles apart from one another on the Isle of Thanet at the northeastern tip of Kent and can be reached via the A253 and A256
Tourist office Ramsgate: 19–21 Harbour Street **t** (01843) 583333; Broadstairs: 6B High Street **t** (01843) 583334

Ramsgate and Broadstairs are Margate's slightly posher, slightly swankier siblings. Broadstairs is easily the most refined of the three despite (according to legend) having been founded on the proceeds of smuggling. A pleasant clifftop resort overlooking a calm bay, it boasts five sandy beaches. The main one, Viking Bay, has a tidal pool, a children's play area and a Punch and Judy theatre, and is cleaned daily during the season – there are lifeguards and a dog ban in operation from May to September.

Broadstairs was the favourite seaside resort of Charles Dickens who came here every summer and eventually rented a clifftop house. It was in this house that Dickens wrote *Bleak House* (after which the house is now named) as well as polishing off *David Copperfield*. The house is open to the public and has a good collection of Dickens memorabilia with four of the rooms decorated as they would have been in Dickens' time.

Nearby Ramsgate can offer just two beaches (they're both sandy, with plenty of children's attractions and have lifeguards and a dog ban in summer), a harbour, a model village, a Motor

Museum where a variety of vintage cars and bikes are displayed in historic settings and scenic coastal walks to Broadstairs.

Just north of Broadstairs stands the North Foreland Lighthouse, which marks the entrance to the River Thames. When converted to automatic operation in 1988, this was the last manned lighthouse in the UK. Tours are offered in summer.

Bleak House
Fort Road, Broadstairs **t** (01843) 862224
Open Feb–July, Sept–mid Dec 10–6; Aug 10–9
Adm Adult £3, child £1.80

North Foreland Lighthouse
Two miles north of Broadstairs on the B252
t (01843) 587765 **www.trinityhouse.co.uk**
Open Easter–Sept Sat and Sun and Bank Hols 11–5
Adm Adult £2, child £1, family £5

Ramsgate Model Village
The Promenade **t** (01843) 850043
www.model-village.com
Open April–Oct 10–6
Adm Adult £3, child £1.50, concs £2, family £8
ice cream kiosk, gift shop

Ramsgate Motor Museum
West Cliff Hall **t** (01843) 581948
Open April–Oct 10.30–5.30
Adm Adult £2.50, child £1.25
Gift shop

Cinemas
Windsor – Broadstairs
Harbour Street **t** (01843) 65726

Whitstable

Getting there Whitstable is 7 miles northwest of Canterbury on the north Kent coast off the A299
Tourist office 7 Oxford Street **t** (01227) 275482

Whitstable offers a calmer, more sedate alternative to traditional seaside resorts. It has few arcades, ice cream kiosks or fish and chip restaurants, just lots of charm. And, despite the rather grown up attractions of its narrow streets, quaint fishermen's cottages and old-fashioned tearooms, there's still plenty for kids to do. There's the beach, of course, a great pebbly expanse surrounded by grassy slopes leading on to a fascinating working harbour where you can experience all the hustle and bustle of the sea harvest – watch the boats unloading their moun-

We all scream for ice cream
Broadstairs is a quaint seaside resort and feels as though it is stuck in the 1950s. This is nowhere more apparent than in its retro Italian milkbars where elaborate ice creams (look out for the Leonardo da Vinci which is served on an artist's palette-shaped plate) are served at brightly-coloured formica tables. Head for Morelli's at 14 Victoria Parade if you feel a knickerbocker glory moment coming on.

tains of shellfish, including the famous Whitstable oysters, which have been the town's principal export since Roman times. Near the harbour stands the Oyster and Fishery Exhibition which offers a seashore touch-pool for kids and oyster tastings for adults.

Oyster and Fishery Exhibition
East Quay, Whitstable Harbour **t** (01227) 280753
Open April–Oct Mon–Sat 10–4; Nov–Dec Sat and Sun 10–4

Activities
AMF Whitstable Bowl
Tower Parade, Whitstable **t** (01227) 274661
Open Daily 10–late
Adm Adult Mon–Fri £2.85, Sat, Sun and Bank Hols £3.35; child Mon–Fri £2.40, Sat, Sun and Bank Hols £2.80; after 6pm, adults and children £3.40, weekend eves and Bank Hols adults and children £3.45. Shoe hire: adults £1, children 65p
24-lane bowling alley.

Nature lovers

Ashdown Llama Farm

Wych Cross, Forest Row **t** (01825) 712040
www.llamafarm.co.uk
Getting there It is on the A22, nr Wych Cross, just
south of the junction with the A275
Open 1 April–30 Sept 10–5 (closed Mon exc Bank
Hols); Sat and Sun only 11–4
Adm Adult £3, child £2.50
Tearoom, knitwear and gift shop, museum

Friendly farm where you can meet sheep, goats
(Angora and Cashmere), llamas and alpacas and
visit the World of Wool Museum housed in an 18th-
century barn. Take a picnic and make a day of it.

Druidstone Wildlife Park

Honey Hill, Blean, Canterbury **t** (01227) 765168
Getting there Blean is 5 miles northwest of
Canterbury off the A290
Open April–Oct daily 10–5.30
Adm Adult £3.50, child £2.50
*Café, gift shop, mother and baby facilities, disabled
access, on-site parking*

Lots of small, friendly animals to meet, including
wallabies, deer, owls and monkeys, plus there's a
woodland walk, an adventure playground and an
under-5s play area.

Hop Farm Country Park

Beltring, Paddock Wood **t** (01622) 872068
Getting there It's about 7 miles east of Tonbridge
on the A228
Open Mar–Oct 10–6; Nov–Feb 10–4
Adm Adult £4.50, child £3
Café, picnic areas, shop, on-site parking

Pleasant country park laid out around the largest
complex of Victorian oast houses (*see* box, left) in the
world. There are exhibitions on hop farming and
traditional farming, nature trails (plus a treasure trail
for kids to follow using mini-metal detectors), a
museum, a farm, a Shire Horse Centre, an adventure
play area, indoor play centre and a pottery workshop.

Horton Park

Horton Lane, Epsom **t** (01372) 743984
Getting there It's 65 miles east of Guildford
off the A246
Open Daily 10–6, till 5 in winter
Adm Child £3.65, accompanying adult **free**
Refreshments

Oast houses

The hop, which is used to give beer its bitter
flavour, has been an important part of the Kent
economy since it was introduced into this country
in the 16th century. Kent's famous oast houses
were originally used to press and dry the freshly
harvested hops. Today breweries still use hops but
they won't have been dried in an oast house – it
would take too long. Many of Kent's oast houses
were pulled down or fell into disrepair. Some,
however, have been renovated (the examples at
the Museum of Kent Life p.58 are particularly fine).
These days it is even possible to stay in an oast
house (*see* 'Where to stay', p.190 for details).

Just south of London, Horton Park is very popular
with the capital's schoolchildren. Its pens are home
to goats, cows and sheep, among others, and there
are special standing platforms so kids can get a
good look at what's going on. They can even get in
with the rabbits and guinea pigs for a quick stroke
if they wish and, if you come in spring or early
summer, you should be able to help bottle-feed the
lambs and goat kids.

Once you've finished bonding, take a wander
through the rest of the complex – you'll come
across numerous free-roaming ducks and chickens
– or, if you want to take the weight off your feet, try
a tractor tour (offered in summer only). Any
remaining energy can be used up at the adventure
playground and children's activity centre, which is
filled with an assortment of climbing equipment.

Howlett's and Port Lympne

These two wild animal parks, founded by the late
conservationist (and controversialist) John Aspinall,
undertake a good deal of important conservation
work. Port Lympne is home to the largest captive
group of black rhinos in the world, while Howlett's
is home to the largest family group of gorillas
outside the African jungle, not to mention the
largest breeding population of elephants in
Europe. Both have successfully reintroduced
captive bred animals back into the wild.
Nonetheless, for all their good works, it has been
Aspinall's rather singular philosophy of zookeeping
– whereby his keepers are expected to form close
social bonds with the (often quite dangerous)
animals they look after – which has kept the zoos
in the news, especially after a number of tragic
incidents involving the keepers of the big cats.

Despite protests from the press and local councils, the practice still goes on and when you visit you may well see keepers in with the tigers or gorillas.

Whatever the controversy, and whatever the merits of such behaviour, there's no doubt that both zoos provide visitors with an excellent day out. The animals are kept in large, natural-looking enclosures and there are regular talks, meet the animals sessions and a whole programme of kids' activities. And, unlike many other modern zoos, there's no doubt here that the animals come first.

Howlett's

Bekesbourne Lane, Bekesbourne, Canterbury
t 0891 800605 www.howletts.co.uk
Getting there It's 5 miles southeast of Canterbury and is signposted from the A2
Open Daily 10–5 (or dusk)
Adm Adult £8.90, child £6.90, under-4s **free**, family £26
Café, restaurant, gift shop, disabled access and toilets, on-site parking

Port Lympne

Aldington Road, Lympne, Hythe t (01303) 264647
Getting there Lympne is about 5 miles inland from Hythe on the Kent coast off the A261 and B0267
Open Daily 10–5 (or dusk)
Adm Adult £8.90, child £6.90, under-4s free, family £26
Café, restaurant, gift shop, disabled access, adapted toilets, on-site parking

Scotney Castle Gardens

Lamberhurst, Tunbridge Wells t (01892) 891081
Getting there It's 6 miles southeast of Tunbridge Wells, just outside of Lamberhurst off the A21
Open April–Oct Wed–Fri 11–6, Sat, Sun and Bank Hols 2–6
Adm Adult £4, child £2, family £10
Café, gift shop, some disabled access, on-site parking

Surrounding the ruins of a 14th-century castle, these beautiful gardens are wonderful for exploring with their thick, lush flowerbeds, over-hanging trees, mossy slopes, grassy lawns and ponds. Look out for the ruins of the castle itself with its tiny child-sized rooms.

South of England Rare Breeds Centre

Woodchurch, Ashford t (01233) 861493
www.rarebreeds.org.uk

Getting there It's 9 miles north of Rye, 6 miles south of Ashford on the B2067 between Hamstreet and Tenterden (J10 from the M20)
Open Summer 10.30–5.30; Winter Tues–Sun 10.30–4.30
Adm Adult £3.50, child £1.90, under-3s **free**
Café, picnic areas, shop, disabled access, parking

This 90-acre working farm has a large collection of rare animals (cows with long twirly horns, shaggy goats, giant rabbits etc). In addition, there is a children's barn where 'meet the animals' sessions are organized and a reconstructed Georgian farmstead. There's also a paddling pool, a sandpit, an adventure playground and lots of special events – including 'piggy picnics', car rallies and 'pudding days' – in summer. Do make sure you pay a visit to the farm's most famous residents, a pair of pigs (nicknamed the 'Tamworth 2' by the press) who escaped from an abbatoir in 1998.

Wilderness Wood

Hadlow Down, nr Uckfield t (01825) 830509
Getting there Hadlow is 4 miles northeast of Uckfield off the A272
Open All year 10–dusk
Adm Adult £1.90, child £1.10
Café, picnic area, playground, visitor centre, baby changing facilities, wheelchair access

The wood is spread out over 62 acres in among the hills of the High Weald. There are walking trails (including a discovery trail for children), exhibition sites (where you can watch furniture-making and camp-building), play areas and picnic spots.

Wildwood Wildlife Centre

t (01227) 712111 www.wildwood-centre.co.uk
Getting there Wildwood is on the A291 between Canterbury and Herne Bay
Open Daily 10-5
Adm Adult £5.25, child £3.75

Over 30 acres of ancient woodland are the setting for this wildlife discovery park which provides children with the opportunity to see a variety of rare and endangered native species from owls to otters and wild boars to beavers (the new wolf cubs, born at the centre, are proving a big hit). Behind the scenes, Wildwood carries out serious conservation work though this is not allowed to intrude on the fun to be had from getting close to the animals.

Look at this!

Biggin Hill International Air Fair

Biggin Hill Airfield, Biggin Hill, Kent
t (01959) 578101
www.airdisplaysint.co.uk
≋ Biggin Hill
Bus 246, 320, 4664, R2
Adm Adult £8.50, child £3, family £19

Every summer, plane enthusiasts from all over the country gather in order to get up close and personal with the truly high-flying machines of the aviation world. Second World War Spitfires and Hurricanes are the biggest draw but there are lots of other planes to see both on the ground and in the sky. A host of displays, fly-pasts and skydives take place over the two days and there's also a funfair and exhibition stands.

Kent Battle of Britain Museum

Aerodrome Road, Hawkinge, Folkestone
t (01303) 893140
Getting there It's 3 miles north of Folkestone off the A260 (J13 from the M20)
Open April–Oct daily 10–5
Adm Adult £3, child £1.50
Snacks, gift shop, disabled access, guided tours, on-site parking

The country's largest collection of Battle of Britain memorabilia is housed, appropriately enough, in this former RAF station. The remnants of over 600 British and German planes are displayed alongside full-size replicas of the Hurricane, Spitfire and ME 109 planes used during the conflict.

Museum of Kent Life

Lock Lane, Sandling, Maidstone t (01622) 763936
Getting there It's a couple of miles north of Maidstone off the A229 (J6 from the M20)
Open April–Oct daily 10–5.30
Adm Adult £4.20, child £2.70, family £12
Tearooms, picnic sites, gift shop, some disabled access, on-site parking

In centuries past, thousands of workers used to come to Kent every autumn to pick hops, a small, bitter fruit used to make beer. Back then, everything was done by hand and it was hard, back-breaking toil for which the workers were paid a pittance. Here on the banks of the River Medway, you can see the hop-pickers tiny huts where they were housed ten or more to a room during the harvest and the strange conical oast houses where the hops were laid out to dry over a hot kiln. You can explore various reconstructed farm buildings, including an 18th-century thatched barn and a granary where there is a gruesome exhibition on rats, the biggest enemy of the harvest. There's also a traditional farm, a craft village, playground and mini-tractors plus acres of delightful countryside.

World Naval Base – Chatham Historic Dockyard

For further information *see* p.51

Steam power

Romney, Hythe and Dymchurch Railway

New Romney Station, Littlestone Road, New Romney t (01797) 362353 www.rhdr.demon.co.uk
Getting there The railway stretches along the Kent coast from Dungeness to Hythe. There are six stations of which New Romney, 10 miles northeast of Rye off the A259 and B2071, is the main one.
Operating times Easter–Sept daily; Oct–Easter Sat and Sun only
Adm £9 return
Cafés, souvenir shops, wheelchair access on trains (but call in advance), adapted toilets

The Romney, Hythe and Dymchurch Railway is a miniature railway built in the 1920s for the racing driver Captain Howey, who hoped to operate it as a full mainline railway carrying freight as well as passengers. Sadly for the Captain, British industry didn't share his vision and the railway was forced to rely on holidaymakers for its main source of income. It fell into disrepair during the Second World War, but was restored and reopened in 1946 (at a ceremony attended by Laurel and Hardy) and, today, can claim the honour of being the world's longest 15inch gauge railway. It runs for 13.5 miles across Romney Marsh close to the coast from Hythe to Dungeness passing through New Romney Station where there's a large collection of toys and models (including one of the largest model train layouts in the country) on the way.

Kent and East Sussex Railway

For further information *see* p.48.

SURREY

SPECIAL TRIPS

Chessington World of Adventures

Chessington **t** 0870 444 7777
www.chessington.co.uk
Getting there Chessington is a couple of miles
north of Epsom, just off the A243, 2 miles from the
A3 and M25 (J9 from the north, J10 from the south).
There are regular train services to Chessington
South Station from London (Clapham Junction)
Open Mar–Nov 10–5.15 (last adm 3); later closing
for Family Fright Nights
Adm Adult £19.50, child £15.50, under-4s **free**
*Fast food outlets, on-site parking, some disabled
access (safety restrictions apply on some rides – call
for detailed leaflet – a limited number of
wheelchairs available on request)*
Note Height restriction: It varies but is usually
1.2m.

With a handful of new rides including the 'Bash
Street Bus' in Beanoland and 'Toadie's Crazy Cars' in
Toytown as well as a new recruit for the 'Trail of the
Kings' (a baby gorilla born in March 2001),
Chessington is expensive but worth it. It's certainly
better value than many other theme parks which
offer free entry to the park itself but charge individually (not to say extortionately) for each ride.
Here you pay a one-off fee which allows you to go
on each ride as often as you like – provided you're
willing to renegotiate the queues, that is (be
warned, in high summer these can be several
hours long which, for some reason, always proves
far more tortuous for parents than children). Arrive
early in the morning and you've got a full day of
fun ahead of you. There are rides for all ages from
top-of-the-range rollercoasters to gentle carousels
and roundabouts. The park's most intense rides are
the 'Samurai' (which spins people round on an
enormous rotor blade), and 'Rameses Revenge',
which looks a bit like a great big bread tin and flips
its passengers over several times before squirting
them in the face with jets of water. In summer, on
'Family Fright Nights', you have the opportunity to
sample all these rides in the dark.

Younger children are well catered for at Toytown,
the Dragon River log flume, Professor Burp's Bubble
Works, the 'Action Man' assault course and the
recently opened Beanoland where you can enjoy a
range of rides themed on Beano characters (such
as Billy Whizz's Waveslinger) and watch costumed
characters acting outing out 'comic' scenes. There's
also a small circus with regular performances by
trapeze artists and clowns.

It's easy to forget that, in among all the hi-tech
gadgetry, there is also a zoo. You can take a quick,
theme-park style look at the resident lions, gorillas
and meerkats aboard the Safari Skyrail, a monorail
that zips over the animal enclosures. There are also
daily displays by sealions, penguins and hawks and,
down in the 'Creepy Cave', you and your kids can go
'urgh!' at the collection of spiders, insects and
other crawling horrors.

Hampton Court

East Molesey **t** (020) 8781 9500 **www.htp.org.uk**
Getting there Hampton Court is just southwest of
London near Kingston-upon-Thames, off the A3
and A309 (J12 from the M25). Trains run regularly
from London (Waterloo) to Hampton Court Station
or you can take a cruise up the Thames with the
Westminster Passenger Service from Westminster
Pier.
Open Oct–Mar Mon 10.15– 4.30, Tues–Sun 9.30–
4.30; Mar–Oct Mon 10.15–6, Tues–Sun 9.30–6
Adm Adult £10, child £6.60, under-5s **free**, family
ticket £29.90
*Café, restaurant, souvenir shops (in particular the
Tudor Kitchen shop which sells a range of Tudor
cooking implements and medieval herbs), guided
tours, disabled facilities, on-site parking*

One of the best loved of all royal palaces,
Hampton Court provides a fabulous day out for
children of all ages. This grand old building is
stuffed full of 500 years' worth of historical treasures including Henry VIII's sumptuous state
apartments, a real tennis court and a Renaissance
picture gallery containing works by Brueghel and
Mantegna. Your children's favourite area, however,
will probably be the huge Tudor kitchens where
everyday a Tudor banquet, complete with spit
roast, is prepared by cooks in full Tudor dress. It's
like stepping into a time-warp where you can see
the sights, hear the sounds and smell the smells of
yesteryear. The guided tours are highly recommended, given by costumed characters who will
regale your children with tales of marriage and
murder (this was where Henry VIII lived,
remember). Children's trails are available and work-

Henry VIII's wives

Everybody knows that Henry VIII, one of the most colourful characters in English history, had six wives. These days it seems quite surprising that he was able to find so many women willing to marry him given the potential risks. Henry was crowned in 1509. He had not expected to succeed his father, Henry VII, but his elder brother Arthur died before their father. So Henry ascended the throne and, aged only 18, married his brother's widow, Catherine of Aragon. Catherine bore Henry six children but only one of these, Mary, lived.

Henry wanted a boy who would grow up to be king and after a lot of struggle and upset he obtained a divorce. Henry married Anne Boleyn, the second of his six wives in 1533. She is known as 'Anne of the Thousand Days', because that's how long she survived as Queen. Anne provided Henry with a daughter, who would grow up to become Elizabeth I, one of this country's greatest rulers! But no sons! Henry grew impatient and had Anne tried for adultery. She was beheaded on May 19, 1536. Henry's third wife, Jane Seymour, died in childbirth a year after the couple were married, giving birth to a son, Edward VI. Henry had his son! But, by now, he was getting into the swing of the marriage business and married Anne of Cleves in 1540. Although the marriage was made for purely political reasons, Henry had been captivated by her portrait in miniature and was so disappointed when he met his new bride that he dubbed her 'The Flanders Mare' and promptly sent her away. The marriage was never consummated and he soon divorced her to marry Catherine Howard. Poor old Catherine fared no better and Henry had her head chopped off after she was convicted of adultery. Finally in 1543 he married Catherine Parr. Luckily for her, Henry died in 1547 and Catherine went on to marry again.

If all this seems a little confusing, there is an easy way to remember Henry's six wives and what happened to them.

Catherine of Aragon April 1506–April 1533 *Divorced*
Anne Boleyn Jan 1533–May 1536 *Beheaded*
Jane Seymour May 1536–Oct 1537 *Died*
Anne of Cleves Jan 1540–July 1540 *Divorced*
Catherine Howard July 1540–Feb 1541 *Beheaded*
Catherine Parr July 1543–Jan 1547 *Survived*

It's fairly simple to remember, just keep repeating: 'divorced, beheaded, died...divorced, beheaded, survived'.

shops and storytelling sessions are organized during the school holidays.

The building itself was begun in the 1520s by Cardinal Wolsey, chief advisor to Henry VIII, who offered the monarch the palace as a gift. Henry refused, only to seize it anyway when Wolsey later displeased him (he failed to secure Henry a divorce from his first wife, Catherine of Aragon). During his reign Henry would spend a staggering £62,000 on Hampton Court (that's around £18 million in today's money), turning it into the most modern, sophisticated palace in England. Only part of the structure we see today, however, dates from this time. Sir Christopher Wren undertook a further £131,000 worth of rebuilding work (today's equivalent would be £9.5 million) in the late 17th century, the most important element of which was the planting of new landscaped gardens.

These beautiful gardens have always been as big a draw as the palace itself, attracting around 1.3 million visitors a year. They contain many wonders: a 1,000-year-old oak tree, the oldest and longest vine in the world planted in 1768 (in the early part of the 20th century the grapes were harvested in baskets made by soldiers blinded in the First World War), 100,000 rose bushes, 250,000 flowering bulbs and, of course, the famous maze. It was planted in 1690 and ensnares around 300,000 people a year. It takes about 20 minutes to reach the centre and at least double that to negotiate the way back.

Anyone for tennis?

Towards the East Gardens, at the north end of the Broad Walk is the Royal Tennis Court which was built in about 1530. It is the oldest tennis court in the world where real or 'royal' tennis is still played today. Henry was passionate about the sport and legend has it that he heard of the execution of Queen Anne Boleyn as he played here. Between April and October you can visit the court and if play is in progress, park yourself on one of the comfortable velvet cushioned seats and attempt to work out the rules of the game.

Need to sit down?

Once you have all made your escape head to nearby Bushy Park (adm free, open dawn till dusk), a wonderful picturesque spot for a picnic with herds of deer, ornamental ponds and a famous 0.75-mile Chestnut avenue which leads from Hampton Court to the Teddington Gate. Laid out by Christopher Wren, these superb trees are best seen in the spring.

Thorpe Park

Staines Road, Chertsey **t** (0870) 444 4466
www.thorpepark.co.uk
Getting there Thorpe Park is on the A320 between
Chertsey and Staines (J11 or 13 from the M25).
There's a regular train service from London
(Waterloo) to Staines and Chertsey, from where
you can catch a bus
Open Mar–Oct, times vary but it usually opens at
9.30–10 and closes between 5 and 7.30
Adm Adult £19.95, child £15.95, under 1m **free**
Fast food outlets, gift shop, baby changing facilities,
first aid centre, some wheelchair access, adapted
toilets, on-site parking

Follwing the success of the bizarrely titled 'X:/No
Way Out', which forced its passengers to travel at
speeds of around 65mph in the dark...backwards,
Thorpe Park has added a trio of brand-name rides
to the list of its attractions. 'Detonator' winches its
riders 100ft up into the air then fires them back
down to the ground at 75mph (major G-force
involved here). 'Vortex' spins its victims round in
great nausea-inducing loops, 65 foot above the
ground and 'Zodiac' turns them upside down
through 360 degrees for a 'whirl-wind circumnavi-
gation of the white-knuckle kind'.

These concessions to modern super-thrill-
seeking trends aside, most of the attractions at
Thorpe Park have clearly been designed to cater for
families rather than adrenaline junkies. Children
are particularly well provided for with various
themed areas such as Mrs Hippo's Jungle Safari
and Mr Monkey's banana ride, as well as Model
World, which features miniature versions of the
Eiffel Tower, the Pyramids and Stonehenge.

Younger children are excluded from some of the
more exhilerating rides, such as Thunder River, for
reasons of safety but they are well catered for elsewhere, especially in the Octopus's Garden. They can
also take a boat ride to Thorpe Farm to bond with
the resident goats, sheep and rabbits.

Swimwear (or a change of clothes) is a must
unless you want to return home with a car full of
bedraggled children. There are more water-themed
attractions here than at most parks, including the
tallest log flume in the country 'Tidal Wave', an
ersatz white-water rafting adventure 'Thunder
River', as well as several pools and water chutes. In
the last week of October, the park holds a number
of firework displays.

The village of Chertsey is worth a visit in its own
right for the vintage costume collection and
hands-on gallery in its local museum. Also, don't
forget to visit the Great Cockrow Railway (*see* p.66).

AROUND AND ABOUT

Bricks and mortar

Hampton Court
For further information *see* p.59.

Lullingstone Roman Villa
nr Eynsford **t** (01322) 863467
www.english-heritage.org.uk
Getting there It's 7 miles north of Sevenoaks, just
outside Eynsford off the A225 (J3 from M25)
Open April–Sept daily 10–6; Oct–March 10–4
Adm Adult £2.50, child £1.90
Shop, on-site parking

One of the largest Roman villas yet found in
Britain, Lullingstone lay buried and forgotten after
the collapse of the Roman Empire in the 5th
century until it was rediscovered some 1,400 years
later in the mid 20th century. Not a great deal
remains – the site mainly consists of a series of
small walls – but there are some well-preserved
mosaics and wall paintings to admire. The audio
guide will help you to fill in the gaps and there's a
children's activity sheet available. It's probably best
to come on one of their numerous English
Heritage-organized event days when children may
have the chance to meet a Roman soldier, eat some
Roman food or try their hand at making a piece of
Roman jewellery or a mosaic.

Did you know...
That in Henry VIII's time, Hampton Court
contained an enormous multiple lavatory. It
could seat 28 people at a time and was known as
'The Great House of Easement'.

Penshurst Place

Penshurst, Tonbridge **t** (01892) 870307
www.seetb.org.uk/penshurst
Getting there Penshurst Place is 6 miles northwest of Tunbridge Wells off the B2176 and B2188
Open April–Oct daily 10.30–6
Adm Adult £6, child £4, family £14
Restaurant, some disabled access, on-site parking

This medieval manor house is surrounded by a wonderful array of gardens (both formal and informal) where you'll find lots of wide grassy spaces, flowerbeds, orchards and ponds, not to mention an excellent adventure playground with a sandpit, slides and some serious looking commando-style climbing equipment. There's also a nature trail through the adjoining woods and, throughout the summer, the gardens play host to a range of special events including falconry displays, craft demonstrations and theatrical performances. The house itself is rather dry and dusty although it does contain a delightful toy room filled with lots of rather overdressed dolls and teddy bears collected from ancient nurseries.

Polesden Lacey

Great Bookham, Dorking **t** (01372) 458203
Getting there Polesden Lacy is a couple of miles north of Dorking off the A246
Open Garden: daily 10–6; house: April–Oct Wed–Sun 1–5
Adm Adult £3, child £1.50, family £7.50
Refreshments, guided tours, some disabled access, on-site parking

This beautiful Regency villa was once one of the most fashionable addresses around, the venue of all the most lavish society parties. Although the chatter, dancing and merriment have long since faded (leaving behind a rather workaday museum-house) it's still well worth visiting for its fabulous gardens. There are rolling lawns for picnicking, woods for exploring and hedges and flowers for admiring (if you're an adult) or playing hide and seek in (if you're a child). For anyone wanting something a little more structured, there are four marked walks through the gardens and woods, ranging in length from 1 to 3 miles, and croquet

sets are available for hire during the summer. Various family events take place here during the year including Easter Egg hunts, country fairs and classical concerts (with firework finales). The famous London–Brighton car run also makes a stop here en-route. There's an activity book and quiz for families wishing to tour the house.

Nature lovers

Birdworld

Holt Pound, Farnham **t** (01420) 22140
Infoline **t** (01420) 22838 **www**.birdworld.co.uk
Getting there It's 3 miles southwest of Farnham off the A325
Open March–Oct daily 9.30–5.30; Nov–Jan Sat and Sun 9.30–4.30
Adm Adult £7.95, child £4.75, under-3s **free**, family £22.95
Restaurant, gift shop, mother and baby facilities, disabled access, on-site parking

There are few better places to come and meet our feathered friends than this imaginatively presented 28-acre animal centre near Farnham. All birdlife is here. You'll see green, squawking parrots, beautiful pink flamingoes and white, haughty-looking pelicans with their huge fish-hungry bills. You'll stand in front of the Ostrich enclosure inspecting these vast birds while they, in turn, inspect you – ostriches must surely be one of the world's most curious animals, a sort of bird version of a monkey. You'll see penguins cavorting underwater and then lining up to be fed their buckets of fish like rows of beaked schoolboys. You'll take a seaside walk among terns and oyster catchers, a tropical tour through an aviary filled with free-flying exotic birds and watch chicks being fed at the incubation centre.

Need to sit down?

There's lots to see, which can be quite hard on little legs, but there's also plenty of opportunity for sitting down. Take a seat at the Heron Centre, where talks are given on the park's inhabitants at 1 and 3 every afternoon (usually accompanied by a demonstration of flying or feeding by one of the park's tamer residents), and you'll be informed and entertained as you rest. Alternatively, take a 10-minute tour of the park aboard the free road train which runs daily from the beginning of June.

As well as a good café and picnic area, the park also contains a small farm, a children's playground and a display of marine creatures 'Underwater World', which is home to several alligators.

Bockett's Farm Park

Young Street, Fetcham **t** (01372) 363764
Getting there Fetcham is a couple of miles south of Leatherhead, a couple of miles north of Polesden Lacey off the A24 and A246
Open Daily 10–6
Adm Adult £3.45, child £2.95, under-2s **free**
Café, mother and baby facilities, disabled access, on-site parking

It may be a proper, working farm, but Bockett's has clearly thought long and hard about how best to present its animals to younger visitors. So you'll find lots of small enclosures surrounded by small fences offering easy viewing for little people. Most of the animals (which include pigs, goats, cows, a donkey and a big, shaggy Shire horse) live in a large open barn, although there is a separate area for small animals where kids can get a little more hands-on with the ever-so-strokable rabbits and guinea pigs, or help feed the free-roaming chickens. Outside, there's a small enclosure of tame red deer and a very good playground filled with the rural equivalent of climbing equipment: hay bales, tyres and even an old tractor (by far the most popular choice) as well as a few more traditional items – swings, slides and a wooden fort. Tractor and pony rides are offered on summer weekends.

Burpham Court Farm

Clay Lane, Jacob's Well, Guildford **t** (01483) 576089
Getting there It's just north of Guildford off the A3
Open Daily 10–6
Adm Adult £3.25, child £2.25, under-2s **free**
Café, on-site parking

Burpham is much less polished and touristy than many of its competitors, but no less enjoyable for that. Unlike other show farms, where the animals are often corralled into one small child-sized area, here they are spread out in the fields and you must follow a trail through the farm to find them. So, pick up some bags at the entrance for feeding the sheep and chickens and get searching. The route starts with a pleasant amble alongside the banks of the River Wey wending your way past overgrown plants and clambering over stiles (not suitable for pushchairs). In summer you should be able to see ducks and butterflies and, if you're lucky, perhaps

Did you know...
That the peregrine falcon is the fastest of all the birds of prey. It hunts by 'stooping', that is, dropping from a great height onto its prey, usually a small bird, which it kills by driving its claws in at speed. During the stoop, the falcon can reach speeds of up to 275mph.
Peregrines are particularly fond of pigeons, which led, in the Second World War, to the government ordering a cull of the falcon, fearing the loss of carrier pigeons carrying vital messages.

the odd dragonfly or two (which will probably delight and terrify your children in equal measure). After that, you come to the open paddocks, separated by wide grassy paths, where you'll find woolly sheep (who'll rush up to be fed) and long-horned cows (who won't) as well as goats, pigs, ponies and even llamas. In spring, kids can help bottle-feed the lambs and goat kids.

One of the great things about Burpham is that at the end of the day, between 4 and 6, depending on the season, you can help the farmer put the animals away for the night (which gives kids a great sense of importance) and collect any hens' eggs that may have been laid during the afternoon. Tea is served in the farmhouse or you can picnic outside.

Chislehurst Caves

Old Hill, Chislehurst **t** (020) 8467 3264
Getting there It's off the A222 on the B264 near Chislehurst railway station
Open Daily during school hols, otherwise Wed–Sun, tours hourly from 10–4
Adm Adult £3, child £1.50
Café, gift shop, on-site parking

These tunnels and caves have played host to Druids, Romans and Londoners trying to escape from the Blitz. Today experienced guides take you on 45-minute tours down into this winding 4,000-year-old network of stoney tunnels and passageways stretching deep beneath the Old Hill.

Coxbridge Rare Breeds Theme Farm

West Street, Farnham **t** (01252) 715539
Getting there It's just north of Farnham on the A31 and A225 at the the Coxbridge roundabout
Open Daily 10–4
Adm Adult £4.50, child £3.50

The North Downs

The North Downs, which rise west of Guildford and undulate their way into Kent, can be the setting for some great family days out.

Box Hill

(just off the A25, east of Dorking)

Surrey's most dramatic viewpoint. The hill covers an area of some 800 acres encompassing wood, heath and downland.

Chatley Heath Semaphore Tower

Ockham Common (just off the A3 between Cobham and Effingham) **t** (01932) 458822
Open Mid March–late Sept, Sat–Sun and Bank Hols, plus Wed during school hols, 12 noon–5; Oct–Mar 1st Sun of month 12 noon–5 **Adm** £2

The country's only surviving semaphore tower, this once formed part of a chain that ran all the way from London to Portsmouth.

Denbies

London Road, Dorking (just off the A24)
t (01306) 876616
Open Mon–Sat 10–5.30, Sun 11.30–5.30; Jan–Mar Mon–Fri closes 4.30 **Adm** £4.50

This is the country's biggest vineyard. Take a tour through the winery and watch a 3-D film of the wine-making process.

Devil's Punchbowl

(just off the A287, 7 miles south of Farnham)

A spectacular natural fold in the downs with numerous nature trails through woodland.

Hambledon

(just off the A283, 3 miles south of Godalming)

Site of a witch's tree: walk around the tree three times to make the witch appear.

Leith Hill

Nr Coldharbour (just off the A25, southwest of Dorking) **t** (01306) 711777

The 18th-century tower at the top of the hill is the highest point in southeast England.

Outwood Post Mill

(just off M23, J9, 5 miles southeast of Reigate)
t (01342) 843458
Open Easter–Oct Sun and Bank Hols 2–6 **Adm** £2

England's oldest working windmill, built in 1665.

Café, mother and baby facilities, disabled access, on-site parking

This is a family-run farm with indoor and outdoor play areas, tractor and trailer rides, horse and wagon rides and picnic areas.

Gatwick Zoo and Aviaries

Russ Hill, Glovers Road, Charlwood, Horley
t (01293) 862312
Getting there It's about 2 miles west of Gatwick Airport and can be reached via the A23 and A24
Open Daily 10.30–6 (last adm 5)
Adm Adults £4.60, under-14s £3.50
Café, gift shop, mother and baby facilities, disabled access, on-site parking

Small zoo where animals are displayed in settings which are as close to their natural environments as possible. There are otters, wallabies, penguins and spider monkeys, as well as two tropical greenhouses full of giant lilies, palm trees and clouds of free-flying butterflies.

Godstone Farm

Tilburstow Hill Road, Godstone **t** (01883) 742546
Getting there Godstone is just south of the M25 (J6) on the A25
Open Mar–Oct daily 10–6; Nov–Feb Sat–Sun and school hols 10–5
Adm Child £3.80, accompanying adult **free**
Café, gift shop, mother and baby facilities, disabled access, on-site parking

England has many children's farms. In recent years, they have become almost as ubiquitous as playgrounds and, in truth, it is sometimes difficult to tell them apart with their standard collections of animals and run-of-the-mill playgrounds. Occasionally, however, you come across a park that surprises you with the range and quality of its attractions. Godstone is one such farm. It's made up of four sections: a 40-acre working farm with enclosures containing goats, sheep, cows and pigs (which kids are encouraged to pet and bond with); a large expanse of fields and woods; a huge outdoor play area with lots of elaborate climbing frames, tunnels, sandpits and even a mini dry-slope toboggan run (not suitable for toddlers) and a large indoor play barn full of toy vehicles and play equipment (perfect for winter visits). There is also an incubation shed where you can help feed the chicks, ducklings and piglets, and in summer sheepdog trials are held. All in all, an excellent day's fun. Unfortunately, its reputation is spreading and it can get very crowded in summer.

Lockwood Donkey Sanctuary

Farm Cottage, Hatch Lane, Sandhills, Wormley, nr Godalming **t** (01428) 682409
Getting there The sanctuary is off the A283 Godalming–Chiddingfold Road
Open Daily 9–5.30
Free
Gift shop, wheelchair-friendly

   Retirement home for old donkeys always on the look-out for children bearing carrots. If you feel particularly moved, you could even adopt one of the shaggy beasts – the cost is £1 per year for children and £2 for adults. The oldest donkey in the country lives in the sanctuary and has appeared in *The Guinness Book of Records*, having reached the ripe old age of 78.

Wisley Gardens

Wisley, Woking **t** (01483) 224234 **www**.rhs.org.uk
Getting there Wisley is just south of the M25 (J10), 5 miles northeast of Guildford. The nearest train station is West Byfleet, 3 miles away
Open Mon–Fri 10–sunset, Sat–Sun 9–sunset. Members only on Suns
Adm Adult £5, child £2, under-6s **free**, disabled helpers **free**
Restaurant, café, plant centre, book and gift shop, disabled facilities, on-site parking

   Set up by the Royal Horticultural Association in 1904, Wisley has become one of the country's best loved gardens. The 240-acre site boasts a traditional country garden, a farm, an orchard, some delightful woodland, a Garden of the Senses and a Temperate Glass House containing a waterfall and pool. There's something to see all the year round although it's definitely at its best on a hot summer's day. Every August there's a popular flower show and a Family Fortnight when children's activities and entertainers are laid on. Garden trails are offered for 7–12 year olds.

Did you know...
That a mule is a cross between a horse and a donkey. You don't get many mules because they can't have baby mules. Not many animals can cross like this. A tigon is another example – it is a cross between a tiger and a lion.

Look at this!

Rural Life Centre

Old Kiln Museum, Reeds Road, Tilford, Farnham
t (01252) 792300 **www**.surreyweb.org.uk/rural-life
Getting there It's 5 miles southeast of Farnham off the A287.
Open April–Sept Wed–Sun and Bank Hols 11–6
Adm Adult £4, child £2
Café, gift shop, guided tours, mother and baby facilities, disabled access, on-site parking

   A collection of traditional farm implements and machinery illustrating over 150 years of rural life. Wander through the buildings in a recreated 19th-century farming village, which include a wheelwright's shop, a smithy, a school room and a village hall. There's also a children's playground, a miniature railway and acres of grounds.

Brooklands Museum

Brooklands Road, Weybridge **t** (01932) 857381
www.motor-software.co.uk
Getting there It's just south of the M3 (J2) and east of the M25 (J11), 2 miles south of Chertsey
Open Tues–Sun 10–4.30
Adm Adult £6, child £4

   Brooklands is the oldest racing circuit in the world, pipping Indianapolis in America to the post by just one year. It was constructed in 1907 and was a wonder of its age. In those days there were no rules for the sport and regulations from horse-racing were adopted including 'handicapping' the cars by weighing them down. The drivers even had to wear silks as a means of identification. Today Brooklands is one of the most romantic names in British racing history, conjuring up images of goggles, flying scarves and dashing men doing daring things in very fast, very unsafe cars.

   This former racetrack is home to a motoring museum with plenty of vintage racing cars on display as well as motorbikes and even a few planes including a Wellington bomber rescued from Loch Ness. Brooklands witnessed the first ever 100mph car ride and, in honour of that feat, there is now a 'Fastest on Earth' exhibition on the history of the speed record – currently held by Britain's *Thrust II*.

Steam power

Great Cockrow Railway

Hardwick Lane, Lyme, Chertsey **t** (01932) 255500
(Mon–Fri), **t** (01932) 565474 (Sun)
Getting there The railway is located 1.5 miles
northwest of Chertsey on the A320
Operating times May–Oct Sun
Fares £1.50

Rides on jaunty miniature steam trains over a
two-mile length of track passing through tunnels
and over viaducts.

Hollycombe Steam Collection

Iron Hill, Liphook **t** (01428) 724900
Getting there It's just south of Liphook off the A3
and B2131
Open April–July and Sept, Sun and Bank Hols 1–6;
Aug daily 1–6
Adm Adult £6.50, child £5, under-2s **free**, family £20
Café, disabled access

At Hollycombe you can experience all the fun of
an old-fashioned fairground. While an antique
barrel organ chortles away excitedly in the background, you can go for a spin on a painted carousel,
check out the views from atop the big wheel or take
a ride on a swingboat. The rides may be steam-
powered (the constant sound of pumping pistons
combined with the noise of the organ makes this
one of the noisiest days out you could ever wish for)
and rather old, but they are still a lot of fun and the
big wheel in particular is more than a little hairy,
although there are also some gentler entertainments – such as a helter-skelter and a chain swing –
for younger children (and nervous adults).

Once you've had your fill of fairground attractions,
you might like to take a ride aboard a narrow-gauge
steam train through a mile and a half of leafy countryside, or climb aboard the steam tractor for a
quick trip down to the centre's small farm to bond
with the resident animals. Or, if you feel like a break
from the constant whirring and hissing, you could
always just go for a wander through the centre's
grounds which are perfect for picnics with their
flower gardens and patches of woodland.

Did you know...
During the 1920s and 1930s the Brookland's track,
designed by record-breaker Malcolm Campbell,
was known by some as the 'Ascot' of motor racing
because of the high society who flocked there.

Arundel

Black Rabbit

Mill Road **t** (01903) 882828
Open Daily 11–3 and 6–11

Pleasant pub offering a children's play area (with a painted wooden play boat), river views, a children's menu and high chairs. Traditional roasts are available on Sundays.

Battle

The Copper Kettle

The Almonry **t** (01424) 772727
Open April–Sept Mon–Sat 9.30–4.30; Oct–Mar Mon–Sat 9.30–3.30

Oak-beamed tearoom with a courtyard garden (and an open fire in winter) serving baguettes, sandwiches, home-made cakes and hot lunches. There's a children's menu but no high chairs. Kids will like the scale model of the town by the tearoom entrance. For 70p (£1 adults) you can see it illuminated and hear a brief audio history of the area.

Gateway

78 High Street **t** (01424) 772856
Open Daily 9–6 (till 5 in winter)

Very child-friendly tearoom with a designated family room leading onto a garden. Kids can either choose from the children's menu – chicken nuggets, fish fingers etc. – or have smaller versions of adult choices. High chairs available.

Whitehart Inn and Restaurant

Netherfield, nr Battle **t** (01424) 838382
Open Mon–Sat 12 noon–3 and 6.30–11, Sun 12 noon–3 and 7–10.30

This pub–restaurant offers traditional pub food (children's menu available) and a large garden with a play area.

Bognor Regis

The Beach Restaurant

Esplanade **t** (01243) 840998
Open restaurant: Daily 10–10, takeaway stays open till 2am Thurs–Sat

Traditional seafront fish and chip shop. Children's menu, children's portions and high chairs available. Eat in or takeaway.

The Regis

The Esplanade **t** (01243) 841763
Open Daily 11–11.30, food till 10pm

Pub with sea-facing restaurant (fish is a speciality). There's a children's menu and a Bruce the Bear Fun Factory play zone for 4–9 year olds (£2 per hour, you get £1 back if you're buying food). High chairs available.

Brighton

Alfresco

The Milkmaid Pavilion, King's Road Arches **t** (01273) 206523
Open Daily 12 noon–10.30

Pleasant, friendly Italian restaurant overlooking the seafront with an outdoor seating area. Although it doesn't have a children's menu, it is popular with families, especially in summer when it can get very full (and when it can be quite difficult manoeuvring a buggy between the narrow-set tables). High chairs available.

Brown's

3–4 Duke Street **t** (01273) 323501
Open Mon–Sat 11am–11.30pm, Sun 12 noon–11pm

High-quality family restaurant near the Lanes. There's a separate children's menu (which includes free ice cream) and high chairs are provided.

Cactus Canteen

5 Bright Square **t** (01273) 725700
Open Mon–Sat 11.30–11, Sun 12 noon–10.30

Lively Tex-Mex diner offering a children's menu. High chairs available.

Café Rouge

24 Prince Albert Street **t** (01273) 774422
Open Mon–Sat 10am–11pm, Sun 10am–10.30pm

Between the seafront and the Lanes, this large branch of the very family-friendly French café chain can offer a children's menu and high chairs.

Devil's Dyke

Poynings **t** (01273) 857256
Open Daily 11.30–10

Family pub overlooking the hugely popular beauty spot of the same name. It offers a children's menu, high chairs, a mother and baby room and outdoor seating on sunny days.

English's

29–31 East Street **t** (01273) 327980
Open 12 noon–10.30pm, Sun 12.30–9.30pm

Seafood restaurant and oyster bar for kids with adventurous culinary tastes (apparently there are some) who wouldn't mind something other than cod and chips (to keep the squeals of horror to a minimum, please don't tell them the oysters are still alive).

Harry Ramsden's

1–4 Marine Parade **t** (01275) 690691

Open 12 noon–9.30, till 10pm Fri and Sat, till 9pm Sun

For kids who do want the usual cod and chips, this branch of the famous northern fish and chip chain is situated opposite the entrance to the pier and, topically, the Sea Life Centre. Inside, there's seating for over a hundred people, so families can spread out and relax. There are two special children's menus: a Postman Pat menu for the little ones at £2.99 and a Cool Kids menu for £3.99. High chairs available. Eat in or takeaway.

The Regency Restaurant

131 King's Road **t** (01273) 325014

Open Daily 9am–11pm

Traditional seafront fish restaurant with white plastic chairs and tables on the pavement shaded by coloured umbrellas and a range of locally caught fresh fish and seafood dishes on the menu. Children's menu and high chairs available.

Broadstairs

Broadstairs Pavilion

Harbour Street **t** (01843) 600999

Open Daily 11–10

Large, very child-friendly modern tavern serving baguettes, pastries, ice creams and pub meals. There is a large, grassy garden which is great in summer and often has a tinkling jazz band tucked away in a corner.

Osteria Pizzeria Posillipo

14 Albion St **t** (01843) 601133

Open Mon, Wed–Sun noon–3, 7–11

Reliable and reasonably-priced Italian food (pizza, pasta, lasagne etc) with a good line in gloopy puds. Children's portions and high chairs available.

Canterbury

Café des Amis

95 St Dunstan's Street **t** (01227) 464390

Open Mon–Sat noon–10, Sun noon–9.30

Popular Mexican diner with an interestingly varied menu. There's no children's menu but most kids are happy to tuck into a plate of nachos, fahitas or suitably tamed (or not) chilli.

Il Vaticano

35 St Margaret's Street **t** (01227) 765333

Open Mon–Sat 10.30–10.30, Sun 11–4

Friendly and moderately priced, Il Vaticano is situated on a pedestrianized street and is a short walk from the cathedral. High chairs, child portions and a flexible menu make this pasta and pizza bar a good bet for a lunchtime or evening nosh up.

PizzaExpress

5a Best Lane **t** (01227) 766938

Open Mon–Sat 11.30–11.00, Sun 11.30–10.30

Yet another branch of this reliably child-friendly pizzeria.

The Moat Tea Rooms

67 Burgate **t** (01227) 784514

Open Daily 10–5

Jolly tearoom housed in a 16th-century building serving sandwiches, hot snacks, pastries, cream teas, etc.

The Old Weavers House

1 St Peter's Street **t** (01227) 464660

Open Daily 11–11

Traditional cream teas and good solid pub fare served in this grand 16th-century half-timbered building overlooking the river. There's a riverside patio garden.

Chichester

Ask Pizza

38 East Street **t** (01243) 775040

Open Sun–Thurs 12 noon–11, Fri and Sat 12 noon–11.30

Serves thin-crust Italian-style pizzas and is very welcoming to families. Pasta portions for kids. High chairs available.

Café Rouge

30 Southgate **t** (01243) 781751

Open Daily 10–11

Family-friendly French restaurant offering a children's menu, high chairs, colouring books and stickers.

Cathedral Cloisters Restaurant

The Cloisters, West Street **t** (01243) 783718

Open Summer Mon–Sat 10–5, winter Mon–Sat 10–4

Pleasant single-level café-restaurant (good for buggies) serving cornish pasties, sausage rolls, lasagnes, cottage pies, home-made cakes and assorted snacks. There's a sunny walled garden for kids to run about in. High chairs available.

King's Head pub

Bognor Road, Drayton **t** (01243) 783576

Open Daily 11–3 and 6–11

Just outside the town centre, children under 12 eat free of charge (up to 3 children) or for just £1.50 on roast days (Sundays). There's one high chair.

PizzaExpress

27 South Street **t** (01243) 786648

Open 12 noon–12 midnight daily, Sun till 11pm

Family-friendly chain serving thin-crust Italian-style pizzas. They do smaller, garlic bread-sized pizzas for kids. High chairs available.

Deal

Hare and Hounds

The Street, Northbourne **t** (01304) 365429

Open Daily Mon–Sat 11–3 and 6–11, Sun 12 noon–3 and 7–10.30

Modern pub–restaurant with a separate section in the bar for families, a nice garden and a children's adventure playground. They take their food very seriously here with lots of organic choices on offer and a children's menu which features scaled down versions of adult choices – baby omelettes, mini steak and kidney pies etc. – rather than the traditional nuggets and fish fingers. High chairs available.

Dover

Park Inn

1-2 Park Place, Ladywell **t** (01304) 203300

Open Mon–Sat 11-10, Sun noon-10

The Park Inn is a friendly pub and good for lunchtime meals if you're in Dover. They have high chairs and a children's menu which includes the standard kiddy fare (pizzas, lasagne, chips and more chips).

Eastbourne

Fusciardi's

19-25 Carlisle Road **t** (01323) 728029

Open Daily 9–6

Opposite the Winter Gardens, Fusciardi's is *the* place to go for all manner of ice cream delights.

PizzaExpress

24 Cornfield Road **t** (01323) 649466

Open Mon 11.30–midnight

Less than five minutes walk from the railway station, this PizzaExpress can be found in the pedestrianized street which leads down to the seafront. All the usual child-friendly touches (crayons, high chairs, mini-portions) are here.

Wildlife Café

6 The Waterfront, Jamaica Way Sovereign Harbour **t** (01323) 470032

Open Mon–Wed 10–4, Thur & Fri 10–8.30, Sat 10–9, Sun 10–8.30

This sister branch of the Wildlife Café in Hastings (*see* below), has the same jungle-themed décor and serves up a good range of child-friendly grub including home-made burgers and gloopy shakes.

Hartfield

Hatch Inn

Coleman's Hatch, nr Hartfield **t** (01342) 822363

Open Mon, Sun noon–2.30, Tue–Sat noon–2.30, 7.30–9.15

Should you find yourself in Pooh Country (see p.38), this old smuggler's pub has bags of character and has two good-size gardens looking out onto Ashdown Forest. There's only one high chair so get there early if you want to grab it. There's a varied menu for the grown-ups which ranges beyond the standard pub grub and also a good seletion of sandwiches and ploughman's lunches. Half-portions are available for dainty appetites.

Honeypots

High Street **t** (01892) 770793

Open Mon, Wed–Sun 10.30–5.30

Just across the road from Pooh Corner (see p.38) this popular café/restaurant serves good value cream teas (including a 'Pooh Bear' variety with honey). There's a nice selection of filling, traditional lunches and a children's menu which includes jacket potatoes, filled baguettes and chips. If the weather is good, there's plenty of outside seating in the Honeypots sunny garden.

Hastings

Castle Tandoori

43 George Street, Old Town **t** (01424) 429685

Open 12 noon–2 and 5.30–12 midnight

Spicy curries in the heart of the old town. Children's portions rather than a children's menu.

The Italian Way

25 Castle Street **t** (01424) 435955

Open Daily 10–10

Friendly Italian restaurant with a typically mediterranean attitude towards children: 'Yes, we take everybody, we are Italian'. There are no children's menu or high chairs but that doesn't seem to put off local families who flock here in summer. The kitchen will happily provide children's portions.

Kingfisher

6 Castle Street **t** (01424) 431932
Open Fri–Sat 12 noon–12.30am, Wed 12 noon–11pm

This restaurant specializes in traditional English dishes. They're very flexible regarding portions and are very family-friendly.

Mermaid Restaurant

2 Rook-a-Nore Road **t** (01424) 438100
Open Daily 7–7

Head to the seafront for some of the best fish and chips in town. Good value with prices ranging from about £3-5 pounds (half-portions start at £2.50) for crisply battered cod or plaice and a healthy portion of chunky chips. If straightforward fish and chips don't appeal, there are other kids' staples including fish fingers, egg and chips and the like. There's only one high chair so you'll need to grab it quick!

New Capels Restaurant

7 Rock-a-Nore Road **t** (01424) 426940
Open Summer Tues–Sun 11–11; Winter Tues–Fri 12 noon–5, Sat and Sun 12 noon–7.30

This specializes in fish but can also provide pies, burgers, sausages, salads and kebabs (all with chips of course). Children's portions come at a reduced price. Eat in or takeaway. High chairs available.

Priory Pub

32 Station Road **t** (01424) 442368
Open Food served Mon–Fri 11–3, Sat 11–5, Sun 12 noon–4

Opposite the railway station, this 19th-century pub can offer kids meals, high chairs and a salty sea dog atmosphere.

Wildlife Café

Priory Meadow Shopping Centre **t** (01424) 434 809
Open Daily 9-7

Fifty per cent of the profits from this theme café go to help endangered animals in the wild. Decked out in the same kind of style as London's Rainforest Café with cascading waterfalls and thick foliage, and alive with the noise of the jungle, it is bound to prove a big hit with kids. The food isn't bad either.

Ramsgate

PizzaExpress

52 Harbour Parade **t** (01843) 592186
Open Mon–Sat 11.30–11.00, Sun 11.30–10.30

Thanet's only branch of this family-friendly pizza parlour which has children's portions, high chairs and some of the best pizza you can find outside Italy. Baby-changing facilities, crayons, paper and a little box of toys and games make it a stress-free place to come for a meal with young kids.

Rye

Cranberries

105a High Street **t** (01797) 224800
Open Daily 10–5

Small, friendly non-smoking café serving morning coffee, light lunches (jacket potatoes, beans on toast etc.), sandwiches, main meals (chilli, cottage pie) and home-made desserts.

Old Forge Restaurant

24 Wish Street **t** (01797) 223227
Open Tues–Wed 6.30–11, Thurs–Sat 12 noon–2.30 and 6.30–11

Seafood dishes at competitive prices. There's no children's menu but they're happy to provide half portions and are popular with local families.

The Queen's Head

19 Landgate **t** (01797) 222181
Open Daily pub: 11.30–11; restaurant: 6.30–9.30

A 17th-century inn with an adjoining olde-worlde restaurant where a hybrid English-French menu is served. Children's portions and high chairs can be provided. There's a non-smoking section.

Whitstable

Pearson's Crab and Oyster House

The Horsebridge **t** (01227) 272050
Open Mon–Sat 12 noon–2.30 and 6.30–10, Sun 12 noon–10

Popular with families, this offers a full children's menu and high chairs.

Due North

Hertfordshire · Bedfordshire Berkshire · Buckinghamshire Oxfordshire · Warwickshire Gloucestershire

Due North

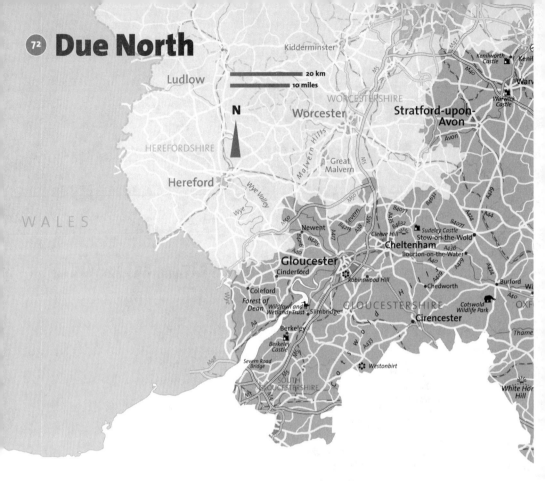

Leaving London and heading north you soon begin the descent into the Thames Valley, a great, green swathe of rolling fields and woodland, flanked by the Chilterns on one side and the Cotswolds on the other. Within this expanse, there's much to attract the parental day tripper or weekend breaker. Oxford, Windsor and Stratford-upon-Avon are rich in child-friendly pickings with enough in or around them to keep grown ups and children amused in equal measure. Legoland, one of the best theme parks in the country, is two miles out of Windsor. Blenheim Palace, birthplace of Winston Churchill, is six miles from Oxford while 10 miles northeast of Stratford is Warwick, home to what is probably the best-preserved medieval castle in the country, which comes complete with a dungeon and its very own ghost. Children looking for a little toothsome fun will enjoy the lions and

Coventry
Coventry Airport
worth
vick
WARWICKSHIRE
NORTHAMPTONSHIRE
CAMBRIDGESHIRE
Cambridge
Northampton
Wilden
Bedford
Sandy
Biggleswade
Banbury
Stewartby
BEDFORDSHIRE
Milton Keynes
Wobum
Buckingham
Woburn Safari Park
Letchworth
Leighton Buzzard
Luton
Stansted Airport
BUCKINGHAMSHIRE
Dunstable
Luton Airport
Whipsnade
Knebworth
HERTFORDSHIRE
Blenheim Palace
Aylesbury
Whipsnade Wild Animal Park
Lea
ESSEX
tney
Oxford
Berkhamsted
St Albans
Hatfield
Hatfield House
Broxbourne
RDSHIRE
London Colney
Didcot
Chiltern Hills
Chalfont St Giles
High Wycombe
Beaconsfield
The Ridgeway Path
se
Greys Court
Maidenhead
LONDON
Basildon
Henley-on-Thames
Bray
Slough
Eton
BERKSHIRE
Windsor Castle
Windsor
Datchet
Heathrow Airport
Old Windsor
Reading
Legoland Windsor
Great Park
Bracknell
Newbury
North Downs Way

tigers (not to mention the baboons, camels, elephants and rhinos) of Whipsnade and Woburn, while mini-miniaturists should make a beeline for Bekonscot, the oldest model village in the country. And for something completely different, they could visit the Wyld Court Rainforest, a little piece of the Amazon in the heart of Berkshire, inhabited by all manner of jungle creatures, from bug-eyed frogs to leaping, squawking squirrel monkeys.

Such a perfect day

Morning: At Windsor Castle (p.78).
Lunch: At PizzaExpress on Thames Street in Windsor (p.106).
Afternoon: A cruise from Windsor Promenade up the River Thames (p.78) to Maidenhead to visit the Courage Shire Horse Centre (p.84).

Special events

February
Oxford: Chinese New Year celebrations
t (01865) 204188
May
Windsor: Royal Horse Show t (020) 7370 8206
www.royal-windsor-horse-show.co.uk
June
Chipping Camden: Cotswold Olympic Games
t (01384) 274041
Blenheim Palace: Fireworks concert t (01993) 811325
www.blenheimpalace.com
July
Henley Royal Regatta, Henley-on-Thames
t (01491) 572 153 www.hrr.co.uk
September
Stow-on-the-Wold: Annual day of Morris Dancing
t (01451) 831082

OXFORDSHIRE & BERKSHIRE

OXFORD

Getting there By road: Oxford is about 48 miles from London and can be reached via the M40. By train: Services arrive frequently from London Paddington. By bus/coach: There are regular National Express coach services to Oxford from London Victoria
Tourist information The Old School, Gloucester Green **t** (01865) 726871 **www.**oxfordcity.co.uk

Oxford, of course, is more than just a pretty town for tourists (and it is pretty with its magnificent college architecture and parks), it's a world famous centre of culture and learning. Indeed, over the centuries, it has become symbolic of a quintessential sort of élitist, flannel-trousered, cloistered Englishness. It is home to one of the country's two most prestigious universities (the other is Cambridge) and, ever since its foundation in the 13th century, has been preparing the great and the good for roles in public life. Tony Blair, Bill Clinton, Margaret Thatcher and even Henry VIII all studied at the university, although the term 'university' is slightly misleading – Oxford actually contains several independently operated colleges which together form the university and define the shape of the city. Most of the colleges are open to the public although, to preserve the academic ambience, many operate restricted opening times and charge hefty admission fees.

With so much accumulated learning and history, you might expect Oxford to be rather dull for children and, approached in the wrong way, it probably would be. But, plan your itinerary carefully and you'll find lots to occupy your days. Oxford actually boasts a good many child-friendly attractions including parks, interactive museums, punts and lots of good viewing spots providing panoramic views of the 'dreaming spires' and surrounding countryside.

Things to see

Bate Collection of Musical Instruments
Faculty of Music, St Aldates **t** (01865) 286261
Open Mon–Fri 2–5, Sat 10–12 noon
Free

A huge selection of musical instruments. It was one of the conditions laid out by the museum's founder that the instruments should be played. As a result the collection is unique in that many of its historic instruments are still used. The museum has a refreshing selection of lesser known instruments including a Javanese Gamelan (a type of orchestra made up of several percussion instruments which produce melodious soft clangings).

Curioxity Science Gallery
The Old Fire Station, George Street
t (01865) 247004
Open Sat, Sun and school hols 10–4
Adm Adult £2.10, child £1.80, family £7.20

Hands-on science museum for children full of interactive games and experiments.

Museum of the History of Science
Old Ashmolean Building, Broad Street
t (01865) 277280 **www.**mhs.ox.ac.uk
Open Tues–Sat 12 noon–4
Free

Recently refurbished, the museum contains displays of scientific instruments dating back to the 16th century (look out for Einstein's blackboard) as well as an education room and library.

The Oxford Story
6 Broad Street **t** (01865) 728822
Open Mon–Sat 10–4.30, Sun 11–4.30; July and Aug daily 9.30–5
Adm Adult £6.10, child £4.90, family £18.50
Gift shop, disabled access

You are transported on an electric cart past three floors of tableaux depicting scenes from the city's long history – student riots, scientific breakthroughs, etc. – with accompanying sound and lighting effects. Obviously, it stresses the academic side of things quite strongly but it's all done in a very entertaining way. There's a children's commentary and special school holiday events.

Pitt Rivers Museum
Parks Road **t** (01865) 270927
Open Mon–Sat 1–4.30, Sun 2–4.30
Free

This elegant Victorian building houses a large ethnographic collection featuring numerous artefacts brought back by Captain Cook from his 18th century journeys of discovery. A witch in a bottle, a puffer-fish lantern, shrunken heads, samurai swords and totem poles are just some of the glorious and gruesome horrors bound to attract the interest of children.

Can you spot?
If you are coming to Oxford by coach or car, keep a close eye out once you get into Headington which is the first part of the city you enter. Look out to the left for 2 New High Street and you will see a huge shark sticking out of a roof as though it has fallen from the sky.

University Museum of Natural History
Parks Road **t** (01865) 272950 **www.oum.ox.ac.uk**
Open Mon–Sat 12 noon–5
Free
Picnic area, some disabled access
Check out the dinosaur galleries and working beehive (summer only).

Views
With its glorious architecture and history, Oxford is a city of many views. Unfortunately, at ground level increased urbanization has meant that many of its best sights are now obscured. Thankfully, there are several more exulted views on offer which allow you to see the 'dreaming spires' in all their glory. Check out the Carfax Tower **t** (01865) 792653, the 22m high remains of a 14th-century church; the University Church of St Mary the Virgin, High Street **t** (01865) 243806 and Oxford's oldest building, St Michael at the Northgate, Cornmarket **t** (01865) 240940, all of which offer panoramic views of the city and surrounding countryside.

Things to do

Parks
Oxford has many parks and open spaces where you can go for walks and picnics. Look out for:

The Botanic Gardens
Rose Lane **t** (01865) 276920
Open Garden: 9–5; glasshouses: daily 10–4.30
Adm Adults £2, under-12s **free** (**free** to all in winter)
Created in 1621, this is the oldest botanic garden in Britain. You can wander through nine small glasshouses filled with tropical and sub-tropical plants, including palms, orchids and giant ferns.

Christ Church Meadow
Access via St Aldate's, Merton Street, Rose Lane
Open Daily 7am–9pm (or dusk if earlier)
Free
Lovely green space near the city centre with a memorial garden and riverside walks. Look out for practising university crews.

Magdalen College Park
High Street **t** (01865) 276000
Open Daily 2pm–dusk
Free
The grounds of Magdalen (pronounced 'Maudlin') contain a deer park and river walks through water meadows.

Port Meadow
Access via Walton Well Road and Thames Towpath
Open Any reasonable time, it is common land
Free
This huge water meadow is the largest green space in Oxford. You can see horses, cows and geese roaming freely.

University Parks
Parks Road **t** (01865) 271585
Open Daily 8am–dusk
Free
Seventy acres of parkland on the west bank of the River Cherwell with gardens, trees, riverside walks and a duck pond.

River trips
Punting, the practice of pushing yourself along the river in a flat-bottomed boat using a long

Tell me a story:
Alice's Adventures in Wonderland
The Oxford mathematics lecturer, Charles Dodgson, took three sisters on a river trip one sunny afternoon in 1862. While having tea on the river bank he told the children a fairytale about a white rabbit which runs down a hole and is chased by one of the sisters, Alice. While underground, Alice meets, among others, a Caterpillar, an Ugly Duchess, a Cheshire Cat, a March Hare and a Mock Turtle. Three years later this unlikely tale was published under the pen-name of Lewis Carroll. While he was writing it, Dodgson struggled over what to call his book. He wrote to a friend of his in 1864: 'I should be very glad if you could help me in fixing on a name for my fairytale. I first thought of *Alice's Adventures Under Ground*, then I took *Alice's Golden Hour*.' Rejecting, too, *Alice Among the Goblins* and *Alice's Hour in Elf-land* he eventually settled on the now famous title of *Alice's Adventures in Wonderland*. In 1898, the year of Dodgson's death, it had sold 86,000 copies in Britain alone.

wooden pole, is particularly associated with England's two great university towns. The image of young men in flannels and straw hats mucking about in boats on hot summer days is, for some, as typically English as teashops, beefeaters and cricket on the village green. It's great fun, if more than a little tricky (young children probably won't be able to handle the heavy pole) but, once mastered, provides a good way of seeing the local countryside. Punts and (for the less adventurous) rowboats for trips on the River Cherwell down past the Botanic Garden and Christchurch Meadow are available for hire from Magdalen Bridge, Folly Bridge and the Cherwell Boathouse. Sightseeing trips to Iffley, Sandford Lock and Abingdon are also offered from Folly Bridge by Salter Brothers **t** (01865) 243421 **www**.salterbros.co.uk

Bus tours

Guide Friday run bus tours of the city in their trademark cream and green open-top buses. For further information contact Guide Friday Tourism Centre, Oxford Railway Station **t** (01865) 790522 **www**.guidefriday.com or simply join the tour at the train or bus station.

Cinemas
ABC

George Street **t** (01865) 723911/0870 333 9064
With a recent £2.5 million investment programme, this mainstream cinema has had its three screens expanded to six.

ABC

Magdalen Street **t** (01865) 725305/0870 333 9063
This former single-screen cinema now has two screens; the old balcony seating has been retained.

Phoenix Picture House

Walton Street **t** (01865) 554909
Art house cinema with a children's club on Saturday mornings.

Ultimate Picture Palace

Jeune Street **t** (01865) 245288
Oxford's first independent cinema (it used to be called the Penultimate Picture Palace); children's film club on Saturday mornings.

Theatres
The Apollo Theatre

George Street **t** (01865) 723834/0870 606 3500
Oxford's major theatre, with a varied range of productions from pop to opera, comedy and children's theatre.

The Burton/Taylor Theatre

Gloucester Street **t** (01865) 793797
Small, experimental venue, founded by film stars Richard Burton and Elizabeth Taylor, with the occasional children's show.

The Old Fire Station Arts and Entertainments

Gloucester Green **t** (01865) 794490
Café, club, bar and theatre, all rolled into one, children's shows are occasionally put on during the summer holidays.

The Pegasus Theatre

Magdalen Road **t** (01865) 722851
Oxford's youth theatre.

The Playhouse

11–12 Beaumont Street **t** (01865) 798600
www.oxfordplayhouse.com
Arthouse theatre which specialises in productions for children under 6.

Activities
Cherwell Boathouse

Bardwell Road **t** (01865) 515978 **www**.cherwell-boathouse.co.uk
Hires out punts, rowboats and Canadian canoes.

C Howard and Son

Magdalen Bridge, High Street **t** (01865) 202643
Hires out punts and rowboats for trips on the River Cherwell.

IPG Marine

Folly Bridge **t** (01993) 868190
Hires out rowing skiffs, punts and motorboats.

Long Leys Riding Centre

Upper Whiteley Farm, Leys Road, Cumnor
t (01856) 864554
Getting there Cumnor is 5 miles west of Oxford, off the A420
Call in advance for opening times and prices

Old Manor Horse Riding Stable

North Hinksey Lane, North Hinksey, Oxford
t (01865) 242274
Getting there North Hinksey is on the western edge of Oxford, off the A34
Call in advance for opening times and prices

Oxford Ice Rink

Oxpens Road, Oxford **t** (01865) 248076
Call in advance for details of times and prices
Ice-skating, ice disco-skating and ice-karting spectaculars – skates can be hired.

Oxford Riding School
Watlington Road, Garsington, Oxford
t (01865) 361383
Getting there Garsington is about 3 miles south-east of Oxford off the B480
Call in advance for opening times and prices

Oxfordshire Narrowboats
Canal Wharf, Station Road, Lower Heyford, Bicester
t (01869) 340348 **www**.oxfordshire-narrowboats.co.uk
Open Mon–Sat 9–5
Fares £85 per boat per day
Self-drive boats for hire on the South Oxford Canal.

WINDSOR

Getting there By road: Windsor is 20 miles west of London, off the M4 exit 6. By train: Services run direct from London Waterloo to Windsor and Eton Riverside (every 30min Mon–Fri) and from London Paddington via Slough to Windsor Central (every 30min Mon–Sun).
By bus/coach: Services leave London from Victoria coach station at regular intervals throughout the day **t** (08705) 808080 for details
Tourist office Royal Windsor Information Centre, 24 High Street **t** (01753) 743900 **www**.windsor.gov.uk. Above the information centre itself is a small exhibition on the history of the town.

Remove all the people and Windsor would be absolutely adorable. Indeed, with its picturesque Georgian houses and demure shops overlooked by the glorious 900-year-old castle, it's almost cartoonishly genteel. People, however, are an integral part of the Windsor experience. Visit on a fine summer weekend and it can seem as if you're stuck in the midst of a travelling Tower of Babel as, hemmed in by tourists on all sides, you shuffle past the town's attractions. Should you manage to escape the the crowds, however, then there's no reason why you shouldn't have a very pleasant time. Although its narrow cobbled streets, full of twee souvenir shops and ye olde tearooms, are fun to explore, Windsor is really a three-site town. Site no.1 is the castle which will be upon you as soon as you leave the train station (either one). It doesn't so much dominate the town as define it, the roads flowing around the fortress walls. It's the official

Can you spot?
As befits this fine royal town, there are two royal blue things to look out for (see also p79): Can you find the blue plaque marking the spot where three men were burnt at the stake in 1543? It's located near the memorial to George V 'The First Sovereign of the House of Windsor', on the corner of Datchet Road and Thames Street.

residence of the Queen and, although a little dry and dusty in places, it's still a castle and thus great fun to explore. Just to the north across the river is the adjoining town of Eton, site of the famous public school (site no.2), first established in the 15th century, where countless government ministers and members of the Royal Family have been educated (including the princes William and Harry; Harry is still there). It is open to visitors throughout the year when you can take a tour of the grounds and see the oldest classroom in the world, its ancient desks scored with generations of schoolboy graffiti. If you come in term time you should be able to see the boys themselves walking around in their distinctive (not to say rather archaic) uniform of top hat and tailcoat. If you think they look adorable and would like to see your little boy dressed the same, you had better start saving – school fees cost around £14,000 a year. Nearby there are lots of grassy meadows for picnicking and watching the boats coming and going on the river. However, you're unlikely to linger long as your kids will no doubt keep reminding you of the *real* reason you're here, to visit site no.3, Legoland (*see* p.81), the exuberant heart beneath the cultured exterior, one of the country's best theme parks. Just two miles out of Windsor, it is full of rides, games, models, activity centres, rollercoasters and, no matter when you visit, hordes of fun-seeking kids.

Things to see
Eton College
Eton High Street **t** (01753) 671177
www.etoncollege.com
Open (term time) 2-4.30pm daily (holidays) 10.30am-4.30pm daily
Adm Adult £2.60, child £2; guided tour £3.80 (adult), £3 (child)
This famous English public school received its Royal Charter in 1440. It was officially named by Henry VI as 'The King's College of Our Lady of Eton

beside Windsor'. The school opened with six choristers and 25 school pupils. Today Eton has more than 500 pupils and is renowned as the training ground for future members of the British establishment. No fewer than 18 of the country's prime ministers have been educated here. Other 'inmates' include George Orwell (creator of *Animal Farm*) and the Earl of Carnarvon, who unearthed the tomb of the ancient Egyptian king Tutankhamen.

Windsor Castle

Windsor **t** (01753) 869898; infoline **t** (01753) 831118
www.royal.gov.uk
Open Mar–Oct 9.45–5.15 (last adm 4); Nov–Feb 9.45–4.15 (last adm 3)
Adm Adult £11, child £5.50, under-5s **free**, family £27.50
Souvenir shop, wheelchair access to most areas of castle; car parking available in town

This splendid concoction of towers, ramparts and pinnacles is, today, the official residence of the Queen and the largest inhabited castle in the world – and it is *big*, almost the size of a small town. In 1992, the State Apartments were ravaged by fire although, following £37 million worth of restoration work, you would be hard pressed to tell. They are today as opulent as they ever were, decorated with hundreds of priceless paintings from the royal collection, including Van Eycks and Rembrandts, as well as porcelain, armour and fine furniture. Children may find them a little dry, however, in which case you should make a beeline for the Queen Mary doll's house which never fails to illicit a gasp of envy (particularly from the girls). This is a fantastic fairytale mini-palace complete with leather furniture, running water in all five bathrooms, lifts and even a working vacuum cleaner (presumably the only hoovering the princess ever did); it's the sort of Doll's House that only a royal child could ever hope to own. If you've got the energy climb to the top of the 12th-century Round Tower where, on a clear day, you can see no fewer than 12 counties. The Changing of the Guard takes place outside the Palace on most days at 11 o'clock sharp.

Things to do

Boat tours

Thirty-five-minute sightseeing tours around Windsor's environs, as well as trips downriver to Runnymede and Hampton Court and upriver to the picturesque villages of Bray and Maidenhead (the largest town in the borough and the site of the Courage Shire Horse Centre, *see* p.84) are offered from **Windsor Promenade**. Special trips for children are also provided along the creeks and backwaters of Windsor to observe the local wildlife (including the famous swans).
French Brothers Ltd, Clewer Boat House, Clewer Court Road, Windsor, **t** (01753) 851900
Fares 35min trip: adult £3.80, child £1.90; 2hr cruise: adult £6, child £3
Fares Motorboats: £30/hr (max 6 people); rowboats: £12/hr (max 4 people)

You can hire rowboats and motorboats for a little self-navigation on the Thames from Gamble and Logie Motorboats, Windsor Promenade, Barry Avenue **t** (0374) 983809.

Bus tours

Bus tours of the city run by Guide Friday in open-top green and cream buses are available daily April–Oct and can be joined at the High Street or at either Windsor Central station or Windsor and Eton Riverside station.
Fares Adult £6.50, child £2.50, family £15.50

For a more elegant, albeit slightly slower, tour climb aboard one of the horse-drawn carriages (4–8 seater) lined up at the taxi rank outside the castle for a 1 and a half hour trip round the town.

Take home a souvenir

With its clusters of well-to-do shops and boutiques lining the pedestrianized triangle of Peascod Street, King Edward Court and the revamped Windsor Royal Station, many people come to Windsor just to shop. Although much of what Windsor has to offer – its antiques, art, crafts and high fashions – will appeal mainly to adults, there are a few emporia designed to capture the

79

OXFORDSHIRE & BERKSHIRE | WARWICKSHIRE & GLOUCESTERSHIRE | BUCKINGHAMSHIRE | BEDFORDSHIRE & HERTFORDSHIRE | WHERE TO EAT

Can you spot?
The blue postbox built to commemorate the first ever air mail flight made by Gustav Hemel in 1911 when he took off in a rickety old Bleriot monoplane and flew from Hendon Aerodrome to Shaw Farm Meadow in Windsor to mark the coronation of George V. It's on the corner of High Street and Park Street.

interest of younger visitors. These include Old Boys Toys, which is full of model cars, and Miniatures on Parade which specializes in dolls' houses. If you visit just one shop during your time in Windsor, however, it should probably be Hawkin's Bazaar, a wonderful assembly of old-fashioned curios and oddities for both children and adults: traditional wooden toys and games, brightly coloured mechanical automata, wind-up dolls, puppets and kits, kaleidoscopes, theatre sets and musical boxes (and not a battery in sight).

Hawkin's Bazaar
134 Peascod Street **t** (01753) 832240
Open Mon–Sat 9–5.30, Sun 11–4

Windsor Great Park
For something a little more sedate, head to Windsor Great Park, a vast 4,800-acre tree-filled green space stretching out to the south of the town. It contains a 35-acre formal botanic garden, the Swiss Garden, and a huge lake, Virginia Water, with a 100ft totem pole standing on its banks. The paths are well marked, so it is pushchair-friendly.

According to legend, the ghost of Herne the Hunter is supposed to haunt the park on moonlit evenings, when he can be seen, dressed in his stag antler headdress riding a black stallion, at the head of a pack of black hounds, which he leads in a midnight chase across the park.

Theatres
Theatre Royal
32 Thames Street **t** (01753) 853888
Overlooked by Windsor Castle this theatre offers a wide repertoire of productions all year round.

Windsor Arts Centre
The Old Court, St Leonards Road **t** (01753) 859336
Local venue with theatre productions, music, classes, educational workshops, comedy and exhibitions.

Activities
French Brothers
Clewer Boat House, Clewer Court Road
t (01753) 851900 www.boat-trips.co.uk
Open Easter–Oct for scheduled sailings; Dec–Easter private hire only
Fares 35min trip adult £4, child £2, family £11; 2hr cruise adult £6.30, child £3.15, family £17.05
Thirty-five-minute sightseeing tours around Windsor's environs, as well as trips downriver to Runnymede and Hampton Court and upriver to the picturesque villages of Bray and Maidenhead, from Windsor Promenade. Special trips for children are also provided along the creeks and backwaters of Windsor to observe the local wildlife (including the famous swans).

Gamble and Logie Motorboats
Windsor Promenade, Barry Avenue **t** 0374 983809
Fares Motorboats: £30/hr (max 6 people), Rowboats: £12/hr (max 4 people)
Rowboats and motorboats for hire on the Thames

Kris Cruisers
The Waterfront, Southlea Road, Datchet
t (01753) 543930 www. kriscruisers.co.uk
Open April–Oct 9–5.30
Fares rowboats from £5/hr, Day boats from £16/hr, 12 seaters from £27/hr
Just south of Windsor, this offers a range of self-drive boats for hire from 6 to 12 seat day boats, 4 to 5 seat rowboats or 2 to 11 berth cabin cruisers.

John Nike Leisure Sport Complex
Amen Corner, John Nike Way, Bracknell
t (01344) 789000 www.nikegroup.co.uk
Getting there Bracknell is about 15 miles north of Guildford, off the A322
Open 8am–10pm (session times may vary)
Adm Skiing per 1.5hrs: adult £8.50, child £6; for other prices call in advance
Café, mother and baby facilities, disabled access, on-site parking
Olympic-size ice rink, 150m dry ski slope and a toboggan ride.

Can you spot?
Queen Charlotte Street in the cobbled area of Windsor between Market Street and High Street. At just 51ft 10in long, this is officially the shortest street in Britain.

Tell me a story:
Who was Winston Churchill?

Winston Churchill was born at Blenheim Palace on November 30, 1874 and educated at Harrow and then Sandhurst. He was on active military service in India and covered the Boer War for a London newspaper, during which he was captured but managed to escape.

Returning to England, he entered politics and became an MP in 1900. From then on, he held many government posts, both as a Conservative and a Liberal, including Home Secretary, Minister of Munitions and Chancellor of the Exchequer. But it was in May 1940, with England at war, that his own 'finest hour' came when he became prime minister. One of the most inspiring orators in history, his speeches helped to restore public confidence and hardened the British determination to resist even when standing alone after the fall of France. In fact, so vital to the war effort was Churchill that some believe without him the war would have been lost. Churchill was more modest: 'It was the nation that had the lion's heart. I had the luck to be called upon to give the roar. I also hope that I sometimes suggested to the lion the right place to use his claws.'

Windsor Leisure Centre

Clewer Mead, Stovell Road, Windsor
t (01753) 850004
Call in advance for opening times and prices
Leisure pool with wave-machine, giant slides, wild water creek, water cannons, fountains and 'Freddie the Frog's Funhouse'. Crêche available.

Windsor Roller Rink

Alexandra Gardens, Windsor t (01753) 830220
Call in advance for details of times and prices
Roller rink with skate and accessory hire. Also bikes for hire by the half-day, day and week.

Wycombe Summit Ski and Snowboard Centre

Abbey Barn Lane, High Wycombe t (01494) 474711
www.ski.co.uk/wycombesummit
Getting there High Wycombe is off J4 of the M40
Open 10am–10pm daily (last adm 9)
Adm Adult £9.50/hr, child £7.50/hr
Café, shop, mother and baby room, picnic areas, disabled access, on-site parking
Lessons for all ages and abilities on England's longest dry ski slope. 'Big Foot Club' for children.

SPECIAL TRIPS

Blenheim Palace

Woodstock **t** (01993) 811325
www.blenheimpalace.com
Getting there Blenheim is about 6 miles northwest of Oxford, just off the A44
Open Palace: mid-March–Oct daily 10.30–5.30 (last adm 4.45); park daily 9–5; gardens, maze and Butterfly House mid March–Oct daily 10–6
Adm Adult £9.50, child £4.80, under-5s **free**, family £25
Shop, restaurants, picnic areas, mother and baby facilities, guided tours, disabled access, on-site parking

One of the best-loved stately homes in the country, Blenheim is associated in most people's minds with the life of Britain's greatest wartime prime minister, Winston Churchill, who was born here in 1874. The house itself is simply vast, covering an area of some 14 acres although, despite its bulk, it's still a very elegant sight with its delicate sandstone colouring and castle-esque pinnacles. The interior is suitably opulent, littered with antiques, statues and tapestries, and holds a small exhibition on Churchill's life, which includes numerous paintings, manuscripts and letters.

However, as with so many of the country's grand stately piles, the house will probably prove much less popular with younger visitors than the grounds which, if anything, are even more magnificent. The gardens immediately surrounding the house are formal and sculpted – landscaped by 'Capability' Brown – although they're still fun to explore with ponds, fountains and water terraces. Beyond this are some grand tracts of open parkland which seem to stretch on and on as far as the eye can see where kids can run about to their hearts' content. You can follow the marked walk, which takes you on an hour long tour of the park passing the large lake on the way (look out for gulping trout), or, if you're feeling a bit lazy (some parts are quite steeply sloped and may be hard on little legs), you could hop aboard the narrow-gauge steam railway which will eventually deposit you at the walled pleasure garden, the undoubted highlight as far as children are concerned with its maze (the largest symbolic hedge maze in the world), giant chess and draughts pieces and model village of Woodstock. Nearby there is a butterfly house with a small collection of fluttering specimens and a well-equipped adventure playground.

The restaurants here are quite expensive and you would be well advised to bring a picnic – which is no great hardship as there are few more elegant spots in which to enjoy a sandwich and a pork pie.

Legoland

Windsor **t** 08705 040404 **www.**legoland.co.uk
Getting there Legoland is 2 miles from Windsor on the Windsor to Ascot Road, signposted from J6 of the M4. The bus service from Windsor town centre to Legoland departs from Thames Street every 15 mins during opening times
Open Daily 10–6, park closes 7 mid July–Aug
Adm Adult £19, child £16
Seven restaurants/cafés and 11 catering stalls, picnic areas, mother and baby facilities, wheelchair access, wheelchair hire available, adapted toilets, on-site parking

The most imaginative of Britain's current breed of theme parks, Legoland is now firmly established as one of the country's top family attractions. The theme is Lego, the Danish multi-coloured plastic building bricks that have become a national institution (27 million of which were used during the construction of the park). Lego kits have always been a good way of getting kids to use and develop their imagination and the park is equally inspiring. It's perhaps best described as a cross between a theme park and an activity centre. It has some good thrill rides, including a dragon-themed roller-coaster that jets its way through a mock-up medieval castle and a log flume, Pirate Falls. Older children (over-10s), however, may find them a little tame compared with what's on offer at places like Chessington. Legoland is geared very much towards the pursuits of younger children.

The most popular attractions are the interactive zones such as Lego Traffic, where children have the chance to drive electrically powered Lego cars through a model town, negotiating traffic lights,

Did you know...
Lego was invented by a Danish carpenter named Ole Kirk Christiansen. Ole's carpentry business was going through some hard times so he set up a separate concern making toys in 1932. In 1934 he named his company Lego from the Danish 'leg godt' which means 'play well' in English. Although his company prospered, it was not until 1949 that he began to produce the famous plastic 'Automatic Binding Bricks'.

pedestrian crossings and roundabouts on the way – the most skilful drivers are awarded their own special Legoland Driving Licence – and the Imagination Centre, where kids are encouraged to erect and destroy model buildings on a special 'Earthquake' table. Older children can create robotic models using the rather eerie concept of 'intelligent' Lego bricks at the Mindstorms Learning Centre or have a go at creating a computer generated driver and car before testing their skills on a futuristic racing circuit, while their younger siblings muck about with the Duplo Gardens' water cannon and go for boat rides. In summer kids can also cool off on the Wave Surfers in My Town, getting a chance to crest the waves on their very own child-sized jet skis.

There's plenty of stimulation for body as well as mind. Many of the park's rides, including the Sky Rider and the Bone Shaker, are pedal-powered, while the Space Tower and Muscle Maker are arm-powered. These are not only a good source of exercise but, because they give children the sensation of being in control, they often prove more popular than the scarier, automatically powered rollercoaster rides.

Adults and children alike will appreciate Miniland with its beautifully constructed model cities – London, Amsterdam, Paris, Brussels *et al*. London features models of St Paul's Cathedral, a hugely out of proportion Big Ben, which towers above everything, and Horse Guards Parade, where you can watch Lego men performing the Trooping of the Colour. You can pick up a (rather annoying) audio guide and even have the chance to watch the model-makers at work in the Creation Centre.

Dotted around the park are numerous Lego characters including Lego trolls, Lego musicians and Lego dinosaurs. Look out for the moving, growling T-Rex which shoots smoke out of its nostrils. As

Can you spot?
The Lego model of St George fighting a Lego dragon. It's located outside the Dragon Knight's Castle.

Rainforests

Around the equator it doesn't get very dry during the summer or very cold during the winter and one day is much the same as another the whole year round. Rain falls almost every day all through the year. These conditions mean that plants can grow and grow. Wherever a plant *can* grow, it *does* grow. Hundreds and hundreds of species thrive.

The result is a dense mass of trees and other plants which are known as rainforests. There are thousands of different kinds of trees in the rainforests. Some of the most common are mahogany, rosewood, walnut and ebony. There are also huge numbers of animals, from large mammals like hogs and monkeys to tiny insects. Many of the animals live in the tree tops where the food is more plentiful.

Rainforests remained largely unchanged for millions of years. These days, however, rainforests are being cut down at a staggering rate in some places. It is estimated that an area the size of England is destroyed every year. The trees make valuable timber and the cleared areas are used for farming and to build roads. And in turn the new roads bring more people who want to cut down more trees so they can clear more land. Without the trees, however, the earth is quickly eroded and within a few years the soil is exhausted and the land becomes useless.

In the short term, cutting down rainforests provides people who don't have very much money with an income and a way to feed their families. But if the rainforest is cut down at the same rate as it is today then it won't be long before there will be no rainforests at all.

well as rides and attractions, Legoland also has several picnic spots (on-site food outlets tend to be pricey, so packing a hearty lunch to bring along is a highly recommended option) and lush grounds to stroll through, plus a train ride to fall back on when little legs become tired.

Look Out Discovery Centre

Nine Mile Ride (opposite Coral Reef), Bracknell
t (01344) 354400 **www**.bracknell-forest.gov.uk
Getting there Bracknell is 15 miles northwest of Guildford, off the A322
Open Daily 10–5
Adm Adult £3.85, child £2.55, under-4s **free**, family £10.20, half price after 4
Café, gift shop, picnic areas, tourist information centre, mother and baby room, disabled access, on-site parking

Superb hands-on science exhibition with over 70 interactive experiments arranged into five themed zones: 'Light and Colour', 'Woodland and Wildlife', 'Forces and Movement', 'Sound and Communication' and 'Body and Perception'. You can do all of the following: balance a beach ball on a jet of air to make it appear as if it's hovering in space; make water dance; listen to your voice in an echo tube; touch a plasma ball and watch electricity flowing towards your fingers; pluck the laser beams of a light harp in a Jean-Michel Jarre sort of way to make a little 'light' music; send a hydrogen rocket shooting up a see-through plastic tube; build an arched bridge; measure your heartbeat; crawl down a mole hole; photograph your shadow and much more. Everything is rendered in brightly coloured plastic and there are helpers on hand to explain the science behind your experiments in easy-to-understand terms.

The centre even has its own resident robotic owl, which answers to the name of Solly. Solly makes regular appearances during the weekends and school holidays at 10.30am, 11.30am, 1.30pm and 2.30pm, which makes him a firm favourite. He can shrug his shoulders, move and spin around. Ask him a question or he may even tell you a joke.

Surrounded by 2,600 acres of Crown Estate woodland, you could easily spend a whole day here. There's a collection of outdoor play apparatus, including several large plastic mushrooms just outside the centre, and you can hire mountain bikes and safety helmets for rides on a special mountain bike trail through the woods – although, do be warned, the course is quite tricky with lots of steep hills. And, should you need cooling off after your exertions, you could always pop along to the Coral Reef Water World just across the road which has chutes, flumes, rapids and a climb-aboard pirate's ship.

Coral Reef Water World

Nine Mile Road, Bracknell **t** (01344) 862525
Call in advance for opening times
Adm Adult £5.50, child £3.95, under-4s **free**,
family £15.90
*Café, shop, mother and baby room, disabled access,
on-site parking*

Wyld Court Rainforest

Hampstead Norreys, nr Newbury **t** (01635) 202444
Infoline **t** (01635) 200221 **www**.livingrainforest.org
Getting there The rainforest is 8 miles from
Newbury, off the B4009
Open Daily 10–5.15
Adm Adult £4.50, child £2.50, under-3s **free**,
family £12
*Café–restaurant, picnic areas, gift shop, mother and
baby facilities, guided tours, disabled access, on-site
parking*

A little piece of rainforest in deepest Berkshire –
here, under 20,000sq ft of glass, are three sweatily
hot simulated tropical environments, 'Lowland
Tropical', 'Amazonica' and 'Cloudforest', full of
dense, lush rainforest vegetation. You take a jungle
tour on wooden duckboards past giant ferns and
palm trees, brightly coloured almost insect-like
orchids and lily ponds filled with giant 8ft lilies, all
inhabited by numerous free-roaming creatures of
the forest: bug-eyed frogs, fluttering brightly
coloured butterflies, slow-moving lizards, parrots
and toucans, shimmering tropical fish and even
leaping, clambering squirrel monkeys. At times,
with perspiration running down your neck, it can
feel as if you really are lost in the jungle. There are
regular talks on conservation and children's events
such as the 'Children's Water Day' and 'Feel the
Heat Activity Day'. Face-painting and art workshops are organized in summer. Unsurprisingly, it
has become a popular venue for children's parties.

As you explore, remember to feel good about
yourself. The project is operated by the Woodland
Trust, a conservation charity, and all the profits of
this enterprise go towards helping save the real
rainforests in Central and South America. So, you're
not just having a good time, you're also helping to
preserve the natural world.

AROUND AND ABOUT

Bricks and mortar

Basildon Park

Lower Basildon, Reading **t** (0118) 984 3040
Getting there Basildon Park lies 7 miles northwest
of Reading, on the west side of the A329
Open Mar–Oct Wed–Sun 12–5.30, house from 1pm
Adm Adult £4.30, child £2.15, family £10.50
*Café, picnic area, shop, mother and baby room,
disabled access, on-site parking*

Surrounding an elegant 18th-century Bath-stone
mansion, this glorious swathe of parkland has
numerous marked walks and plenty of open spaces
for running about on. The house contains a
number of features that may appeal to children
including the jungle mural that adorns the walls
and ceiling of the small tearoom and the collection
of shells in the Shell Room. Events for families, such
as craft fairs and theatre shows, are put on in
summer.

Blenheim Palace

For further information *see* p.80.

Greys Court

Rotherfield Greys, Henley-on-Thames
t (01491) 628529
Getting there Greys Court is 3 miles west of
Henley-on-Thames, off the B481
Open April–Sept, garden Tues–Sat and Bank
Holiday Mon 2–6; house Wed, Thurs, Fri and Bank
Holiday Mon 2–6
Adm Adult £4.60, child £2.30, family £11.50
*Tea room, picnic area, shop, mother and baby room,
some disabled access, on-site parking*

This beautiful 16th-century house is set in
charming grounds that will delight children.
There's a brick maze to explore, a wheelhouse
(where donkeys were once used to power the
wheel that drew water from a deep underground
well) and, in among the ruins of a medieval forti-
fied manor, a series of 'secret' gardens which are
linked by 'doorways' in the walls.

In the 17th century, the house acted as a sort of
informal prison for Robert and Francis Carr who
were banished here by James I after they were

found guilty of murdering a fellow courtier – you can probably think of a lot worse places to be imprisoned.

The nearby town of Henley-on-Thames is famed for its summer sailing festival known as the Royal Regatta, which is one of the highlights of the traditional upper-class social season and an important amateur rowing tournament. At any time of the year, though, you can see rowers practising on this short stretch of the river. Row-boats can be hired for a little self-guided sightseeing if you want.

Nature lovers

Cotswold Wildlife Park

Bradwell Grove, Burford **t** (01993) 823006
www.cotswoldwildlifepark.co.uk
Getting there Burford is about 18 miles west of Oxford, off the A40
Open April–Sept daily 10–6; Oct 10–5; Nov–Mar 10–4.30
Adm Adult £6.50, child £4, under-3s **free**
Café, picnic areas, gift shop, mother and baby room, disabled access, on-site parking

These 160 acres of woodland and gardens surrounding a Victorian manor house provide an idyllic environment for a whole range of creatures. There are large, natural-looking enclosures for the outdoor animals to roam about in, which include lions (these are the rare Asiatic variety), leopards, white rhinos and zebras (with raised viewing areas so little people can have a good look), as well as a walk-through aviary, an aquarium, an insect house and a bat house where you can watch bats flying beneath you from an observation platform. Kids itching to get involved can stroke the animals in the small children's farm, take a rubbing in the brass-rubbing centre before hitting the adventure playground which has slides and a helter-skelter. There's also a narrow-gauge railway.

Courage Shire Horse Centre

Cherry Garden Lane, Maidenhead **t** (01628) 824848
Getting there The centre is 2 miles west of Maidenhead, on the A4
Open March–Oct 10.30–5 (last adm 4)
Adm: Adult £3.50, child £2.50
Tea room, picnic areas, gift shop, mother and baby room, guided tours, on-site parking

You can stroke and pet the great Shires with their shaggy flared legs at this popular equestrian centre and watch them being groomed and having their tails plaited. On certain days you may also be able to see the harness-maker and farrier at work.

Wellington Country Park

Odiham Road, Riseley, Reading **t** (0118) 932 6444
Open Mar–Oct 10–5.30 daily (last adm 4.30)
Adm Adult £4, child £2
Café, picnic areas, gift shop, disabled access, on-site parking

This 350-acre country park, five miles south of Reading, has marked nature trails through and around meadows, woodland and lakes (row and pedal boats can be hired). For the less actively inclined, there's a miniature railway providing good views of the deer park while children are catered for with a small adventure playground.

Wyld Court Rainforest

For futher information *see* p.83.

Look at this!

Cogges Manor Farm Museum

Church Lane, Witney **t** (01993) 772602
Getting there Witney is about 13 miles west of Oxford, off the A40
Open April–Oct Tues–Fri and Bank Hol Mon 10.30–5.30, Sat and Sun 12 noon–5.30 (last adm 4.30)
Adm Adult £4, child £2, under-3s **free**
Café, picnic areas, mother and baby room, disabled access, on-site parking

The aim at Cogges is to provide an all-encompassing Victorian farmyard experience, so visitors can see what farm life was like before the advent of industrialization. Not only will you find a working Victorian farm with vintage breeds of horses, donkeys, cows and pigs, but there's also a 13th-century manor house complete with Victorian furniture, fixtures and fittings, a Victorian kitchen where bread and cakes are baked every day (in a Victorian style of course), a Victorian dairy and even a Victorian activities room where children can try on Victorian costumes and play with Victorian toys and games. You can see demonstrations of Victorian crafts such as blanket-weaving and corn-dolly making and there are occasional Punch and Judy shows in summer. And, even if your interest in Victoriana isn't that great, you will probably still enjoy the museum's riverside setting. You can picnic on the riverbanks and take walks through the adjoining woodland.

Look Out Discovery Centre
For further information *see* p.82.

Steam power

Didcot Railway Centre
Didcot **t** (01235) 817200
www.didcotrailwaycentre.org.uk
Getting there Didcot Railway centre is 10 miles south of Oxford and is signposted from J5 of the M4 and the A34
Open April–Oct Sat, Sun and Bank Hol Mon 10–5; July–Aug Wed, Sat, Sun and Bank Hol Mon 10–5; Nov–Feb Sat and Sun 10–4
Fares Adult £8, child £6.50
Refreshments, shop, disabled access, on-site parking

A wonderful day out for mini steam enthusiasts. Although the town's industrialized setting is hardly inspiring, you'll barely notice as you examine the 20 or so huge, shiny GWR (Great Western Railway) locomotives in the engine shed, many of which can be boarded and explored. Kids can stand in the driver's cabin for that all-important pretending-to-drive-the-train experience; still a thrill even in today's virtual reality age. On steam days you can take train rides up and down a short length of track, watch engines being turned around on a turntable and see how mailbags are collected by a moving train or 'Travelling Post Office'. There's also a small collection of railway memorabilia, including several model trains, and the chance to see trains being repaired in the locomotive works.

Around Christmas, and on other special occasions, Didcot is transformed into the the land of talking trains, home to the famous loco *Thomas* who takes delighted fans on a journey round the mythical island of Sodor. These jolly trips sell out quickly so it is essential to book well in advance (phone for details).

STRATFORD-UPON-AVON

Getting there By road: Stratford is 80 miles from London and 10 miles from Warwick. By train: the best service direct to Stratford from London is from Paddington with Thames Trains. By bus/coach: National Express run services from Warwick and London Victoria
Tourist office Bridgefoot **t** (01789) 293127
www.shakespeare-country.co.uk. Ask for a copy of the leaflet 'Children's Stratford' or phone 'where to take the children' infoline **t** (0900) 131 1419

Stratford to most people, of course, means just one thing, William Shakespeare. This is where the country's most famous and celebrated dramatist was born, where he married and lived for twenty-odd years before moving to London, and where he returned later in life having made his fortune. The association has turned this small, pretty but otherwise unremarkable market town into one of the country's top tourist attractions. In summer its streets welcome an almost ceaseless procession of coaches come to disgorge their Will-obsessed human cargo. Join the throng and take a tour through five of the buildings where Shakespeare spent much of his early and later life. Once you've seen how he lived, you can catch a performance of his work at one of the three theatres in Stratford operated by the Royal Shakespeare Company: the Royal Shakespeare Theatre, The Swan Theatre and The Other Place, all of which overlook an idyllic stretch of the River Avon (backstage tours available).

Children, of course, can quickly overdose on Shakespeariana; one house should probably do it – Mary Arden's with its animals and hawk displays will probably prove the most popular. Thankfully, the town does boast several alternative distractions for when the thought of seeing one more framed sonnet becomes too much to bear. There's a very good teddy bear museum (owned by the author and former MP, Gyles Brandreth), full of furry favourites, a brass-rubbing centre, a Butterfly Farm with over 1,500 free-flying butterflies and, perhaps best of all, the Ragdoll TV shop (Ragdoll is the company responsible for the *Teletubbies, Rosie*

& *Jim* and *Brum* among other programmes) where there's a designated play area for children. The Shire Horse Centre, where you can watch parades by the great shaggy beasts and meet some friendly farmyard animals, is just south of Stratford.

Things to see

Cox's Yard
Bridgefoot **t** (01789) 404600 **www**.coxyard.co.uk
Open 9.30–5.30
Adm Adult £3.95, child £2.50, family £11
Café–restaurant, shop
Historical dioramas 'The Stratford Tales', interactive games and a camera obscura giving sneaky peeks of modern Stratford.

Mary Arden's House
Station Road, Wilmcote **t** (01789) 204016
www.shakespeare.org.uk
Open April–Oct Mon–Sat 9.30–5, Sun 10–5;
Nov–Mar Mon–Sat 10–4; Nov–Mar Mon–Sat 10–4
Adm Adult £5, child £2.50, family £12.50
On-site parking, café, picnic area, shop, guided tours
The former home of the playwright's mother, this is perhaps the most kid-friendly of the five Shakespeare Houses. There's a Victorian farm and you can see displays of falconry daily in summer.

The Ragdoll Shop
Chapel Street **t** (01789) 404111
Open Mon–Sat 9.30–5.30, Sun 12–4
Free
Kids can explore the Tots Secret House, watch Ragdoll programmes and speak to their favourite tellytubby on the phone.

The Shakespeare Houses
The Shakespeare Birthplace Trust, the Shakespeare Centre, Henley Street **t** (01789) 204016
www.shakespeare.org.uk
Tours of the five houses cost: adult £12, child £6, family ticket £29
The Shakespeare Houses is a tour around the five buildings in Stratford-upon-Avon where the bard spent much of his early and later life. These are the small house on Henley Street where he was born in 1562 (decked out with period furniture, it contains an interactive display on his life and a garden planted with trees and flowers mentioned in the plays); the home of his mother, Mary Arden; the thatched Tudor farmhouse where Will's bride Anne Hathaway lived; New Place, which in the early 17th

> **Did you know...**
> *Teddy Bears, the world's best-loved children's playthings, were 'invented' in 1902. According to the Brooklyn toy maker who gave the cuddly bears their name, it came from an incident in the life of American President 'Teddy' Roosevelt. During one of his regular hunting trips he spared a female bear and her cubs. When the incident was recreated in a political cartoon the toy maker saw his chance and started naming his toy bears after the president.*

century was one of the largest houses in Stratford and was bought by Will with wealth accrued in London (the building was destroyed in the 18th century although the foundations and Elizabethan knot garden survive), and Hall's Croft, the home of Dr John Hall who married Shakespeare's daughter.

Stratford-upon-Avon Butterfly Farm
Tramway Walk, Swan's Nest Lane **t** (01789) 299288
www.butterflyfarm.co.uk
Open Summer 10–6; winter 10–dusk
Adm Adult £3.75, child £2.75, family £10.75
Restaurant, shop, disabled access, on-site parking
Europe's largest butterfly farm is also home to an Insect City, full of stick insects, beetles and leaf-cutter ants, as well as a spider-infested Arachnoland (look out for tarantulas and giant scorpions) in addition to the many tropical butterflies fluttering around the centre's rainforest and tinkling waterfalls.

Teddy Bear Museum
19 Greenhill Street **t** (01289) 293160
www.theteddybearmuseum.com
Open Mar–Dec 9.30–6; Jan–Feb 9.30–5
Adm Adult £2.50, child £1.50, family £7.50
Shop
Thousands of bears (including favourites like Paddington and Sooty) are displayed in a house that once belonged to Henry VIII. Children's quiz sheets available.

Things to do

Avon Cruises
Swan's Nest Lane **t** (01789) 267073
www.avon-boating.co.uk
Open Easter–Oct daily
Fares Guided cruises adult £3, child £2; boat hire per hour adult £2.50, child £1.50

Tell me a story:
Was Shakespeare really Shakespeare?

He's the most famous playwright in the world. His works have been staged and filmed more times than any other author and yet the man himself remains something of a mystery. Little documentary evidence of Shakespeare's life survives. It is known that he was born in Stratford-upon-Avon in 1564, the son of a local glovemaker, that at age 18 he married a local girl, Anne Hathaway and, in his mid-twenties, moved to London. He became an actor and, later, a playwright before, at the end of his life, returning to live in Stratford where he gave up writing to concentrate on business. Beyond that, however, details are sketchy and many questions remain unanswered. Who, exactly, was Shakespeare? What prompted this working-class lad from the Midlands to seek his fortune in the theatres of Elizabethan London and, perhaps more intriguingly, where did he find the inspiration to write his collection of plays that are still being performed around the world 400 years later?

Very few personal documents relating to Shakespeare's private life have survived. There is not one single existing copy of a Shakespeare play or poem in his own handwriting. Indeed, he seems to have been strangely unconcerned with preserving his own work. His will contains no mention of any manuscripts or books (although it does mention his 'second best bed' which he left to his wife) and his works weren't even compiled into an anthology until 1623, some six years after his death. This has led some people to question whether the low-born man from the Midlands was indeed the same man responsible for some of the finest works in the English language. How, they ask, could a man with little education (Shakespeare's own father could neither read nor write) have transformed himself into a writer of such stature? Some have even argued that 'Shakespeare' was in fact a pseudonym used by one of the other (higher-born and better educated) men of letters of the time – Sir Francis Bacon and Christopher Marlowe have been put forward as possible alternatives.

The Marlowe theory would seem to be undermined by the small fact that Marlowe was actually murdered in a bar brawl early in Shakespeare's career. Conspiracy theories abound, however, and it has been claimed that Marlowe faked his own death in order to avoid being jailed for a criminal charge he was on at the time. It is known that Marlowe was a close friend of Sir Thomas Walsingham, one of the most powerful men in the country and one of the few capable of arranging Marlowe's 'disappearance'. It should also be noted that Christopher Marlowe had worked as a spy for the government and so may have had other reasons for wanting to duck out of public view. Once officially declared dead, the conspiracy theorists believe that Marlowe, still wanting to continue working as a playwright, hired a young, jobbing actor on the London theatre scene called William Shakespeare to act as a front for his work, in the same way that blacklisted writers did in America in the 1950s.

Shakespeare and the English language

Shakespeare wasn't just a playwright, he was perhaps the single greatest linguistic innovator in the history of the English language who fundamentally changed the way English was written and spoken. He coined well over 2,000 words, many of which are still in use today. Everytime you're 'critical', tell a 'barefaced' lie or find something to be 'excellent', you have Shakespeare to thank. Mountaineers would never reach the 'summit', money-savers could never be 'frugal' and the wind would never 'gust' without Shakespeare's help. He was the first to 'castigate', 'hint' and 'hurry' and the first to describe things as 'monumental', 'majestic' or 'obscene'.

As a phrasemaker, he was even more influential: 'one fell swoop', 'my mind's eye', 'play fast and loose', 'to be in a pickle', 'more in sorrow than in anger', 'flesh and blood', 'cruel to be kind' – these are all phrases regularly uttered in everyday discourse that were first introduced to the language by the Bard of Avon.

Shakespearean theatre

Today, we often regard theatre-going as something rather refined and elegant but in Shakespeare's day it was seen as a rough and ready form of entertainment and a chance to let off steam. The audiences at Shakespeare's plays were a rowdy lot. Mostly drunk, they were determined to enjoy the show, and would cheer for the goodies, hiss at the baddies and pitch rotten food at the stage (and each other) if they were displeased with the performance.

Offers half-hour guided river trips on motorized river launches plus punts and rowboats for hire. You can jump on board a cruise at any point along its route. If you're lucky, you may even see boats being built back at the workshops.

Bus tours

Open-top double decker bus sightseeing tours of Stratford are run by Guide Friday in summer.
t (01789) 294466 **www.guidefriday.com**
Fares Adult £9, child £2.50, family £20.50

Guided walks

Ghost walks of the city are offered by Grimm's Ghostly Tours between April and September
t (01789) 204106

Royal Shakespeare Company

Waterside **t** (01789) 403403 **www.rsc.org.uk**
Tour times Mon–Fri at 1.30 and 5; Sun at 12 noon, 1, 2 and 3
Adm Adult £4, child and concs £3

Forty-five-minute tours of the Royal Shakespeare Company and Swan Theatre are available all year round – you can stand on the stage, watch the scenery being changed and see how the costume department gets the fake blood to look so realistic.

The Shakespeare Express

Snow Hill Station **t** (0121) 605 7000
www.vintagetrains.co.uk
Open Late May–Sept daily, selected Suns during rest of year
Fares adult single £10, child single £3
Some disabled access

The fastest steam trains in the land run between Stratford-upon-Avon and Birmingham every day in summer. The journey lasts 50mins.

Stratford Brass Rubbing Centre

The Royal Shakespeare Theatre Summer House, Avon Bank Gardens **t** (01789) 297671
Open Summer daily 10–6; winter Sat and Sun 11–4
Free, each rubbing costs £1–20
Shop, garden, disabled access, on-site parking

Cinemas
The Picture House

Windsor Street **t** (01789) 415500
Stylish little cinema, located between the town centre and Shakespeare's birthplace. Rooftop bar.

Theatres
Royal Shakespeare Theatre

Waterside **t** (01789) 403403 **www.rsc.org.uk**
Home to the Royal Shakespeare Company. Plenty of Shakespeare on offer as well as backstage tours.

Activities
Cotswold Country Cycles Bicycle Hire

Longlands Farm Cottage, Chipping Camden
t (01386) 438706 **www.cotswoldcountrycycles.com**
Getting there Chipping Camden is about 18 miles east of Camden on the B4035
Open April–Oct 9–5.30, otherwise by prior appointment only
Hire From £10 per day

Stocks adult bikes, children's bikes, tag-a-longs and panniers and can provide details of cycle routes through the Cotswolds.

THE COTSWOLDS

The Cotswolds is quite simply one of the most beautiful regions in the entire country – a rolling limestone escarpment running for a hundred miles or so between Chipping Campden and Bath. Beautifully unspoilt, it's an area characterized by its gently undulating stone-walled landscape, clusters of historic villages (many little changed in hundreds of years), honey-coloured cottages, snug pubs, steep wooded valleys, winding streams, duck-filled ponds, sheep-dotted fields and other such picture postcard staples. It has inevitably become something of a tourist Mecca and in fine weather its walks and trails (including the Cotswold Way which runs the entire length of the region) are thick with ramblers. There's so much of it, however, that it's easy to get off the beaten track to admire some of the most dramatic and photogenic scenery the country has to offer. There are also plenty of attractions for children to get their teeth into – animal parks, model villages, museums, etc. – many of which can be found in the almost impossibly picturesque towns (with equally picturesque names) of Bourton-on-the-Water, Stow-on-the-Wold and Moreton-in-Marsh – the average Cotswold village is a very hyphenated affair.

Bourton-on-the-Water

Getting there Bourton is 15 miles east from Cheltenham on the A429, off the A40
Tourist information centre Victoria Street
t (01451) 820211

One of the most touristy villages in the Cotswolds, Bourton is also one of the most fun for children. Nestling among its honey-coloured cottages is a fine array of attractions that should keep you and the kids happily occupied in between your bouts of countryside rambling. There's Birdland, a 70-acre bird sanctuary which is home to over 130 species of birds including parrots, penguins and flamingoes; the Cotswold Motor Museum, with its large collection of vintage cars (and slightly smaller collection of vintage toys), and the Bourton Model Railway, one of the largest model railways in the country. For some reason, miniaturization has become big business in Bourton where everyone, it seems, has some sort of Gulliver complex. You can also visit Miniature World, a collection of mini-shop and house interiors inhabited by 6-inch high figures, and The Model Village, a replica of Bourton itself complete with a miniature version of the River Windrush flowing through the town. Bourton also boasts a Perfumery Exhibition where you can see scents being manufactured, a large yew tree maze and, just outside the town is Folly Farm, a show farm-cum-wildfowl centre with hordes of hand-reared (and thus extremely friendly) ducks, geese, chickens, goats, cows and even llama – all ready and waiting to be fed.

Bourton can be crowded and, whatever the locals might say, it is actually a bit tacky and over-developed but, from a kid's perspective (and most of the town's attractions appeal to them), it will probably prove to be the most popular Cotswold village.

Can you spot?
Bourton's model village is a 1/10 scale model of Bourton itself. As a complete model, it also has a model of itself. Can you spot it? This is a 1/100th scale model of Bourton. If it were to be completely accurate, this 1/100th scale model would also contain a model of Bourton. This would be a 1/1000th scale model of the scale model of the scale model of Bourton, and on and on to infinity.

A few miles to the southwest in the village of Northleach you'll find the Cotswold Heritage Centre, housed in a former 18th-century prison building, which has an exhibition on rural life. You can visit the re-created workshops of a wheel-wright and blacksmith as well as the restored cell block and courtroom. Children's events, such as dressing up in period costumes, are regularly organized. Also in Northleach is Keith Harding's World of Mechanical Music which houses a diverse collection of antique music boxes, automata and musical instruments.

Birdland Park and Gardens
Rissington Road **t** (01451) 820480
Open April–Oct daily 10–6; Nov–Mar 10–4 daily
Adm Adult £4.25, child £2.50, under-4s **free**
Café, shop, disabled access, mother and baby room

Bourton Model Railway
Box Bush High Street, **t** (01451) 820686
Open April–Sept 11–5.30; Oct–Mar Sat and Sun 11–5
Adm Adult £1.75, child £1.50

Bourton Model Village
The Old New Inn **t** (01451) 820467
Open Summer daily 9–6; Winter daily 10–4
Adm Adult £2.75, child £2, under-4s **free**
Shop

Cotswold Heritage Centre
Northleach **t** (01451) 860715
Open April–Oct Mon–Sat 10–5, Sun 2–5, Bank Hol Mon 10–5
Adm Adult £2.50, child 80p, family £5
Café, picnic area, shop, mother and baby facilities, disabled access, on-site parking

Cotswold Motor Museum
The Old Mill **t** (01451) 821255
Open Mar–Oct daily 10–6
Adm Adult £2.25, child £1.25, under-5s **free**
Gift shop, disabled access

Folly Farm
t (01451) 820285
Getting there It is on the A436, about 10 miles east of Cheltenham
Open Summer daily 10–6; Winter 10–3.30
Adm Adult £3.50, child £1.50
Restaurant, farm shop, disabled access, on-site parking

Keith Harding's World of Mechanical Music

High Street, Northleach **t** (01451) 860181
www.mechanicalmusic.co.uk
Open Daily 10–6
Adm Adult £5, child £2.50, family £12.50
Shop, guided tours, disabled access

Miniature World

t (01451) 810121
Open April–Oct 10–5; Nov–Mar Sat and Sun
10–4.30
Adm Adult £2.50, child £1.50, under-4s **free**

Perfumery Exhibition

Cotswold Perfumery, Victoria Street
t (01451) 820698
Open Mon–Sat 9–5, Sun 10–5, mid summer open
until 6
Adm Adult £2, child £1.75
Shop, disabled access

Stow-on-the-Wold

Getting there Stow is 16 miles northeast of
Cheltenham and can be reached via the A429
Tourist Information Centre Hollis House, The
Square **t** (01451) 831082

'Stow-on-the-Wold where the wind blows cold.'
Set on a plateau some 240m up, this picturesque,
albeit occasionally windswept, town is the highest
in the Cotswolds. The usual collection of charming
stone cottages and houses are here laid out around
a large central marketplace that's vaguely reminiscent of a medieval piazza. Note the narrow
alleyways surrounding it. Originally designed to
make it easier for farmers to drive their sheep to
market, they are now lined with shops and stalls. A
good base for exploring the Cotswolds, the town's
most child-friendly attraction is probably the Toy
and Collectors Museum on Park Street, which
houses a collection of antique toys.

Stow straddles the old Roman Fosse Way which
also takes in Moreton-in-Marsh, a few miles to the
north, where a lively market is held every Tuesday
when over 200 stalls open for business. It's also
home to the Cotswold Falconry Centre where you
can watch eagles, hawks and owls being flown daily.

Between Stow and Moreton lie the tiny villages
of Upper and Lower Slaughter which, despite their
rather macabre names, are actually among the
most picturesque of all the Cotswold villages (and
that's saying something).

SPECIAL TRIPS

Warwick Castle

Warwick **t** 0870 442 2000
www.warwick-castle.co.uk
Getting there It's 2 miles from the M40 (J1), off the
A429 in the centre of Warwick town. The nearest
train station is Warwick, 5-mins walk away which
operates a direct service with London Marylebone
Open April–Oct daily 10–6; Nov–Mar 10–5
Adm Adult £11.50, child £6.75, under-4s **free**,
family £30
*Two restaurants, gift shops, limited wheelchair
access, disabled parking spaces available, on-site
parking*
House unsuitable for pushchairs

Run by the Tussaud's Group, this has got to be the
country's most well-presented castle – a cross
between a medieval fortress, an interactive
museum and a historical pageant.

There has been a castle on this spot as far back as
the 10th century when it was home to Ethelfleda,
daughter of Alfred the Great, although most of
what you see is 14th century with a few 19th-
century adornments. It's made up of a main house
linked to a series of unsymmetrical towers – the
largest, Caesar's tower, is 147ft tall – by a crenel-
lated curtain wall and is surrounded by 60 acres of
picnic-perfect landscaped gardens where free-
roaming peacocks strut their haughty stuff. The
castle's interior has been divided into a series of
lively exhibits in which costumed guides lead you
through some of the more notable episodes from
the castle's medieval heyday. You can visit the
Ghost Tower, said to be haunted by the spirit of Sir
Fulke Greville, murdered here by his servant in 1628,
descend into the dungeon to see the terrifying
collection of torture instruments used to extract
confessions from French prisoners during the
Hundred Years War and tour the ramparts to see
the Murder Holes through which boiling tar was
poured on potential invaders.

The castle reached the height of its status and
importance in the 15th century when it was the
home of Richard Neville, the Earl of Warwick, one of
the major players in the Wars of the Roses. During
his illustrious career he helped depose both the
Lancastrian Henry VI and the Yorkist Edward IV
(thereby earning himself the nickname 'The

Kingmaker') before being killed in battle by Edward's troops in 1471. The Kingmaker exhibition in the castle's undercroft makes full use of the Tussaud's Group's visual and sound trickery to create an atmospheric tableaux, showing the preparations for the Earl's final battle.

The castle is highly interactive throughout, the owners clearly having realized that in today's virtual reality world, dusty displays guarded by 'do not touch' signs don't really cut it. At the recently opened Death or Glory Exhibition, which show-cases the castle's magnificent collection of medieval armour and weapons (one of the largest in Europe), you can attempt a few thrusts and parries with a mighty broadsword, try on a knight's helmet and see how longbows were used.

By the 19th century, the country's civil wars had all been fought and fortresses were no longer much in demand. Consequently, Warwick's mighty walls now became the setting for lavish society parties rather than fearsome battles. The Royal Weekend Party – 1898 is a waxwork re-creation of one of these swanky soirees showing Daisy, the Countess of Warwick, playing the elegant hostess to a group of society notables including the Prince of Wales and a young Winston Churchill. You can also see the opulent great hall and state rooms adorned with priceless furniture and paintings by Rubens and Van Dyck.

The best time to visit the castle is definitely between May and September when its river island plays host to a vibrant medieval festival. In a recon-structed medieval village you can watch knights jousting and engaging in hand to hand combat, see demonstrations of archery and bird of prey handling and take part in a range of medieval games.

The Doll Museum which occupies a half-timbered Tudor house near the castle entrance is also well worth a visit. It holds a large collection of antique toys and dolls.

Cinemas
The Dream Factory
Shelley Avenue t (01926) 419555

Activities
International Warwick School of Riding
Guys Cliffe, Coventry Road, Warwick
t (01926) 494313
Lessons, hacks and daily riding in the Warwickshire countryside.

AROUND AND ABOUT

Bricks and mortar

Chedworth Roman Villa
Yanworth, nr Cheltenham t (01242) 890256
Getting there The Villa is situated off the A429, 10 miles southeast of Cheltenham
Open Mar 11–4; April–Oct 10–5.30; Nov 11–4
Adm Adult £3.70, child £1.85, family £9.30
Shop, some disabled access, on-site parking

Pay a visit to Roman Britain via the remains of this 4th-century villa, one of the largest in Britain. Clearly the property of some very wealthy Roman citizen, the house came equipped with all mod cons (Roman style) including central heating, two bath houses and a lavatory. There are also some very well-preserved mosaics and an introductory video and audiovisual guide which will help you to picture what the villa would have looked like when first built all those centuries ago. Children's activi-ties are put on during the school holidays.

Kenilworth Castle
Castle Green, Kenilworth t (01926) 852078
www.english-heritage.org.uk
Getting there It's in Warwickshire on the western edge of Kenilworth town off the A46. Follow the signs
Open April–Sept daily 10–6; Oct daily 10–5; Nov–Mar daily 10–4
Adm Adult £4, child £2
Tearoom (open in summer), picnic area, shop, disabled access, on-site parking

This gloriously grizzled ruddy monster with its 20ft thick walls is the largest ruined castle in the country. It was built sometime in the 12th century and you can still see the remains of the Norman keep as well as the Strong Tower and Great Hall added in later centuries. In the 16th century it was often frequented by Elizabeth I who came here to meet with her favourite Robert Dudley, the Earl of Leicester. At that time the castle would have stood in the middle of a great lake, now replaced by lawns although a Tudor Barn and Tudor Garden still survive (the barn houses the castle shop, café and a small interactive museum with a model showing how

Kenilworth used to look). Following the Civil War, the castle was deliberately left to fall into disrepair.

This is no wet weather option. Every part of the site is open to the elements and a great deal of the soft red sandstone has been eaten away by centuries of wind and rain. Nonetheless, the lack of preserved formality means you can tour the castle and grounds more or less at will, the ruins providing a perfect impromptu climbing frame for adventurous children. Audio guides are available and there's a free children's activity leaflet and (as with most of the English Heritage sites of this type) there are lots of events and activities to attend over the course of the year ranging from demonstrations of medieval combat to plays, performances of medieval music and songs and even sheepdog demonstrations and Hallowe'en tours for the kids.

Lunt Roman Fort

Baginton, Coventry **t** (024) 7683 2381
Getting there Located in Baginton, near Coventry Airport
Open Easter–Oct Sun and Bank Hol Mon, every day during school hols 10–5
Adm Adult £2.60, child £1.30
Picnic area, gift shop, guided tours, disabled access
Reconstruction of a wooden 1st-century Roman Fort (on the site of an original fort) where you can watch demonstrations of Roman military training and fighting (very realistic, they even shout and swear at each other in Latin).

Sudeley Castle

Winchcombe **t** (01242) 602308
www.stafford.co.uk/sudeley
Getting there Sudeley Castle is on the A46, just south of Winchcombe
Open Castle apartments and church April–Oct 11–5; grounds and gardens Mar–Oct 10.30–5.30
Adm Adult £6.20, child £3.20, family £17
Restaurant, shop, on-site parking
This grand medieval castle was a popular hang-out for an assortment of Tudor royals. Henry VIII, Anne Boleyn, Lady Jane Grey and Elizabeth I all stayed here, while Catherine Parr, Henry VIII's luck-iest wife (she survived him and married again) lived here and is buried in the chapel. Largely remodelled in the 19th century, the castle is in wonderful condition, its grand apartments filled with sumptuous furnishings and paintings by a number of big name painters including Van Dyck,

Rubens and Turner. The equally lavish grounds (which cover some 1,500 acres) contain the famous rose-filled Queen's Garden, a Tudor Knot Garden, with a water feature modelled on a pattern of one of Elizabeth I's dresses and a well-equipped adven-ture playground.

Warwick Castle

For further information *see* p.90.

Nature lovers

Coombe Country Park

Visitor centre, Brinklow Road, Binley, Coventry
t (0247) 645 3720
Getting there It's on the B4027 between Coventry and Rugby
Open Park daily dawn–dusk; visitor centre summer 9–6, winter 9–4
Free
Café, picnic areas, shop, mother and baby facilities, guided tours, most of the park is wheelchair acces-sible with all weather pathways in place and easirider vehicles available free of charge (these must be booked at least a day in advance), on-site parking (charge)
These 400 acres of woodland, historic parkland and beautiful formal gardens have lots to offer children. The Visitor Centre has a special Discovery Centre for younger visitors with inter-active games – they can learn how to distinguish between different woodland scents, types of tree bark and fish – and sells pond-dipping and insect-collecting kits. The Young Rangers Club, also based at the centre, offers guided nature walks around the park.

In addition, the park contains two adventure playgrounds (one near the visitor centre), a lake (unfenced) full of friendly ducks and an arboretum full of enormous, imported American redwoods.

Cotswold Farm Park

Guiting Power, Stow-on-the-Wold **t** (01451) 850307
Getting there The farm is about 15 miles east of Cheltenham and 5 miles from the B4682 at Winchcombe
Open April–Oct Mon–Sat 10.30–5, Sun and Bank Hol Mon 10.30–6
Adm: Adult £4.50, child £2.30

Café–restaurant, picnic areas, shop, mother and baby room, guided tours, disabled access, on-site parking

Home to over 50 rare (and sometimes rather odd looking) farm breeds including sheep, cows, pigs, horses and goats – look out for the 'Golden Guernsey' with its huge curved horns and long white beard. There are baby animals to cuddle and feed in the touch barn (including lambs in early summer which can be bottle-fed), a pets' corner, shearing demonstrations in summer and, all year round, you can take an audio tour of the farm entitled 'Animals through the Ages'. There's also a well-stocked adventure playground and a recently opened tractor driving school, where children get the chance to drive mini tractors and trailers loaded with bales of hay around a mini farm.

National Bird of Prey Centre

Newent **t** 0870 990 1992 **www**.nbpc.co.uk
Getting there The centre is about 12 miles west of Gloucester, and is signposted from the B4215, off the A40
Open Feb–Nov daily 10.30–5.30 (or dusk if earlier); flying demonstrations April–Sept daily 11.30, 2 and 4; Feb–Mar and Oct–Nov 11.30, 1.30 and 3.30
Adm Adult £5.75, child £3.50, under-4s **free**, family £16.50
Café, gift shop, guided tours, disabled access, mother and baby room, on-site parking

Perhaps the best place in the whole country to watch birds of prey in flight – you'll see vultures, eagles and falcons taking to the skies and flying from keeper to keeper to pick up titbits of food. Close-up, you can really get a feel for just how large and powerful these magnificent creatures are, particularly when you watch the eagles with their 2m wingspans swooping down onto their keeper's outstretched hand with a mighty swoosh, or a falcon diving or 'stooping' from a great height.

In between the flying demonstrations, which take place three times a day, you can explore the centre's 110 barn-like aviaries which house over 80 species of bird and inspect the assorted hawks, falcons and owls at close quarters. The centre organizes falconry experience days when you can come and learn how to handle and fly the birds yourself.

Prinknash Abbey Bird and Deer Park

Cranham **t** (01452) 812727
Getting there It is 2.5 miles northeast of Painswick on the A46

Open April–Sept 10–5; Oct–Mar 10–4
Café, picnic area, gift shop, mother and baby room, on-site parking

Described as the largest pets' corner in the country, Prinknash gives animal-mad children the opportunity to view and interact with a variety of animals. As you enter you'll see peacocks parading their plumage on the grassy lawns while, beyond, is a lake teeming with waterfowl – swans, ducks, geese – all waiting to be fed their daily ration of bread. You'll even find yourself approached by tame fallow deer on the lookout for tasty treats – something which always thrills children. The park's idyllic grounds are also home to aviaries full of song birds and there's a wonderful two-storey Tudor-style Wendy house for children to play in. At the abbey itself you can watch pottery demonstrations.

Stratford Shire Horse Centre

Clifford Road **t** (01789) 415274
Getting there Located a couple of miles south of Stratford off the B4632
Open Mar–Oct daily 10–5; Nov–Feb Sat–Wed 10–5
Adm Adult £5.50, child £4.50
Licensed restaurant, picnic areas, shop, mother and baby facilities, disabled access, on-site parking

Watch the great shaggy beasts in their stables and shuffling around a parade ring (at 11am and 2pm every day) and take a cart ride through a mock 19th-century village. There's an adventure playground for kids as well as a range of friendly farm animals to meet.

Wildfowl and Wetlands Trust

Slimbridge **t** (01453) 890333 **www**.wwt.org.uk
Getting there Signposted from the M5, J13 or J14, the Trust is about 13 miles south of Gloucester
Open Summer daily 9.30–5; Winter 9.30–4
Adm: Adult £6, child £3.60, family £15.60
Restaurant, café, shop, mother and baby room, guided tours, disabled access, on-site parking

The Wildfowl and Wetlands Trust operates eight centres across the UK, of which this one at Slimbridge was the first and, thanks to a large investment of lottery cash, perhaps the best. You follow a zig-zagging path though a vast expanse of soggy wetlands on the hunt for the 8,000 or so waterfowl who make the park their home at various times of the year (there are many more birds in winter than in summer). Armed with a bag of bird food, your children will no doubt have a whale of a time as flocks of ducks, swans and even flamingoes approach, demanding, often noisily, to be fed. There's also a Tropical House, home to a number of free-flying tropical birds hiding amongst the lush green rainforest-esque vegetation (if you're lucky you may even spot a tiny hummingbird), a birdwatching tower offering elevated views of the park and the River Severn, and a PondZone where you can go pond-dipping for insect and amphibian life and then examine what you've found, magnified on a TV screen in the Discovery Centre. There are quiz sheets for older children.

Look at this!

Hatton Country World

Dark Lane, Hatton, Warwick **t** (01926) 843411 **www.**hattonworld.com
Getting there It's off the A4177 Warwick–Solihull road, J15 from the M40
Open Daily 10–5
Free
Café, restaurant, mother and baby facilities, disabled access, on-site parking (£4.25 per car)

A sort of rustic shopping centre with over 30 shops selling a range of traditional craft produce, gifts and antiques housed in a series of Victorian farm buildings (known collectively as the Craft Village) with a family farm, a pets' corner, a guinea pig village, an adventure playground and a soft play area attached. Nature trails lead from here to the Canal Locks.

Shambles Museum

Church Street, Newent **t** (01531) 822144
Getting there Newent is 12 miles from Gloucester, on the B4215
Open Mid Mar–Dec 10–6 or dusk if earlier (last adm 5)
Adm Adult £2.85, child £1.85
Refreshments, shop

It seems fitting that such a pretty, unspoilt, historic-looking town should have a museum dedicated to preserving historic buildings. The Shambles is a small recreated Victorian town laid out around a central courtyard where you can wander along cobbled streets, wend your way through narrow alleys and browse the period shops which include a pawnbroker's, a jeweller's and, best of all, a toy shop. There's lots to see, so pick up a guide at the entrance

which will point you towards all the most interesting bits. It's all very charming in a twee sort of way. Once you've had your fill of looking at Victoriana, you could always eat some at the Victorian teashop.

Steam power

Gloucestershire and Warwickshire Railway

The Railway Station, Toddington, Winchcombe
t (01242) 621405 **www.gwsr.plc.uk/**
Getting there Toddington is 13 miles northeast of Cheltenham, on the B4632
Open Mid March–Oct Sat, Sun and Bank Hol Mon 10–5; school hols Tues–Thurs, Sat, Sun and Bank Hol Mon 10–5; some Christmas weekends
Fares Adult £7, child £4, under-5s **free**
Refreshments, gift shop, on-site parking

Perhaps the most pleasant way to tour the Cotswold area around Cheltenham is by taking a ride aboard one of the gently puffing steam trains of the Gloucestershire and Warwickshire Railway. The trains run along a 6.5-mile long stretch of track between Toddington and Winchcombe, passing over bridges, through fields and woodland and past tiny stone villages. You even get to travel through a short (693-yards) stretch of the dark Greet Tunnel, something which never fails to illicit squeals of delight from youngsters. On your journey look out for the Welsh Mountains rising in the west far away beyond the Vale of Evesham.

The whole experience is hugely atmospheric with the smoke billowing from the engine funnel, the smell of engine oil and the guard in his peaked cap blowing his whistle and waving his flag to set the train in motion. While waiting for your train at Toddington you can explore the railway's large collection of steam-powered contraptions which, in addition to the trains themselves, also include traction engines and fairground organs. If you're lucky, they may be fired up and playing happily (not to say very noisily) when you visit.

Lots of children's events are laid on throughout the year including Easter Egg Hunts, Santa Specials and, of course, Thomas the Tank Engine days.

BUCKINGHAMSHIRE BEDFORDSHIRE & HERTFORDSHIRE

THE CHILTERNS

A sweep of rolling hills stretching across southern Buckinghamshire and beyond, the Chilterns are just 30 miles from London and, although hardly spectacular in a Cotwolds sort of way, have been justly designated an area of outstanding natural beauty. Throughout the year they attract walkers who come to tackle the less than demanding (indeed, highly child-friendly) summits, admire the views and explore the various pretty villages – like the Thames-side Marlow and Hambleden and the National Trust-owned West Wycombe – which dot the area. The region also boasts several grand landscaped parks, such as the 300-acre West Wycombe Park and Cliveden with its geometric topiary and mazes, not to mention plenty of child-orientated attractions, most notably Whipsnade Wild Animal Park (p.97); Bekonscot Model Village (the oldest model village in the country) (p.96); Odds Farm Park (p.97), one of the best family-orientated farms around; and the Hell Fire Caves, a network of natural caves extending deep beneath West Wycombe Hill (*see* below).

Ashridge Estate

Ringshall, Berkhamsted, Herts **t** (01442) 851227
Getting there It is situated just off the B489
Visitor centre open April–Oct daily, afternoons only, except Fri
Refreshments, gift shop, on-site parking

This grand area of woodland, which covers 4,500 acres and takes in the famous Ivinghoe Beacon, is one of the most popular walking spots in the region. The beacon is over 230m tall and, on a clear day, it is possible to see no fewer than eight counties from the top. It was once the site of an Admiralty Beacon, which formed part of a chain between London and the coast, and would have been lit to warn the capital of potential invaders.

Bluebell Woods

Getting there From J5 of the M40 at Stokenchurch, follow the signs to Christmas Common. It is 5 miles from the turning for the A40, just off the B481 between Stokenchurch and Watlington
Free
Not suitable for pushchairs, car park

Bluebell Woods is the site of the Chiltern Sculpture Trail, run by the Forestry Commission, a continually changing display of modern, nature-themed art. There is a signposted walk and you can occasionally see the artists at work on their sculptures in the beech wood. It's a good idea to take a pair of wellies.

Coombe Hill

At 260m (or 850ft), this is the highest peak in the Chilterns (by way of comparison, it's only slightly taller than Canary Wharf) and provides both good panoramic views and perfect kite-flying conditions. The nearby village of Wendover, with its woodland nature trails and collection of cafés and teashops, should provide the perfect base camp for your explorations. It's just off the A413.

Dunstable Downs

Dunstable Downs Countryside Centre, Whipsnade Road, Kensworth **t** (01582) 608489
Getting there On the B4541 Dunstable to Whipsnade road
Open Countryside Centre April–Oct Tues–Sat 10–5, Sun and Bank Hols 10–6; Nov–Mar Sat and Sun 10–4
Free
Picnic areas, mother and baby room, on-site parking

Large open area of countryside just east of London and north of Whipsnade that marks the very northern tip of the Chilterns. There are lots of good walks and viewing spots (this is the highest spot in Bedfordshire – you can see right over the Vale of Aylesbury) among the rolling grasslands, plus the remains of a Bronze Age burial site, 'Five Knolls'. On most weekends you should be able to see groups of kite-flyers clustered on the highest peaks, plus daredevil hang-gliders taking advantage of the perfect thermal soaring conditions.

Hell Fire Caves

West Wycombe Park, High Wycombe
t (01494) 533739
Open Mar–Oct daily 11–5.30; Nov–Feb Sat and Sun 1–5
Adm Adult £3.50, child £2
Café, on-site parking

These originally natural caves were extended in the 18th century at the behest of Sir Francis Dashwood (according to legend, they provided a suitably secret venue for the wildly debauched parties of his notorius Hell Fire Club) and now stretch a third of a mile beneath West Wycombe

Hill. With their huge flinty entrance and collection of weird and wonderful tableaux and models, they provide the perfect venue for an afternoon of spooky exploration.

The Ridgeway Path

Claimed to be the oldest path in Britain, the Ridgeway may have been in use for well over 5,000 years, although it's obviously difficult to tell with any great degree of accuracy. It runs from Overton Hill in Wiltshire to Ivinghoe Beacon in Buckinghamshire, taking in the Chilterns and Coombe Hill on the way.

Thames Path

The section of this 180-mile long route that passes through the Chilterns is mostly flat walking and takes in the scenic villages of Hambleden and Marlow. You can also hire boats for trips along the river.

Country parks in the Chilterns

There are numerous country parks nestling among the Chiltern slopes. The most famous of all is Burnham Beeches (off the A355 between Slough and Beaconsfield), a National Nature Reserve – made up of dense beechwood forest and inhabited by colonies of free-roaming deer – that has provided the location for numerous films including *Robin, Prince of Thieves*.

Chiltern Open Air Museum

Newland Park, Gorelands Lane, Chalfont St Giles
t (01494) 871117 **www.coam.org.uk**
Getting there The museum is 13 miles north of Windsor and is signposted from J17 of the M25
Open April–Oct daily 10–5
Adm Adult £5.50, child £3, under-5s **free**, family £15, special prices apply for event days
Café, picnic areas, gift shop, mother and baby room, disabled access, on-site parking

A collection of old and not-so-old farm buildings rescued from all over Buckinghamshire and reassembled here where they provide a fascinating insight into the rural life of centuries past. Children always seem to connect more deeply with history when it's presented in this sort of living hands-on way rather than in textbooks or lectures. There are around 25 buildings to explore, including a Victorian farm with cows, ducks, chickens, sheep and horses, an Iron Age house, a tin chapel, a fully furnished 1940s prefab and even an Edwardian lavatory. The staff (some of whom may be in period

dress) are always more than happy to fill you in on the background history to the exhibits and you can watch demonstrations of traditional crafts such as blacksmithery. On one of its numerous event days, including the 'Museum Alive' summer festival, children can dress up in period costumes (chain mail armour for the boys, Victorian bonnets for the girls), listen to storytellings and take part in a range of activities, including puppet-making, kite-making, brick-making, straw-plaiting and brass rubbing. In addition to all its historic exhibits, the park also boasts nature trails through leafy woodland (look out for bluebells in the spring) and an adventure playground.

SPECIAL TRIPS

Bekonscot

Warwick Road, Beaconsfield **t** (01494) 672919
www.bekonscot.org.uk
Getting there The village is in Beaconsfield which is 2.5 miles from J2 of the M40
Open Mid Feb–Oct daily 10–5
Adm Adult £4.50, child £2.75, family £12.50
Refreshments, shop, picnic area, on-site parking

Bekonscot may be the country's oldest model village, but it's still one of the best. First opened in 1929, it's continually being added to and refined and now provides the perfect Lilliputian experience for would-be giants. You follow a set path through the village (it's actually made up of six different villages), which is quite long, although there are numerous picnic spots and an adventure play-

How Bekonscot began

The idea for Bekonscot came from a London accountant named Roland Callingham who bought a few patches of land here and decided to dig a pond. He then thought a few model houses would look nice and his friend, James Shilcock, decided that a model railway would complete the picture. From these humble beginnings the model village gradually grew and was opened to the public in 1929. Today it takes three full-time and two part-time gardeners, three electrical enginners, two model makers and a whole army of volunteers to keep the miniature world open.

ground (with slides, swings and a climbing castle) on hand for when the urge to do finally overcomes the urge to see. This shouldn't come for a while, however, as children are invariably fascinated by this miniature world – the weeny thatched cottages, churches and schools; the titchy zoo complete with miniscule animals, the tiny harbour with its minute colourful sailing boats and the model train that wends its intermittent way through the site – while parents will relish the corny names on all the shops. The 'burning' cottage is always a particular favourite, as is the fairground with its carousels and helter-skelter. See if you can spot the carp living in the brook that trickles over the model water wheel.

Odds Farm Park

**Woburn Common, High Wycombe t (01628) 520188
www.oddsfarm.co.uk**
Getting there The farm is about 10 miles north of Windsor and is signposted from the A4, A40 and A355
Open Feb half-term–Oct daily 10–5 (last adm 4); Nov–Feb half-term Thurs–Sun 10–4 (last adm 3)
Adm Adult £3.95, child £2.95, under-2s **free**
Tea room, gift shop, picnic area, mother and baby room, disabled access, on-site parking

Famously friendly, Odds Farm is one of the most popular farms in the whole of southern England. Although it holds the usual collection of show farm essentials – an animal handling area, a pets' corner, a play barn, an adventure playground, etc. – it's all so imaginatively presented that it's easy to see why it's generally considered a cut above the competition. Here, you're not expected simply to traipse around the paddocks looking at the animals but are invited to actively involve yourself in the life of the farm. Numerous activities for children are organized throughout the day, many of which, such as bottle-feeding, egg-collecting and hand-milking, are farm related – while some, such as face-painting, are not.

The signs on the paddocks are mostly written in easy-to-understand child-friendly language so you can identify the various unusual looking species of cows, sheep and goats as you tour the farm (look out for the shaggy highland cattle with their long fringes covering their eyes – how do they see?) and understand the role the farm plays in preserving these breeds for future generations. In summer there are demonstrations of sheep-shearing and

Did you know...
Giraffes give birth standing up, so when a baby giraffe is born it has to withstand a 6.5ft (2m) drop to the ground. Don't worry. It doesn't hurt them and this unexpected jolt is thought to stimulate the calf to breathe.

sheepdog trials out of doors while in winter most of the animals are safely ensconced within a large snug barn. The pets' corner, with its collection of long-eared rabbits, stays open all year.

Of course, for the modern show farm, imaginative displays of animals are no longer enough to attract the fickle fancy of the public, the play equipment must also come up to scratch with discerning young judges, and Odds Farm's certainly does. There's a barn full of hay bales which give kids the opportunity to leap about safely while tyres and sit on toys constructed from farm tractors. provides for for rustic-themed play. Benches and tables are close by so tired parents can sit down and watch their charges rush about. There's also an adventure playground with climbing equipment for more modern-style fun and games. Very young children can play in a special toddlers' area which has a sandpit and soft toys. And, once you've finished learning about farm life and being active and the hunger pangs begin, remember there are plenty of picnic tables and a teashop selling farm produce.

Whipsnade Wild Animal Park

**Whipsnade, Dunstable t (0990) 200123
www.whipsnade.co.uk**
Getting there It's signposted from the M25 (J21) and the M1 (J9 and J12). Green Line buses run from London Victoria t (020) 8668 7261. The nearest train stations are Luton (served by King's Cross Thameslink) and Hemel Hempstead (served by Euston)
Open Easter–Sept Mon–Sat 10–6, Sun and Bank Hol Mon 10–7; Oct–Easter please call in advance
Adm Adult £10.70, child £8, under-3s **free**, car entry **free**
Café, picnic areas, shop, disabled access, mother and baby room, disabled access, on-site parking

No wildlife park in Britain gives its animals as much space to roam about in as Whipsnade which, at the last count, boasted no less than 6,000 acres of paddocks. Whipsnade is home to over 2,500 animals, and the number is constantly growing. Among the latest arrivals are a female giraffe cub, a trio of youthful Siberian tiger cubs and four baby Bactrian camels.

There are four ways to tour Whipsnade: on foot, which can be tiring (especially for little legs) although you will get to wander among free-roaming wallabies, peacocks and deer; in the safety of your car, for which you have to pay extra; aboard the Whipsnade narrow-gauge steam railway, for which you also have to pay extra but which takes you on a tour through herds of elephants and rhinos; or, perhaps the best option, aboard the free open-top sightseeing bus which not only offers elevated views of the animals but can deposit you at all the best walking spots.

There's a vast range of animals to see including Asian elephants (their numbers having been swelled by the addition of London Zoo's herd), who get to enjoy Europe's largest elephant paddock; white rhinos, who also have plenty of space to run about in (a rhino in motion is a pretty fearsome sight, they can shift a lot faster than their huge bulk would seem to allow); hippos, permanently submerged in muddy water; tigers (come at feeding time when you can see these magnificent beasts on the prowl, a tiger that's not eating tends to be a tiger that's not moving); wolves, giraffes, iguanas, flamingoes, penguins and chimps.

Many of the animals (thanks to the park's successful captive breeding programme) come with babies in tow. In particular, look out for the white rhino calf, the two baby tigers, Kira and Kharia, and the baby crocodiles basking on their mother's back or being carried tenderly in her mighty jaws.

The only noticeable absentees are lions, although Whipsnade is currently trying to raise the money to build a new lion enclosure. So, if you're missing the king of the jungle, you'll have to make do with the famous 'Whipsnade Lion', a 460ft wide chalk picture cut into the Chiltern Hillside in 1932 which stares benignly down upon the park.

Need to sit down?

As you would expect, the park has a very good children's play area with lots of wooden climbing equipment, clamber nets and enclosed slides so the kids can let off steam and you can have a breather. In addition, there are a couple of good cafés (much improved in recent years) and numerous picnic areas overlooking the park's lake.

Woburn Safari Park

Woburn Park, Woburn **t** (01525) 290407
www.woburnsafari.co.uk
Getting there Woburn is just off the A4012, J13 from the M1
Open Mar–Oct daily 10–6.30 (or dusk if earlier, last adm 5); Nov–Feb Sat and Sun and school hols 11–3
Adm Summer adult £12, child £8.50; Winter adult £6.50, child £5
Café, picnic areas, shop, mother and baby room, guided tours, disabled access, on-site parking

The outbreak of foot-and-mouth led to a difficult time for safari parks such as Woburn, which had to put a number of its projects, including the outdoor sealion pool, on hold. Matters are beginning to improve now, however, and the sealion pool (which will have an underwater viewing facility) is scheduled for completion in 2002.

The sealions, like the other animals here, have to work slightly harder for their money than they do at Whipsnade, Bedfordshire's other animal attraction. The elephants are introduced to guests in the showring. Sealions leap through hoops in the pool – and there are plenty of opportunities for kids to interact with the residents. In the walk-through aviary, they can feed cups of nectar to beautiful, multicoloured lorikeets while, at the Wild World Leisure Area, tame lemurs will take bread from their hands. Best of all, you and the kids can walk through the monkey enclosure inspecting at close quarters the assorted squirrel monkeys (while they in turn inspect you).

The car-based parts of your tour (the 'Safari Drive Thru') will be equally exciting, especially when you take a tour through the lion and tiger enclosures. With just the car window to separate you from the fearsome beasts, this provides an adrenalin-pumping experience for both parents and children – even if, as is usually the case, the big cats are doing nothing more aggressive than sleeping in the shade. You'll also see elephants, giraffes, hippos, bears, ostriches, camels, rhinos and penguins on your travels, all living in large enclosures. So large, in fact, that you may not always be able to see a particular enclosure's residents close-up – the bears, in particular, are masters at hiding, which makes the few glimpses you do get all the more rewarding.

Did you know...

Elizabeth I, the daughter of Henry VIII and Anne Boleyn, lived at Hatfield until 1558 when she became Queen. Many attempts were made to persuade her to marry but she preferred to remain single all her life and she was known as the 'virgin queen'. During her 45-year reign Francis Drake defeated the Spanish Armada and William Shakespeare wrote many of his most famous plays including Romeo and Juliet. Elizabeth is said to have kept a sword by her at all times in her office. When she grew old she used to lose her temper fairly easily and would crossly thrust the sword through the tapestries that hung on the walls.

You can find out a bit more about the animals in the park on the My World Education Centre's computer terminals, before burning up a little energy at the park's great collection of play equipment which includes an excellent indoor play area shaped like Noah's Ark, full of slides and ball pools; an outdoor adventure playground, the 'Tree-Tops Action Trail'; Swan Lake, where you can take rides in swan shaped pedaloes; the 'Bob-Cat' toboggan run; a Tiny Tots Safari trail and a small steam railway. A full day of fun for around two-thirds of what you'd pay at a theme park (a lot less in winter).

AROUND AND ABOUT

Bricks and mortar

Claydon House

Middle Claydon, nr Buckingham **t** (01296) 730349
Getting there Claydon House is 13.5 miles north-west of Aylesbury and is signposted from the A413 and A41
Open April–Oct Sat–Wed 1–5; grounds 12–6
Adm Adult £4.30, child £2.15, family £10.50
Tea room, mother and baby room, some disabled access, on-site parking

Built by the noble Verney family in the early 17th century, Claydon House is said to be haunted by the ghost of Edmund Verney who was Charles I

standard-bearer at the Battle of Edgehill in 1642 (the first major battle of the Civil War). Captured by the Roundheads, poor old Edmund had his hand chopped off before finally being killed. His body was never recovered and his ghost is now said to haunt Claydon, searching for his missing limb.

Should Edmund's apparition prove elusive, you could always pay a visit to the room where Florence Nightingale used to stay when visiting her sister. Within are displayed some of her letters, detailing events from the Crimean War (where she was employed as a field nurse) and her horror at the conditions soldiers had to face in the makeshift hospitals there. Various events, including spring walks through the grand gardens and children's theatre performances, are put on during the year.

Hatfield House

Hatfield **t** (01707) 262823
Getting there Hatfield is 15 miles north of London, 7 miles from the M25 (J23), 2 miles from the A1 (J4) and is signposted from the A414 and A1000. Hatfield train station is immediately opposite. There are regular services from King's Cross which take approximately 25-mins
Open Late March–late Sept House: Tues–Thurs guided tours only 12 noon–4pm, Sat–Sun and Bank Hol Mon 1pm–4.30pm; Park: Sat–Thur 10.30am–8pm, Fri 11am–6pm
Adm House and Park adult £4.20, child £3.10; Park only adult £1.80, child 90p
Restaurant, picnic areas, shop, mother and baby room, guided tours, disabled access, on-site parking

Come to Hatfield to see how a real-life princess lived. This grand red-brick Jacobean mansion was built in the early 17th century on the site of the Tudor Palace where Queen Elizabeth I spent her childhood days. A wing of the original palace still survives adjoining the main house. The vast 4,000-acre grounds will probably be of most interest to children with their formal gardens full to bursting with hedges, paths, ponds and fountains and wilderness areas to explore. Horse and carriage rides are offered in summer and there are 5 miles of marked walks. On your travels see if you can spot the oak tree under which the young princess supposedly learned of her succession following the death of her sister Mary in 1558.

The house itself is very grand inside with its imposing rows of paintings (look for the portrait of Elizabeth) and vast oak staircase (appropriately named the Grand Staircase) decorated with carved figures. Kids will like the National Collection of Model Soldiers which has over 3,000 miniature figures arranged in positions of mass combat. For a little bit of fun, you could book a table for one of the five-course Elizabethan banquets occasionally held in the Elizabethan wing with minstrels and court jesters on hand to provide period entertainment.

Knebworth House

Knebworth **t** (01438) 811908
www.knebworthhouse.com
Getting there Knebworth House is 2 miles from Stevenage; the entrance is directly off J7 of the A1
Open School hols House: 12 noon–5; park and gardens: 11–5.30
Adm Adult and child £5.50, under-4s **free**, family £19
On-site parking, café–restaurant, picnic areas, gift shop, guided tours

Built in the 16th century, Knebworth was originally a simple Tudor mansion, but was covered in over-the-top gothic adornments in the 1800s at the behest of the Victorian author Edward Bulwer-Lytton who wanted the house to resemble one of the romantic locations from his books – look out for the rearing heraldic dragons and crenellations. The interior will be of only passing interest to children, with its collections of paintings and armour (quiz sheets available), it's the grounds which are the real draw. As you head south away from the house you'll encounter a sunken garden surrounded by trees, followed by an exquisite rose garden (just to the right is a pet cemetery), a wildflower meadow and a small maze. Beyond this is a wilderness area and a huge 250-acre park where herds of red deer roam free.

The biggest attraction for children, however, will inevitably be the Fort Knebworth adventure playground, one of the biggest and best around with lots of derring-do climbing equipment and a great selection of slides, including a suspension slide (you travel down clutching on to a rope), the four-lane Astroglide, where you travel on a helter-skelter-type rush mat down a bumpy plastic chute, a twisting corkscrew slide and a vertical-drop slide. There is also a bouncy castle and a miniature railway, which provides looping 15-minute tours of the grounds.

Nature lovers

Bedford Butterfly Park

Renhold Road, Wilden **t** (01234) 772770
www.bedford-butterflies.co.uk
Getting there Wilden is 4 miles north of Bedford off the A421 (it's signposted). The nearest train station is Bedford, which has regular connections to London St Pancras
Open Mid Feb–Oct 10–5 (last adm 4)
Adm Adult £4, child £2.50, under-3s **free**
Tea room, gift shop, guided tours, mother and baby room, disabled access, on-site parking

In a small re-created rainforest environment, heated to a constant 28°C, you can study the life cycle of the butterfly from egg, through to caterpillar and larvae, to fully formed fluttering creature. There's also a bug room where you can see giant snails, tarantulas and scorpions and, outside the glasshouse, an adventure playground, a painting barn for children, a pygmy goat enclosure and wildflower meadows with nature trails.

Mead Open Farm and Rare Breeds

Stanbridge Road, Billington, Leighton Buzzard **t** (01525) 852954
Getting there Leighton Buzzard is 10 miles north-east of Aylesbury on the A418
Open Feb–Oct daily 10–5; Nov–Jan Sat–Tues 10–4
Adm Adult £3.75, child £2.95
Mother and baby room, disabled access, on-site parking

Standard show farm fare – there's a wide range of farm animals for kids to meet including cows, sheep, pigs and goats, a pets' corner housing rabbits, guinea pigs and chipmunks, a large indoor play barn, wooden outdoor play equipment and two old tractors to clamber over. There are fortnightly falconry displays and tractor rides are offered around the farm in summer.

Oak Farm Rare Breeds Park

Broughton, Aylesbury **t** (01296) 415709
www.pebblesculpt.co.uk/oakfarm
Getting there Broughton is on the eastern edge of Aylesbury and signposted from the A41. Then follow the brown tourist signs to the farm
Open Feb half-term–Oct daily 10–5.30 (weather permitting)
Adm Adult £2.50, child £1.50
Refreshments, picnic area, shop, on-site parking

Small, traditional farm where children can meet and, on occasion, feed the residents. Demonstrations of lambing, shearing and donkey grooming are put on and there are marked nature trails through the fields and paddocks and numerous picnic spots as well as a play area with old tractors to climb over.

Odds Farm Park

For further information *see p.97.*

Paradise Wildlife Park

White Stubbs Lane, Broxbourne **t** (01992) 470490
www.pwpark.com
Getting there Broxbourne is about 15 miles east of St Albans, off the A10
Open April–Oct daily 10–6; Nov–Mar 10–dusk
Adm Adult £7.50, child £5, under-2s **free**
Café, picnic areas, mother and baby room, on-site parking

This fast expanding, albeit still quite small, park boasts an interesting selection of animals including camels, cheetahs, meerkats, zebras, donkeys and tigers. It has a children's play area with a slide, go-karts, a 'Pirate's Cove' adventure playground, an indoor play area for under-5s, a 'Dinosaur Wood' and a woodland railway. Animal handling sessions and birds of prey flying demonstrations are also organized.

RSPB Nature Reserve

The Lodge, Patton Road, Sandy **t** (01767) 680541
www.rspb.org.uk
Getting there Sandy is about 26 miles north of St Albans on the A1. The reserve is 1 mile east of Sandy, on the B1042
Open Park: daily dawn–dusk; Visitor Centre: 10–5
Adm: Adult £3, child £1, family £6
Refreshments, picnic areas, shop, mother and baby room, disabled access, on-site parking

RSPB headquarters with 104 acres of woodland, heathland and wildlife gardens where you can see woodpeckers, nuthatches and other common woodland birds. Lots of picnic areas.

Standalone Farm

Wilbury Road, Letchworth Garden City
t (01462) 686775
Getting there Letchworth Garden City is about 18 miles north of St Albans, off the A1
Open Mar–Sept daily 11–5
Adm Adult £2.95, child £1.90

Refreshments, picnic area, shop, disabled access, on-site parking

A 170-acre working farm with pigs, sheep, Shire horses, cows, picnic areas, a pets' corner and a children's play area.

Stowe Landscape Gardens

Buckingham **t** (01280) 822850
Infoline **t** (01494) 755568
Getting there The gardens are 3 miles west of Buckingham via Stowe Avenue, off the A422
Open Gardens: Mar–Oct Wed–Sun and Bank Hol Mon 10–5.30; Dec 10–4; House is only open at certain times during the Easter and Summer period so phone in advance for details
Adm Adult £4.60, child £2.30, family £11.50
Café, picnic area, shop, mother and baby facilities, manual wheelchairs cannot be accommodated, on-site parking

These 18th-century landscaped gardens are full of monuments and temples inspired by ancient Greece and Rome. There is the Temple of British Worthies where kids can try and spot some celebrities from British history, a Grotto, an Obelisk and the Congreve Monument with a monkey perched precariously on top. Maps are available to help you plan your route round the fairly extensive gardens.

Whipsnade Wild Animal Park

For further information *see p.97.*

Woburn Safari Park

For further information *see p.98.*

Look at this!

Bekonscot

For further information *see* p.96.

Chiltern Open Air Museum

For further information *see* p.96.

Gulliver's Land

Livingstone Drive, Newlands, Milton Keynes
t (01908) 609001 **www**.gullivers-themeparks.com
Getting there The theme park is signposted from
J14 of the M1
Open Mid April–mid Sept 10.30–5; Oct half-term
10.30–5. For special Christmas events call in
advance
Adm adult £8.80, child under 90cm **free**
*Café–restaurant, fast food, shop, picnic areas,
mother and baby room, on-site parking*

Small theme park where all the rides, attractions,
shows and food are aimed at 3–13 year olds and
which boasts a suitably child-sized entrance fee
(just £8.80), around half of what you'd pay at one
of the bigger name parks. There are several gentle-
ish rollercoasters, including a log coaster and the
'Wild Mouse'; a log flume plus a number of themed
areas such as Adventureland, where you can take a
Jeep Safari through a mock jungle; Discovery Bay,
which has pump carts; Toyland, which boasts a soft
play area for toddlers; and, the centrepiece of the
park, the Lilliput Land Castle.

Roald Dahl Gallery

Buckinghamshire County Museum, Church Street,
Aylesbury **t** (01296) 331441
Open Call in advance
Adm Adult £3.50, child £2.50, under-3s **free**
Café, shop, garden
No pushchairs allowed

There is only one contender for the title of 'all
time children's literature champ' – Roald Dahl,
author of such classics as *James and the Giant
Peach, George's Marvellous Medicine, The Witches,
The BFG, Charlie and the Chocolate Factory, Danny
the Champion of the World* and *The Fantastic Mr
Fox*. No other author has offered children such a
pleasingly subversive view of the world or has been
as ruthlessly unsympathetic in their portrayal of
adults (of all the authors of children's fiction only
Dahl has been willing to admit what children have
known all along, that adults are the enemy) and no
other author has created such a memorable collection of disparate characters still loved by
generations of children the world over.

Dahl spent most of his life (and indeed wrote
most of his books) in Buckinghamshire, prompting
the county council to create this small hands-on
gallery themed on the characters from his books.
It's a colourful, lively affair decorated throughout
with cut-outs of Quentin Blake's famous illustra-
tions. As you enter, you pass the multi-coloured
Great Glass Elevator itself which will shoot you up
into the stars (or, at least, to the next floor) while
inside is an imaginative, not to say slightly subversive (hip replacements fashioned into door
handles, labels written in mirror writing) array of
games and experiments fully in keeping with the
imaginative and quirky nature of the books. You
and the kids can tick off the settings and characters from the books together. There's the Giant
Peach with the centipede, the ladybird and all the
other friendly bugs living inside (which you can
examine through microscopes and magnifying
glasses); the Fantastic Mr Fox's Tunnel, which you
can crawl along, and Miss Catchpole's cupboard.
Everywhere you go there are things to press, holes
to peer through and games to play. You can try the
shadow-making machine, create your own
jewellery and watch demonstrations of optical
trickery by the great Willy Wonka himself. The only
downside is that your visit will be on a timed ticket
giving you just an hour to explore the gallery, so it's
best to whizz through. If ever there was an attraction designed to get kids away from their
Playstations and Game Boys and back to reading,
it's this one. There's plenty of space outside for
letting off steam too and the County Museum,
packed with local artefacts and crafts) to explore at
your leisure afterwards.

Did you know...
*Though Roald Dahl is most famous for his chil-
dren's books he was also a bit of a daredevil and
served as a fighter pilot with the RAF during the
Second World War. He didn't just write children's
books either. In 1967 he wrote the screenplay for
the James Bond blockbuster You Only Live Twice.*

Shuttleworth Collection

Old Warden Aerodrome, Biggleswade
t (09068) 323310 **www.shuttleworth.org**
Geting there Old Warden is 6 miles southeast of Bedford off the A600
Open April–Oct 10–5; Nov–Mar 10–4, call in advance for details of flying days
Adm Adult £6, accompanied children free
Restaurant, shop, disabled access

On its infrequent flying days you can see all sorts of rickety old historic aircraft taking to the skies from the traditional grass airstrip, including a model of the plane in which Louis Bleriot became the first man to fly across the English Channel in 1909, and a Spitfire. There are also numerous vintage motor vehicles and a coach room full of 19th-century horse-drawn carriages. The adjacent Warden Park boasts a beautiful 19th-century Swiss Garden laid out around a central lake.

Verulamium Museum and Park

t (01727) 751810
Getting there Follow signs to St Albans from J21a from the M25 or J6, 7 or 9 from the M1, then follow signs to Verulamium
Open Mon–Sat 10–5.30, Sun 2–5.30
Adm Adult £3.20, child £1.85, family £7.90
Shop, picnic area, disabled access, on-site parking

Verulamium has one of the finest collection of artefacts relating to daily Roman life on display in Britain. Among the featured displays are areas entitled food and farming, which depicts the villas and agricultural production; making a living, which shows a broad cross section of the jobs and crafts performed by the town's populace; recreation and rites, which highlights the bath houses and temples of the town; and merchants and markets, featuring the goods traded to and from Verulamium and the methods of transport employed to do this.

In addition, there are a range of reconstructed rooms based on excavated evidence, featuring a kitchen, carpenter's workshop, living room and office. You can wander through these rooms which come complete with decorative wall plasters and mosaics (see if you can spot the famous half-shell mosaic), look at the many Roman artefacts through microscopes and find out about everyday life in the Roman city of Verulaminum on touch-screen computers. Quiz sheets are available for children.

The museum is set in a hundred acres of attractive parkland where you can see more Roman remains including walls, a theatre, a bathhouse and even a hypocaust building – hypocausts were the Roman version of central heating consisting of a system of underfloor furnaces which heated the houses from below.

The park also contains tennis courts, a crazy-golf course, a children's paddling pool and a lake where you can feed the ducks.

Zoological Museum

Akeman Street, off the High Street, Tring
t (01442) 824181
Getting there Tring is about 13 miles west of St Albans, on the A41
Open Mon–Sat 10–5, Sun 2–5
Adm Adult £3.50, child **free**, **free** for all after 4pm
Picnic areas, shop, disabled access

You've never seen so many mammals, insects, birds and fish together in one place. And, because they're all stuffed, there's no chance that on the day you visit they'll be hiding in the bushes or asleep under a tree as so often happens at the zoo. Here, you can go right up to the fearsome beasts and examine them as much as you like – and even if it has been dead for over a hundred years, it's still quite a thrill to look a lion straight in the eye.

The museum is a museum piece in itself, little changed since it first opened in the late 19th century. It's a wonderfully atmospheric place with its gnarly wooden cabinets stuffed full of stuffed exotica. In particular, look out for the extinct creatures like the Quagga, the Moa and, of course, the most famous ex-animal of them all, the dodo. It certainly is different.

Steam power

Buckinghamshire Railway Centre

Quainton Road Station, Quainton, Aylesbury
t (01296) 655450 **www. bucksrailcentre.org.uk**
Getting there The railway is 5 miles northwest of Aylesbury and is signposted off the A41 and A413
Open April–Oct Sun and Bank Hol Mon 10.30–5.30, also Wed in July–Aug
Fares Call in advance for details
Café, gift shop, picnic areas, mother and baby room, on-site parking

Anytime you visit you'll find a whole host of vintage steam locomotives and engines to explore in the beautifully preserved Victorian station at Quainton Road, although it's probably best to come on one of the centre's special event days (these include a 'Miniature Traction Engine Rally', a 'Fire Fighting Day' and an 'Autumn Steam Spectacular') when you can actually take a ride along a short length of track. The Christmas steam days always prove popular when kids are joined on their journey by a jolly Santa Claus, handing out presents and mince pies as the train happily puffs along. For dads, there's a chance to live out that schoolboy dream by learning to drive a steam engine on one of their special courses.

Leighton Buzzard Steam Railway
Pages Park Station, Billington Road, Leighton Buzzard **t** (01525) 373888 **www.buzzrail.co.uk**
Getting there Leighton is about 10 miles northeast of Aylesbury, off the A418
Open Mar–Oct Sun, for other times call in advance
Fares Adult £5, child £2, under-2s **free**
Café, gift shop, picnic area, mother and baby room, disabled access, on-site parking

In deepest Bedfordshire the largest collection of narrow gauge locomotives in the country is regularly put through its paces along the tight curves and hard climbs of a country-roadside track. Here you can experience the English light railway as it was 80 years ago, with a wide variety of coaches and wagons in use and on display. The railway celebrated its 80th birthday in 1999 and regularly organizes special events for children including a 'Teddy Bear's outing', a 'Mad Hatter's Extravaganza' and the annual 'September Steam-Up' when you can take steam train rides along a 2.5-mile long stretch of line near the Grand Union Canal.

WHERE TO EAT

Bourton-on-the-Water

Bay Tree
Victoria Street **t** (01451) 821 818
Open Daily 9–5, 6.30–9

Most of Bourton-on-the-Water's restaurants and cafés are limited for space because of the nature of the buildings they are in. Most, however, make an effort to welcome children with high chairs and children's menus. The Bay Tree is non-smoking and can accommodate pushchairs/strollers. There is a little toddler crawling space at the front and the restaurant (licensed) serves a varied menu including fish and chips, roast dinners and after-noon teas.

The Mad Hatter
Victoria Street **t** (01451) 821508
Open Summer 10–9; Winter 10–4.30

The Mad Hatter has outside seating looking onto the river and a children's menu (which includes such delights as turkey dinosaurs and chicken teddies). They can provide high chairs and there's room for pushchairs/strollers. Non-smoking inside.

The Old New Inn
Rissington Road **t** (01451) 820 467
Open Mon–Sat 11-11, Sun noon-10.30

This friendly public house serves a good range of pub grub (lasagne, ploughman's etc) and can provide children with half portions from the main menu as well as having a children's menu (£3). There's a family room at the back of the pub with french windows opening out onto a play area.

Oxford

Browns
5–11 Woodstock Road **t** (01865) 511995
Open Mon–Sat 11–11, Sun 12 noon–11

Pleasant, friendly branch of the extremely family-friendly chain. It can offer a children's menu, plastic bibs and high chairs, a non-smoking area, a buggy-parking area and nappy-changing facilities.

Donnington Doorstep
Townsend Square **t** (01865) 727721
Open Mon–Sat 10–4

Good for a snack or a simple lunch, this drop-in centre has nappy-changing facilities, high chairs and toys for children.

Edgar's Café
Carfax Gardens **t** (01865) 790622
Open Mon–Sat 9–6

Once you've finished gazing at the views from the top of the Carfax Tower, you can race down to enjoy a pleasant lunch at this small café situated at its foot.

Florence Park Family Centre
Rymers Lane **t** (01865) 777286
Open Mon, Thurs and Fri 10–3

Good for a snack or a simple lunch, this drop-in centre has nappy-changing facilities, high chairs and toys for children.

Gourmet Pizza
2 The Gallery, Gloucester Road **t** (01865) 793146
Open Sun–Thurs 11–10.30, Fri and Sat till 11

An excellent pizza chain, it can offer a full children's menu plus games and colouring books.

The Isis Tavern
On the towpath between Donnington Bridge and Iffley Lock **t** (01865) 247006
Open Daily 11–11 (children till 7)

Good pub food and a garden with swings.

Old Orleans Restaurant
George Street **t** (01865) 792718
Open Mon–Sat 11–11, Sun 12 noon–10.30

This is an extremely child-friendly restaurant with a children's menu, high chairs, and crayons and a colouring menu to keep the kids occupied while they wait for their food.

The Turf Tavern
Bath Place **t** (01865) 243235
Open Daily 11-11

Characterful 13th-century tavern away from the bustle of the city centre. Lunchtime and evening meals available. Quiet pub garden.

Stow-on-the-Wold

Shepherd of the Hills Tea Shop
Lyndhurst House, Sheep Street **t** (01451) 831526
Open Daily 10–5

This friendly little tea shop serves a selection of home-made cakes as well as light lunches. Unlike some of the restaurants and cafés here, it isn't too cramped so there is plenty of room to stack away pushchairs/strollers.

Hunters Restaurant & Tea Rooms
Church Street **t** (01451) 832463
Open Mon, Wed–Sun 11–2, 3–5

With only 12 tables this quaint little tea shop is fairly short on space but makes up for it with a friendly welcome. There's no children's menu as such but the staff do their best to accommodate small appetites with a mixture of light lunches, snacks and cakes.

Stratford-upon-Avon

Bella Pasta

32 Wood Street **t** (01789) 297261

Open Daily 12pm–10pm

Large pasta chain offering a kids' menu, high chairs and a non-smoking section. Kids are provided with colouring sets and balloons to keep them occupied while they wait for their food.

Bensons of Stratford

4 Bards Walk **t** (01789) 261116

Open Daily 9–5.15

Elegant, but still very child-friendly establishment offering sandwiches from its café and cakes from its patisserie. Children's portions available.

Desports

13–14 Meer Street **t** (01789) 269304

www.desports.co.uk

Open Tues–Sat 12–2, 6–10.30

This hugely popular, multi-award winning restaurant housed in a 16th-century building serves up a hybrid Mediterranean–Thai menu. Children are welcomed although, as the entrance is up a set of stairs, it's not very buggy friendly. The chefs will, however, willingly tailor their dishes according to kids' preferences. High chairs provided.

Sorrento... A Taste of Italy

8 Ely Street **t** (01789) 297999

www.sorrentorestaurant.co.uk

Open Lunch Tues–Sat 12–2; dinner Mon–Sat 6–11

The restaurant displays a warm and welcoming, typically Mediterranean, attitude towards families. The chef is very flexible and will happily provide child-friendly meals and portions. Children are welcome in the lounge and bar.

Warwick

Pizza Piazza

33–35 Jury St **t** (01926) 491641

Open Daily 12pm–11pm

High chairs available

Environmentally conscious restaurant offering stone-baked pizzas and a children's menu featuring the 'O-People'; five cartoon characters designed to teach children all about the exciting world of organic produce and (bad) GM foods. The restaurant's organic menu was designed by Jamie Oliver.

> ### *Poor Knights of Windsor*
> The Poor Knights would probably have enjoyed tucking into this simple pudding. Slices of stale bread are soaked in milk and sherry, then rolled in egg-yolk, fried and finally topped with cinnamon, raspberry or strawberry jam.

Windsor

Crooked House Tea Rooms

51 High Street **t** (01753) 857534

Open Daily 10–6

Tearoom housed in the oldest free-standing building in Windsor.

Cyber Café

36 St Leonard's Road **t** (01753) 793164

Open Mon–Fri 9–5, Sat and Sun 10–4

Surf the net while you munch your sandwiches.

Good Measures

Boots Passage 18a Thames Street **t** (01753) 860720

Open Mon–Sat 12–2.30 and 6–10.30, Sun 12–3.30

Quality bistro with an outdoor patio – accompanied children eat for free.

Haagen Dazs ice cream emporium

22 Thames Street **t** (01753) 832973

Open Daily 10–10

Wide variety of delicious ice creams, for a kid's (and adult's) treat.

New College Inn

55 High Street, Eton **t** (01753) 865516

Food served 12–2.30 and 6–9

For a traditional English cream tea try this inn near the bridge in Eton.

PizzaExpress

7–8 Thames Street **t** (01753) 856424

Open Mon–Sat 11.30am–12am, Sun 11.30am–11pm

Large branch of the family-friendly pizza chain.

Royal Oak

Datchet Road (opp Windsor and Eton Riverside Station) **t** (01753) 865179

Open 11–11

This attractive pub is festooned with flowers in summer, and has a children's menu and high chairs.

Sally Lunn's

11 Peascod Street **t** (01753) 862627

Friendly branch of the original tearoom in Bath (p.183).

East is East

Cambridgeshire · Essex
Norfolk · Suffolk

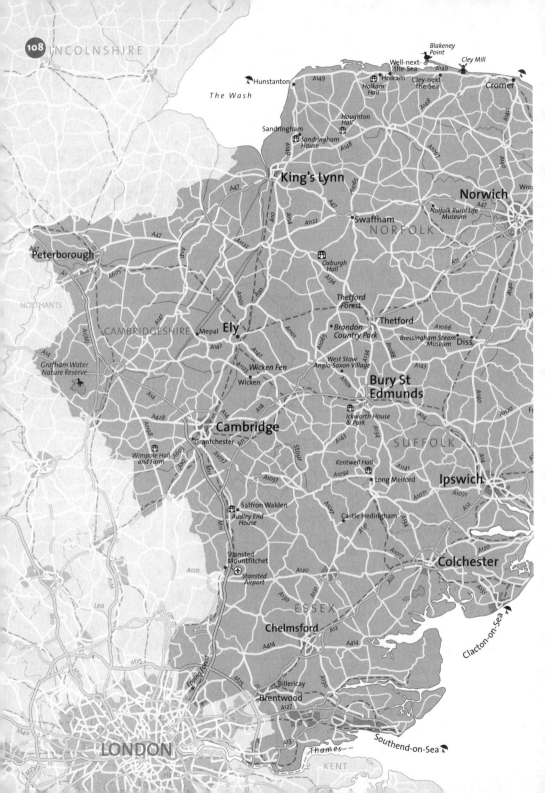

The Wash

Hunstanton

Well-next-the-Sea

Blakeney Point

Cley Mill

Cley-next-the-Sea

Cromer

Holkham

Holkham Hall

A149

A149

A148

A149

A140

Wro

Houghton Hall

Sandringham

Sandringham House

A149

A148

A47

King's Lynn

NORWICH

A47

A47

A10

A134

A1122

Swaffham

Norfolk Rural Life Museum

A47

A11

NORFOLK

Peterborough

A47

A47

A1122

A1101

A10

A47

A605

A1

NORTHANTS

Oxburgh Hall

A134

Thetford Forest

Thetford

A1066

Diss

A1

A14

CAMBRIDGESHIRE

Mepal

Ely

A142

A10

A142

A1101

Brandon Country Park

A1065

Bressingham Steam Museum

A1088

A143

A14

Grafham Water Nature Reserve

A1123

Wicken Fen

Wicken

West Stow Anglo-Saxon Village

A1101

Bury St Edmunds

A140

A14

A14

A14

A428

A1198

Cambridge

Grantchester

A11

A1037

Stour

Ickworth House & Park

A143

A134

SUFFOLK

A120

Wimpole Hall and Farm

A603

A10

M11

A1037

Kentwell Hall

A1141

Ipswich

A1071

A1071

A14

A1092

Long Melford

A1071

Saffron Walden

Audley End House

M11

A1017

Castle Hedingham

A131

A134

A1017

Colchester

A120

A133

Stansted Mountfitchet

Stansted Airport

A120

A120

A130

ESSEX

Chelmsford

A12

A414

A414

Lea

M11

M25

A10

Epping Forest

M25

Billericay

A130

Clacton-on-Sea

Brentwood

A127

A12

A13

Thames

Southend-on-Sea

LONDON

M25

M40

KENT

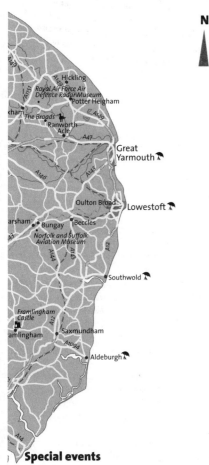

40 km
20 miles

N

Of the four regions in this guide, East Anglia is likely to come as the biggest surprise. It has a reputation for being flat, yet much of Suffolk is made up of gently undulating hills, while parts of north Norfolk's coastline are defiantly craggy. Many of the seaside towns and villages, including Southwold, Dunwich and Walberswick are beautifully unspoilt and often ignored. Even the larger resorts, such as Great Yarmouth and Lowestoft hide their lights under bushels of deceptive familiarity. There's plenty for kids to enjoy, from the trains and waggons at Bressingham Steam Museum to the jets and fighters at Duxford Air Museum. Simpler pleasures include pottering round Cambridge's shops and museums or a day's birdwatching at the RSPB Nature Reserve, Minsmere, while active types might favour a weekend exploring the Norfolk Broads' 120 square miles of interlinked streams, rivers and lakes.

Such a perfect day

Morning: Punting along the scenic waterways of Cambridge (p.113).

Lunch: Head for Trumpington Street for family favourites at Brown's (p.149).

Afternoon: Drive or take the free bus service from Cambridge train station to Duxford, 7 miles south, to see Europe's largest collection of planes and play on its hi-tech simulators (p.117). Alternatively, you could drive to Linton Zoological Gardens, 10 miles southeast, to meet its assorted tigers, lions, zebras and snakes (p.116).

Special events

May
Bury St Edmunds: Festival **t** (01284) 764667
Stilton: Stilton Rolling **t** (01783) 241206
June
Aldeburgh: Festival of Music and the Arts
t (01728) 453637
Cambridge: Camfest **t** (01223) 322640
Cambridge: Midsummer Fair **t** (01223) 322640
Norwich: Royal Norfolk Show **t** (01603) 748931
July
Cambridge: Big Day Out **t** (01223) 322640
Hunstanton: Carnival **t** (01485) 532610
August
Cromer: Carnival **t** (01263) 512497
Southend-on-Sea: Carnival Week **t** (01702) 215120
November
Cambridge: Bonfire fireworks **t** (01223) 322640

Highlights

Animal fun, Blakeney Point, p.137
Birdwatching, RSPB Minsmere, p.142
Boating fun, the Broads, p.132
Punting on the Cam, p.113
Castle fun, Mountfitchet Castle, p.121
Crabbing, Walberswick, p.145
Cycling, the Broads, p.132
Getting lost, Great Leigh's Great Maze, p.123
Plane fun, Duxford Air Museum, p.117
Rollercoaster fun, Great Yarmouth Pleasure Beach, p.135
Roman fun, Colchester Castle, p.119
Steam train rides, Nene Valley Railway, p.117
Top town, Cambridge p.110
Tudor fun, Kentwell Hall, p.143

CAMBRIDGESHIRE

CAMBRIDGE

Getting there By air: Stansted airport is about 30 miles south of Cambridge and is linked to the city by a regular bus service (and the M11). By road: Cambridge is 55 miles north of London and can be reached by the M11 from the south and A14 from the north. Driving into Cambridge city centre, which is largely pedestrianized and ringed by an impenetrable mass of one-way streets, isn't really an option. You'll either have to come by train (the train station is a good mile and a half south of the centre; there's a regular bus service) or take advantage of the city's Park & Ride scheme. There are four car parks on the outskirts of Cambridge: Cowley Road on the A1309 to the north, Newmarket Road on the A1303 to the east, Babraham Road on the A1207 to the south and Madingley Road on the A1303 to the west. Parking is free and buses leave for the city centre every 10–15 mins between 7am and 8pm. For more details contact Stagecoach Cambus **t** (01223) 423554. By train: there are frequent rail services to London King's Cross (50min) and London Liverpool Street (1hr 10min). By coach: an hourly coach service from London Victoria coach station is provided by National Express
Tourist office The Old Library, Wheeler Street **t** (01223) 322640 www.tourismcambridge.com. The centre has a souvenir shop and can provide details of guided walking tours led from here by Blue Badge Guides throughout the year (dramatic tours with costumed characters take place in summer)

Cambridge, like its great rival Oxford, is principally famous for its university, one of the oldest and most respected in the world (although it's not quite as old as Oxford, as Oxford graduates are always at pains to point out). Also like Oxford, it's an exceedingly beautiful place to visit with some of the country's prettiest architecture, several beautiful parks and, of course, the River Cam, a great sash of water flowing around the north and west of the city.

Being smaller and more condensed than Oxford, it's a great place for pottering, be it on foot, by bike or on the river,. The city's modern, hi-tech industries are mainly confined to the suburbs, so the centre of town, where you'll find most of the colleges and university buildings, is largely pedestrianized. The two main thoroughfares, Bridge Street (which

turns into Sidney Street, St Andrew's Street and Regent Street) and St John's Street (which becomes Trinity Street, King's Parade and Trumpington Street) are lined with shops, tearooms and (for the students) bookstores – look out for Heffer's Children's Bookshop at 30 Trinity Street – and there's a bustling market held every day on Market Square, selling general produce (fruit 'n' veg, books clothes, flowers) from Monday to Saturday, and arts and crafts, antiques and farmers' produce on Sundays. As you might expect of a city so steeped in academia, there are lots of museums, some of which will be of interest to children (*see* below) and in term time you can tour the magnificent crenallated college buildings, although this may prove somewhat frustrating as you are usually not allowed to walk on their inviting expanses of neatly manicured grass. Indeed, some of the more popular colleges are becoming increasingly less tolerant of the disruption to study caused by tourists; you may be expected to pay a rather exorbitant entrance fee. For the record, Peterhouse is the oldest college, Trinity the largest, famed for its Great Hall and statues of former illustrious students including Tennyson, Francis Bacon and Isaac Newton and King's is probably the most beautiful with its glorious 15th-century chapel from which a beautiful carol service is broadcast every Christmas. In its chapel exhibition you can read about the history of the college and see a model showing how the chapel ceiling was constructed. Look out for the branch of the English Teddy Company opposite the entrance to King's, guarded by a 6ft teddy dressed in a mortar board and gown.

The city and the surrounding flat countryside are perfect for cycling, which explains the rows and rows of parked bikes you'll see everywhere you go, outside the colleges, alongside the shops, by the railway station, everywhere. It really is the everyday transport of choice here and there are numerous bike hire shops. You can follow the towpath along the banks of the River Cam all the way to the cathedral town of Ely. The best way to see Cambridge, however, at least in summer, is in a punt, poling yourself along the Cam in a flat-bottomed boat through the 'Backs', the most picturesque part of town (so-called because the university buildings 'back' on to it). With its elegant bridges, lush, green riverside vegetation overhung with willow trees and gorgeous views this kind of trip is a must on a summer afternoon.

A popular destination for a longer punt trip is to head for the nearby town of Grantchester (about two miles upstream) where you can enjoy some refreshment at the Orchard Tea Gardens. The War Poet Rupert Brooke lived here while he was an undergraduate and it was about Grantchester that he penned the now famous lines 'Stands the Church clock at ten to three? And is there honey still for tea?'. One of Grantchester's three pubs is named after Brooke; its clock is set permanently at ten minutes to three.

Despite all the well-preserved history, Cambridge is no museum city. The large student population helps it to retain its youthful vigour – there are lots of theatres, live music and comedy venues, including the famous Corn Exchange opposite the tourist office – and it has a justly deserved reputation as one of the most vibrant cities in southern England.

Things to see

Cambridge and County Folk Museum
2–3 Castle Street **t** (01223) 355159
Open Tues–Sat 10.30–5, Sun 2–5; also open Mon from April–Sept 10.30–5
Adm Adult £2, child 50p, under-5s **free**
Gift shop, guided tours

Housed in a 16th-century, half-timbered farmhouse, this looks at the non-academic side of life in Cambridge, with displays on the people who have lived and worked in this area for the last 400 years. Activity days for children aged 6–10 are organized on some Saturday afternoons and children's workshops for 7–11 year olds are held during the school holidays.

Cambridge Museum of Technology
The Old Pumping Station, Cheddars Lane
t (01223) 368650 **www.cam.net.uk/home/steam**
Open Easter–Oct Sun 2–5; Nov–Easter first Sun of every month 2–5
Adm Steaming £4, non-steaming £2
Shop, disabled access

Can you spot?
The Mathematical Bridge in the grounds of Queen's College; you can see it from the Silver Street Bridge or from aboard a punt on the river itself. So clever was its design – it was originally supposed to have been built without bolts and fastenings – that in the 18th century some engineers took it apart to see how it worked, only to find they couldn't put it back together again. The bridge you see is a copy of the original.

Housed in a preserved Victorian pumping station, this is filled with the noisy contraptions of the industrial age: boilers, engines and pumps, which are set in motion during the museum's occasional 'steam days'.

Fitzwilliam Museum
Trumpington Street **t** (01223) 332906
www.fitzmuseum.cam.ac.uk
Open Tues–Sat 10–5, Sun 2.15–5
Free
Café, gift shop, guided tours, mother and baby facilities, limited wheelchair access
Not suitable for pushchairs although babyslings/harnesses available

The city's most respected museum, parts of which will be of interest to children, although you may want to skip all the endless cases full of European porcelain, Chinese vases and Korean ceramics (there's only so much fun to be had from old plates) and head straight to the mummies and painted coffins in the Antiquities gallery, or the room full of armour and weapons in the Applied Arts section. Family activity sheets are available.

Great St Mary's Church
Market Hill **t** (01233) 350914
Open May–Sept Mon–Sat 9–6; Oct–April Mon–Sat 9–4.15
Adm £1.75

Climb to the top of the 113ft tower for great views out over the colleges and nearby marketplace, or clamber up the steep Castle Mound on Castle Hill, just north of the river off Castle Street (it marks the spot where the Norman Cambridge Castle once stood), for views out over the medieval city.

Museum of Archaeology and Anthropology
Downing Street **t** (01223) 333516
www.cumaa.archanth.cam.ac.uk

Open Tues–Sat 2–4.30; phone to check extended summer hours June–Sept
Free

The ground floor 'Rise of Civilization' gallery, full of ancient pots and bits of flint, is only worth a cursory inspection. Instead, make a beeline for the ethnographic collection on the first floor, a wonderful array of treasures brought back by 18th- and 19th-century explorers: native American feathered headresses, Eskimo canoes and parkas (made from dried walrus hide), scary African tribal masks and suits of Japanese ceremonial armour, all arranged around a 50ft high totem pole.

Sedgwick Museum of Earth Sciences

Downing Street **t** (01223) 333456
www.esc.cam.ac.uk/SedgwickMuseum
Open Mon–Fri 9–1 and 2–5, Sat 10–1
Free (Discretionary donation encouraged)
Shop, some wheelchair access/assistance available

Houses the oldest geological collection in the world (although, in geological terms, this is a pretty slight claim) with various multi-million-year-old rocks and minerals displayed in antique walnut cases. It also has a large collection of fossil dinosaurs. Look out for the iguanadon, here assembled as if it were a four-legged animal with a horn on its nose. In fact, when this dinosaur was alive (some 65 million years ago) it would have walked on its two back feet, much like a T-Rex or a person. The reason this model is on all fours is because, when the first iguanadon fossil skeletons were found at the beginning of the 19th century, they were put together incorrectly; as a result, this model was assembled inaccurately too. The iguanadon's spike didn't go on its nose at all but on its hand in place of its thumb. It's an understandable mistake; remember, the scientists who assembled these bones were working blind, and had no previous models to refer to. If you dug up a pile of old bones, would you know how to put them back together again? It would be hard, especially if you had no idea what the animal looked like.

You can bring your own specimen fossils along to show the museum staff, who will be happy to identify them and give you tips on how to look after them.

Note *During 2001 the museum began a process redevelopment and about 40% of it was closed to the public. Following the project's completion (set for spring 2002), the museum will have even more space dedicated to the weird and wonderful world of nature; planned displays include exhibits on giant dragonflies, how volcanoes work, and whether there might be life on other planets.*

University Botanic Garden

Cory Lodge, Bateman Street **t** (01223) 336265
www.plantsci.cam.ac.uk/Botgdn/index.htm
Open Jan, Nov, Dec 10–4; Feb and Oct 10–5; March–Sept 10–6
Adm (March–Oct, weekends and Bank Hols) adult £2, child £1.50, under-5s **free**
Café–restaurant (summer only), picnic areas, gift shop, mother and baby facilities, guided tours by arrangement, disabled access

The 40-acre University Botanic Garden, just south of Cambridge's centre, was founded in 1762 and is the city's most beautiful open space with lots of trees and flowers, several glasshouses, a lake, a geographical rock garden and numerous rare plants laid out amid an elegant landscaped setting. It may prove a little formal for younger tastes, however. If you're after a spot where kids can enjoy more uninhibited play, try Jesus Green, to the north of the city centre near the river, a large, open grassy space with a children's play area and an open air swimming pool in summer. Otherwise, just to the west, you'll find Midsummer Common, a huge riverside meadow that plays host to fairs and circuses in summer and a large firework display on 5 November.

University Museum of Zoology

Downing Street **t** (01223) 336650
www.zoo.cam.ac.uk/museum
Open Term-time Mon–Fri 2–4.45; university holidays 10–1 and 2–4.45
Free
Wheelchair access

Contains a wide range of natural history displays including numerous fossils and animal skeletons, as well as several items collected by the greatest naturalist of them all, Charles Darwin, on his famous *Beagle* voyage. Look out for the 70ft whale skeleton hanging above the entrance (it's pretty hard to miss) and the reconstruction of a prehistoric rocky shore with a killer whale, an extinct, giant ground sloth and a giant spider crab.

Things to do

Bike hire

Geoff's Bike Hire, 65 Devonshire Road
t (01223) 365629
Open April–Sept daily 9–6; Oct–Mar daily 9–5.30
Hire charges 3 hrs £4.50, 1 day £7, 1 week £15. A £25 deposit is also payable. Guided tours (2.5 hours) £9.50 including bike hire

Bikes, trailer bikes and child trailers for hire by the hour, day or week. Guided cycle tours of the city are also offered between April and September.

Cambridge Brass Rubbing Centre

The Round Church, Bridge Street **t** (01223) 871621
Open Summer daily 10–5; winter daily 1–4

This brass rubbing centre is housed in a 12th-century 'round' church, one of only five such churches in the entire country, and looks a bit like a giant cottage loaf with a tower stuck on top. Each brass rubbing costs £2 and will take approximately 20 minutes to complete.

Punting

The archetypal Cambridge pursuit can be enjoyed every day between Easter and October. Punts can be hired from Magdalene Bridge, Mill Lane, Garret Hostel Lane, the Granta Pub on Newnham Road and the Rat and Parrot pub near Magdalene Bridge. A deposit of around £25 is usually required while the punts themselves will cost something in the region of £6–8 per hour. Chauffeured punt trips are also available.

You'll be shown how to use the pole before you set off although it will still take a lot of getting used to – and you should also prepare your children for disappointment as they will probably be unable to deal with the pole's considerable weight, although on sightseeing trips they may be allowed to hold the wooden oar-rudder.

Do be aware that it can be a pretty wet and soggy experience, especially during the initial learning process, although the Backs do provide an idyllic space in which to dry off and have a quick picnic while you refine your technique. Remember to stick to the left.

Heffer's Children's Bookshop

30 Trinity Street **t** (01223) 568551
Open Mon–Sat 9–5.30, Sun 11–5

Touch Wood Creative Toys

10 Mill Road **t** (01223) 507803
Open Tues–Sun 10–5

Wooden toys, kits and games.

Walking tours

In summer (June–Oct) you can join one of the Ghost Walks which depart from outside King's College Gatehouse on King's Parade (**t** 01284-756717), while in winter Cambridge Junior Explorers offers tours of the city for children aged 9–12 in the company of a qualified guide. The tour leaves from outside the Guildhall on Market Square at 2pm and tickets, which cost £2 per child (accompanying adult free), should be purchased from the guide **t** (01233) 301615.

Cinemas

Arts Picture House

38–39 St Andrews Street **t** (01223) 504444

Independent, three-screen cinema in the heart of the city.

Warner Bros Cinema

The Grafton Centre, East Road
t (01223) 460225

Large eight-screen multiplex located within a shopping mall. Creche service available.

Theatres

ADC Theatre

Park Street **t** (01223) 359547/503333

The oldest university playhouse in England, established in the middle of the last century by the Amateur Dramatic Club. Managed by the University of Cambridge, it puts on a wide variety of shows including the occasional kids' event.

Cambridge Drama Centre

Covent Garden, Mill Road **t** (01223) 322748
www.dramacentre.co.uk

A year-round programme of drama and workshops. In addition to a broad spread of children's theatre, CDC runs a term-time programme involving drama, movement, circus and voice , followed by a six week programme during the summer holidays.

Corn Exchange

Wheeler Street **t** (01223) 357851

The city's main venue, housed in a former 19th-century trading hall.

Activities

Abbey Indoor Pool

Whitehill Road, off Newmarket Road, Cambridge **t** (01223) 213352

Call in advance for details of times and prices

Small indoor pool and soft play area for children.

Cambridge Parkside Pools

Gonville Place, Cambridge **t** (01223) 446100
Open Call in advance
Adm adult £2.50, child £1.30

Children's pool and leisure pool with two flume rides.

Geoff's Bike Hire

65 Devonshire Road, Cambridge **t** (01223) 365629
Open April–Sept daily 9–6; Oct–Mar daily 9–5.30
Hire charges 3 hrs £4.50; 1 day £7; 1 week £15. A £25 deposit is also payable. Guided tours (which last 2.5 hrs) cost £9.50, including bike hire

Bikes, trailerbikes and child trailers for hire, by the hour, day or week. Guided cycle tours of the city are also offered April–Sept.

LaserQuest and Kids' Kingdom

2nd floor, 13–15 Bradwells Court, Cambridge **t** (01223) 302102
Open Call in advance
Adm Laser Quest: weekdays £2.95, evenings and weekends £3.50; Kids' Kingdom £2
Café

Laser-shooting games and an indoor adventure play area for under-7s with a bouncy castle, aerial runways and ball pools.

SPECIAL TRIPS

Wimpole Hall and Wimpole Home Farm

Arrington, near Royston **t** (01223) 207257
www.wimpole.org
Getting there It is 8 miles southwest of Cambridge off the A603. Take J12 from the M11
Open Hall: April–Sept Tues–Thurs and Sat–Sun 1–5; Aug Tues–Sun daily 1–5; Oct–Nov Sat and Sun 1–4. Park: daily dawn–dusk. Farm: mid Mar–Oct Tues–Thurs and Sat–Sun 10.30–5; July–Aug Tues–Sun and Bank Hol Mon 10.30–5; Nov–Mar Sat and Sun 11–4
Adm Estate: adult £8.50, child £4.20, family £21; farm only: adult £4.70, child £2.70; garden only: adult £2.50, child **free**
Café–restaurant, gift shop, disabled access, on-site parking

There are three main attractions here. Begin in the grand 17th-century hall itself which, though rather stuffy (few children can get that excited about a library no matter how many priceless leather-bound volumes it has) does contain a few nooks and crannies worth seeking out, such as the clever trompe l'oeil ceiling, the enormous room-size bath and the servants' quarters. Look out for the row of bells on the wall, each inscribed with the name of a servant, which would be rung to summon that particular domestic 'above stairs'. The children's guide available at the gift shop will point you to all the most interesting things and can offer a few 'can you spots?' to help pass the time.

The lavish hall grounds (landscaped, of course, by Capability Brown) contain many marked walks taking you through woodland and past lakes and follies. You can picnic anywhere and there's an adventure playground and an enclosed toddlers' area with toy tractors to ride on. The real highlight of your visit, however, will be the restored Georgian farm. On weekends you can take a wagon ride (pulled by two enormous shire horses) to the farm from the stableblock near the hall. The farm has been carefully preserved to look more or less the same as it did in the 18th century, which translates into lots of weird looking traditional breeds (including orange Tamworth pigs, heavily fleeced Leicester sheep and White Park cows), thatched-roof barns and good old-fashioned muck. Manure appears to have been big business in Georgian times and its thick, pungent smell hangs heavy in the air. Head to the centre of the farm (doing your best to avoid the free-roaming geese and chickens as they peck between your feet) where you'll find all the headline animals: pigs, sheep, goats and horses (piglets and lambs, too, in early summer). Pick up a bag of animal feed and get acquainted. Activities such as mucking out the pigs (great fun?), milking the goats, collecting eggs and sheep-shearing are organized and children can try on traditional farm costumes. There's also a small wagon museum full of painted carts and barrows. Special events, such as 'Children's Fun Days', 'Heavy Horse Shows' and 'Lambing Weekends', are regularly organized.

AROUND AND ABOUT

Nature lovers

Ferry Meadows Country Park

Getting there It lies 3 miles from Peterborough, off the A605 to Oundle. Follow the brown tourist signs to Nene Park
Open All year daily
Free Car parking charge April–Oct weekends and Bank Hols
Cafés, visitor centre, watersports centre, caravan club, on-site parking

500-acre park within the larger Nene Park with two huge boating lakes and several children's play areas. Miniature railway and pony and trap rides are available in summer.

Grafham Water Nature Reserve

The Wildlife Cabin, Mander Car Park, Huntingdon **t** (01480) 812660/811075
Getting there Lies just west of Perry Village in Huntingdon, Cambridgeshire. Follow the signs from the A1
Open Daily dawn–dusk
Free
Café, picnic areas, guided tours, disabled access, on-site parking (Mon–Fri £1, Sat–Sun £2)

There are nature trails, woodland walks and a 10-mile family cycle trail around this large body of water, as well as birdwatching hides (you can see grebes, woodpeckers and sparrowhawks), bird-feeding stations and a dragonfly pond.

Activities

Grafham Water Cycling

Marlow car park, Grafham Water, Huntingdon
t (01480) 812500

Miles of tracks around this enormous reservoir with various nature reserves and birdwatching sites on the way.

Lakeside Bowl

Fen Road, Pidley, Huntingdon **t** (01487) 740968

Hamerton Zoo Park

Hamerton Road, Steeple, Giddking **t** (01832) 293362
Getting there It's signposted from the A1 (J15) and A14 (junction with the B660)
Open Daily 10.30–6 (dusk in winter)
Adm Adult £4.95, child £3.95
Café–restaurant, picnic areas, gift shop, disabled access, on-site parking

This dedicated wildlife breeding centre is home to over 120 different types of animal, including gibbons, wildcats, meerkats, wallabies, cheetahs and 2-toed sloths (the only such sloths in the entire country). There's also a children's zoo and indoor and outdoor play areas.

Hinchingbrooke Country Park

Brampton Road, Huntingdon **t** (01480) 451568
Getting there Situated a few miles west of Huntingdon, off the A14
Open All year daily
Free
Café, picnic areas, on-site parking

180 acres of woodland, rivers, lakes and ponds which provide a home to a variety of wildlife including woodpeckers, herons and foxes. There are numerous marked walks (guided walks are led from the visitor centre most weekends) and the lake has facilities for watersports.

Activities

Northbrook Equestrian Centre

New Road, Offord Cluny, Huntingdon
t (01480) 812654

Lessons for all ages and levels of experience.

Linton Zoological Gardens

Hadstock Road, Linton **t** (01223) 891308

Getting there It's 10 miles southeast of Cambridge on the B1052 just off the A1307. From the M11, take J9 (northbound) or J10 (southbound)
Open Summer 10–6, winter 10–dusk (last adm 1hr before closing)
Adm Adult £5, child £4, under-2s **free**
Café (summer only), picnic areas, gift shop, disabled access, on-site parking

Small, very pretty zoo set in 16 acres of beautifully landscaped gardens. Home to the Cambridgeshire Wildlife Breeding Centre, the zoo's primary purpose is the conservation of endangered species, but it nonetheless presents itself in a friendly, entertaining way and the animal enclosures, though occasionally a bit on the small side, are well designed; the tiger enclosure, for instance, has glass windows allowing you to get right up close. In addition to visiting the animals, which include zebras, snow leopards, lions and giant tortoises, kids can attend animal handling sessions where they can stroke an owl or have a boa constrictor draped around their neck; in summer, there's a family quiz trail and a bouncy castle.

Shepreth Wildlife Park
Willersmill, Station Road, Shepreth **t** 09066 800031 (calls cost 25p per min)
www.sheprethpark.f9.co.uk
Getting there Lies on the A10 between Cambridge and Royston, 7 miles south of Cambridge. Shepreth train station is just a 2-minute walk away
Open Daily 10–6 (dusk in winter if earlier)
Adm Adult £3.95, child £2.95
Café, picnic areas, souvenir and toy shop

Since its foundation in 1979 as a refuge for orphaned and injured British birds and mammals, Shepreth has grown into one of East Anglia's very best animal attractions, with a wide variety of native and exotic wildlife on display including peacocks, tortoises, wolves, owls, otters, coati, wallabies, squirrel monkeys and capybara (the largest rodent in the world, in case you're wondering, a sort of giant guinea pig). There are lots of interactive opportunities for the kids, too: a special petting field where kids can meet deer, donkeys and sheep; a Fish Farm where huge colourful koi carp will eat from your fingers; an insect display, 'Bug City', where you can watch leaf-cutter ants building a 'fungus city', before checking out the assorted sting rays, puffer fish and seahorses at the next door Waterworld. You'll also find a children's playroom, a play area

with a sandpit, an adventure fort and a pet's corner. Pony rides are available on summer weekends.

Wicken Fen
Lode Lane, Wicken, Ely **t** (01353) 720274
Getting there It's 8 miles south of Ely and is signposted form the A1123 and A142. The nearest train station is Ely
Open Fen: daily dawn–dusk; visitor centre, cottage and windpump: daily 10–5
Adm Adult £3.70, child £1.20
Refreshments, guided walks, on-site parking
Boardwalk suitable for pushchairs

The last surviving patch of unspoilt fenland, this 297-acre area is the country's oldest nature reserve. Within its confines you'll find a tiny, original fen cottage, the area's last surviving windpump as well as a vast array of wildlife. It's particularly good for birdwatching and nature-themed events are organized here throughout the year. Trail guides are available and you can hire binoculars; be sure to check out the views from Tower Hide.

Wildfowl and Wetlands Trust – Welney
Hundred Foot Bank, Welney, Wisbech
t (01353) 860711 **www**.wwt.org.uk
Getting there Located 12 miles north of Ely off the A1101
Open March–mid Nov daily 10–5; mid Nov–Feb Wed–Sun 10–8
Adm Adult £3.50, child £2, under-4s **free**, family £8.50
Tearoom, gift and book shop, binocular hire, disabled access, on-site parking

One of eight Wildfowl and Wetlands Trust centres dotted around the country, Welney is home to thousands of birds. At the visitor centre, you can find out about the many different species who visit over the course of the year, and watch live video feeds of various parts of the site, before setting off along the nature trails to visit the centre's network of hides. Welney is definitely at its most exuberant in winter, when great living carpets of ducks and clouds of swans fly in every afternoon to claim their nightly nesting spot, and at its most beautiful in summer, when the wild flower meadows come into bloom. The centre organizes family events throughout the year.

Wimpole Hall and Wimpole Home Farm
For further information *see* p.114.

Look at this!

Duxford Airfield Museum

Imperial War Museum, Duxford, Cambridge
t (01223) 835000 **www.iwm.org.uk**
Getting there It's about 7 miles south of
Cambridge at J10 of the M11. There's a free bus
service from Cambridge train station and the
Crowne Plaza
Open Summer daily 10–6; winter daily 10–4. For
airshow dates, call in advance
Adm Adult £7.70, child **free**; adm **free** after 4.30 in
summer and 3 in winter
*Café–restaurant, gift shop, disabled access, on-site
parking*

Run by the Imperial War Museum, Duxford is
home to Europe's largest collection of military and
civilian aircraft. There are around 140 flying
machines in all, ranging from First World War bi-
planes to modern jet fighters, all housed in
enormous, looming hangars. Obviously, it's best to
visit during one of the museum's numerous
airshows when you can see the spectacular craft in
action: you'll see jets roaring above your head
(seemingly only feet away), recreated bi-plane dog
fights and demonstrations of precision formation
flying, as often as not by the famous Red Arrows.
Be warned, though, these shows are incredibly
noisy and will probably prove a bit much for very
young children.

Don't let that put you off altogether, however, as
the museum is well worth visiting on non-flying
days too, when kids will actually be able to climb
aboard some of the sleek machines – no matter
what age you are, it's always quite a thrill to sit at
the controls of a jet fighter – and put their dog-
fighting skills to the test on the hi-tech Battle of
Britain simulator. During the real battle, Duxford
was one of the country's main fighter aerodromes
and you can find out all about the nation's 'finest
hour' at the restored control tower and operations
room. There is also a small section dedicated to
land warfare where you can see realistic reconstructions of battle scenes and, outside, an
adventure playground. Trips around the site aboard
a narrow-gauge railway are available in summer.

Farmland Museum and Denny Abbey

Ely Road, Waterbeach, Cambridge **t** (01223) 860988

Getting there It's about 7 miles northeast of
Cambridge off the A10
Open April–Oct daily 12–5
Adm Adult £3.50, child £1.30, under-5s **free**, family
£8.30
*Café at weekends, picnic areas, gift shop, some
disabled access, adapted toilets, on-site parking*

Museum of farming with interactive displays and
recreated period interiors including a village shop,
a medieval schoolroom and a farmworker's
cottage. A range of family events is put on during
the year, including falconry displays, art workshops
and craft demonstrations (butter-making, print-
making, basket-making).

Steam power

Nene Valley Railway

Wansford Station, Stibbington, Peterborough
t (01780) 784444; talking timetable **t** (01780)
784440
Getting there Wansford station is off the A1
between the A47 and A605 junctions.
Peterborough NVR station is half a mile from
Peterborough BR station and is signposted from
the A605 Oundle Road. The nearest mainline
railway station is Peterborough
Open End Feb–Oct Sat–Sun; April–Oct Wed;
July–Aug Tues–Fri
*Refreshments, souvenir shops, wheelchair access to
most locations; most trains have a specially
adapted carriage; adapted toilets at Wansford
station, parking at Wansford, Ferry Meadow, Orton
Mere and Peterborough NVR stations*

Nene is one of the county's most famous and best
loved railways, probably because it's the home of
Thomas, everyone's favourite steam engine. It's
been the location for dozens of films including
Octopussy and *Goldeneye* and recently celebrated
its 21st year of operation. It can offer 15-mile round
trips from Wansford (where there's a large collection of locomotives and rolling stock from all over
Europe), passing through scenic Yarwell and on to
Orton Mere where you can alight for a walk in the
500-acre Nene Park, with its model railway circling
the central lake, before re-embarking for the final
leg to the restored Peterborough NVR station. Look
out for the haunted tunnel where train drivers have
seen the ghosts of 19th-century railway workers.

COLCHESTER

Getting there By road: Colchester can easily be reached via the A12 from London and the A1037 and A1124 from Cambridge. By rail: there are frequent intercity services between Colchester and London Liverpool Street (50min) and Norwich (1hr). By bus/coach: daily National Express coach services link Colchester to all the principal towns and cities in Britain.

Numerous short stay, long stay and NCP car parks are located near the centre of town, particularly in the area around Colchester train station. There are 24-hour car parks on Priory Street, Osborne Street and Magdalen Street

Tourist office 1 Queen Street **t** (01206) 282920. The centre can provide details of Blue Guide tours of the city. There are three tours to choose from: a walking tour of the town centre, an open-top bus tour (both available summer only) and a tour of the castle

Colchester's heyday was long ago. Once upon a time it was the most powerful and important city in the whole country. Archaeological evidence has shown that there was a settlement here as far back as the 5th century BC, making it (as the town's tourist signs will constantly remind you) Britain's oldest town. When the Romans invaded in the 1st century AD, they made it the capital of the new province of Britannia (naming it *Camulodunum*) and built the country's first temple and bathhouse here. Sacked by Boudicca and the rampaging Iceni army in AD 60, its influence gradually faded over the succeeding centuries as London (or *Londinium* as it was then) began her inexorable rise.

Although it enjoyed prosperity in the Middle Ages, thanks to a thriving textile industry established by Dutch and Flemish refugees fleeing religious persecution on the continent, the only other distinguished episode in Colchester's history came in the Civil War when the town (rather unwisely) declared itself for the Royalist side. This resulted in a three-month siege by the parliamentary forces, during which time the trapped population ate every living thing within the city walls: cats, dogs, rats, mice...everything.

Once the queen of all she surveyed, present-day Colchester is now a rather frumpy old dowager, respected more for what she was than what she has become. Although the self-styled 'cultural capital of Essex' (which is saying something), it no longer enjoys national significance – which is not to say that it is in anyway run-down or decrepit. Modern Colchester is, in fact, a very pleasant, middle-ranking university town with lots of old buildings, plenty of good shopping and a youthful atmosphere bolstered by its large student population. It boasts several supremely child-friendly visitor attractions, including a Natural History Museum, a 12,000sq ft indoor play area 'Go Bananas' an excellent park, an award-winning zoo and (I bet you didn't know this) the only international-standard roller skating rink in Britain.

There's no escaping the past, however, and remnants and remains of Colchester's illustrious history are everywhere. Around two and a half miles of the Roman wall survives along with the country's largest Roman gateway, and you can visit St Botolph's, the oldest Augustinian priory in the country, where a medieval fair with storytellings and demonstrations of medieval crafts is held in summer. If you see just one sight in Colchester, however, it should be the wonderful Norman castle (construction began a few years after the Battle of Hastings in 1066) where you can learn all about Roman Britain at its excellent interactive museum and explore acres of landscaped parkland.

The heart of the town is the High Street, which still follows the original Roman route, around which are grouped most of the town's attractions. The main shopping area – which is made up of narrow lanes lined with specialist shops, three large covered shopping centres and a market, held every Friday and Saturday in Vineyard Street – is just to the south while the Dutch Quarter and Castle Park are to the North. The River Colne flows in a loop around the north and east of the town. Remember, Colchester is just a dozen or so miles from the sea and the bustling resort of Clacton is just a short drive or train ride away.

Can you spot?
Jumbo, the 134ft, 19th-century water-tower that dominates the skyline to the west of the city. It was named after the famous elephant of the same name living at that time in London Zoo.

Things to see and do

Colchester Castle and Castle Park

Castle Park **t** (01206) 282931
Open Mar–Nov Mon–Sat 10–5, Sun 1–5
Adm Adult £3.80, child £2.50, under-5s **free**
Picnic areas, shop, guided tours, disabled access, on-site parking

At first sight, your kids may find Colchester's great castle, which sits atop the remains of a Roman temple just northeast of the High Street, disappointing. It's a bit boxy, with few of the features you usually associate with medieval fortresses. The interior, however, more than makes up for any exterior deficiencies, with a host of bloodthirsty displays on the town's gory past. You can find out all about the warrior queen Boudicca

---

Tell me a story:
Boudicca – warrior queen

Who was Boudicca?

She was the Queen of the Iceni, a British tribe living in East Anglia during the first few decades of the Roman occupation of Britain.

Why is she famous?

Because she led a bloody revolt against the Romans in AD 60 during which she and her army sacked and destroyed numerous Roman towns and massacred many thousands of Roman citizens.

Why did she do that?

The Romans conquered many countries in their time – at its height the Roman Empire stretched from the north of England to the eastern edges of Europe and Africa – but they didn't always conquer by fighting. Obviously, if the people of a particular country didn't want to be conquered, the Romans would fight them, but the Romans often found it much easier (and a lot cheaper) simply to persuade people to let them rule them.

The Romans' favoured method of persuasion was to do deals with local leaders offering them money and status within the Roman Empire in return for their co-operation. They would even be allowed to continue ruling, except they would now have to do so in the name of Rome. This is exactly what happened in East Anglia in AD 43 when the Romans 'came to an arrangement' with Prasatagus, the Chief of the Iceni (and Boudicca's husband). When Prasatagus died, however, the local Roman Governor, Suetonius Paulinus, decided that he'd had enough of deals. He seized Prasatagus' wealth and land and attempted to turn East Anglia into a slave province. When Boudicca protested she was publicly flogged by the Romans. Bad move.

What happened?

Boudicca mobilized the Iceni army and launched a furious assault against the Romans in AD 60. The Roman army didn't know what hit it as the Iceni rebelled. They destroyed Colchester, the capital of Roman government, and burnt the Temple of Claudius, the ultimate symbol of Roman rule, to the ground (Colchester Castle now stands on the site), before laying waste to London and St Albans. In all, her army killed an estimated 70,000 Romans and tortured many more – pulling a Roman's arms out of their sockets was a favourite Iceni ploy.

So, did she win?

No. When Boudicca started her rebellion, most of the Roman army was busy in Wales putting down an insurrection (they were much less keen on 'deals' in Wales) and so her army actually faced little armed opposition. When the Roman army returned, however, things began to go very wrong for Boudicca. Hers was a rag-bag, disorganized army that had achieved most of its success as a result of the surprising speed of its attacks. Despite outnumbering the Romans by many thousands, the Iceni proved no match for the highly disciplined Roman troops. The two sides met in pitched battle at Epping Forest (*see* p.123) where the Iceni were practically destroyed. Boudicca's army lost thousands of lives while the Roman casualties numbered just 400. With the battle lost, Boudicca committed suicide by poisoning herself rather than face the wrath of the Romans who then took a terrible revenge on all of the surviving rebel tribes.

Where is she now?

No-one knows for sure where Boudicca is buried. According to some experts her grave is to be found under platform 8 at King's Cross railway station in London. What could be her grave was found by archeologists in 1988. British Rail, who had recently made improvements to the platform, refused all requests to have the site excavated and we'll probably never know for sure.

(who burned the original temple to the ground), the devastating Civil War siege and Matthew Hopkins, the notorious Witchfinder General who, in the 17th century, used to interrogate suspected witches in the castle. The museum houses one of the finest collections of Roman antiquities in the country, with mosaics, tombstones, jewellery, coins and a bronze statue of the messenger God Mercury, although kids will be much more excited about the fact that they are allowed to try on a toga or a Roman helmet.

Stretched out behind the castle are 33 acres of beautifully landscaped gardens with a sensory garden, a children's play area, a crazy golf course, a putting green and a children's boating lake. It's also home to the Hollytrees Museum (*see* below) and, at the northern end, you can trace part of the city's Roman wall. Punch and Judy shows and children's craft and circus workshops are held in summer.

Colchester Zoo

Maldon Road, Stanway **t** (01206) 331292
www.colchester-zoo.co.uk
Getting there Follow the brown elephant signs from A1124 exit from the A12, just south of the town. It's just 10 min from Colchester train station by bus or taxi
Open Daily 9.30–5.30 (or dusk if earlier)
Adm Adult £8.25, child £5.25, under-3s **free**
Café–restaurant, picnic areas, shop, mother and baby facilities, disabled access (be warned, the site is hilly), on-site parking

Colchester Zoo has been revamped in recent years, which is just as well. Previously the epitome of the depressingly cramped city zoo, Colchester's residents, including snow leopards, lions, orang-utans, elephants and chimps, now have a good deal more space to roam around in. It's still not exactly a safari park, but it is a distinct improvement. The zoo is divided into several themed areas: 'Penguin Shores', 'Wilds of Africa', 'Serengeti Plains' (wishful thinking, I'm afraid) and the 'Spirit of Africa', a modern hi-tech enclosure which is home to giraffes and hippos. There are over 30 animal displays and feeding sessions to choose from every day, including reptile encounters (kids can have a 12ft

boa constrictor draped around their neck), birds of prey flying displays, the penguin parade (you can watch them swimming underwater from a special viewing area) and elephant bath time. There's also a Jungle Safari Train as well as a soft play complex and four outdoor adventure play areas.

Hollytrees Museum

High Street **t** (01206) 282939
Open Tues–Sat 10–1 and 2–5
Free

If you continue on down the High Street, east of the castle you reach a row of attractive Georgian houses. One of these, opposite the tourist office, is the Hollytrees Museum. This museum, which has been undergoing a period of refurbishment, houses a large, colourful collection of toys and costumes from the 18th to the 20th century, and reopened in August 2001.

Dedicated to the life of the family over the years, Hollytrees is likely to appeal to children. Kids can see what kind of games their grandparents might have played when they were children (no GameBoy then!) and learn about the lives of the people, both rich and poor, who lived in this beautiful Georgian town house.

Natural History Museum

All Saints Church, High Street **t** (01206) 282941
Open Tues–Sat 10–1 and 2–5 (last adm 4.30)
Free
Shop, disabled access

Excellent (though rather small) museum of natural history with numerous interactive exhibits including 'feely boxes' for the kids. Various events such as 'Animal Magic', when children can build model animals, and 'Animals close up', when children can examine a range of beasties through microscopes and magnifying glasses, are organized throughout the year.

Cinemas
Odeon

Crouch Street **t** 0870 50 50 007/(01206) 544869
Multi-screen cinema in the middle of town.

Theatres
Arts Centre

St Mary-at-the-Walls, Church Street
t (01206) 500900
Varied programme from rock to dance with the occasional children's performance.

Mercury Theatre
Balkerne Gate **t** (01206) 573948
Colchester's principal venue for drama.

Activities

Go Bananas
9–10 Mason Road, Cowdray Centre, Colchester
t (01206) 761762
Open Daily 9.30–6.30
Adm Child £3.75, under-5s £3.20, accompanying
adult **free**
Café, mother and baby facilities, on-site parking
Three-storey soft play area for 5–12 year olds with
ball pools, slides, swings, webs and 'spook rooms'.

Megabowl
Cowdray Avenue, Colchester **t** (01206) 560500

Rollerworld and Quasar
Eastgates, Colchester **t** (01206) 868868
www.rollerworld.co.uk
Call in advance for opening times and prices
*Café–restaurant, mother and baby facilities, on-site
parking*
Roller skating for all ages and abilities plus laser
combat games in the Quasar centre.

SPECIAL TRIPS

Mountfitchet Castle and Norman Village

Stansted **t** (01279) 813237 **www.**gold.enta.net
Getting there Lies 2 miles from J8 of M11 and five
minutes' walk from Stansted Mountfitchet station,
which is on the London–Cambridge line
Open Mar–Nov daily 10–5
Adm Adult £4.80, child £3.80
Café, shop, on-site parking
Mountfitchet, a reconstruction of a classic
Norman motte and bailey castle, is a great place for
kids to come and find out what life in a medieval
castle was really like: not all that pleasant, to be
honest. The romanticized image of dashing knights
in armour and princesses in long velvet dresses
and strange pointy hats is a long way from the
truth. While life for the castle's handful of nobles
may indeed have been terribly luxurious, for the
majority of people it was gruesome. You may be
surprised to find an entire replica Norman village
inside the castle walls, complete with church,
thatched cottages, charcoal burner's hut, pottery
kiln and blacksmith's forge, but then, in medieval
times, castles were more than simple fortresses. In
times of siege these noble bastions also provided a
home for many hundreds of people, most of whom
lived in cramped, gloomy living quarters, here
recreated in all their squalor. Inside, animated wax
figures dressed in period costume will tell you their
rather miserable stories – the blood-spattered
victims in the prison have a particularly gruesome
tale to tell – while outside, free-roaming farmyard
animals such as goats, hens and tame deer
scrabble about between the houses. Once you've
had enough of all the dirt, grime and squalour
head to the castle itself to see how the other half
lived, in the aptly named Great Hall, laid out for a
magnificent medieval banquet.

Mountfitchet is a fascinating place that will really
help to bring history alive for children (it's particularly helpful if they happen to be studying medieval
life at school), although it should be noted that, in
the interests of authenticity, the site is very hilly and
you'll have to put in some serious walking to see
everything. On your travels, look out for the replica
siege tower (which can be climbed), from where
medieval soldiers would have fired arrows and cata-
pulted large stones at potential invaders; your
children will no doubt volunteer to help with a
reconstruction. For a top day out you could also pay
a visit to the Mountfitchet toy museum, just five
minutes up the hill, which has over 80,000 vintage
toys displayed over two floors (p.124).

AROUND AND ABOUT

Bricks and mortar

Audley End House
Audley End, Saffron Walden **t** (01799) 522399
www.english-heritage.org.uk
Getting there It's a mile west of Saffron Walden on
the B1383. There's a path leading directly to the
mansion from Saffron Walden High Street (1 mile)
Open April–Sept Wed–Sun and Bank Hols
House: 12–5; Grounds: 11–6; Oct House: Wed–Sun
11–3; Grounds: Wed–Fri 11–4, Sat–Sun 11–5

Adm House and grounds: adult £6.75, child £3.40, family £16.90; grounds only: adult £4.50, child £2.30, family £11.30

Café–restaurant, picnic area, gift shop, mother and baby facilities, some disabled access, on-site parking

This exceedingly grand Jacobean mansion, which looks a bit like an enormous, square horseshoe, was built by the Earl of Suffolk in the early 17th century. One of the largest houses in the entire country at the time, it was generally considered 'fit for a king'; so fit, in fact, that Charles II actually bought it for £50,000 (an enormous sum of money in those days, the equivalent of many millions today). It's a good deal smaller now; the courtyard and east wing (amounting to around two-thirds of the original structure) were demolished in the early 18th century. Even so, it's still terribly swish, with grand gardens landscaped by Capability Brown, and thirty sumptuously decorated rooms to explore. For kids, the interior highlights will probably be the lavishly furnished Victorian dolls' house and the 19th-century collection of stuffed birds and animals (there are over a thousand on display). A free children's activity sheet is available. However, although interesting, it has to be said that inside the house it's all a bit whispery and quiet and your kids may soon be eager to explore the grounds where they can run around and make a bit of noise. They'll find sculpted hedges where they can play hide and seek, walks down by the River Cam and a miniature steam railway, very much aimed at children (oversize toys and teddies line the route). Medieval themed attractions and a special 'Children's Day' with puppet and magic shows are put on in summer.

Buckets and spades

Southend-on-Sea

Getting there Southend lies at the southernmost tip of East Anglia, at the mouth of the Thames estuary, 40 miles east of London (reached by the A127). Trains depart from London Fenchurch Street to Southend Central station regularly (1hr), and National Express run a frequent service from London Victoria (2.5hrs)

Tourist office 19 High Street **t** (01702) 215120 www.southend.gov.uk

Southend, situated on the north bank of the River Thames estuary, is within easy reach of the East End of London; indeed, for decades it seemed as if the two were linked by some sort of vacation umbilical cord. Every Bank Holiday, coachloads of East End families would descend on the Essex town looking to enjoy their annual day in the sun – only to discover that they were once again about to enjoy their annual day in the pub waiting for the rain to clear. The lure of cheap Spanish package holidays may have weakened the bond slightly, but the resort is still going strong and has plenty to offer families looking for that archetypal British seaside experience. There's a seven-mile-long stretch of sandy beach where you'll find facilities for sailing, water-skiing and windsurfing; a promenade lined with typically seasidey things: crazy golf courses, arcades, children's playgrounds, beach showers etc. (there's a seafront shuttle train in summer) while jutting out from the front is the town's most famous feature, revered since its cockney heyday, Southend Pier, which at over 1.3 miles is the longest pier in the world – it's quite a walk to the tip although you can hop aboard the pier train if you don't feel quite up to it.

Otherwise, the town's most exciting places for children are the Central Museum and Planetarium and Peter Pan's Adventure Island.

Central Museum and Planetarium

Victoria Avenue, Southend-on-Sea **t** (01702) 215640
Open Museum: Mon–Sat 10–5; planetarium shows: Wed–Sat 10–4 on the hour
Adm Museum: **free**; planetarium: adult £2.25, child £1.60, family £7

Archaeology and natural history displays plus one of the few planetariums to be found outside London.

Peter Pan's Adventure Island

Sunken Garden, Western Esplanade **t** (01702) 468023 www.adventureisland.co.uk
Open Times vary, call in advance
Adm Unlimited rides wristband £15, children's mini-wristband £9 (restricted rides only), or individual rides 60p each

This is a full-on fun park with several hi-octane thrill rides including the Thrill River log flume, the Green Scream giant rollercoaster and the Barracuda (which looks a bit like an enormous pair of metal legs; you sit in the feet as they spin over and over and over) as well as lots of dedicated kiddy-friendly attractions such as Flying Jumbo rides, junior go-karts (senior go-karts also available) and dodgems.

Cinemas
Odeon
Victoria Circus **t** (01702) 393543/0870 50 50 007

Activities
Mr B's Quasar Spacechase
5–9 Marine Parade, Southend-on-Sea
t (01702) 603947
Lazer fun for kids of all ages.

Kids Kingdom
Garon Park, Eastern Avenue, Southend-on-Sea
t (01702) 462747
Large indoor adventure centre with slides, climbing frames and ball pools.

The Kursaal
Eastern Esplanade, Southend-on-Sea
t (01702) 322322
A chance to brush up on your bowling skills after a dip in the sea.

Nature lovers

Barleylands Farm Museum
Barleylands Road, Billericay **t** (01268) 290229
Getting there It's just off the A176; take J29 from the M25
Open daily Mar–Oct 10–5 (last adm 4.30)
Adm Adult £3.50, child £2, family £10
Tearoom, shop, mother and baby facilities, disabled access, on-site parking

The museum holds over 2,000 farm-related exhibits including over 50 tractors (you'll see every size, shape and colour machine imaginable), several steam engines (often set in motion on summer weekends) as well as an animal petting area with goats, pigs and cows. In summer, you have the chance to pick (and, of course, eat) your own strawberries in the farm's fields and take tractor-trailer rides or a trip on a miniature railway.

Great Leigh's Great Maze
Rochester Farm, Great Leighs, Chelmsford
t (01245) 361411 **www.**rochesterfm.freeserve.co.uk
Getting there It's on the A131 2 miles from Braintree and 4 miles from Chelmsford
Open Mid July–early Sept daily 10–7 (last adm at 5)

Adm Adult £4, child £2.50, wheelchairs and pushchairs **free**
Refreshments, souvenir shop, on-site parking

A maze with a difference: this particular labyrinth is made entirely out of full-grown corn-on-the-cob plants (it's a maize maze, get it?) which means it must be grown afresh each year. In 1999 it was declared the largest maze in the world. You must find the route (and there is only one) to the Sunny Sunflower Centre where you can find out how well (or how badly) everyone else is doing from the viewing platform. Every child receives a free maze puzzle.

Epping Forest
Epping Forest Field Centre, High Beech Road, Loughton **t** (020) 8508 7714
Getting there It's within easy reach of London: take the tube to Loughton (Central Line) or catch one of the following buses: 20, 167, 210, 214, 215, 219, 220, 240, 250, 301, 531, 532, 549
Open (Field Centre) Mon–Sat 10–5, Sun 11–5
Free
On-site parking

A little piece of ancient Britain on the outskirts of modern London. Once part of a huge swathe of woodland that stretched from the River Lea to the sea, Epping Forest came into existence some 8,000 years ago, or just after the last Ice Age. Six thousand years later, Queen Boudicca (see p.119) supposedly fought her last battle here against the Roman Army. Today, this 10-mile crescent is a wonderful mixture of thick dense woodland, grassland, heathland and ponds inhabited by a wide range of wildlife including deer, woodpeckers, foxes and badgers.

It's perfect walking territory with paths suitable for pushchairs and plenty of clearings for a picnic. In autumn, the brambles are thick with sticky, messy blackberries – kids can colour themselves purple from head to toe in a little under half an hour. The excellent field centre, which can provide leaflets and maps of the area, organizes various activities for children, including mini-safaris, nature trails and pond dippings. It's a great place to come and escape the rigours of city life with its miles of winding paths; the farther you go into deep, dark forest, the farther away the modern world seems.

Lee Valley Park Farm
Stubbings Hall Lane, Crooked Mile, Waltham Abbey
t (01992) 892781
Getting there Lies 2 miles north of Waltham Abbey
off the B194; take J26 from the M25
Open Mon–Fri 10–4.30, Sat–Sun and Bank Hol Mon
10–6
Adm Adult £2.75, child £1.80
Picnic areas, farm shop, mother and baby facilities,
disabled access, on-site parking
Farm animals, a milking exhibition (where you
can see over 150 cows being milked each afternoon), an incubation room (where you can see
chicks being born), a farm trail, picnic areas, a pets'
corner and a play area are the main attractions of
this twin-farm site.

Marsh Farm Country Park
Marsh Farm Road, Woodham Ferrers, Chelmsford
t (01245) 321552
Getting there Follow the brown tourist signs from
the A130, it is 9 miles northwest of Southend-on-
Sea
Open Mid Feb–Oct Mon–Fri 10–4.30, Sat–Sun and
Bank Hol Mon 10–5.30
Adm Adult £2.40, child £1.60, under-2s **free**
Café, picnic areas, farm shop, mother and baby facil-
ities, disabled access
There are various kinds of farm animals,
including cattle, sheep and pigs to feed and an
adventure playground with a soft play area for
toddlers.

Mistley Place Park Animal Rescue Centre
New Road, Colchester **t** (01206) 396483
Getting there It's 8 miles northeast of Colchester, 8
miles west of Harwich off the A137
Open Daily 10–5.30
Adm Adult £2.50, child £1.50, under-4s **free**
Sanctuary for abused, abandoned or injured
domestic and farm animals with over 1,500 residents ranging from horses, dogs and birds to
guinea pigs and mice, many of which roam freely
in the centre's 25 acres of parkland. The
surrounding area, which overlooks the beautiful
Stour Valley, is particularly good for walks.

Mole Hall Wildlife Park
Widdington, Saffron Walden **t** (01799) 540400
Getting there Lies a few miles south of Saffron
Walden, signposted from the B1383
Open Daily 10.30–6

Adm Adult £4.50, child £3.20, under-3s **free**
This wildlife park is set in the grounds of a
moated manor house (private, unfortunately)
which provides a home to a whole range of
animals including otters, chimpanzees and free-
roaming deer. There's also a butterfly house.

Look at this!

Central Museum and Planetarium
Victoria Avenue, Southend-on-Sea **t** (01702) 215640
Open Museum: Mon–Sat 10–5; planetarium
shows: Wed–Sat 10–4 on the hour
Adm Museum: **free**; planetarium: adult £2.25, child
£1.60, family £7
Archaeology and natural history displays and the
only planetarium in the southeast outside London.

Dedham Art and Craft Centre and Toy Museum
High Street, Dedham **t** (01206) 322666
Getting there It is one mile off the A12 between
Colchester and Ipswich
Open Museum: Tues–Thurs, Sat–Sun and Bank Hols
10–4; craft centre: daily 10–5, Jan–Mar closed Mon
Free
Restaurant–tearoom
Watch artists and craftsmen at work and see toys
being nursed in the dolls' and toys' hospital.

House on the Hill Toy Museum
Grove Hill, Stansted **t** (01279) 813237
www.gold.enta.net
Getting there It's 2 miles from J8 of M11 and a 5min
walk from Stansted Mountfitchet station, which is
on the London Liverpool Street– Cambridge line
Open Daily 10–4
Adm Adult £3.80, child £2.80
Gift shop
This collection has been over 50 years in the
making and it shows. The owner bought his first
Hornby train set in 1946 and has been collecting
ever since. The museum is run by the same people
responsible for Mountfitchet Castle just five
minutes down the hill (*see* p.121). This is the
largest privately owned toy collection in the
world with over 80,000 toys and games spread
over two floors.
The collection includes huge numbers of tin toys
including Japanese tin space toys that look like

they could come alive at any moment. Wind up tin robots from the 1950s and '60s, bug-eyed Martians, and space craft in all shapes and sizes.

Then there are puppets galore, including ventriloquist's puppets and even a puppet theatre as well as a vast array of board games, teddy bears, dolls and dolls' houses and action figures (including the world's largest collection of Action Man paraphernalia; check out the old-style 'eagle eyes' version) all housed in glass cabinets.

Unfortunately, the museum is a look-but-don't-touch sort of a place in the main, although there are some push-button interactive toys, as well as a few coin-operated slot machines and the occasional puppet show in summer.

Mountfitchet Castle and Norman Village
For further information *see* p.121.

Secret Nuclear Bunker
Kelvedon Hatch **t** (01277) 364883
www.japar.demon.co.uk
Getting there Lies off the A128 Brentwood to Chipping Ongar Road
Open Mar–Oct Mon–Fri 10–4, Sat–Sun, Bank Hols 10–5; Nov–Feb Thurs–Sun 10–4
Adm Adult £5, child £3, under-5s **free**, family £12
Refreshments, disabled access

It wasn't too long ago that many people were convinced that a nuclear war between the two so-called Superpowers (America and Russia) was just around the corner. The British government came up with all kinds of contingency plans for what it would do in the event of a nuclear war (despite the fact that some experts predicted there would only be a three-minute warning) and a network of secret and not so secret hideaways and communications systems were built so that the business of governing could continue after the bomb had dropped (not, given the devastating effects of a nuclear explosion, that there would have been too many people left to govern).

Cunningly concealed beneath an ordinary looking bungalow is this now defunct three-storey bunker. Fitted out with a staggering 110 tonnes of equipment, it was designed to support 600 government personnel during a nuclear war. An audio tour takes you around the site (kids get their own version), with en-route films, military uniforms and gas masks to try on and there's a computer quiz at the end.

Site of Essex's Secret Bunker
Shrublands Road, Mistley **t** (01206) 392271
Getting there It's on the B1352, 8 miles northeast of Colchester, 8 miles west of Harwich off the A137
Open April–Oct daily 10.30–5
Adm Adult £4.95, child £3.65, family £15

Restored Cold War nuclear command centre (it was operational until a few years ago) you can find out how the great and the good of Essex would have coped had the bomb gone off.

Steam power

Colne Valley Railway
Yeldham Road, Castle Hedingham **t** (01787) 461174
www.cvr.org.uk
Getting there Situated 20 miles northwest of Colchester on the A1017, 2 miles north of Sible Hedingham
Open Mar–Dec 11–5; steam days take place Mar–Oct most Suns with extra midweek days in July and Aug
Adm Static viewing: adult £3, child £1.50, family £7.50; steam days: adult £6, child £3, family £16
Pullman restaurant train, buffet, picnic area, wheelchair access to most of the site, on-site parking

This beautifully restored, one-mile long riverside stretch of the former Colne Valley and Halstead railway offers two very different train-themed experiences. On non-steam days kids and parents can examine the railway's 60 or so vintage engines and carriages, see how the signal box works, try the guard's flag and whistle and (always a thrill) walk along the train tracks. On steam days you can actually ride one of the puffing steam trains as it trundles along the line. Parents will relish the opportunity to dine in the luxurious Pullman carriage, although kids will probably prefer to picnic on the grass overlooking the Colne River or in the grassy grounds of the adjoining Castle Hedingham, a beautifully preserved Norman keep, where jousting tournaments and re-enactments of medieval sieges are held in summer.

NORWICH

Getting there By road: Norwich is 115 miles from London, 63 miles from Cambridge and can be reached via the M11 and the A11 (from London) and the A14, A11 and A47 (from Cambridge). By train: regular train services run to Norwich from London Liverpool Street (1hr 45min). The station is a 10min walk from the centre. By bus/coach: there are regular National Express coaches from London Victoria to Norwich (3hrs) and from Cambridge (2hrs). There are numerous pay and display car parks in and around the city centre as well as a handful of multi-storeys, including one just off St Giles Street near the City Hall. There are also three NCP car parks just outside the centre; one to the south, two to the north

Tourist office The Guildhall, Gaol Hill **t** (01603) 666071 www.norwich.gov.uk

Norwich is East Anglia's biggest town and the region's unofficial capital. A good-looking, old city with plenty of fine architecture, it makes a convenient base for exploring the Norfolk Broads, the vast agglomeration of inland waterways just northeast of the town, and the east Norfolk coast. Great Yarmouth, the area's principal resort, is about 20 miles to the east. Norwich is home to a handful of child-orientated attractions – the best of which are the Inspire Hands-On Science Centre, the Norwich Puppet Theatre and the Bridewell Museum – and is within easy reach of several more.

Norwich was founded by the Angles who, with their better known countrymen the Saxons, invaded and colonized much of the country in the centuries following the collapse of the Roman Empire. In the Middle Ages it became the site of a thriving textile industry as a result of trade links built up with the Netherlands. In fact, during this time, it probably enjoyed a closer relationship with the low countries across the North Sea than it did with London and, by the early 1700s, was the country's second most prosperous city. From this point on, however, its position began to slip. Slow to adapt to new manufacturing methods pioneered during the industrial revolution, it found itself undermined by the large, new textile factories of the northern cities and fell into a decline.

These days, however, thanks to a boom in its new hi-tech manufacturing industries, its star is once again in the ascendant and it is now a busy, lively

city, albeit one with a distinctly olde-worlde-village feel to it. The streets still follow the rather jumbled Angle layout (with cobbled alleyways jutting off from the main roads hither and thither) and are lined with medieval buildings. In the middle of the city's pleasant pedestrianized centre is the market place, the real heart of the city, where every day around 200 stalls set up for business under coloured awnings, selling clothes, jewellery, sweets and fruit and vegetables. As you browse, look out for the very brave (or very stupid) starlings darting between your legs looking for scraps.

The town's two principal sights are also its two principal landmarks, which at least makes them easy to find. The squat Norman castle sits atop a mound just to the south of the city centre, while the magnificent cathedral is just to the east. The cathedral's spire, which is the second tallest in the country, hardly dominates the skyline, but you will see it every now and then poking through the rooftops, although the rather random layout of the streets makes it appear that, rainbow-like, the harder you try to reach it, the further away it seems to get.

Things to see

Assembly House

Theatre Street **t** (01603) 626402
www.assemblyhousenorwich.co.uk
Open Mon–Sat 11–6
Adm Adult £3.50, child £2
Tearoom and restaurant

Elegant 17th-century townhouse where children's activities, such as their 'design a plate competition', are occasionally held.

Bridewell Museum

Bridewell Alley **t** (01603) 667228
Open Feb–Sept Tues–Sat 10–5
Adm Adult £1.80, child 90p
Shop
Not suitable for pushchairs

Good local museum telling the story of Norwich (from small provincial town to economic powerhouse and back again) with lots of exhibits on the two principal themes of Norwich life: clothes and mustard. Art and craft workshops (where kids can learn block printing, the techniques of forensic science, i.e. finger-printing, or how to be a newspaper editor) as well as storytelling sessions are organized during the school holidays.

Did you know...
The first ever long-distance telephone call was made by Mr Adams from Colman's mustard factory in Norwich to their head office in London in 1878.

City of Norwich Aviation Museum

Old Norwich Road, Horsham St Faith
t (01603) 893080
Getting there The museum lies a few miles north of the city off the A140
Open April–Oct Tues–Sat 10–5, Sun and Bank Hol Mon 12–5; Nov–Mar Wed and Sat 10–4, Sun 12–4
Adm Adult £2.50, child £1.50, family £7
Refreshments, shop, disabled access, on-site parking

Military aviation museum with plenty of planes on display including a Vulcan Bomber; kids can sit in the pilot's seat.

Colman's Mustard Shop

15 Royal Arcade **t** (01603) 627889
Open Mon–Sat 9.30–5, Sun 11–4

No visit to Norwich would be complete without a trip to Colman's Mustard Shop where you can discover the secret history of mustard and find out how the fiery condiment is made. Kids can follow the cartoon adventures of Jeremiah Colman around the shop, while their parents examine the Art Deco mustard pots and wartime tins.

Inspire Hands-On Science Centre

St Michael's Church, Coslany Steet **t** (01603) 612612
www.science-project.org
Open Tues–Sun 10–5.30 (last adm 4.30)
Adm Adult £3.50, child £2.90, family £10, under-3s **free**
Café, science shop

Small but well-equipped science museum housed in the medieval St Michael's Church where, among other things, kids can step inside a bubble, build an arch bridge and discover the secrets of lightning.

Norwich Castle

t (01603) 493625
Open Mon–Sat 10.30–5, Sun 2–5
Adm Call in advance to check prices

After the Tower of London, this squat, square little castle (21m high, 28m square) is the best preserved Norman military fortress in the country. Built in the mid 12th century, it was converted into a prison in the late Middle Ages and was the site of numerous public executions – the last of which took place in the early 19th century.

The castle has recently undergone a period of restoration. It reopened in June 2001 and visitors can once again tour the dungeons to see the castle's collection of torture instruments and original plaster casts of the heads of hanged murderers. These were cast for the purposes of phrenological study, the now discredited science of testing someone's predisposition to crime by measuring the shape and size of their head and prominent facial features.

The adjacent Regimental Museum, which is linked to the castle by an underground tunnel contains galleries full of military paraphernalia, as well as a reconstruction of a First World War trench.

Norwich Cathedral

12 The Close **t** (01603) 764385
www.cathedral.org.uk
Open Mid May–mid Sept daily 7.30–7; mid Sept–mid May 7.30–6
Free (Voluntary donation of £2 requested)
Restaurant, shop, guided tours, adapted toilets, some disabled access and parking

Passing through the great gateway to the city's medieval cathedral close is like stepping back in time. In among the close's grassy lawns, overhanging trees and narrow alleyways, the modern world suddenly seems very far away. Filled with graceful architecture from medieval to Georgian, nothing too modern or fancy – it's like a mini town within a town. At its heart is the honey-coloured, spired cathedral, one of the country's best. Begun in 1092, it was completed some 50 years later and was built entirely from stone sailed across from Normandy (the builders clearly didn't think much of the domestic stone on offer). You can still see the remains of special channels dug to float the stones from the river to the site.

The great spire, which is surrounded by four mini-spires, was added in the 15th century and at 315ft tall is the second highest in the country (only Salisbury's is taller). The interior is peculiarly light and airy (peculiar, that is, for cathedrals which usually specialize in darkness) with lots of clear glass illuminating the nave. There are spectacular stained glass windows at the west and east ends and a wonderfully ornate ceiling decorated with round lattice-like stones: known as bosses, which have been carved with intricate representations of biblical stories. You can study them (without the need to crane your neck) in the mirrors positioned along the aisle although, to be honest, you can't really pick out that much detail (the ceiling is a good 60ft up) and, if you're particularly interested, you should check out the similar designs adorning the cloisters (the largest in the country), which are only about 15ft above your head.

Look out for the huge thick pillars supporting the roof, a speciality of Norman architecture (and in particular the two either side of the choir which, with their diagonal line motifs, look as if they're being screwed into the ground) and the tombs lining the floors of the side aisles; the thought of walking over dead bodies always gives kids a spooky thrill. There are also quiz sheets for children.

Norwich Puppet Theatre

St James, Whitefriars **t** (01603) 629921
www.geocities.com/norwichpuppets
Performance times Call in advance, box office open Mon–Fri 9–5 and from one hour before the performance on weekends
Adm Performances: adult £5, child £1; workshops: £5

The Norwich Puppet Theatre puts on award-winning marionette, glove and rod puppet shows for children aged 3–10 which are staged most Saturdays at 10.30am and 2.30pm (there are extra weekday shows during the school holidays). Most are based on fairy tales – Cinderella, Jack and the Beanstalk, Snow White – although there are occasional performances of more modern children's classics such as Roald Dahl's *George's Marvellous Medicine*. The centre also organizes puppet-making workshops for children aged 5 and over where they can create their own puppets and learn manipulation skills from one of the centre's puppeteers.

Sainsbury Centre for Visual Arts

University of East Anglia, Earlham Road
t (01603) 593199 **www.**uea.ac.uk/scva
Getting there Located off the B1108 (Watton Road), just outside the city centre
Open Tues–Sun 11–5
Adm £2 (includes entry to all exhibitions and displays), £1 concs, under-5s **free**

The city's latest pride and joy: a collection of 19th- and 20th-century European art, African tribal sculpture, Egyptian and Asian artefacts housed in a state-of-the-art Norman Foster-designed building on the Norwich University campus. Special events are put on throughout the year.

Stranger's Hall

Charing Cross **t** (01603) 667229
Open Guided tours only: Wed and Sat only at 1 and 3pm, also from April–Sept at 11am
Adm Adult £2.50, child £1.50, under-5s **free**; tickets can be booked at the Bridewell Shop **t** (01603) 629127.

This is a medieval merchant's house that's been turned into a museum of domestic life, with each of its rooms furnished in a different period style (Tudor, Regency, Victorian, etc.).

Things to do

St Peter Hungate Church Museum

Princes Street **t** (01603) 667231
Open Mon–Sat 10–5
Free

Children can take brass rubbings from a number of replica brasses.

Boat trips

For the clearest and best views of the city's castle and cathedral, take a boat trip along the River Wensum, which flows in a loop around the centre of the town. For information on boat tours through Norwich and the Norfolk Broads contact Southern River Steamers **t** (01603) 624051.

Bus tours

During the summer months Guide Friday offers open-top bus tours of the city, **t** (01789) 294466. For more general information on public transport contact NORBIC **t** 0845 300 6116.

Walking tours

Sightseeing tours of the city in the company of a Blue Badge Guide are organized by the tourist office **t** (01603) 666071.

Cinemas

Cinema City

Stuart Hall & Suckling House, St Andrew's Street
t (01603) 622047

UCI

Wherry Rd, Riverside Development
t (0870) 0102030

Theatres

Norwich Playhouse
42–58 St George's Street
t (01603) 633635
Art theatre with the occasional children's show.

Norwich Puppet Theatre
St James, Whitefriars **t** (01603) 629921
www.geocities.com/norwichpuppets.
For further information *see* opposite.

Theatre Royal
Theatre Street **t** (01603) 630000
Big west end productions and the inevitable Christmas panto.

SPECIAL TRIPS

Bressingham Steam Museum

Bressingham, Diss **t** (01379) 687386
Getting there The museum is just off the A1066, 2 miles west of Diss; follow the brown tourist signs. There's a regular train service to Diss Station which is on the main line from Norwich to London Liverpool Street
Open April–October daily; special events in December
Adm Full (including rides): adult £10, child £8, family £35; adm only: adult £7, child £5, family £23; rides only £3.50; under-3s **free**
Restaurant, souvenir shop, gardens and plant centre, wheelchair access, adapted toilets, on-site parking

Bressingham offers a wide array of steam attractions set in six acres of pretty gardens. There are three different narrow-gauge lines: the Nursery Railway, which passes the nearby lake and woodland and gives views of Roydon Church; the Waveney Valley Railway, which runs over watermeadows and through rhododendron banks; and the Garden Railway, home to the 'Alan Bloom', built from scratch by the Bressingham team.

Pride of place goes to the standard gauge locomotives which includes a number on loan from the National Railway Museum in York. Many of these are brought out for display on the museum's 1/4-mile demonstration line and include 'little phutters' such as the 1893 *Granville* through to the Royal Scot, used on the west-coast express service from London to Glasgow. Also of note is the *Oliver*

Cromwell which, in 1968, became the last steam loco to haul a British passenger train.

Not all of Bressingham's collection is track-based. There are steam wagons, road rollers, tractors, stationary engines and impressive road locomotives such as the *Black Prince* which was last used in 1942 to demolish buildings damaged in the Blitz. Young visitors will probably head for the 'Galloper' – a Victorian merry-go-round with ornate paintwork and horses three-abreast which spins round to the melodies of a chirpy steam-powered organ. This mechanical marvel was built in 1900. It came to Bressingham in 1967 and underwent an extensive period of renovation to bring it up to its near-mint condition. These days it requires a permanent member of staff whose sole responsibility it is to keep it running. The 'Galloper' still gives rides on steam days.

Dinosaur Adventure Park

Weston Park, Lenwade, Norwich **t** (01603) 870245
www.dinosaurpark.co.uk
Getting there It's 9 miles northwest of Norwich off the A1067 and is signposted from both the A1067 and A47
Open April–mid Sept 10–5; mid Sept–mid Oct Fri–Sun 10–5; 22–28 Oct Mon–Fri 10–5
Adm Adult £5.95, child £4.95, under-3s **free**
Restaurant, picnic areas, barbeque area, disabled access, on-site parking

All kids love dinosaurs, it's the law. And while examining old fossils in a museum is all very well, it's no substitute for being able to climb over, around and even inside models of the great beasts, which is exactly what kids can do at this excellent little adventure park. There's a dinosaur trail with various life-size fibreglass models hidden amid the foliage, a woodland maze, a 75ft long 'climb-a-saurus' – kids can climb up into the body, along the neck and take a look out through the fearsome jaws – a crazy golf course, 'Jurassic Putt', a soft play area for under-5s, 'Tiny Pterosaurs', and an education centre with a fossil workshop which provides fun facts about different kinds of dinosaur and looks at the competing theories as to why dinosaurs became extinct (was it a meteor which caused an ice age or did they all suffer from constipation after eating too many flowers?).

Natural history rambles through the local countryside are arranged and the park has picnic areas with gas-fired barbeques as well as a dinosaur-themed diner.

At the recently opened 'Secret Garden' children can meet and stroke a range of animals (sadly no dinosaurs) including deer, pigs and guinea pigs.

AROUND AND ABOUT

Bricks and mortar

Blickling Hall
Blickling, Norwich **t** (01263) 738030
www.nationaltrust.org.uk
Getting there Blickling Hall is 15 miles north of Norwich on the B1354 and is signposted off the A140
Open April–Oct Wed–Sun and Bank Hol Mon house: 1–5 (4 in Oct), garden: 10.15–5.15; Nov–Dec Thurs–Sun garden: 11–4; Jan–Mar Sat and Sun garden: 11–4; park and woods all year daily dawn–dusk
Adm Adult £6.70, child £3.35
Restaurant, picnic area, mother and baby room, disabled access, on-site parking

Grand, 17th-century mansion built on top of the house where Anne Boleyn, Henry VIII's second wife, spent much of her childhood. Today, she is said to haunt the site; her headless ghost has been seen arriving at the doors of the hall in a carriage drawn by a team of headless horses. Pretty spooky. Ghostly goings-on aside, the house is still well worth a brief detour. Though a touch stuffy and, as you would expect, richly furnished with a grand, oak staircase, it does have a few interesting what-nots to look out for, including a statue of Anne (in her pre-headless state), a tapestry of Peter the Great and a Long Gallery which has all manner of bizarre creatures moulded into its plaster ceiling.

Cley Mill
Cley-next-the-Sea, Holt **t** (01263) 740209
Getting there The windmill is situated 11 miles west of Cromer, on the A149
Open Easter–Sept 2–5
Adm Adult £1.50, child 75p, under-5s **free**
Gift shop

Not suitable for pushchairs or wheelchairs
First built in the 18th century, though much altered since, Cley Mill fell into disrepair in the early part of the 20th century and was converted into a holiday home in 1921, before finally opening as a guesthouse in 1983. There are wonderful views from the balcony out over Blakeney Harbour, Cley Bird Sanctuary and the salt marshes.

Felbrigg Hall
Roughton, Norwich **t** (01263) 837444
www.nationaltrust.org.uk
Getting there It's 2 miles southwest of Cromer, off the B1436 and signposted from A148 and A140
Open April–Oct Sat–Wed house: 1–5; Bank Hol Mon and Sun 11–5; garden: 11–5.30
Adm Adult £5.80, child £2.90, family £14.50
Restaurant, tea room, picnic area, mother and baby room, disabled access, on-site parking

The last squire of Febrigg bequeathed this 17th-century hall to the National Trust back in the 1960s, since when it has been spruced up and turned into one of Norfolk's most popular stately homes. Inside are a number of oddities that should appeal to the kids. Children's guide in hand (available from the ticket office), see if the kids can track down the false door, the extremely elaborate Gothic-style library and the bath with a difference: designed to preserve one's modesty while servants were in the room, it enabled bathers to wash without revealing the more private parts of their body. Do also look out for the large collection of stuffed rare birds (most of which you wouldn't be allowed to shoot today) and, outside, the beautiful walled garden and avenue of beech trees.

Great Bircham Windmill
Bircham, King's Lynn **t** (01485) 578393
Getting there Lies 7 miles southeast of Hunstanton
Open April–Sept daily 10–5
Adm Adult £2.75, child £1.50, under-5s **free**

Great Bircham is located on one of Norfolk's very few hills and can offer great views. Its sails still turn on windy days and it contains a bakery where you can buy freshly baked bread. You can also hire bikes here to explore the local countryside (adults £6, children £4).

Holkham Hall
Holkham **t** (01328) 710227

Getting there Situated 3 miles west of Wells-next-the-Sea on the A149; follow the brown tourist signs
Open Easter–May Sun and Mon 11.30–5; June–Sept Sun–Thurs 1–5
Adm Adult £6, child £3

With grand, landscaped gardens and a wonderful collection of paintings by artists such as Rubens, Van Dyck and Gainsborough, Holkham is nonetheless principally worth visiting for its Bygones Museum, which contains over 4,000 domestic and agricultural artefacts – from Victorian matchboxes and vintage cars, to gramophones and fire engines – housed in a converted stable.

Houghton Hall

Houghton, King's Lynn **t** (01485) 528569
Getting there The hall is on the A148 King's Lynn–Cromer Road, 11 miles from King's Lynn
Open Easter–Sept Thurs, Sun and Bank Hol Mon 1–5.30
Adm Adult £6, child £2, under-5s **free**
Café–restaurant, gift shop, disabled access, on-site parking

A grand stately home with sweeping landscaped gardens built by Robert Walpole, Britain's first prime minister, in the 18th century. It houses the Cholmondeley (pronounced 'Chumley') Soldier Museum, which has over 20,000 model soldiers arranged in a series of spectacular battle scenes. In the grounds, look out for a small obelisk. This marks the spot where the village of Houghton once stood: when Walpole wanted his house built, he simply had the village moved a couple of miles down the road.

Oxburgh Hall

Oxborough, King's Lynn **t** (01366) 328258
www.nationaltrust.org.uk
Getting there Oxburgh Hall is 17 miles south of King's Lynn, off the A134
Open April–Oct Sat–Wed House: 1–5, Bank Hol Mon 11–5; Garden: 11–5.30; Aug daily, March Sat–Wed 11–4
Adm Adult £5.30, child £2.65
Restaurant, picnic, shop, mother and baby room, some disabled access, on-site parking

Thanks to a good deal of 19th-century prettification, this 15th-century manor looks almost castle-esque with its grand battlements and moat. It was owned by the same Catholic family, the Bedingfelds, for over 500 years, hence the priest's hole which would have been used to hide the family priest when Catholicism was outlawed following the Reformation in the 16th century. Oxburgh Hall produces a children's guide which points out some of the more interesting items on display, including the collection of weapons and armour from the Civil War, and the display of embroidery sewn by Mary Queen of Scots while she was held in captivity by Elizabeth I. Outside, there are attractive woodland walks.

Sandringham House

Sandringham **t** (01553) 772675
www.sandringhamestate.co.uk
Getting there Located 8 miles northeast of King's Lynn off the A148
Open Easter–early Oct daily 11–5 (house closed late July–early Aug)
Adm Adult £6, child £3.50, family £15.50
Café–restaurant, gift shop, mother and baby facilities, guided tours, disabled access, on-site parking

This is where the Queen makes her broadcast to the nation at 3pm every Christmas Day and it has a much more relaxed and intimate feel to it than some of the other Royal residences with a good many more family rooms open to the public than at Buckingham Palace or Windsor Castle.

It's only a relative distinction, of course. Nobody could describe this grand collection of priceless porcelain, enamelled Russian silver, old master paintings and antique furniture as homely. It's as well-to-do and plush as you'd hope.

The house itself is 19th century, although built in Jacobean style (it was bought by Queen Victoria for her son Edward, the future king, in 1862 – that's some birthday present) and contains a collection of royal cars, a collection of royal photographs, a collection of royal big-game trophies (lions, tigers, etc.) and (of most interest to kids) a collection of miniature royal cars and dolls made for successive generations of princes and princesses. Lucky things! Surrounding the house are landscaped gardens and over 2,000 acres of rolling country parkland, which provide a home for game birds (who must make themselves scarce every New Year when the Royal Party enjoys its annual hunt) and contain an adventure playground.

The Norfolk and Suffolk Broads

This dense network of inland waterways just east of Norwich provides the location for perhaps the ultimate boating holiday: 120 square miles of interlinked streams, rivers and lakes adding up to no less than 125 miles of navigable waterways. It's a resolutely wet landscape. In addition to the waterways themselves – the region is dissected by six rivers in total, including the Bure which is joined by the Ant and the Waveney before tipping into the sea at Great Yarmouth – you'll find vast areas of marshland, watermeadows, bogs and fens. It's water, water everywhere, as far as the eye can see.

It's also a fantastic place for nature lovers with its nature reserves and bird sanctuaries, the whole area having been given 'national protected status'. The Broads Information Centres can provide details of guided tours and a list of bird-watching sites. The most accessible site is probably Ranworth, eight miles northeast of Norwich, where there's a quarter-mile boardwalk through reed beds and marshes and a viewing platform from where you can see herons, crested grebes and terns. At the conservation centre you can see a display on the history (and natural history) of the Broads. Also check out the Toad Hall Cottage Museum at How Hill (see below) which has displays on Victorian country life. Guided wildlife cruises are offered on weekends.

If you want to explore the area fully, taking a boat is the only realistic option. There are few roads worthy of the name, although the Bure Valley Steam Railway (p.141) does cover part of the Broads on its route from Aylsham to Wroxham, the 'Capital of the Broads' (combined train rides and broad cruises available). The waterways are, in effect, the region's roads. The main centres for boat hire are listed below.

The term 'Broads' itself refers to the large lake-like expanses of water that dot the area. For centuries they were thought to be purely natural phenomena until medieval records were discovered which showed that they were, in fact, the result of extensive peat excavation in the Middle Ages (in an area where wood was scarce, peat was a valuable source of energy). Large holes cut by the peat diggers filled with water when the sea level rose in the 13th and 14th centuries and, hey presto!, the Broads – home to some of the countries rarest birds.

Broads information centres

A handful of information centres are dotted around the Broads and can help with accommodation, restaurants and hiring a boat (don't bother trying to explore the Broads by car; they're rivers after all!).

Main centre
The Broads Authority, Thomas Harvey House, 18 Colgate, Norwich **t** (01603) 782281
Beccles
The Quay, Fen Lane, Beccles **t** (01502) 713196
Great Yarmouth
North West Tower, North Quay, Great Yarmouth **t** (01493) 332095
Hoveton
Station Road, Hoveton, Norwich **t** (01603) 782281
How Hill
Toad Hole Cottage Museum and 'Electric Eel' Wildlife Water Trail, How Hill, Ludham, Great Yarmouth **t** (01692) 678763
Loddon
The Old Town Hall, 1 Bridge Street, Loddon, Norwich **t** (01508) 521028
Potter Heigham
The Staithe, Bridge Street, Potter Heigham, Great Yarmouth **t** (01692) 670779
Ranworth
The Staithe, Ranworth, Norwich **t** (01603) 270453

Boat trips

If you want to see the Broads at their best then hire a boat to explore the 100 or so miles of easy-to-navigate waterways. Day hire prices vary. Expect to pay £9–15 per hour, £40–65 per day depending on the size of craft. The main booking agents are:
Blakes Holiday Boating
Hoveton, Norwich **t** (01603) 739333
Hoseasons Holidays Ltd
Sunway House, Lowestoft **t** (01502) 500505
Norfolk Broads Direct
t (0800) 917 3206 **www**.broads.co.uk

The latter can supply cabin cruisers and sailing yachts. The boats are easy to handle and include fully-equipped galleys, TVs, showers and all deck gear (including life belts), and all linen (including duvets). Prices for a boat sleeping four to six people start at £265 for a short-break (three nights).

River Ant

Ludham Bridge Services
Ludham Bridge **t** (01692) 630486
  Motor launches, electric boats, dinghies, rowing boats.

Stalham Yacht Service
The Staithe, Stalham **t** (01692) 580288
  Motor launches, sailing dinghies, canoes, rowing boats.

River Bure

Broad Tours Ltd
The Bridge, Wroxham **t** (01603) 782207
  Motor launches.

Camelot Craft
The Rhond, Hoveton **t** (01603) 783096
  Dinghies and canoes.

Fineway Launch Hire
Riverside Road, Hoveton **t** (01603) 782309
  Motor launches, electric boats.

Island Boat Hire
Coltishall **t** (01603) 737589
  Canoes and rowing boats.

River Thurne

Herbert Woods
Broads Haven, Potter Heigham **t** (01692) 670711
  Motor launches, electric boats.

Whispering Reeds
Hickling **t** (01692) 598314
  Electric boats, dinghies, rowing boats.

River Waveney

Day Launch Hire
Oulton Broad Yacht Station **t** (01502) 513087
  Motor launches, rowing boats.

HE Hipperson
Gillingham Dam, Beccles **t** (01502) 712166
  Motor launches, dinghies, electric boats.

River Yare

Highcraft
Griffin Lane, Thorpe St Andrew **t** (01603) 701701
  Motor launches, rowing boats.

Guided boat trips

Electric Eel Wildlife Water Trail
How Hill Nature Reserve, Ludham
t (01692) 678763
Fares Adults £3, children £2, family £6
  50-minute boats trip taking eight people on an Edwardian-style electric boat through dykes and marshes. The trail runs on weekends, Bank Holidays and school holidays in April, May and Oct and June–Sept daily from 10–5.

Hickling Boat Trail
t (01692) 598276
  Water trail trekking on Hickling Broad National Nature Reserve.

Other boat trips

Broad Tours
The Bridge, Wroxham **t** (01603) 782207
Mississippi River Boats, Lower Street, Horning
t (01692) 630262

Southern River Steamers
Elm Hill and Thorpe Station Quays, Norwich
t (01603) 624051

Cycle hire

  Broads cycle hire points are located at:
Acle
Acle Bridge Stores, Acle Bridge **t** (01493) 730355
Bungay
Outney Meadows Caravan Park **t** (01986) 892338
Hickling
The Pleasure Boat Stores, Staithe Road
t (01692) 598211
Hoveton
Bure Valley Railway **t** (01603) 783096
Camelot Craft, The Rhond, Hoveton **t** (01603) 783096
Loddon
Broadland Riverine Boatcraft Ltd, Norwich
t (01508) 528735
Ludham
Ludham Bridge Boat Service **t** (01692) 630486
Norwich
Norwich Yacht Station, City Boats **t** (01603) 701701
Thorpe, Highcraft **t** (01603) 701701
Sutton
Sutton Staithe Boatyard **t** (01692) 581653
Thurne Staithe
Thurne Stores **t** (01493) 369235

Buckets and spades

Cromer and the North Norfolk Coast

Getting there Cromer is easily reached via the A148 from King's Lynn (approx. 35 miles) or the A140 from Norwich (approx. 20 miles). Local bus services run to Cromer from Norwich, and there are rail links to both King's Lynn and Norwich
Tourist information Cromer Bus Station, Prince of Wales Road **t** (01263) 512497
www.north-norfolk.gov.uk

There are few better ways to spend a sunny afternoon than crabbing in rockpools, and there are few better places to go crabbing than Cromer: all you'll need is a bit of bacon tied on a string and a bucket (*see* also p.145). The town itself, though once refined and classy, the most fashionable of Victorian resorts, is these days rather frayed around the edges. Wind-battered and exposed on low craggy cliffs, Cromer's charms have faded slightly with the years, as if the raging sea wind (which comes straight down from the North Pole) has blown all the glamour and elegance from the streets. Its natural attributes, however, still hold strong: its long sandy beach recently won a Blue Flag Award, its rugged coast is good for walks and can offer imposing views out over the sea and, of course, its waters are still home to the crabs that have for so long been the town's biggest draw.

There are also several worthwhile attractions within easy reach of the town including the Norfolk Shire Horse Centre, a couple of miles west along the coast, which has a large collection of working horses and ponies (p.138). You can see demonstrations of harnessing, pulling and ploughing and kids can take cart rides and meet the animals at the children's farm. A mile or two further west is Sheringham (site of the landscaped Sheringham Park with its rhododendron bushes and viewing towers), where you can clamber aboard the North Norfolk Railway (p.141), while just beyond this is Weybourne, home of the Muckleburgh Collection. Blakeney Point, one of the nation's foremost nature reserves (and home to large colonies of birds and seals), is about five miles west of Weybourne (p.137).

In summer Cromer plays host to a week-long carnival with a Grand Parade, children's activities and firework display and there are variety shows held every day at the end of the pier.

Muckleburgh Collection
Weybourne, Holt **t** (01263) 588210
Getting there Lies on the A149 coast road, a few miles west of Cromer
Open Mid Feb–Oct daily 10–5
Adm Adult £4.95, child £2.50, under-5s **free**, family £12.50
Café–restaurant, shop, disabled access, on-site parking

The largest private collection of military paraphernalia in the country with masses of tanks, missiles, bombs and uniforms on display. There are tank-riding demonstrations every Sunday when kids also have the opportunity to ride in a US personnel carrier.

Activities
Funstop
Exchange House, Louden Road, Cromer
t (01263) 514976 **www.**funstop.co.uk
Open May–Sept daily 10–6; Oct–April Fri, Sat and Sun only 10–6

Indoor play centre for under-10s.

Great Yarmouth

Getting there The town can be reached via the A47 from Norwich (17 miles), the A12 to Ipswich (40 miles) and the A143 to Bury St Edmunds (25 miles). There is a rail link with Norwich (30min), and buses connect with Lowestoft and Norwich. National Express, which runs a service from London, has a coach stop at the Market Gates (east side)
Tourist offices Town Hall (near main post office) **t** (01493) 846345; Marine Parade (Easter–Sept only) **t** (01493) 842195
www.great-yarmouth.gov.uk/tourism

A slightly faded sign at the train station welcomes you to 'Britain's greatest seaside resort'. All the seaside regulars are here: the shops selling novelty hats and postcards, the face painters, the chip shops (so many chip shops) and the legion of souvenir shops that always seem to flourish in these sorts of resorts. The seafront itself provides a grand sweep of simple entertainments: arcade after arcade, bingo halls, crazy golf courses and video game parlours, all lit up with clusters of coloured bulbs.

There are two piers: the Britannia, which has a funfair and a dedicated kids zone 'Joyland' with various rides and a hall of mirrors, and the

Wellington, which has an entertainment complex where B-list TV stars undertake summer seasons. At the western edge of town is the Pleasure Beach, the region's most popular fun park with roller-coasters, log flumes and numerous other rides.

Kids love the place. Everywhere they go they'll find games to play, teddies to win, rides to be ridden and 'wobbly worlds' to negotiate. On the seafront, or Marine Parade as it is called, there is a Reptile House, 'Amazonia', with lizards, snakes and crocodiles living in a replica jungle, a model village with over 200 miniature buildings, from castles to cottages, set in landscaped gardens, a 120ft observation tower providing good views of the town from the telescopes at the top, a 'Rock Factory' where you can watch demonstrations of rock-making and a Sea Life Centre, one of the country's biggest, where you can take a sea-bed stroll past seahorses, sharks and jellyfish.

And then, of course, there's the Blue Flag beach, the town's undoubted highlight: wide, sandy and covered with a smattering of the sort of flat, round stones that are so perfect for skimming. There are lifeguards, warning flags and it's cleaned daily during the summer season. Pony and cart rides along the front are offered from Britannia Pier.

Amazonia World of Reptiles

Marine Parade, Great Yarmouth **t** (01493) 842202
Open Mar–Oct daily 10–5 (7 in summer)
Adm Adult £3.95, child £2.95, under-4s **free**

Britain's largest collection of reptiles, which includes snakes, lizards and crocodiles, occupies a lush botanical setting on the seafront at Great Yarmouth.

Elizabethan House Museum

4 South Quay **t** (01493) 855746
Open April–Sept Mon–Fri 10–5, weekends 1.15–5
Adm Adult £2, child £1, family £4.70

16th-century house with a (rather incongruous) display on 19th-century domestic life, an exhibition on the execution of Charles I and a toy room for children.

Old Merchant's House and Row 111

Row 111, South Quay **t** (01493) 857900
Open April–Oct 10–1 and 2–5
Adm Adult £2.40, child 1.20, under-5s **free**

A pair of 17th-century houses decorated in period style: late 19th century and Second World War respectively. Visits are by guided tour only.

Pleasure Beach

South Beach Parade **t** (01493) 844585
www.pleasure-beach.co.uk
Open Mar–Sept, dates and times vary, call in advance
Free entry; rides can be paid for either with tokens (50p each) or wristbands (£8)
Fast food, tearoom, sweet shops, some disabled access, adapted toilets

The Pleasure Beach was, when it first opened in the early part of the century, a rather gentle, charming little place with a scenic railway, a small joy wheel and little else. In the 90 odd years since, however, it has transformed itself into one of the country's top fun parks with 70 or so daredevil rides spread over nine seafront acres.

Try the Ejector Seat, an ingenious variation on the traditional bungee jump in which passengers in a two-seater cage are flung by the 'mother of all elastic bands' up to a height of 160ft, going from 0–70mph in just under a second, or the Top Spin, a large 360° spinning gondola, or Sheer Terror, a walk-through attraction, where performing arts students from Great Yarmouth College dress up in scary costumes (mad axe man, Hannibal Lecter, etc.) and then try to terrify the visitors. There's also a go-kart track, a log flume, a waltzer, an adventure golf course as well as numerous children's rides, a boating lake and a

---

Great Yarmouth – a town with a past

In among all the modern attractions, elements of Great Yarmouth's past do remain. Despite appearances, this is a town with a history. Founded as long ago as the 11th century, Great Yarmouth boasts one of the most complete medieval walls in the country and, in the 19th century, it was the centre of the European herring industry. It even provided the setting for part of Charles Dickens' *David Copperfield*. On the historic South Quay you'll find the Elizabethan House and the Tollhouse Museum, where activities for children – such as treasure hunts, storytellings and histori-cally-themed craft workshops (mask-making, quill-making, hat design) – are organized during the school holidays. Nearby are two 17th-century houses, the Old Merchant's House and Row 111. Heritage walks through the town are offered in summer; contact Great Yarmouth Heritage Walks **t** (01493) 859307.

traditional, seafront tearoom pavilion. The park's showpiece ride, however, harks back to its earlier days. It's a traditional wooden rollercoaster that's been operating here since 1932 and can offer that proper, hollow sound of wooden slats banging together.

Tollhouse Museum

Tollhouse Street **t** (01493) 858900
Open Easter and late May–Sept Sun–Fri 10–5
Adm Adult £1.10, child 70p under-5s **free**

This was once the town's prison. You can visit the restored dungeons and make brass rubbings.

Cinemas
Hollywood Cinema

Marine Parade **t** (01493) 842043

Theatres
St George's Theatre

King Street **t** (01493) 858387

Wellington Theatre

Marine Parade **t** (01493) 843635

Britannia Pier Theatre

Marine Parade **t** (01493) 842209

Activities
Caister Riding School

Beach House Farm, Yarmouth Road, Caister, Great Yarmouth **t** (01473) 720444

Lessons for all ages and abilities.

Caldecott Hall Equestrian Centre

Caldecott Hall, Fritton, Great Yarmouth
t (01473) 488488

Instruction and trekking by arrangement.

Croft Farm Riding Centre

Croft Farm, Thrigby, Great Yarmouth
t (01473) 368275

Hacking and lessons.

Marina Leisure Centre

Marine Parade, Great Yarmouth **t** (01493) 851521

Leisure pool with wave machines, water chute and indoor beach.

Wizard Racing

Marine Parade, Great Yarmouth (just south of the Pleasure Beach) **t** (01493) 854041
Open Call in advance
Adm Arrive and Drive 12 laps £7; 24 laps £13; 35 laps £16

Cadet kart racing for children aged 8 and over around a 300m track.

Hunstanton

Getting there It's on the northwest coast of Norfolk within easy reach of King's Lynn via the A149 (20 miles)
Tourist office Town Hall, The Green
t (01485) 532610 **www**.west-norfolk.gov.uk

Norfolk's largest resort after Great Yarmouth, Hunstanton is a slightly more genteel affair. Its Victorian front, which was purpose-built in the mid 19th century by the wonderfully named, local landowner Henry Styleman le Strange, still manages to exude a rather refined air with its elegant gardens and carrstone cottages. And this is despite being lined with the usual collection of arcades and crazy golf courses. In summer, there's a land train to carry visitors between the front's attractions. These include the Oasis Leisure Centre (**t** (01485) 534227), which boasts a tropically heated outdoor pool complete with an aquaslide and giant inflatables, the Jungle Wonderland (**t** (01485) 535505), an indoor soft play area with ball pools, giant slides and aerial walkways, and the Sea Life Aquarium (**t** (01485) 533576), one of the best aquariums around, which, in addition to its touch pool, underwater tunnel and array of sharks, seahorses, octopi and jellyfish, has a seal hospital. You can join in the daily feeding sessions and even take a trip out to see the seals living in their natural habitat further along the coast aboard a Second World War amphibian craft.

The beach, which is long, sandy and gently shelved with rock pools at the northern end, has won Seaside Awards for cleanliness for the past eight years. You can take donkey rides and boat trips in summer. There is a full-time lifeguard service from May through to September.

Nature lovers

Banham Zoo

Kenninghall Road, Banham **t** (01953) 887771
www.banhamzoo.co.uk
Getting there It's on the B1113: follow the brown tourist signs from the A11 Cambridge–Norwich road and the A140 Ipswich–Norwich road
Open April–June 10–5; July–Sept 10–5.30; Oct–Mar 10–4 (last adm 1hr before closing)

Adm Adult £7.50, child £5.50, under-3s **free**
Café–restaurant, picnic areas, gift shop, mother and baby facilities, disabled access and parking, guided tours, on-site parking

Run by the same people responsible for the Suffolk Wildlife Park near Lowestoft, these 35 acres provide a home to some 150 species of animal including red pandas, penguins, seals, lemurs and kangaroos, although it's the zoo's big cats which are very much the feature presentation. You'll see tigers and snow leopards living in large (albeit hardly safari park-size) enclosures with glass-fronted windows which allow you to get within a few inches of the fearsome beasts. You can attend feeding sessions throughout the day (penguins at 11.30, seals at 12 noon and tigers at 3.45) and there are regular birds of prey flying demonstrations. At the recently opened children's farm, kids can meet and pet the resident donkeys, goats and sheep.

Blakeney Point

Information centre, Morston Quay **t** (01328) 830401
Getting there It's off the A149 Cromer–Hunstanton Road. There's a car park, although access to the beach itself is by foot only from Cley Beach
Open Daily dawn–dusk
Free
Refreshments (summer), shop, on-site parking (charge)

One of the country's best known bird sanctuaries, this 3.5-mile long National Trust sand and shingle spit provides a home for vast colonies of breeding terns, oyster catchers, plovers, redshank as well as common and grey seals. There are several companies offering seal-watching trips from Morston Quay, including:
Bishop's Boats **t** (01263) 740753
Jean Bean Boat Trips **t** (01263) 740038
Jim Temple Boats **t** (01263) 740791

Fritton Lake Countryworld

Fritton, Great Yarmouth **t** (01493) 488208
Getting there It's on the A143, southwest of Great Yarmouth. The nearest train station is Haddiscoe, just over 2 miles away
Open April–Sept 10–5.30; Oct Sat–Sun and half term 10–5.30
Adm Adult £5.30, child £3.90, under-3s **free**
Disabled access, disabled toilets, disabled boats for fishing, on-site parking

Woodland and landscaped gardens surrounding a 150-acre lake where rowboats and pedaloes can be hired. There's also a Heavy Horse Centre where

> **Do you know...**
> The difference between a butterfly and a moth? There are several features which distinguish them. One of the easiest to remember is that the antennae of butterflies are clubbed at the tip while the ends of moth's antennae can be a variety of shapes (none of them clubbed).

Shires and Suffolk Punches give wagon rides, a children's farm, an adventure playground and, in summer, you can take a ride on a miniature railway and watch falconry displays.

Long Sutton Butterfly and Wildlife Park

Long Sutton, Spalding **t** (01406) 363833
www.butterflyandwildlifepark.co.uk
Getting there It is off the A17 between King's Lynn and Sleeford: follow the brown tourist signs
Open Daily end Mar–Oct 10–5
Adm Adult £4.90, child £3.50, under-3s **free**, family £16.00
Tearooms, picnic areas, gift shop, guided tours, on-site parking

Long Sutton has one of the country's largest walk-through tropical houses containing hundreds of free-flying butterflies, as well as reptiles and insects. Daily flying demonstrations by eagles, owls and falcons can be seen at the on-site Lincolnshire Birds of Prey Centre and kids, big and small, can exhaust themselves in the adventure playground and tiny tots area.

Norfolk Wildlife Centre

Fakenham Road, Lenwade, Norwich **t** (01603) 872274
Getting there Lies just off the A1067, about 10 miles northwest of Norwich
Open Easter–Oct 10.30–5.30 (or dusk if earlier)
Adm Adult £4, child £2.50, under-4s **free**
Café, gift shop, disabled access, on-site parking

Forty acres filled with the sort of animals found living (at least once upon a time) in Britain and Europe, so don't go expecting to see lions, tigers and elephants. Instead, you'll have to make do with rather less exotic fare: foxes, wild boar, badgers and wallabies which, though hardly mind-bogglingly exciting, are all nonetheless presented in interesting and imaginative ways. You can watch badgers (sleeping mainly, since they're nocturnal) through a glass window looking in on their set, wander in among (and feed) the wallabies and climb a specially erected tower for views of the nests built here every spring by visiting herons. Young children are also well catered for at the rabbit and guinea pig village and there are a couple of large play areas for letting off steam.

North Norfolk Shire Horse Centre

West Runton Stables, West Runton, Cromer
t (01263) 837339
www.norfolk-shirehorse.centre.co.uk
Getting there Follow the brown tourist signs from the A149 Cromer–Sheringham Road, or the A148 Cromer–Holt Road. West Runton Station is served by Anglia Railways
Open April–Oct Mon–Fri, Sun and Bank Hols 10–5 (last adm 4), also Sat in Aug
Adm Adult £4.75, child £2.75
Café, picnic areas, gift shop, on-site parking

Dedicated to the country's great working horses, the centre is home to a variety of different Shire horse breeds and native UK ponies and has various restored wagons, carts and pieces of old machinery on display. You can meet the horses, help feed the foals and farm animals, watch harnessing and working demonstrations and go for cart rides.

Pensthorpe Waterfowl Park and Nature Reserve

Fakenham **t** (01328) 851465
Getting there Signposted from the A1067 Norwich–Fakenham Road
Open Mar–Oct 10–5; Nov–Feb 10–4.30
Adm Adult £4.90, child £2.40, family £12.50
Restaurant, countryside shop, binocular hire, disabled access, on-site parking

A wide variety of wildfowl, including spoonbills, oyster catchers, scarlet ibis and, that great British favourite, kingfishers, can be seen here in the idyllic Wensum Valley. The waterfowl on the lakes can be viewed from the very swish heated observation gallery and there are wild flower meadows and lakeside nature trails to explore.

Pettits Animal Adventure Park

Camphill, Reedham **t** (01493) 701403
Getting there Situated just off the A47, 7 miles west of Great Yarmouth. Follow the brown tourist signs from Acle
Open April–Oct daily 10–5
Adm Adult £6.75, child £6.50, under-3s **free**, family £26.50
Restaurant and burger bar, picnic areas, shop, mother and baby facilities, disabled access, on-site parking

Did you know...
That horses are pretty clever. They know, for instance, how to walk on just one toe. Well actually, they have no choice. This toe is better known as 'the hoof'; the other toes have reduced over time to small digits.

Three attractions in one: there's a small fun park with a rollercoaster, a jet plane ride, an astro-glide slide, a miniature railway and a toboggan run; an adventure play area with ball ponds, a giant snake slide and a crazy golf course and, last but by no means least, a small zoo, home to miniature horses, wallabies and birds of prey, as well as an animal petting area.

Redwings Horse Sanctuary

Caldecott Hall, Fritton, Great Yarmouth
t (01493) 488531 **www.**redwings.co.uk
Getting there It is 1 mile northeast of the village of Fritton on the A143 about 7 miles southwest of Great Yarmouth
Open April, end May–beg Oct daily 10–5; May and Oct Sun–Mon 10–5
Adm Adult £3.50, child £1.50, under-3s **free**
Café, shop, disabled facilities, leisure facilities at Caldecott Hall, free on-site parking

At Redwings Horse Sanctuary there are around a hundred horses, ponies and donkeys for children to look at, pet and feed. All the animals you can see living here have been rescued from dire circumstances, be it neglect, misfortune or potential slaughter. There are clearly marked walks though the paddocks and 'Humane Horse Handling' demonstrations are available to visitors every Wednesday at 2pm.

RSPB Titchwell Marsh Nature Reserve

Main Road, Titchwell, King's Lynn **t** (01485) 210779
Getting there Situated just off the A419, 6 miles east of Hunstanton
Open Reserve: daily dawn–dusk; visitor centre: April–Oct 10–5; Nov–Mar 10–4 **Free**
Café, picnic areas, guided tours, disabled access, on-site parking (£3, limited space available)

Coastal reserve with hides, a visitor centre, a café and picnic areas. It is particularly good for wading birds such as the avocet (the one with the funny upturned bill).

Snettisham Park Farm

Manor Lane, Snettisham, King's Lynn **t** (01485) 542425

Getting there Lies 9 miles north of King's Lynn, off the A149, close to the church, 4 miles south of Hunstanton
Adm Adult £7, child £5, family £23.50
Tearoom, shop
   You can meet and feed a range of farmyard animals and take a safari through a red deer park where the deer will happily eat from your hand. There's also a children's farmyard and a very good adventure playground.

Thrigby Hall Wildlife Gardens
Filby, Great Yarmouth **t** (01493) 369477
Getting there It is 7 miles northwest of Great Yarmouth off the A1064
Open Daily 10–5
Adm Adult £5.50, child £3.90, under-4s **free**
Café, gift shop, picnic area, disabled access, on-site parking
   250 year-old park providing a dwelling place for various exotic creatures from Asia including gibbons, red pandas, toucans, otters, monkeys, leopards and crocodiles (living in the Forest House). The monkeys are fed at 3.30 and the otters at 4. There is a children's play area and a tree walk.

Tropical Butterfly Gardens
Great Ellingham **t** (01953) 453175
www.tropicalbutterflyworld.com
Getting there It's off the A11 Norwich–Thetford road, on the B1077
Open Mon–Sat 9–5.30, Sun 10–5.30
Adm Adult £3.50, child £2.50
Café, shop, guided tours
   Butterflies, exotic birds and fish, and falconry displays held at 11.45 and 2.45, Sunday 12.30 and 2.45.

Look at this!

Caister Castle Car Collection
Caister-on-Sea, Great Yarmouth **t** (01572) 787251
Getting there It's 1 mile from Caister-on-Sea just off the A1064 and about 3 miles north of Great Yarmouth. Follow the brown tourist signs
Open Late May–Sept Mon–Fri and Sun 10–4.30
Adm Varies, call in advance
Picnic area, refreshments, disabled facilities, on-site parking
   The resort of Caister, a few miles north of Great Yarmouth, boasts a long, sandy beach in addition to this large collection of vintage motor cars in the grounds of a 15th-century castle. There are over 200 exhibits, including an 1893 Panhard et Levassor, the first 'real' car ever made.

Cockley Cley Iceni Village and Museum
Cockley Cley, Swaffham **t** (01760) 721339
Getting there It's 3 miles south of Swaffham off the A1065
Open April–Oct 11–5.30 (July–Aug from 10)
Adm Adult £3.50, child £1.80
On-site parking, tea room, gift shop, disabled access
   Recreation of an Iceni settlement believed to have existed here 2,000 years ago.

Dinosaur Adventure Park
For further information *see* p.129.

Ecotech
Swaffham **t** (01760) 726100 **www.**ecotech.org.uk
Getting there It's signposted from the A47 King's Lynn–Norwich Road
Open Easter–Sept daily 10–5; Oct–Easter Sun–Fri 10–4
Adm (All inclusive) adult £5.90, child £4.55, family £17.40
Café–restaurant, shop, disabled access, adapted toilets, on-site parking
   It calls itself an 'environmental discovery centre' and its aim seems to be to get children interested in the environment by showing them the various potential disasters that have and, indeed, could befall it. You can discover what scientists think happened to the dinosaurs (hit by a meteorite seems to be the most popular explanation), learn about floods, volcanoes and hurricanes and find out how climate change is likely to make all of these increasingly common in years to come. You can also find out what you can do to prevent the world's imminent destruction. Housed in East Anglia's largest timber-framed building with a computer-controlled heating system to save energy and a rainwater recycling scheme, the centre has certainly put its money where its beliefs are. Although a little worthy and a tad alarmist, it's all presented in a fresh and lively way and is actually a lot of fun. The most fun part of your trip, however, is bound to be your climb to the top of the country's largest wind turbine, for fantastic panoramic views out over East Anglia.

Norfolk and Suffolk Aviation Museum

Buckeroo Way, The Street, Flixton, Bungay
t (01986) 896644
Getting there It's on the B1062, off the A143, 1 mile west of Bungay
Open April–Oct Sun–Thurs 10–5; Nov–Mar Tues, Wed and Sun 10–4
Free
Picnic areas, shop, mother and baby facilities, guided tours, disabled access, on-site parking

During the early years of the Second World War, when Britain was under almost constant attack by the German Air Force (who hoped to establish dominance of the skies in preparation for a land invasion), it was the RAF bases of East Anglia and Kent that led the fight back, and sent out the planes for the Battle of Britain which finally thwarted Hitler's plans.

Several of the region's former bases have now been turned into museums where you can find out more about the conflict and see (and often climb aboard) some of the great flying machines that secured Britain's freedom.

At the Norfolk and Suffolk Aviation Museum, for instance, (which is made up of the 446th Bomber Group Museum, Royal Observer Corps Museum, RAF Bomber Command Museum and the Air Sea Rescue and Coastal Command Museum), there's a vast array of aviation paraphernalia and a World War II hangar with over 25 historic aircraft on display.

Norfolk Rural Life Museum and Union Farm

Beech House, Gressenhall, East Dereham
t (01362) 860385
www.norfolk.gov.uk/tourism/museums/charges.htm
Getting there The museum is 3 miles west of Dereham and is signed from the A47 and B1146
Open Mid May–Nov daily 10–5
Adm Adult £4.80, child £2.70, family £10.95
Café–restaurant, gift shop, picnic areas, guided tours, mother and baby facilities, disabled access, on-site parking

Displays of agricultural and village rural life in a former workhouse adjoining a recreated 1920s farm with working horses (cart rides available) and traditional East Anglian animal breeds such as large, black pigs, red poll cattle and Norfolk horn sheep. There are regular talks on workhouse life

and quizzes and quests for the children taking them all over the museum and farm. In July, kids can help with the annual haymaking.

Royal Air Force Air Defence Radar Museum

RAF Neatishead, Norwich **t** (01692) 633309
www.neatishead.raf.mod.uk
Getting there It's signed from the A1062 Wroxham–Horning Road
Open Tues, Thurs, Bank Hol Mon and 2nd Sat each month 10–3
Adm Adult £3, child £1
Refreshments, guided tours, on-site parking

At the Royal Air Force Air Defence Radar Museum, which is housed in an original 1942 building, you can visit a restored Battle of Britain Ground Control Interception room and see films and documentary footage about the use of radar (Radio Direction and Range) during the Second World War. The museum won't be of much interest to younger children but older kids will enjoy learning how the perfection of this technology, which was largely thanks to the work of the British scientist Robert Watson-Watt, provided a vital early-warning system for this country and played such a large part in helping the RAF win the Battle of Britain.

The Village Experience

Burgh St Margaret, Fleggburgh **t** (01493) 369770
www.thevillage-experience.com
Getting there It's on the A1064 between Acle and Caister, 7 miles northwest of Great Yarmouth. The nearest train station is four miles away in Acle
Open Easter–Oct daily 10–5
Adm Adult £5.95, child £3.95, under-4s **free**, family £17.50

> ### Tell me a story: RADAR
> The invention of RADAR is largely thanks to the work of the scientist Robert Watson-Watt who gave the first demonstration of his *Radio Direction and Range* apparatus (hence RADAR) in 1935. Watson-Watt had been experimenting with a primitive form of RADAR as early as 1919, when he used radio waves to spot incoming thunderstorms. From 1935, as Europe moved steadily towards war, he began working in secret on the military version which was able to provide Britain with a vital early-warning system throughout World War II.

Café, tearoom, lakeside barbeque, picnic areas, mother and baby facilities, on-site parking

Recreated 19th-century village offering old-fashioned fairground rides, puppet shows, a miniature steam railway, vintage motorbikes, a working sawmill, farmyard animals and 35 acres of leafy woodland to explore, not to mention a large, indoor, soft play area and a science centre: the 'Exploratorium'.

Wroxham Barns

Turnstead Road, Hoveton **t** (01603) 783762
Getting there It's 7 miles from Norwich along the A1151
Open Barns: daily 10–5; fair: April–Sept 10–5; dates vary, so call in advance
Adm Barns and fair: **free** (individual charges for fairground rides); junior farm: £2.25, under-3s **free**
Tearooms, craft shops, on-site parking

Traditional East Anglian crafts such as decorative glass-making, pottery, woodworking, stitchcraft, furniture-making, printing and cider-pressing, demonstrated in a collection of 18th-century barns. There's also a Junior Farm and, in summer, a traditional fair with swing boats, roundabouts, a ferris wheel and old end-of-the-pier slot machines.

Steam power

Bressingham Steam Museum

For further information *see* p.129.

Bure Valley Railway

Norwich Road, Aylsham **t** (01263) 733858
www.bvrw.co.uk
Getting there Aylsham station is midway between Norwich and Cromer on the A140. Wroxham Station is adjacent to the Anglia Railways Bittern Line Wroxham (Hoveton) Station which receives direct services from Norwich, Cromer and Sheringham
Fares Return: adult £6.90, child £3.75, family £19; train and cruise: adult £11, child £7.50, family £37.50. Under-5s **free**
Restaurant, picnic areas, shop, tourist office, wheelchair access on to some carriages, on-site parking at both stations

North Norfolk Railway

The Station, Sheringham **t** (01263) 820800
www.nnrailway.co.uk; talking timetable **t** (01263) 820808
Getting there Sheringham Station is on the opposite side of the road to the Anglia Railways station of the same name and signposted from the A1082
Open Mar Sat–Sun; April–Oct daily; Nov Sat only; Santa and Mince pie Specials in Dec
Fares Standard steam fares adult £7.50, child £4, under-4s **free**, family (2+3) £21
Buffet at Weybourne, bookshop, souvenir shop, model railway shop at Sheringham, wheelchair access, on-site parking at both stations

Full-size steam and diesel railway, known as the 'Poppy Line', running along a scenic stretch of the North Norfolk coast between Sheringham and Holt. Plenty of opportunities for getting off and exploring the wooded countryside. At Holt you can ride the 'Holt Flyer' horse-drawn carriage into the town.

Wells and Walsingham Light Railway

Stiffkey Road, Wells-next-the-Sea **t** (01328) 710631
Getting there It's just off the A149, 300 yards east of the A149 Wighton and Walsingham Road junction. Follow the brown signs
Open Easter–Sept daily
Refreshments served from Wells signal box, on-site parking

Steam train rides along the North Norfolk coast, between Wells-next-the-Sea and Walsingham. Here you can visit the ruins of an Augustinian Priory and visit the cells or enter a restored Georgian courtroom in the Shirehall Museum, where you can choose between standing in the dock or sitting in the judge's chair.

SPECIAL TRIPS

RSPB Nature Reserve, Minsmere

Westleton, Saxmundham **t** (01728) 648281
Getting there It's off the A12, about 8 miles north of Aldeburgh
Open Reserve: Wed–Mon 9–9 (dusk if earlier); visitor centre: summer 9–5; winter 9–4
Adm Adult £5, child £3, family £10 (2+4)
Café, picnic area, shop, mother and baby facilities, guided tours, disabled access, on-site parking

At 2,300 acres, Minsmere is one of the largest nature reserves in the country and at different times of the year it is home to 333 species of bird, 35 species of mammal (including otters and red deer), 640 species of plants and 33 species of butterflies. Despite the abundance of wildlife, it is for the birds that people principally visit.

Start off at the visitor centre (which has a tearoom and gift shop), where you can hire binoculars and pick up leaflets before heading off along a variety of trails through heath, woodland and marshes, stopping off every now and then to see what you can you can spot from the observation hides.

Minsmere is home to some of the country's rarest birds. During the summer visitors are likely to see avocets and hear booming bitterns (Minsmere has a quarter of the British population of both species). In the winter many wading birds and wildfowl including wigeon, teal and Bewick's swan make the reserve their home. Step quietly through Minsmere's 143 acres of woodland and you might see woodpeckers, nightingales and warblers.

A host of activities are put on throughout the year including guided walks, birdwatching classes for beginners, and safaris.

Watch the birdie!

Some people find birdwatching boring. Others really enjoy it, to the point where it becomes a passion. Birdwatching demands a high degree of patience and this will not suit everyone. You also have to learn to be very, very quiet so that birds will not be disturbed.

Birds are all over the place, even in big cities and towns and you don't need to go to a nature reserve to study them. But nature reserves have the advantage of playing host to rare birds or birds which need a special type of environment to survive, and so they attract large numbers of bird watchers (or 'twitchers').

To be a bird watcher you need a pair of binoculars. Some nature reserves (such as Minsmere) have binoculars available to rent.

A notebook is also essential for birdwatching. This allows you to write or sketch obvious features about a bird, which will help you to identify the bird you have spotted. Noting the date and time when you saw the bird is also useful, as are any features of the bird's behaviour or its call.

There are a number of birdwatching clubs (Minsmere has a society especially for children). Joining one of these is a good way to find out more about how and where to go birdwatching by talking to more experienced members.

AROUND AND ABOUT

Bricks and mortar

Framlingham Castle

Castle Street, Framlingham, Woodbridge
t (01728) 724189 **www**.english-heritage.org.uk
Getting there Situated on the B1116 about 20 miles northeast of Ipswich
Open April–Sept daily 10–6; Oct daily 10–5, Nov–Mar daily 10–4
Adm Adult £3.20, child £1.60
Shop, guided tours, disabled access, on-site parking

This 12th-century castle has been, in its time, a royal residence (this is where, in 1553, Mary I heard of her succession upon the death of her brother Edward VI, and where she waited while Lady Jane Grey enjoyed her brief nine day reign), an Elizabethan prison, a poorhouse and even a school. Extremely well preserved, the medieval curtain wall linking the castle's 13 towers still survives; in fact, you can walk along it. Framlington Castle puts on a range of medieval-themed events over the summer including plays, music recitals and archery competitions. Activity books for children are available.

Ickworth House and Park

The Rotunda, Ickworth, Bury St Edmunds
t (01284) 735270 www.nationaltrust.org.uk
Getting there It's on the A143, 2 miles south of Bury St Edmunds
Open House and garden: April–Oct Tues–Sun and Bank Hol Mon 1–5; park: daily 7–7
Adm House and garden: adult £5.20, child £2.20; park only: adult £2.20, child 70p
Café–restaurant, picnic areas, shop, disabled access, mother and baby facilities, on-site parking

The people who run Ickworth have done their best to make the stately home as interesting for children as possible. You can pick up a 'handy' box at the entrance full of interesting whatnots and doodahs – candles, pieces of chandelier – which you must match with the ones displayed somewhere in the house. There are also quizzes and trails and children can take part in a free 'touch' tour of the house. Nonetheless, for all their efforts, your kids will probably still prefer the grand Italianate gardens. There is also a deer park, woodland walks, a family cycle trail and an adventure playground. A new, luxury family hotel opened in the house's east wing at the end of 2001 (p.195).

Kentwell Hall

Long Melford **t** (01787) 310207 www.kentwell.co.uk
Getting there It's 11 miles south of Bury St Edmunds, off the A134
Open 1 April–10 June, 11 July–23 Sept, 30 Sept–28 Oct daily 12–5
Adm Adult £5.70, child £3.50, under-5s **free**
Café–restaurant, gift shop, on-site parking

Kentwell Hall is a large Tudor Manor house that, on selected weekends, is turned into a sort of Tudor theme park when around 250 costumed volunteers attempt a mass recreation of Tudor domestic life. All aspects are covered: they cook Tudor meals in the Tudor kitchen, play Tudor music in the Tudor minstrels gallery, bake Tudor bread in the Tudor bakehouse, spin Tudor pots on the Tudor pottery wheel, make Tudor butter and cheese in the Tudor dairy and tend to the Tudor-style animals in the Tudor farmyard, stables, dovecote and goathouse. The volunteers are even expected to speak in Tudor style, adopting mid 16th-century speech patterns throughout the day. It's all tremendous fun and fascinating for children who will have lots of opportunities to join in the fun and games.

Obviously, during the rest of the year, the house is a good deal quieter but, nonetheless, still well worth a visit.

In the house, look out for the Brueghel-style ceiling in the parlour, which is decorated with pictures depicting Tudor children's games and, in the grounds, for the Tudor Rose-shaped maze and (if you fancy getting away from the overwhelming Tudorishness for a while) the peaceful woodland walks.

Buckets and spades

Aldeburgh and the Suffolk Heritage Coast

Getting there Take the A12 from London or Colchester and follow the signs east. The nearest train station is Saxmundham, about 10 miles away, from where you can catch the hourly no.81 bus to Aldeburgh. A taxi from Saxmundham should cost in the region of £10
Tourist office The Cinema, 51 High Street (open April–Oct only) **t** (01728) 453637

There could be no greater contrast between the seaside towns of Aldeburgh and Lowestoft, and yet both are strangely typical of the region. Suffolk's coast is a peculiar entity. At its north end is Lowestoft, a typically English, typically vibrant, slightly downmarket seaside resort. To the south is the functional freight ferry port of Felixstowe, while in between lie Aldeburgh and the Suffolk Heritage Coast, a 40-mile stretch of some of the most beautifully unspoilt coastline in the country, with numerous areas of 'special scientific interest' and clusters of tiny seaside villages ignored by public transport, and only accessible via the minor roads running east of the A12.

Beautifully unspoilt by man that is; the sea is doing its best to do a bit of spoiling, hungrily eating away at the coast. Half of the old town of Dunwich, about 6 miles north of Aldeburgh, is now underwater (locals say that on stormy nights you can hear the submerged church bells ringing out), although Aldeburgh itself has fared slightly better – the sea still has a few yards to go before it reaches the town – and, for the moment at least, it makes a pleasant, peaceful base from which to explore this grand coastal sweep. You can follow the pebble beach all the way from here to Thorpeness, about 3 miles north, without seeing a single building (and probably not a single person – outside of the high season and weekends) along the way.

Aldeburgh has no specific attractions beyond the Elizabethan Moot Hall, which is the town's museum, but it nonetheless welcomes its fair share of visitors bent on 'getting away from it all' among the painted cottages and historic buildings – watching fishermen winching their boats onto the shingle beach and sampling the excellent cod and Dover sole served up at the town's surprisingly trendy collection of restaurants.

In June, the town does comes to life for its annual music festival, first founded by the composer Benjamin Britten, whose grave is in the churchyard, and again for the town carnival in August, when there's a parade and firework display.

About five miles south of here is Orford Castle, a 90ft 18-sided keep offering fantastic views out over the countryside and North Sea. A range of events including puppet-making workshops, storytelling sessions, mask-making demonstrations and music recitals are put on throughout the year and there's a free children's activity sheet available. When the castle was first constructed in the 12th century, it was actually positioned right on the shoreline, but the sea subsequently retreated. You can find out more about the shifting nature of the coastline in these parts at the nearby Dunwich Underwater Exhibition, which has finds recovered by divers from the submerged town.

Other local areas of interest include Walberswick, about 10 miles north, which is well known locally for its excellent crabbing (it even holds competitions in summer (see box); Dunwich Heath, 5 miles north, an area of ancient heathland home to numerous rare breeds of wildlife including night-jars, antlions, damselflies and red deer (it also has

an outdoor playground and guided walks and nature trails are offered from the information room at the Coastguard Cottages t (01728) 645805) and the nearby Minsmere Beach, which is made up of a mixture of sand and pebbles and makes a pleasant spot for a paddle. Display boards by the beach show where the village of Dunwich originally stood before it fell into the sea. Various events for children such as beach art and gorse shakes are organised here during the summer and there is a holiday club for 6–12 year olds focusing on environmental activities. Minsmere RSPB Nature Reserve is is also nearby (p.142).

Dunwich Underwater Exploration Exhibition

The Craft Shop, Front Street, Orford, Woodbridge t (01394) 450678
Getting there Orford lies on the B1084, 20 miles northeast of Ipswich
Open Daily 11–5
Adm 50p
(*See* above)

Orford Castle

Castle Terrace, Orford t (01394) 450472
www.english-heritage.org.uk
Getting there It's in Orford, on the B1084, 20 miles northeast of Ipswich
Open April–Sept daily 10–6; Oct daily 10–5; Nov–Mar Wed–Sun 10–1 and 2–4
Adm Adult £3.10, child £1.60
Shop, on-site parking

Lowestoft

Getting there Lowestoft lies on the east coast of Suffolk, just south of Great Yarmouth (approx. 10 miles via the A14) and southeast of Norwich (22 miles approx, via the A146)
Tourist office East Point Pavilion, Royal Plain t (01502) 533600

Britain's most easterly town is a thriving holiday resort which, if not quite as overwhelmingly touristy as Great Yarmouth , is still pretty lively. There are six beaches in all, most of which are sandy with some shingle and the most popular, South Beach, has two piers and a children's play area, and is patrolled by lifeguards in summer. Young kids will like the Discoverig 2, on the Esplanade (housed in the same building as the tourist office) a multi-level play area, while older kids will probably prefer a trip to the Pleasurewood

Catch crabs at Walberswick

The British Open Crabbing Championships, held every August in Walberswick (just a short distance for Southwold), attracts hundreds of contestants. Some grown ups take the event extremely seriously, closely guarding the reciepe for what they hope will be prize-winning bait but in the main its just a bit of fun with the proceeds of the entry money going to charity. It's a giggle for kids who need only turn up with a bit of bacon or chicken. The rules are simple. Over a 90 minute period and with a single line, the prize (last year it was £50!) and trophy goes to the person landing the single heaviest crab. For a few hints on technique see below. It only costs a £1 to enter, and don't worry if you've left your crab-catching equipment at home. All equipment (buckets, bait and line) is available on site for a small charge. T-shirts advertising the event, with the charming slogan 'I caught crabs at Walberswick', generally prove to be a big hit with parents and children alike. For further details t (01502) 722359.

If you miss the competition, you can easily go crabbing on your own. All you need is a bit of bacon (or a chicken carcass), string and a small bucket (filled with water).

Tie a piece of bacon (or, if you want to catch many little crabs at once, the carcass of a chicken) to the string and weight it with a stone. Drop it into the water so that the bait sits on the bottom. Then, wait. When a crab grabs the bacon, pull it out and shake it off into the bucket. See how many you can catch. Make sure children are well supervised at all times. Once you've finished, the crabs should be gently tipped back into the water.

Hills theme park, just outside the town, which has over 50 rides. Also look out for the East Anglia Transport Museum, set in three acres of woodland a few miles southwest of the town (p.148) and the Suffolk Wildlife Park (5 miles south, p.147).

Discoverig 2

East Point Pavilion, Royal Plain t (01502) 533600
Open Summer daily 9.30–5.30; winter Mon–Fri 10.30–5, weekends 10–5
Adm Over 3s £2.50 Mon–Fri, £2.95 weekends and school hols; under-3s £2
Refreshments

A North Sea oil rig with ropes, scramble nets, tubes, ball pools and a giant slide.

Pleasurewood Hills

Leisure Way, Corton t (01502) 586000
www.pleasurewoodhills.co.uk
Open Times vary, call in advance to check
Adm Over 1.3m tall £12.75, 1–1.3m tall £10.75, under 1m tall **free**; conc £8
Various cafés, fast food restaurants and picnic areas, some disabled access, on-site parking

This fun park includes a 'Tidal Wave' water-coaster, a 'Megadrive' spinning ride and, its most hi-tech offering, the 'Cannonball Express', a replica train which plunges around tight curves and down into dark tunnels. There are also dodgems, mini motorbikes and a special area for under-9s, 'Woody's Little Big Park', which has 10 rides including a Waltzer and a Sky Diver Slide.

Cinemas
Marina
The Marina t (01502) 573318
Hollywood
London Road South t (01502) 588355/ 564567

Theatres
Marina Theatre
The Marina t (01502) 573318
Seagull Theatre
Morton Road t (01502) 562863

Southwold

Getting there Southwold is situated midway between Lowestoft and Aldeburgh. Take the A12 from London or Colchester and follow the signs for the A1095. By rail: travel to Ipswich from Liverpool St, change onto the Lowestoft line and get off at Hailsworth where you can pick up the X99 bus or take a taxi (20-30 mins, £12).
Tourist office 69 High Street t (01502) 724729

Once a busy fishing port, Southwold is today an unspoilt and sleepy coastal town. Its Blue-Flag sand and shingle beach is lined with colourful beach chalets which can be hired for the day (t 01502-724818). There's a full lifeguard service and plenty of traditional fun to be had, such as putting, boating and a model yacht pond all within easy reach of the beach. The privately-owned pier is in the process of major refurbishment and is currently home to an amusement arcade and café which is open all day during the summer months.

The big name in Southwold is Adnams Brewery which owns the town's two best hotels (the Crown and the Swan). Everything about the place is understated: the High Street has none of the tackiness of larger seaside resorts, the Market Place is little bigger than a handkerchief and the town's diminutive museum and Sailors' Reading Room are hardly buzzing and hold an eclectic mix of model ships and nautical memorabilia. Another slant on the area's nautical history can be obtained at the Alfred Corry Museum which provides an insight into the lives of the Southwold Lifeboat crews. Housed in the old Cromer Lifeboat shed, which was removed from Cromer Pier in 1997, the museum's star attraction is the *Alfred Corry* lifeboat which was built in 1893 at a cost of £490.7s.6d.

Otherwise, the best place to head for is the harbour. Set at the mouth of the River Blythe this pretty spot has a pronounced salty tang about it with fishing smacks bobbing on the water, wooden jetties and the occasional sea dog repairing his nets. From here there is a footpath which leads to a tiny ferry which crosses the river to nearby Walberswick (*see* p.145). Here there are rustic fisherman's huts, plenty of crabs for sale and some of the best fish and chips in the area, courtesy of The Harbour Inn (*see* p.152).

Alfred Corry Museum

Ferry Road **t** (01502) 723200
Open Mon, Tues, Thurs & Fri: 2–5pm, Sat & Sun 10am–noon, 2–5pm; Nov-Mar (Bank Holidays & fine weekends only) 10.30–noon, 2–3.30pm)
Free

Southwold Ferry

Operates Easter-May Sat-Sun 10–12.30, 2–4.30; Jun-Aug daily 10–12.30, 2–4.30
Cost 40p

Southwold Museum

9-11 Victoria Street **t** (01502) 723374
Open from March daily 2.30–4.30pm
Free

Sailors' Reading Room

East Cliff
Open Daily 9–5
Free

Nature lovers

Baylham House Rare Breeds Farm

Mill Lane, Baylham **t** (01473) 830264
Getting there It's 6 miles northwest of Ipswich off the B113
Open Easter–Sept Tues–Sun and Bank Hol Mon 11–5
Adm Adult £3.50, child £1.75, under-4s **free**
Picnic areas, gift shop, refreshments, disabled access
Show farm on the site of a former Roman settlement with rare breeds of cattle, pigs, sheep and goats as well as a children's paddock.

Brandon Country Park and Thetford Forest

Visitor Centre, Bury Road, Brandon **t** (01842) 810185
Getting there Situated 1 mile south of Brandon on the B1106, and about 12 miles north of Bury St Edmunds
Open Park: daily dawn–dusk; visitor centre: April–Sept daily 10–5; Oct–Mar daily 10–4
Brandon Country Park is located within Thetford's thick pinewood forest and boasts a walled garden, four waymarked forest walks (including a 'find the tree' trail and a history trail) and numerous cycle paths. The visitor centre has interactive displays and can provide information and leaflets.

The Forestry Commission organizes numerous events in and around Thetford Forest, including Red Deer Safaris, Fungi Walks, Desert Rat Memorial Tours (the 7th Armoured Division hid themselves away in the forest while they prepared for the Normandy Landings of 1944) and walks to look at the forest's bat boxes. Contact the Recreation Department, Forest District Office, Santon Downham, Brandon **t** (01842) 810271.

British Bird of Prey and Nature Centre

Stonham Barns, Pettaugh Road, Stonham Aspel **t** (01449) 711425
Getting there It's off the A140 between Ipswich and Norwich
Open daily 10.30–5.30
Adm Adult £2.95, child £2, under-4s **free**, family £9.50
Café, picnic areas, crafts shops, on-site parking
Collection of aviaries housing numerous birds of prey including owls, vultures, hawks, buzzards, peregrine falcons and eagles with flying demonstrations held daily at 12 and 2.30 in summer. In the

nature centre you'll find rabbits, chinchillas and guinea pigs for kids to feed, as well as goats, Shetland ponies, ferrets, a butterfly walk, a bath-house and a special dipping pond. There is also a play area and a crazy golf course.

Easton Farm Park

Easton, near Wickham Market **t (01728) 746475**
www.eastonfarmpark.co.uk
Getting there It's about 12 miles northeast of Ipswich, follow the brown tourist signs from the A12
Open mid March–Sept Tues–Sun and Bank Hol Mon 10.30–6
Adm Adult £4.10, child £2.60, under-3s **free**
Tearoom, picnic areas, gift shop, mother and baby facilities, disabled access, on-site parking

Victorian model farm situated in the picturesque Deben River Valley. Kids can watch cows being milked in the dairy centre, feed the goats and sheep, take pony and cart rides at weekends and during the school holidays visit the working black-smith and play on the toy tractors in the adventure playground.

Orford Ness

Quay Street, Orford, Woodbridge
Getting there Ferry from Orford Quay. Orford is 14 miles northeast of Ipswich, take the A12, B1078, then the B1084
Open April–Oct Thurs, Fri and Sat 10–2
Adm Adult £5.20, child £2.60, under-3s **free** (ferry included in price)
Guided tours

This isolated shingle spit provides a home to numerous nesting coastal birds but is accessible only by ferry (maximum stay 3.5 hours). There's a children's 'spy-trail', too.

Otter Trust

Earsham, Bungay **t (01986) 893470**
Getting there Situated just off the A143, 1 mile west of Bungay
Open April–Oct daily 10.30–6
Adm Adult £5, child £3, under-3s **free**
Shop, tearoom, picnic area, play area, disabled access, on-site parking

This is the largest and oldest otter conservation organization in Britain and the only one dedicated to breeding otters (including both the British and the Asian short-clawed otter) in order to return them back into the wild. The trust has, so far, rein-

troduced around a hundred captive-bred otters back into the British countryside. Though they're easily the cutest of our native mammals, they're also the shyest, so while you're waiting for them to put in an appearance, get acquainted with some of the centre's other residents: you'll come across geese, grebe and muntjac deer living in and around three large lakes. There is also a children's play area and there are a number of riverside walks.

Rede Hall Farm

Rede, Bury St Edmunds **t (01284) 850695**
Getting there It is 6 miles south of Bury St Edmunds on the A143
Open April–Sept daily 10–5 (last adm 4)
Adm Adult £4, child £2.50
Café–restaurant, gift shop, mother and baby facilities, disabled access, on-site parking

A themed 1940s farm where children can help bottle feed lambs and take pony and wagon rides.

RSPB Nature Reserve, Minsmere

For further information *see* p.142.

Suffolk Wildlife Park

Kessingland, Lowestoft **t (01502) 740291**
www.suffolkwildlifepark.co.uk
Getting there It's on the A12, 20 miles south of Great Yarmouth, 5 miles south of Lowestoft
Open April–June daily 10–5; July–Sept daily 10–5.30; Oct–Mar daily 10–4 (last adm 1hr before closing)
Adm Adult £6.95, child £4.95, under-3s **free**
Café–restaurant, picnic areas, gift shop, mother and baby facilities, disabled access, on-site parking

All African wildlife is here: you'll find lions, chee-tahs, giraffes, chimps, hyenas, zebras and ostriches living in this 100-acre walk-through safari park (you can climb aboard the free road train if you don't fancy tackling the whole thing on foot). Feeding talks and animal handling demonstrations are given throughout the day: at 12.30 you can help feed the giraffes – their great necks swooping down to take the leaves delicately from your hand – before watching the big cats being fed at 3.15 (thankfully, you are not expected to give the meat directly to the lions or to get the cheetahs to chase after you), while at 4 you may have the opportunity to handle a snake. Birds of prey flying displays take place on Tuesdays and Wednesdays during the summer. There are also explorer trails, play areas, a bouncy castle and a crazy golf course. Various special events aimed at children are laid on over the summer, including their 'Bugs Week', when kids can come and handle a range of creepy crawlies.

Valley Farm White Animal Collection

Wickham Market, Woodbridge **t** (01728) 746916
www.valleyfarm.demon.co.uk
Getting there It is signposted off the B1078 towards Charlesfield, off the A12
Open Daily 10–4
Free (A donation to charity is suggested)

Valley Farm is home to a slightly odd collection of animals including Baa the sheep, Camelot the camel, Muffin the mule and Billy and Gruff the goats, as well as the only breeding herd of Carmargue horses (they come from the south of France) in the UK, which are available for rides.

Look at this!

Museum of East Anglian Life

Iliffe Way, Stowmarket **t** (01449) 612229
www.suffolkcc.gov.uk/central/meal
Getting there Lies in the centre of Stowmarket opposite the Asda supermarket, signposted from the A14 and B115. It's a 10min walk from Stowmarket train station
Open April–Oct Mon–Sat 10–5, Sun 11–5
Adm Adult £4.50, child £3, under-4s **free**, family (2+3) £14.75
Restaurant, picnic areas, gift shop, some disabled access, adapted toilets

This 70-acre site contains just a dozen or so historic buildings and you'll have to put in a lot of walking if you hope to see them all. Nonetheless, the riverside setting is very pretty and all the exhibits are presented in an informative and entertaining way. As you enter you'll find yourself in Home Close, which is surrounded by various old buildings: an Abbots Hall Barn, a stable , a cart lodge and a couple of converted barns where you can see displays and videos on East Anglian farming life. Beyond this is an area of woodland before you reach the charcoal-maker, the adventure playground (look out for Remus, the Suffolk Punch horse whose enclosure is nearby) and, the real highlight of the site, the riverside area where you'll find a watermill, a Victorian kitchen and a windpump. Demonstrations of traditional crafts,

such as basket-making, are given at weekends and Family Fun days, dressing-up days, treasure hunts, country fairs and craft days are held in summer.

West Stow Anglo Saxon Village

Visitor centre, Icklingham Road, West Stow, Bury St Edmunds **t** (01284) 728718
www.stedmundsbury.gov.uk/wtseesub.htm
Getting there It's off the A1101 5 miles northwest of Bury St Edmunds. Follow the brown tourist signs
Open Daily 10–5 (last adm 4)
Adm Adult £4.50, child £3.50, family (2+3) £13
Refreshments, gift shop, picnic areas, mother and baby facilities, some disabled access, on-site parking

This replica village has been reconstructed on the site of a real Anglo Saxon village originally built here sometime in the 5th–6th century AD. The seven buildings have been erected using the same techniques, tools and building materials that would have been used by the original builders, so it's pretty authentic. Nothing is roped off, so you're free to examine the buildings from every possible angle (and kids usually do) and meet the pigs and chickens who also live on the site. Original finds from the site are displayed in the visitor centre and the village is surrounded by a 125-acre country park with woodland, heathland and trails along the banks of the River Lark. Activity days, when kids can try on Saxon costumes and go on guided walks, are organized during the summer.

Steam power

East Anglia Transport Museum

Chapel Road, Carlton Colville **t** (01502) 518459
Getting there Situated 3 miles southwest of Lowestoft on the B1314, signposted from the A12 and A146. Nearest train station at Oulton Broad
Open Easter and May Sun and Bank Hol Mon 11–5.30; June–Sept Wed and Sat 2–5, Sun, Bank Hol Mon 11–5.30; Aug daily 2–5
Adm Adult £4.50, child £3, under-5s **free**
Café, picnic areas, bookshop, mother and baby facilities, tours, some disabled access, on-site parking

You can clamber aboard trams, steam rollers, lorries, cars, buses and trolley-buses, and even go for a ride through a 1930s street scene. Rides are included in the entry price.

WHERE TO EAT

Aldeburgh

The Captain's Cabin
170 High Street **t** (01728) 452520
Open Daily 10–5 (lunches served noon; last orders 3.30 weekdays, 5pm Saturdays)

With outside seating, a couple of high chairs and a convenient location in the centre of town, this is a good place to head for. The menu is reasonably varied and includes simple snacks through to fish and chips. Children's menu.

Regatta
171 High Street **t** (01728) 452011
Open Daily noon–2, 6–10

Smart and trendy bistro with a blackboard showing a daily selection of fresh fish. A good choice of modern British and traditional favourites. If you fancy a picnic but can't be bothered to make one, Regatta can provide a hamper for the beach (they'll even include the plates and cutlery).

Cambridge

Bella Pasta
The Mill, Newnham Road, Cambridge
t (01223) 367507
Open 12 noon–11

Children's menu full of mini Italian favourites, plus colouring books and crayons to keep the kids occupied while they wait for their food.

Brown's
23 Trumpington Street **t** (01223) 461655
Open Mon–Sat 11.30–11.30, Sun 12 noon–11

Housed in Addenbrooke Hospital's former outpatient unit opposite the Fitzwilliam Museum, this huge branch of the ever family-friendly chain serves a combination of French and American cuisine (and a good line in meaty pies) and can offer a range of children's choices; the hamburgers are particularly recommended. The pale yellow dining-room is kept cool by overhead fans and a mother and baby room and high chairs are provided.

Café Rouge
24–26 Bridge Street **t** (01223) 364961
Open Mon noon–11, Tue–Sat 10–11, Sun 10–10.30

Well-situated for Cambridge's major sights, this child-friendly café chain has a good supply of high chairs as well as activity packs and a separate children's menu which includes mini-portions of the adult fare.

Cambridge Blue
85-87 Gwydir Street **t** (01223) 361382
Open Daily 11-11

Family friendly pub which serves evening and lunchtime meals. Children are allowed in the conservatory and in the large garden which has a Wendy house and various toys. Children's menu available.

Cambridge Tea Room
1 Wheeler Street **t** (01223) 357503
Open Daily 10–6

Opposite the tourist information centre, this tearoom serves good cream teas, as well as baked potatoes and sandwiches.

Copper Kettle
King's Parade **t** (01223) 365068
Open Daily 8.30–6

A Cambridge institution where generations of undergraduates have come to discuss the meaning of life over coffee and a Chelsea bun. Overlooking the glorious vista of King's College, it is a good place for a 20-minute sandwich pit-stop. No credit cards accepted.

Don Pasquale
12 Market Hill **t** (01223) 367063
Open Mon–Thur 8–6, Fri & Sat 8am–9.30pm, Sun 9–6

With seating on the market square and a plentiful supply of high chairs this is a fun place to come for a slice of pizza, if blood sugar is running low, and watch the world go by.

Fitzbillies
52 Trumpington Street **t** (01223) 352500
Open Mon–Fri 8.30–5, Sat–Sun 8.30–5.30

Good for cakes and scones.

Hobbs Pavilion Restaurant
Park Terrace **t** (01223) 367480
Open Daily noon–2.30 and 6.30–10.30

Cricket-themed restaurant opened by the great England and Surrey batsman Jack Hobbs himself. It is housed in a former cricket pavilion and is decked out with mountains of memorabilia. There are mini portions for the children who can play on the grass of Parker's Piece.

The Milton Arms
205 Milton Road **t** (01223) 505012
Open Daily 11–11

Outside the centre of town, this is a good family-orientated pub with an outdoor play area.

PizzaExpress

7a Jesus Lane **t** (01223) 324033
Open 11.30–midnight
Tasty pizza in the marbled hall of this gentleman's club close to Trinity College. Another, cosier, branch can be found at 28 St Andrew's Street **t** (01223) 361320.

Around Cambridge

Orchard Tea Rooms

45 Mill Way **t** (01223) 845788
Open Daily 10–6
Idyllic spot to partake of a cream tea or a light lunch. The nicest way to get here is by punt from Cambridge (see p.113).

The Red Lion

High Street, Grantchester **t** (01223) 840121
Open Daily 11–11
Good pub food (there's a children's menu), a grassy garden and a special indoor play area, 'Bumpy's Kingdom'.

The Queen's Head

Newton **t** (01223) 870436
Open Mon–Sat 11.30–2.30, 6–11, Sun noon–2.30, 7–10.30
This country pub is friendly and unspoilt and full of olde-world charm. They do a good line in olde-world food too which includes such delicacies as 'brown soup' and 'toast and dripping'. Well behaved children are welcome in the games room which includes such favourites as darts, shove-ha'penny, table skittles and dominoes.

Colchester

Clowns

61 High Street **t** (01206) 778631
Open Daily 11–10
Solid English fare served in impressively large portions. Children's menu and high chairs are provided.

PizzaExpress

1 St Runwald Street **t** (01206) 760680

Colchester oysters

For hundreds of years, Colchester and Whitstable were the most important centres of oyster fishing in Britain. It's hard to believe today, but until the 1860s, oysters were so cheap that oyster bars were the contemporary equivalent of fish and chip shops.

Open Daily 12–11.30
Large, comfortable branch of the ever impressive chain serving thin-crust Italian-style pizzas, pastas, garlic breads, salads and sticky puddings. High chairs available.

Red Lion Hotel

High Steet **t** (01206) 577896
Open Daily 12 noon–10
Hearty pub food and cream teas.

Tilly's Tea Rooms

22 Trinity Street **t** (01206) 560600
Open Daily 9–6
Cakes, scones and sandwiches.

Warehouse Brasserie

12 Chapel Street **t** (01206) 765656
Open Mon–Sat 12 noon–2.30 and 7–11
Colchester's swankiest restaurant can provide a very reasonably priced family lunch, based around a combination of French and English staples.

Dunwich

The Ship Inn

St James Street **t** (01728) 648219)
Open Daily 11–11
This traditional boozer is Dunwich's only pub. It has a cosy bar with low wooden beams and an open fire. There is a family room and a pleasant garden and excellent sea food dishes on the menu both at lunchtime and in the evenings. Children's portions and baby changing facilities are available.

Great Yarmouth

Atlantis Fish Restaurant

60 Marine Parade **t** (01493) 332723
Simple, seaside fish and chips.

Harry Ramsden's

112 Marine Parade **t** (01493) 330444
Perhaps the best of the town's galaxy of fish and chip shops, this huge, 140-seat version of the great northern chain serves large portions of proper, thick-cut, chunky chips, along with a range of choices for children.

North Drive

North Drive **t** (01493) 844194
Open Daily 9–6
Cheery coffee shop serving sandwiches, cakes and rolls, overlooking a boating lake and gardens.

The Yankee Traveller

36 King Street **t** (01493) 857065

Ribs, fried chicken, steaks and burgers are the specialities of this American-style diner. There's a special children's menu.

Hunstanton

The Lodge Hotel and Restaurant

Old Hunstanton Road, Old Hunstanton
t (01485) 532896
Open Mon-Fri 12.30–2.30 and 6.30–9,
Sat, Sun 12 noon–9

This friendly restaurant serves pub food and cream teas and has a carvery at weekends. Children's menu available.

Norwich

Adlard's

79 Upper St Giles **t** (01603) 633522
Open Mon 7.30–10.30, Tues–Sat 12.30–1.45 and 7.30–10.30

Adlard's is Norwich's swankiest restaurant. Serving up a mixture of Modern European and seasonal dishes, it is one of only two restaurants in the whole of East Anglia to currently hold a Michelin star. Children will have to be very well behaved but are made very welcome. High chairs available. Expensive.

Andersons Café-Restaurant

52 St Giles **t** (01603) 617199
Open Mon–Thurs 9.30–6.30, Fri and Sat 9.30–9.30

Good for a pit-stop, this café serves tasty filled baguettes, jacket potatoes (to eat in or take away) and all-day breakfasts.

The Assembly House

The Georgian Restaurant, Theatre Street **t** (01603) 626402 **www**.assemblyhousenorwich.co.uk
Open Mon–Sat 10–8

With home-made scones, pastries and sausage rolls on the menu, this is a good place to come for tea. The food is served in an elegant Georgian dining-room. The house itself holds regular food-themed exhibitions (phone for details).

Caffè Uno

2–3 Tombland **t** (01603) 615718
Open Daily 10am–11pm

Treacle tart
Norfolk treacle tart should be sticky, flavoured with lemon zest, and served with custard. A tasty treat.

This excellent Italian restaurant is a stone's throw from Norwich Cathedral in the evocatively named Tombland. There's a special children's menu.

Courtyard Restaurant

Maids Head Hotel, Tombland **t** (01603) 209955
Open Mon–Fri 7–10am, 12 noon–2 and 7–10pm; Sat 8–10am, 12 noon–2 and 7–10pm; Sun 8–10am, 12 noon–2 and 7–9.30pm

For something a little bit different, the Courtyard can offer ostrich and bison steaks, as well as traditional favourites such as sausage and mash and shepherd's pie. Children's menu and high chairs available.

Fatso's Speakeasy Restaurant

63–67 Prince of Wales Road **t** (01603) 762763
Open Mon–Sat 11–11, Sun 11–10.30

Serves up simple American-style food including ribs, burgers and fried chicken. Children's menu and high chairs are available.

Jarrod Department Store

London Street **t** (01603) 660661
Open Mon–Sat 9.15–5.50

This huge department store has three child-friendly eateries. The second-floor, self-service restaurant, with its views over the market, is perhaps the best.

Linzers

67 London Road **t** (01603) 630745
Open Mon–Sat 9–5

Patisserie and pavement café offering a tasty range of cakes and pastries.

Pizza One Pancakes Too!

24 Tombland **t** (01603) 621583
Open Mon–Wed 12 noon–10, Thurs 12 noon–10.30, Fri and Sat 12 noon–11, Sun 12 noon–9

Pizzas, pastas and French crêpes served in this lively café situated in the cathedral wall. High chairs are available.

Around Norwich

Blue Boar Pub and Restaurant

259 Wroxham Road, Sprowston **t** (01603) 426802
Open Mon–Sat 11–11, Sun 12 noon–10.30

This family-friendly pub is just outside the city centre, on the Norwich–Wroxham road, and has a children's play area and a no-smoking sun lounge.

The Green Man

Wroxham Road, Rackheath **t** (01603) 782693

Open Mon–Sat 11–2.30 and 5.30–11, Sun 12–3 and 7–10.30

Pleasant country pub serving excellent hearty meals. Children's menu available.

Orford
Butley Orford Oysterage
Market Hill **t** (01394) 450277
Open Mon–Fri noon–2.15, 7–9, Sat & Sun noon–2.15, 6.30–9

With formica tables and bare walls, this may not look like much but the food is delicious. Out the back they smoke their own fish. There are also oysters on the menu and fish so fresh it fairly leaps off the plate. A real treat and the kind of place the kids will remember.

Southend-on-Sea
Liberty Belle
10-12 Marine Parade **t** (01702) 466 936
Open Daily 11-11

Sea-front pub close to Southend's pier. As well as serving real ale, the pub has a family room and a garden with a variety of toys. Food is only served at lunchtimes. Children's portions are available.

Southwold
The Crown
90 High Street **t** (01502) 722275
Food served Daily 12.30–1.30, 7.30–9.30

This up-market hotel is both the best place to stay (see p.195) and the best place to eat in Southwold. Under-5s are not encouraged in the main restaurant (which has an ambitious modern European menu) but the hotel has a children's 'high tea' from 5.30–7 in the bar area which can furnish kids with pretty much anything they fancy from fish and chips to pasta or even something more exotic.

Drifters Bistro
36 East Street **t** (01502) 724806
Open Tue–Sat 10– 2.30, 7–9 (for evening meals), Sun noon–2 (for Sunday lunch).

Close to the Nelson Public house, this informal non-smoking restaurant serves up local produce at reasonable prices, from morning coffee through to lunch and evening meals. It's fairly small (with seating for only 30) and there isn't much room for pushchairs/strollers. Book in advance.

The Red Lion
2 South Green **t** (01502) 722385
Open Daily 11-11

Pleasant 17th-century pub, once popular with fishermen and now popular with families, especially during the summer. It has a family room and garden, good beer and freshly caught fish on the menu. Children's portions available.

Walberswick
The Harbour Inn
Blackshore **t** (01502) 722381
Open Mon–Sat 11–11, Sun noon–10.30; food served noon–2.30, 6–9

Walberswick's main pub has a relaxed atmosphere and a good sized garden. A reasonable range of home-cooked food is on offer. The best time to turn up is either on Friday night or Saturday lunch time when you can have a traditional meal of fish and chips served in paper.

Go West

Hampshire · Somerset
Wiltshire · Dorset

Go West

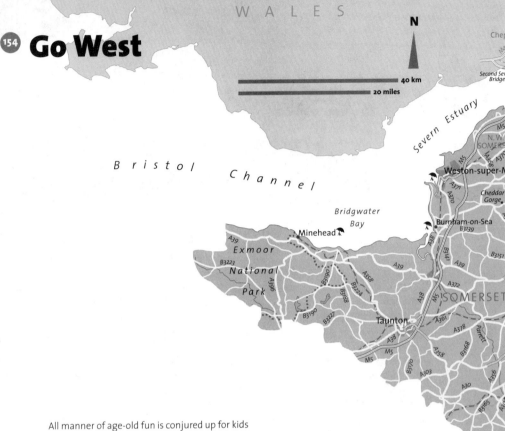

All manner of age-old fun is conjured up for kids in the mystical landscape west of London. There are the ancient and unexplained monuments of Stonehenge and Avebury to ponder over for starters. Alternatively, kids can kit themselves out with a magnifying glass and bag to go in search of 200-million-year-old dinosaur fossils on the Isle of Wight. Meanwhile, in the city of Bath, there is the chance to see how they scrubbed up in Roman times while in Portsmouth kids can step aboard HMS *Victory*, the vessel in which Horatio Nelson led the fight to scupper Napoleon at the Battle of Trafalgar in 1805. At Beaulieu there are classic sports cars from the earliest days of motor racing to marvel at, and at Longleat, the first stately home to open its doors to the public, there is the world's longest hedge maze to negotiate. Along the coast of Dorset, the beaches and myriad attractions of Bournemouth, Christchurch and Poole provide all the fun of a traditional seaside break while in the New Forest (which is anything but new) kids can catch sight of free-roaming ponies which are said to be descended from Spanish horses captured from the Armada in the late 16th century.

Such a perfect day

Morning: Checking out England's rich nautical history at Flagship Portsmouth (p.162).
Lunch: Make for Ye Olde Oyster House, a family-friendly pub with a beer garden and games room (p.186).
Afternoon: hover across to the Isle of Wight from Southsea to make the most of Ryde's sandy beaches and numerous attractions including Brickfield's Horse Sanctuary, Flamingo Park and the Isle of Wight Steam Railway (p.166).

Special events

April

Salisbury: St George's Spring Festival

May

Bath: Bath Children's Festival, also known as 'Glastonbury Festival for kids'

Bath: International Music Festival

t (01225) 463362

July

Bournemouth: Festival of Fun

Cowes Week **t** (01983) 295744

Highlights

Ancient monument, Stonehenge p.180

Beach fun, Bournemouth, p.172

Fossilised fun, Isle of Wight p.169

Horse-riding, New Forest, p.175

Motorized fun, Beaulieu p.171

Nautical fun, Flagship Portsmouth p.162

Roman Baths, Bath p.158

Safari Park, Longleat p.180

Shopping fun, Salisbury Market p.179

Steam train ride, The Watercress Line, p.177

Top town, Bath p.156

BATH & NORTHEAST SOMERSET

BATH

Getting there By road: Bath is 118 miles from London, take J18 of the M4, then the A46. Car parking: Parking is always tricky in Bath and you'd be better off using the park-and-ride facilities at Lansdown, just north of the city (signposted from the A46). Double decker buses will deposit you in Queen's Square in the city centre (handy for sights and shops) and provide you with panoramic views of the area as they negotiate the city's steep outlying hills – children always seem to enjoy this rather precipitous ride. By train/coach: Both Bath Spa train station and the bus station are on Manvers Street, near to the city centre. Trains arrive here from London (Paddington), Salisbury and Portsmouth while National Express services arrive from London, Salisbury, Portsmouth, Oxford and Stratford-upon-Avon
Tourist office Abbey Chambers, Abbey Church Yard **t** (01225) 477101 **f** (01225) 477787
email tourism@bathnesgov.uk

Bath is elegant and unspoilt and has its fair share of child-friendly attractions. Kids will certainly like the Roman Baths, the costume museum, the parks and a cruise along the River Avon. Some of this fine city's charms however – the glorious 18th-century architecture, the fine art museums, the narrow lanes lined with antique shops – are perhaps best appreciated by adults.

The city can also get very, very crowded. Indeed, as the site of the country's only hot spring, it's been attracting hordes of visitors for well over 2,000 years now. The Romans built a bathing complex here, as did the Tudors some thousand or so years later, although it wasn't until the 18th century, when doctors began prescribing spa water as a cure for a quite bewildering range of ailments, that Bath became really popular. It was these Georgian health-seekers who were responsible for much of

Special event
Bath Children's Festival
In May a programme of activities, workshops and entertainments is held in Royal Victoria Park which has become known as 'the Glastonbury Festival for kids'.

the town's elegant architecture, who rediscovered and restored the Roman Baths and who turned the Pump Room into one of the country's most fashionable meeting-places – where you might come across Jane Austen scribbling a quick note or Gainsborough indulging in an idle doodle.

The city's air of refinement has been carefully preserved ever since. Upon arriving, the first thing you'll notice is the overwhelming architectural uniformity of the place. There are no modern unsightly blemishes here. Every building, whether old or new, has been built from the same honey-coloured Bath stone and there are strict building regulations in place to make sure nobody bucks the trend. It has proved an inspired decision. Framed by green hills, the city is undeniably beautiful with a certain, timeless feel to it.

Things to see

American Museum
Claverton Manor **t** (01225) 460503
www.americanmuseum.org
Getting there The museum is 2 miles east of Bath off the A36
Open April–Oct Tues–Sun 2–5; open Mon in Aug
Adm Adult £5.50, child £3
Café, picnic area, gift shop, mother and baby room, guided tours, limited wheelchair access (phone in advance), on-site parking

The only museum in the country devoted solely to the good ol' US of A, these 18 rooms have been decorated and furnished to look like historic American house interiors, while in the grounds there's a replica of George Washington's garden at Mount Vernon, a teepee, a colonial herb garden and an American arboretum. The children can sample free home-made gingerbread. Various events are held throughout the year including a Native American Weekend, a Civil War Weekend, a French and Indian War re-enactment and, of course, Independence Day celebrations.

Bath Abbey
Abbey Churchyard **t** (01225) 422462
Open April–Oct 9–6; Nov–Mar 9–4.30

Free (recommended donation £2)
Shop, disabled access

The entrance to Bath Abbey stands about 10m from the entrance to the Roman Baths and a further 5m from the entrance to the Pump Room, making the three a perfect afternoon combination. Known as the 'Lantern of the West' since Tudor times, owing to the sheer amount of stained glass adorning its walls, inside the Abbey is as grand and dry as most religious buildings. Its famous scalloped fan vaulting will be of little interest to children but they should like the Heritage Vaults, a lively exhibition on the religious history of the town housed in the south side of the abbey.

Building of Bath Museum

Countess of Huntingdon's Chapel, The Vineyards
t (01225) 333895
Open Mid Feb–Nov Tues–Sun 10.30–5, last adm 4.15
Adm Adult £4, child £1.50, family £10
Shop, guided tours, disabled facilities

If you're having trouble finding your way around the town, this museum should help you get your bearings. The centrepiece is a huge, scale-model of the city itself with every street and building beautifully rendered in miniature detail. It is fully illuminated so you can press buttons and light up different sections of the town. Elsewhere, there are exhibits illustrating the different stages of Bath's construction – Celtic, Roman, Saxon, Tudor, Georgian – and showing how, since the 1960s, Bath has been preserved as a sort of Museum City with regulations in place to make sure that all new buildings are made of Bath stone, so as to match the historic surroundings.

The Impossible Microworld Museum

4 Monmouth Street **t** (01225) 333003
www. TheImpossibleMicroworld.com
Open Daily 10–6 (last adm 5.30)
Adm Adult £3.95, child £2.95, under-6s **free**, family £11.95

This museum, a collection of almost impossibly tiny hand-crafted statues, is guaranteed to get the whole family going 'Aah!'. And by tiny, they really mean tiny, the statue's titles should give some idea of the scale involved: *The Scales of Justice on a Pin Head*, *Adam and Eve in the Lead of a Pencil*, *A Polar Bear on a Granule of Sugar*, *Posh 'n' Becks in a Cocktail Stick*, *A Ballerina Dancing on a Pin Head*, *Samson inside a Human Hair*, *A Camel in the Eye of a Needle*, *Birds Tending a Nest on an Eyelash*, each

displayed under a powerful magnifying glass allowing you to pick out the extraordinary miniature detail. These amazing examples of craftsmanship are all the work of Willard Wigan, a native of Birmingham, who suffered from learning disabilities as a child and began his career carving mini cartoons of his teachers as a sort of revenge 'because they made me feel so small'. The carving process, as Mr Wigan describes it, sounds frighteningly intense. He has trained himself to hold his breath for up to three minutes, during which time he stands completely immobile, apart from the hand holding the scalpel. The slightest movement or tremor could cause a wayward cut which is why, during the most crucial moments, he claims to work between heartbeats. Whatever the process, the results are truly astonishing.

Museum of Costume and Assembly Rooms

Bennet Street **t** (01225) 477752
www.museumofcostume.co.uk
Open Daily 10–5, last adm 4.30
Adm Adult £4.20, child £3, under-6s **free**
Shop, mother and baby room, disabled facilities, guided tours

A comprehensive display of changing fashions featuring over 200 figures dressed in costumes from the 16th century to the present day. There is a free audio guide.

Parade Gardens

These gardens near Pulteney Bridge overlooking the river provide a nice spot for a picnic. Look out for the organic statues of baby dinosaurs emerging from their eggs. See if you can also spot the leafy T-Rex leering out of a nearby hedge.

Postal Museum

8 Broad Street **t** (01225) 460333
Open Mon–Sat 11–5, Sun open only by special arrangement
Adm Adult £2.90, child £1.20

Lively displays on the history of written communication from 'clay-mail to email' housed in the building in which the world's first postage stamp, the Penny Black, was sent on 2 May 1840. There are hands-on activities for children and Postman Pat figures on sale in the museum shop.

Need to sit down?

Royal Victoria Park is a large, grassy, open space, and is the best place to take kids when they

Roman Baths

Stall Street **t** (01225) 477785
www.romanbaths.co.uk
Open Jan–Feb and Nov–Dec 9.30–5.30; Mar–June and Sept–Oct 9.30–6; July–Aug 9am–10pm
Adm Adults £7.50, children £4.20, family £18.50
Café, shop, guided tours

In Roman times, every major town boasted a large public bathhouse. Bathing was one of the Romans' favourite activities, perhaps second only to conquering countries and trying on new togas. To the Romans, bathing was more than just a means of getting clean, it was an important social experience. The bathhouse fulfilled much the same function for the average wealthy Roman as the pub or café does for people today. It was an informal meeting-place, somewhere for people to come and relax and talk about the day's events. When the Roman Empire collapsed, however, in the 5th century AD, their bathhouses went out of fashion. The invading Saxon tribes had little need for such fancies and most were either destroyed or left to decay. The bathhouse in Bath was built over and forgotten until the 18th century when workmen stumbled on it by accident. Remarkably, it had survived more or less intact and was quickly spruced up and re-opened to the public, whereupon it soon became one of the country's top tourist attractions – something it has remained to this day.

The complex, which looks a bit like a cross between an ancient temple and a modern swimming-pool, is beautifully preserved and, wandering through it today, you can really get a feel for what it must have been like in Roman times, full of chattering, gossiping people. On arrival, you are given a self-paced audio guide which will lead you through the complex and adjoining museum to the hot, bubbling spring itself which still produces a staggering 250,000 gallons of water a day at a constant temperature of 45.6°C or 116°F – the bubbles you see are a result of escaping gas rather than the heat. The Romans channelled this water into a whole range of different baths: a large hot bath, a number of small tepid pools and treatment baths as well as a cold, circular plunge pool into which the bathers would jump after their hot dip to freshen themselves up. There would also have been steam rooms and saunas heated by underfloor hypercausts (the Roman version of central heating). Today, although you can see the remnants and remains of all these facilities, only the main bath and the plunge pool still contain water which flows along lead pipes laid down by Roman engineers. You're free to explore both, although you should on no account drink the water.

In Roman times, the source of the spring was marked by a shrine to the Goddess Sulis Minerva where people would come to worship and throw curses written on sheets of lead into the water. You can see examples of these requests for supernatural intervention (most seem to have been the result of quite everyday disputes between neighbours) at the museum along with a bust of the goddess herself. This tradition continues today (albeit in diluted form) at the plunge pool which is littered with coins tossed in by visitors for luck. The museum also contains various models and dioramas showing what the complex would have looked like in AD400, as well as a number of mosaics and a collection of everyday objects such as coins and hairpins.

The pleasant, pedestrianized square outside the Baths, where you'll also find the Pump Room and Bath Abbey, is often frequented by street performers – musicians, jugglers, etc. – and there's a branch of the English Teddy Bear Company guarded by a 6ft bear in a Beefeater uniform.

Tip The complex can get very crowded, especially in summer, so try to pick your time carefully. Also, do be aware that it takes at least an hour to go round which can be tiring and frustrating for younger children.

Pump Room

Come to the Pump Room, the epitome of 18th-century elegance (it's basically just a very well-to-do tearooom), for a refreshing glass of hot spa water pumped from the same spring that feeds the Roman Baths next door. It is supposed to be very good for you.

Bath Spa Project

t (01225) 477710 **www.**bathspa.co.uk

A new £17-million bathing complex is due to open in October 2002. The only place in the UK where you'll be able to bathe in natural, hot spring water, the complex will be housed in a futuristic-looking building and contain two new bathing spas, a rooftop pool (where you'll be able to swim and admire a stunning view of Bath at the same time) a spa water drinking fountain, cafés and shops as well as water-therapy treatments.

develop cultural overload. It contains an aviary, a botanical garden and a safe, well-equipped children's adventure playground with toilets and refreshments nearby. Every year, during the last week in May, a big top is erected for the Bath Children's Festival, a big kids' jamboree which, in part, aims to promote environmental issues through a range of green-themed activities and events.

William Herschel Museum

19 New King Street **t** (01225) 311342
www.bath-preservation-trust.org.uk
Open Mar–Oct 2-5; Nov–Feb 2–5 Sat, Sun
Adm Adult £2.50, child £1, family £5

William Herschel, the distinguished astronomer, scientist and musician, lived in this house during the 1770s and early 1780s together with his sister Caroline. Caroline was a talented astronomer in her own right but, times being what they were, she acted as her brother's assistant. Both were fascinated by the idea of manufacturing the perfect instrument to investigate the stars and, whenever time allowed, they would experiment with different telescopes of their own making. You couldn't just go down to the shops and buy a telescope in those days. You couldn't even buy the parts and Herschel would spend days constructing mirrors and lenses. This work demanded such patience and concentration that Herschel's sister took it upon herself to spoon-feed him so that he could work on uninterrupted.

In 1781 this dedication paid off and the pair discovered the planet Uranus and later several of its satellites. With this important discovery, Herschel doubled the size of the known universe and uncovered a rich vein of schoolboy jokes for succeeding generations.

Following a recent refurbishment, the modest Georgian townhouse now looks very much as it would have in the late 18th century from the furniture and fabrics down to the door handles. The workshop is particularly worthy of note and still contains Herschel's treadle lathe and his workbench. Even the flagstones are authentic – the crack in the stone came about when molten metal was accidentally spilt on the floor.

As well as the rooms, the garden from which Herschel first discovered the seventh planet shining dimly in the night sky has also been restored to give a true representation of a Georgian

town house garden and contains plants and herbs which were popular at the time.

Things to do

Boat trips

Boats leave the shop-lined Pulteney Bridge every half-hour in summer for sightseeing trips up the River Avon. For up-to-date information on river and canal trips call (**t** (09068) 360396).

You can hire rowboats, punts, canoes and traditional wooden skiffs from the Boating Station on Forester Road, a restored Victorian structure with a pleasant tea garden and restaurant.

The Bath Boating Station

Forester Road **t** (01225) 466407
Open April–Sept daily 10–6
Café, picnic area

Guide Friday

t (01225) 444102 **www.**hoponhopoff.com
Fares Adult £8.50, accompanied child £3,
under-5s **free**, family £20

Open-top bus tours provide an excellent introduction to the city with enough to see to keep even the liveliest toddler interested. Guide Friday is probably the best (and therefore the most expensive) tour. It lasts one hour and can be joined at any stop along the route – these include the Bath Bus Station, Terrace Walk, High Street, Milsom Street and Great Pulteney Street.

Walking tours

The company of Mayor's Honorary Guides gives free walking tours of the city. Try the 'Bizarre Bath' tour or the 'Ghost Walk', a night-time trawl past the city's most haunted sites (**t** 09068 360393).

Cinemas

ABC

23–24 Westgate Street **t** (01225) 462959/461730
Old-fashioned single-screen cinema with seating for 700.

Little Theatre

St Michael's Place **t** (01225) 466822
Bath's arthouse cinema with a children's show at the weekend.

Robins Cinema

St John's Place **t** (01225) 461506
Bath's very own multiplex (three screens) showing the latest blockbusters.

Theatres

Theatre Royal

St John's Place **t (01225) 448844**

Bath's main theatre venue. Companies come here before moving on to London's West End. The place to come for a good Christmas panto.

Activities

Avon Valley Cyclery

Behind Bath Spa Station **t (01225) 461880 f (01225) 446267 www.bikeshop.uk.com**

You can hire bikes for day trips along the traffic-free Bristol and Bath Railway Path which wends its way through the local countryside and follows the River Avon for part of its length.

Bath Sports and Leisure Centre

North Parade, Bath **t (01225) 462563**

Call in advance for details of times and prices

Excellent children's play pool with two long, twisting slides.

AROUND AND ABOUT

Nature lovers

Avon Valley Country Park

Pixash Lane, Keynsham, Bath **t (0117) 986 4929**

Getting there Take the A4 from Bath and follow the signs

Open April–Oct daily 10–6

Adm Adult £3.50, child £2.50, under-2s **free**

Café, picnic areas, disabled toilets

No dogs allowed

Upon arriving at the park, the kids will probably insist on heading straight to the adventure playground with its fabulous collection of climbing frames, rope bridges and vertical drop slides. Once they have burnt off some energy, pick up a leaflet from the visitor centre and head off along the riverside trail, stopping here and there for a little pond dipping. If you're lucky, you may spot a wild mink or even a wallaby or two. There are lots of picnic sites along the way – if you bring your own coal, you may use the barbecues – and the fields alongside the trail are dotted with children's play equipment which, in total, make up a one-mile

long children's assault course. Also, look out for the lake where there are rowboats for hire, the miniature railway and the pens of farm animals including sheep, ponies and rabbits.

Norwood Farm

Bath Road, Norton St Philip, Bath **t (01373) 834356**

Getting there The farm is 4 miles south of Bath on the B3110 Bath–Frome road

Open Mar–Sept daily 10.30–6

Adm Adult £4.25, child £2

Café, picnic area, gift shop, disabled facilities

Organic, environmentally-friendly show farm set in acres of beautiful countryside. It has over 30 different types of animal which means that, depending on the time of year, your kids should be able to see some or all of the following: lambs, goat kids, piglets, calves, foals and chicks.

Steam power

Avon Valley Railway

Bitton Station, Bath Road, Willsbridge **t (0117) 932 5538 Infoline t (0117) 932 7296 www.avonvalleyrailway.co.uk**

Getting there The railway is just off the A43, midway between Bristol and Bath. The nearest railway station is Keynsham, on the Bristol–Bath line

Open April–Oct every Sun, Aug additional mid-week service and around Christmas

Fares Adult £3.50, child £2, under-3s **free**, family £10

Refreshments and snacks, picnic area, children's play area, converted carriage for wheelchair use, on-site parking at Bitton Station

Steam train rides operate most Sundays between April and October along this two-mile stretch of the former Midland Railway line just southeast of Bristol. The railway also organizes numerous special event days including Mother's/Father's Days, Children's Fun Days (when kids can meet Postman Pat), Teddy Bears' Picnics, Santa Specials and, of course, Thomas the Tank Engine Days. The line was designed by Bristol's favourite son, Isambard Kingdom Brunel.

HAMPSHIRE & THE EAST DORSET COAST

PORTSMOUTH

Getting there By road: Portsmouth is 75 miles southwest of London on the south Hampshire coast, just south of the M27. By rail: Trains arrive at Portsmouth Harbour Station daily from London (Victoria and Waterloo) and Brighton. By bus/coach: National Express services run from London (Victoria and Heathrow) and Brighton
Tourist offices 102 Commercial Road
t (023) 9282 6722; The Hard **t** (023) 9282 6722.
www.portsmouthcc.go.uk/visitor.
The tourist information centre organizes guided walks of the city costing £1 per person (accompanied children **free**).

Ships, ships and more ships – if you and the kids are thinking of coming to Portsmouth it would help if you're interested in ships. The city is the current headquarters of the British Navy and its huge 7-mile square harbour is simply full of them. Spend a day here and you'll see almost every type of naval craft imaginable, from Tudor warships and 19th-century gunboats to Second World War submarines and modern aircraft carriers. The city's main draw is Flagship Portsmouth, the umbrella organization which runs Portsmouth's four main naval attractions in and around the historic dockyard. These are: HMS *Victory*, Admiral Nelson's flagship at the Battle of Trafalgar (you can see the spot where he was fatally wounded by French sniper fire); HMS *Warrior*, the most fearsome fighting vessel of the 19th century; the *Mary Rose*, Henry VIII's Tudor flagship (sunk by the French in 1545, it was only rediscovered in 1965) and the Royal

Naval Museum. These, along with the Submarine Museum in Gosport, and the Royal Marines Museum and D-Day Museum in Southsea, provide the most comprehensive overview of naval history you could ever wish for. Of course, if the sight of all these ships makes you yearn for a life on the ocean waves, you could always put your sea legs to the test on a sightseeing tour of the harbour or a trip out to Spitbank Fort, a brick and iron fortress one mile out to sea, which has a network of spooky passageways to explore. You could even pay a visit to the Isle of Wight, which lies just two miles off the coast (p.164).

Portsmouth town's multimillion pound facelift is in full swing. The first results of this are the Gunwharf Quays leisure complex (with shops, restaurants, cinemas, a bowling alley and a craft market); the Millennium Promenade, a 6-mile-long walkway linking the old town with the historic dockyard, and the 165m Spinnaker Tower which affords wonderful views of the town. To be honest, all the prettifying in the world won't make Portsmouth one of the country's beauty spots. Bombed heavily during the Second World War, its skyline is blighted by some rather ugly tower blocks. Nonetheless, what it lacks in aesthetic appeal, it more than makes up for in exuberance and atmosphere, particularly in the neighbouring resort of Southsea where you can enjoy a range of traditional seaside attractions including a Sea Life Centre, a long pebble beach, a pier, a waterpark and a castle.

Things to see and do

D-Day Museum
Clarence Esplanade, Southsea **t** (023) 9282 7261
Open Daily 10–5
Adm Adult £4.75, child £2.85, family £12.35
Gift shops, café, adapted toilets, baby changing facilities, on-site parking

On 6 June 1944, in the dead of night, thousands of allied soldiers landed on the Normandy coast in the largest seaborne invasion ever staged. This would be the turning point of the war, the moment when the allied forces were finally able to drive the Nazis back towards Germany. The story of this remarkable achievement is retold in this fascinating and surprisingly child-friendly museum. There are lots of audiovisual displays and you can even climb aboard one of the landing craft yourself. The centrepiece of the display, however, is the

> **Did you know...**
> That the phrase 'to turn a blind eye' dates back to the time Nelson, then second in command at the Battle of Copenhagen, ignored what he considered to be silly signals from other ships by holding his telescope up to his blind eye so that he could not see them. In fact a number of phrases owe their origins to our nautical heritage. To have 'three square meals a day', for instance, harks back to the time when sailors aboard HMS Victory had to survive on three stingy meals which were served on square plates.

extraordinary 272ft long Overlord Tapestry
('Overlord' was the invasion's code name), based on
the famous Bayeux Tapestry in France, a sort of
enormous comic strip detailing every stage of the
great invasion.

Explosion!

Priddy's Hard, Priory Road **t** (023) 9250 2490
Open Daily 10–5
Adm Adult £5, child £2.50
Shop, disabled access

Recently opened, Explosion! is dedicated to
tracing the history and development of naval
armaments – in other words, things (on ships) that
go bang! – from cannons to cruises missiles.
There's lots of interactivity for children.

Flagship Portsmouth

Historic Dockyard, Portsmouth Harbour
t (01705) 861512 **www.**flagship.org.uk
Open Mar–Oct 10–5.30; Nov–Feb 10–5
Adm Ticket to all attractions adult £14, child £10,
family £33
Single ship tickets adult £5.75, child £4.25
*Gift shops, restaurant, café, adapted toilets, baby
changing facilities, on-site parking*
*Note Your Flagship Portsmouth ticket also allows
you entry to the Fighting Top Playship, a naval-
themed adventure playground, the Dockyard*

*Apprentice Exhibition where you can try your hand
at a range of shipbuilding skills and the Warships by
Water tour, which takes you out into the harbour
for a close-up look at the modern warships and
aircraft carriers stationed there.*

The Mary Rose

In 1982, when the *Mary Rose* was raised from the
Solent silt, in one of the greatest recovery operations in archaeological history, the ship turned out
to be a genuine Tudor time-capsule laden with
hundreds of unique artefacts. She was built in 1509
on the orders of Henry VIII and led the King's fleet
in his wars against the French before sinking in the
Solent during a skirmish in 1545, where she lay for
over 400 years until rediscovered in 1965. It would
be a while yet, however, before she saw the light of
day. Between 1978 and 1982 divers recovered some
19,000 objects from around the wreck – made up
of a mixture of the ship's military hardware,
including heavy guns and longbows (the only
examples to survive from Tudor times), and sailors'
personal effects: painted pocket sundials, embroi-
dered pouches, rosary beads and lice combs –
before the hull itself was carefully brought back to
the surface. Today, the great ship sits in a specially
constructed gallery where the environment is carefully controlled to prevent her from decaying and
can be observed from a viewing gallery. Audio
guides are available.

Royal Naval Museum

Housed in an 18th-century dockside building, this
museum tells the story of the Royal Navy from its
beginnings to the Falklands War. As you would
expect, it holds a good deal of Nelson memorabilia,
including his uniform, the furniture from his cabin
on HMS *Victory*, his watch and a miniature of
Emma Hamilton. In a recently opened exhibition,
'Horatio Nelson, the Hero and the Man', you can
stand next to a waxwork model of the great man
(shorter than you'd think) and watch an audiovisual presentation on his life. Elsewhere, there's lots
of interactivity for the kids, especially in the 'Sailing
Navy' gallery which aims to show what life was like
aboard a 19th-century warship – children can hold
a musket, climb inside a leaguer barrel and even
take the wheel of a virtual 74-gun ship – and the
recently opened 'Action Stations' exhibition on
modern warships. Do also look out for the
delightful exhibition tracing the evolution of the

sailor's uniform – from frogging and riband to bell bottom trousers.

HMS *Victory*

It was aboard this ship that Vice Admiral Nelson commanded the British naval victory at Trafalgar in 1805 over the combined Franco–Spanish fleet. Fatally wounded in the battle, it was also where he spent his final hours before being brought home, preserved in a barrel of brandy, to a hero's funeral.

The ship, commissioned in 1759, was the most awesome fighting machine of its day. It carried 100 cannons and was manned by 821 officers and crew including 153 Royal Marines 'to provide accurate musket fire in battle'. It has been beautifully restored to look exactly as it would have done on that fateful day in 1805, with its huge cannon lined up along the gun deck, and, although not quite as awe-inspiring as HMS *Warrior*, it is still a hugely impressive sight.

HMS *Warrior*

With her masts and rigging, gangways and stairways, cannon and armour, this huge 19th-century warship provides the perfect setting for an afternoon of serious exploring. When she was built in 1861, HMS *Warrior* was the fastest, most heavily armed, most heavily armoured warship in the world. She was the first to be fitted with an iron hull and the first to carry 110lb guns. Overnight, she made all other warships obsolete and was described by Napoleon III, the Emperor of France, whose naval threat she had been designed to curb, as 'a black snake among rabbits'. Just 15 years later, however, and without ever having been used in battle, she too was obsolete, surpassed by faster, nastier, craft. For much of the 20th century she languished in a state of disrepair before being restored to her former splendour in the early 1980s and, in 1987, returned to Portsmouth.

Portsmouth Harbour Cruises

Departs from Ferry Pontoon, The Hard
t (023) 9273 9459
Fares Adult £3.50, child £3, family £8
Fifty-minute cruise around the harbour to view HMS *Warrior*, HMS *Victory*, Porchester Castle and the warships in Fountain Lake.

Portsmouth Sea Life Centre

Clarence Esplanade, Southsea **t** (023) 9287 5222
Open Daily 10–6
Adm Adults £5.50, under-14s £4, under-4s **free**
Café, gift shop, adapted toilets, baby changing facilities

Overlooking the Solent, this is a great place to introduce kids to the wonders of the marine world. In addition to the assorted sharks, rays and jellyfish, there's an Underwater Adventure Trail, a scratchcard trail and a soft play area for toddlers.

Royal Marines Museum

Eastney Esplanade, Southsea **t** (023) 9281 9385
www.royalmarinesmuseum.co.uk
Open June–Aug 10–5; Sept–May 10–4.30
Adm Adult £4, child £2.15, family £12
Gift shop, café, adapted toilets, on-site parking

Most parents, when trying to come up with somewhere to take the kids, tend to avoid museums prefixed with the word 'royal'. Royalty, in museum terms, more often than not means dullness. The Royal Marines Museum, however, breaks the mould. This is a very lively museum with plenty of interactive exhibits and lots of opportunities for kids to pretend to be soldiers. In particular, check out the Jungle Room where you can experience the conditions of a tropical campaign and see the type of hazards marines have to deal with (like snakes, scorpions and blowpipe darts), the multimedia cinema where you can watch footage of various derring-do campaigns and, outside, the excellent junior assault course.

Southsea Castle

Clarence Esplanade **t** (023) 9282 7261
Open April–Oct daily 10–5.30; Nov–Mar Sat and Sun 10–4
Adm Adults £2, under-13s **free**
Gift shops, adapted toilets

Built as a coastal defence in 1544 on the orders of Henry VIII, Southsea Castle proved such a success that it was in continuous use by the military until 1960. In its 'Amazing Time Tunnel' exhibition a costumed guide will lead you through a series of gruesome waxwork tableaux depicting the most dramatic (i.e. the most bloodthirsty) scenes from the castle's long history – prisoners being whipped in a damp, dark Victorian cell is always a particular favourite. During the summer months various events such as battle re-enactments and birds of prey days are staged.

Submarine Museum

Haslar Jetty Road, Gosport **t** (023) 9252 9217
www.rnsubmus.co.uk

Getting there The museum is reached by passenger ferry from the Harbour train station. Alternatively, take the water bus which gives you a half-hour tour of the harbour first
Open April–Oct 10–5.30; Nov–March 10–4.30
Adm Adult £3.75, child £2.50, family £10
Gift shops, Jolly Roger Café, waterfront picnic area, adapted toilets, guided tours, on-site parking

This museum recreates the life of the undersea soldier through a variety of exhibits and audiovisuals. The highlight is a guided tour through the narrow, clunking decks of HMS *Alliance*, a genuine Second World War submarine, to see its periscope, torpedo launchers and cramped sleeping quarters.

Cinemas

Odeon
London Road **t** (023) 9266 4623/0870 50 50 007

UCI
Port Solent **t** (023) 9264 030

Theatres

Kings Theatre
Albert Road **t** (023) 9282 8282

New Theatre
Guildhall Walk **t** (023) 9282 4355

Activities

Play Zone
Unit A4, Oak Park Industrial Estate **t** (023) 9237 9988 **www**.theplayzone.co.uk
Open Daily 10–7
Adm Adults 50p, under-11s £3.20 (weekdays) £3.70 (weekends, school hols), under-4s £2.20 (weekdays) £2.70 (weekends, school hols), under-1s **free**
Café, baby-changing facilities, on-site parking

Huge 6,500sq ft indoor playground full of giant slides and climbing frames. For children aged 1–11.

The Pyramid Centre
Clarence Esplanade, Southsea, Portsmouth **t** (023) 9279 9977
Open Sat and Sun 10–6, Mon closed, Tues and Thurs 2–7, Wed 11–6, Fri 2–8
Adm Adult £4.60, child £3.60
Family changing rooms, disabled access

Tropical pools (heated to 84°F) with superflumes, toddlers' pool, animal slides, and inflatables, video games, gift shop, fast food and licensed café–bar.

THE ISLE OF WIGHT

A roughly diamond-shaped piece of land a couple of miles off the coast of southern England, the Isle of Wight has long been one of the country's favourite family getaways. Its appeal is perhaps best characterized as a sort of detached Englishness as it is both removed from and, at the same time, an essential part of the country itself. It is often said that the Isle of Wight languishes some 20 years behind the mainland, so it is presumably just entering the 1980s now. You certainly shouldn't go expecting the latest whizz-bang Disney-ish thrills. This is a walking, horse-riding, cycling, sea bathing, pottering about sort of place – somewhere to relax and enjoy the abundant summer sunshine. The south side of the island, in particular, has an almost balmy climate. It is also one of the country's prime fossil-hunting regions with soft clay cliffs revealing dozens of preserved dinosaur skeletons each year – thus giving rise to the isle's nickname, 'Jurassic Island'.

Cowes

Getting there By road/boat: Cowes lies on the northern tip of the island, the closest town to mainland England, 4 miles north of Newport (via the A3020) and 6 miles northwest of Ryde (via the A3054 and A3021). Red Funnel operates a car ferry service between Southampton and East Cowes (the journey should take just under an hour) **t** (01703) 334010. By train/boat: Trains run from London (Waterloo) to Southampton Central Station, from where passengers can make their way to the Town Quay Terminal where a high-speed Red Jet passenger-only catamaran will whisk them up Southampton Water and across the Solent to West Cowes in a little over 20 minutes **t** (023) 8033 4010. Car ferries from Southampton arrive at East Cowes
Tourist office The Arcade, Fountain Quay **t** (01983) 813818 **www**.islandbreaks.co.uk **www**.netguides.co.uk/wight/index.html

Principally known for its boat-building industry and terribly posh yachting regatta (held here every August), Cowes, at the northern tip of the island, is a lively, rather upmarket sailing town with lots of interesting shops lining its narrow high street (including boatyards and chandlers) and plenty of good walking along the nearby cliffs. Osborne House, Queen Victoria's favourite home (and, following the success of the film *Mrs Brown* in the late 1990s, English Heritage's most visited property) is in East Cowes across the River Medina (reached via a chain ferry).

Cowes Library and Maritime Museum
Beckford Road **t** (01983) 293394
Open Mon–Wed and Fri 9.30–6, Sat 9.30–4.30
Free
Disabled access
   The maritime history of the island, plus a few model boats.

Isle of Wight Model Railways
The Parade **t** (01983) 280111
Open Mon–Sat 11–5
Adm Adult £2.50, child £1.25
Disabled access
   Large display of model trains with a rocky mountain scene, a special large-scale kids' layout and a shop selling Thomas the Tank Engine models .

Osborne House
York Avenue, East Cowes **t** (01983) 200022
www.english-heritage.org.uk
Getting there It's just east of East Cowes off the A3021
Open April–Sept 10–5; Oct 10–4
Adm Adult £6.90, child £3.50, family £17.50
Café, tearoom, souvenir shop, guided tours, wheelchair access to ground floor and gardens only,
   If ordinary people resemble their dogs, then perhaps it could be said that monarchs resemble their palaces. This certainly seemed true in the 19th century when the flamboyant, iconoclastic George IV ordered the construction of the flamboyant, iconoclastic Brighton Pavilion while the staid, conservative Queen Victoria (who quickly rejected her predecessor's effort) made her personality manifest in the form of the staid, conservative Osborne House.

Can you spot?
In the Swiss Cottage, look out for the rather odd collection of marble arms modelled on the royal children – Queen Victoria had them commissioned as souvenirs.

Built during the 1840s according to plans drawn up by Victoria's beloved Albert, Osborne was intended to be a 'quiet, modest retreat'; a simple country house where the family could holiday together. Of course, the vast Italianate palace that resulted does not conform to many people's ideas of 'modest' but, in royal terms, it is rather restrained; certainly when compared with grand palaces like Windsor and Buckingham.

Osborne was very much Victoria's house. Responsible for much of the interior decor, she referred to it as a 'place of one's own, quiet and refined' and would eventually see out her final days here in 1901. Her son Edward VII's decision, soon after her death, to bequeath the house to the nation had the effect of turning it into a sort of unofficial memorial to the country's longest reigning monarch and its apartments have been carefully restored to look as they would have done during Victoria's day. Though ornate and, as you would expect, beautifully furnished, the rooms have a distinctly sombre quality to them. Following Albert's death in 1861, the Queen remained in mourning for the rest of her life and Osborne's rooms are littered with reminders of her grief – you can see Albert's personal bathroom preserved just as he left it, a specially commissioned portrait of the Prince Consort which sat by the Queen's bed as well as a starkly melancholic study of the Queen herself 'The Queen Called Sorrow' by Landseer. In parts, the house feels a little mausoleum-like, although it does have its more lighthearted areas including a billiard room where the Queen used to challenge her ladies-in-waiting to games and a room filled with furniture made entirely from antlers.

The most charming part of the whole estate, however, and the area that will most appeal to children is the Swiss Cottage built in the gardens in the 1850s for the royal children to play in – there's a toy fort, a miniature kitchen and a collection of miniature gardens which the children were encouraged to tend. The cottage can be reached from the house aboard a wonderfully grand horse-drawn carriage – check out the views of the Solent on the way. There's a free activity sheet for children.

Can you spot?
The 20 brass cannon by the harbour used to start yacht races.

Ryde

Getting there By road/boat: Ryde, in the island's northeast corner (6 miles southeast of Cowes off the A3054) provides the main link with the mainland. Car and passenger ferries run from Portsmouth to Fishbourne (just east of Ryde) every half-hour in summer (every hour in winter). The journey takes just over half an hour. A passenger-only ferry also operates from Portsmouth to Ryde Pier (the craft dock at the tip, 25 minutes) **t** (0870) 582 7744 for both. Hovercraft travel (in good weather) from Southsea, just south of Portsmouth, to Ryde **t** (01983) 811000. By train/boat: Trains link London (Victoria and Waterloo) with Portsmouth. Passengers are deposited directly onto The Hard (where the ferry terminals are situated). Train arrivals are arranged to coincide with ferry departures. The Isle of Wight's own mainline railway runs from Ryde down the east coast of the island to Shanklin via Sandown and connects with the Isle of Wight Steam Railway at Smallbrook Junction

Tourist office 81–83 Union Street **t** (01983) 562905

The island's largest and liveliest town, Ryde is a typically seasidey affair with six miles of sandy beaches, a pier (at half a mile, it's the second longest in the country) and a large number of family-orientated attractions lining its esplanade including an ice rink, a swimming-pool (with retractable roof) and a bowling alley with a children's play area plus numerous arcades and fish restaurants. The promenade stretches from the Esplanade past Appley Gardens and Appley Tower, a Victorian folly, to Puckpool Park where you'll find tennis courts, a crazy golf course and a children's playground. It's only a short ride from Ryde aboard the island's mainline railway to Smallbrook Junction where you can connect with the Isle of Wight Steam Railway.

Brickfields Horse Country

Newnham Lane, Binstead, Ryde **t** (01983) 566801
www.brickfields.co.uk
Getting there It's just southwest of the town off the A3054
Open Daily 10–5
Adm Adult £4.50, child £3.25, family £14
Café, picnic areas, shop, mother and baby facilities, guided tours, disabled access, on-site parking

Lots of good horsey stuff. You can take wagon rides, go for tours of the stables, see the blacksmith

at work in his forge, meet Bud and Weiser (giant twin shires) and watch the lively twice-daily horse parades (12 noon and 3.30) when mounted cowboys and indians will show off their riding prowess and engage in mock pistol versus tomahawk battles. There are also occasional 'Shetland Grand Nationals' and pig races are held three times daily. Miniland is a dedicated children's area with animals to meet and pet.

Butterfly and Farm World

Staplers Road, Wootton **t** (01983) 884430
Getting there It's 4 miles west of Ryde on the coastal A3054 road
Open April–Oct 10–5
Adm Adult £4, child £2.50
Café, picnic areas, shop, guided tours, disabled access, on-site parking

This is a 5-acre garden centre with water gardens, 'jumping' fountains and a tropical butterfly house.

Flamingo Park

Seaview **t** (01983) 612153
Getting there It's just east of Ryde off the B3330.
Open Easter–Sept 10–5 (last adm 4); Oct 10.30–4 (last adm 3.15)
Adm Adult £4.75, child £3.50
Shop, disabled access, on-site parking

Flamingoes may be the main draw – there are over a hundred in residence – but it's the opportunity the park offers for visitors to interact with a range of animals that really sets it apart. Depending on when you visit you may find yourself hand-feeding penguins or parrots or, even, giant carp. There's also an aquarium and an indoor bird and plant house.

Isle of Wight Steam Railway

The Railway Station, Havenstreet **t** (01983) 882204
Open April–Oct Thurs and Sun; June–Sept daily
Café, gift shop, picnic area, children's play area, limited wheelchair access (call in advance), on-site parking

A truly historic experience – the geographic isolation of the Isle of Wight's railway means that a greater proportion of its Victorian and Edwardian rolling stock has survived from at most other restored lines. At Havenstreet Station, the nerve centre of the railway, you can see a collection of Island Railway artefacts and watch locomotives being shunted and worked upon. From here you can take a 2-mile journey to Wootton Station, a traditional country terminus with an old wooden booking office and signal box, before travelling back along the line's entire 5-mile length to Smallbrook Junction where you can connect with the island's mainline railway and rejoin the modern world (or, at least, the 1930s, which is when most of the mainline rolling stock dates from). The Railway plays host to various events throughout the year, including brake van rides, barbeque evenings, a Summer Extravaganza and Santa Specials.

Little Canada

Little Canada Centre, New Road, Wootton, contact 3-D Education t 0870 607 7733
www.3deducation.co.uk
Getting there It's a couple of miles west of Ryde off the A3054
From £314 per child for a 7-night stay. Day boarders are charged £22 a day including lunch.

Little Canada, just outside Ryde, is one of the most famous and well-respected children's activity centres in the country. It's primarily residential, with room for up to 600 children (aged 7–16) to stay (six to a centrally heated chalet) for anything from a day to a week, although they do also welcome day guests. There's a vast range of expertly organized, carefully supervised activities to choose from including abseiling, archery, canoeing, dragon-boating, fencing, quad-biking, ten-pin bowling, trampolining and zip-wiring. Kids are free to do as much or as little as they choose. Incidentally, it's called Little Canada because of the log cabins built here during the 1920s.

Sandown and Shanklin

Getting there Sandown and Shanklin are a couple of miles apart on the island's east coast off the A3055. Shanklin marks the southernmost station of the island's mainline railway which links it to Ryde
Tourist office Sandown: The Esplanade t (01983) 403886; Shanklin: 67 High Street t (01983) 862942

Sandown is a popular Victorian resort with a pleasure pier lined with entertainments, several fine gardens – including Los Altos and Sandham Gardens – a boating lake, a zoo, a fossil museum and a bustling market. The beach is wide and sandy and stretches for 2 miles along the coast to the neighbouring resort of Shanklin which can offer a similar array of seaside attractions including a crazy golf course, arcades and a fun fair

as well as a wonderful natural gorge to explore, Shanklin Chine (*see below*).

Isle of Wight Zoo

Yaverlands, Seafront, Sandown t (01983) 403883
Open Easter–Nov 10–6; Feb–Easter 10–5
Adm Adult £4.95, child £3.95
Café, shop, guided tours, on-site parking
Although it can count monkeys, birds, snakes (there are snake-handling displays in the summer) and giant spiders among its many residents, most people come here for the big cats which live in a dedicated extension, the Tiger Sanctuary. As the name suggests, tigers are the star attractions. They have long been zoo owner Jack Corney's obsession and he has spent 20 years plus overseeing a captive breeding programme resulting in the birth of dozens of tiger cubs, including over 30 born to the world's most productive pair of captive tigers, Tamyra and Shere Khan. A Millennium Commission-funded dinosaur museum built in the shape of a pterodactyl is due to open here shortly.

Museum of Isle of Wight Geology

High Street, Sandown t (01983) 403344
Open Mon–Sat 9.30–4.30
Free
Café
Fossils, life-sized dinosaur models and guided fossil hunts along the coast.

Shanklin Chine

12 Pomona Road, Shanklin t (01983) 866432
Open April–Oct 10–5 (till 10pm in summer, depending on the weather)
Adm Adult £2.50, child £1
Café, souvenir shop, mother and baby facilities
One of the island's great beauty spots, the Chine is a natural sandstone gorge filled with dense jungle-like vegetation and traversed by numerous paths and trails leading to its most spectacular feature, a 45ft waterfall. The gorge is lit up at night with fairy lights and the heritage centre can provide information on the local flora and fauna.

Ventnor

Getting there By road: Ventnor lies in the island's southeast corner, 3 miles south of Shanklin on the A3055
Tourist office 34 High Street t (01983) 853625
The Victorian spa town of Ventnor has been built on a series of terraces below St Boniface Down

(which, at 787ft, is the island's highest point) and is linked by a collection of seriously steep, seriously windy roads (Zig Zag Road is particularly aptly named). Famed for its sunny climate (the result of its sheltered, southerly aspect) and with beautiful botanic gardens, it's one of the island's most well-to-do resorts. Look out for the elegant flower-lined cascade which leads down to the esplanade where you'll find a narrow sand and shingle beach as well as arcades and winter gardens. The pretty village of Bonchurch, with its working blacksmith's forge, lies just east of the town while the Isle of Wight Rare Breeds and Waterfowl Park is just west.

Appuldurcombe House

Appuldurcombe Road, Wroxall, Ventnor
t (01983) 852484 www.english-heritage.org.uk
Getting there It's 3 miles northwest of Ventnor off the B3327
Open April–Oct 10–6
Adm Adult £2, child £1
Picnic areas, shop, disabled access, on-site parking

Once one of the grandest buildings on the island, the 18th-century Appuldurcombe House has, since it was vacated in the early part of the 20th century, been allowed to slowly decay. The result is rather odd. Like a faded movie queen, Appuldurcombe looks grand and stately from a distance and it's only when you get close that you can see how the ravages of time have taken hold. You can still visit the rather ghost-like rooms within and the 11 acres of orna-mental gardens (designed by Capability Brown, which are in much better condition) although the real draw here is the Isle of Wight Owl and Falconry Centre housed in some of the restored out-build-ings. Daily flying displays are given at 11 and 2.

Blackgang Chine Fantasy Park

Blackgang, Ventnor **t** (01983) 730330
www.blackgangchine.com
Getting there Blackgang is on the south coast, 5 miles west of Ventnor off the A3055
Open April–Oct 10–5.30 (till 10 during the summer hols)
Adm Adult £5.50, child £4.50, family £18
Café, restaurant, shop, mother and baby facilities, disabled access

Don't go expecting Disneyland-style hi-tech amusements. The attractions at this 40-acre fun park are more of the water garden, pirate ship, hedge-maze variety with plenty on hand to amuse younger children including Bodger the Badger's

fairground which has three gentle rides. Lightweight it may be (its most razzle-dazzle offering is probably its high-speed water chute) but it has an undeniable charm with its replica Wild West town, haunted mansion and fairy castle and there are always the steep wooded slopes of the Chine itself to explore, where you'll find various themed areas populated by models of goblins, trolls, dinosaurs and nursery rhyme characters.

Rare Breeds and Waterfowl Park

Undercliff Drive, St Lawrence **t** (01983) 852582
Getting there It's just east of St Lawrence on the south coast, a couple of miles west of Ventnor off the A3055
Open Easter–Oct 10–5
Adm Adult £3.70, child £2.20, under-5s **free**
Shop, picnic areas, disabled access, on-site parking

Miniature horses, deer, pigs, otters, llamas, meerkats, owls, pygmy goats and over a hundred species of waterfowl living in 30 picturesque coastal acres.

Ventnor Botanic Gardens

Undercliff Drive **t** (01983) 855397
Open Gardens: Mar–Oct 10–5; Nov–Feb Sat and Sun 11–4; Museum of Smuggling: Easter–Sept 10–5
Adm Gardens: **free**; Museum of Smuggling: Adult £2.20, child £1.10
Café, picnic areas, shop, guided tours, disabled access, on-site parking

These 22 acres of landscaped gardens are the town's biggest draw and are filled with subtropical blooms which flourish in the balmy, south-facing climate. Vegetative highlights include the collec-tion of 100-year-old palm trees, the medicinal herb garden, the temperate house and the recently opened Millennium Commission-funded exhibi-tion centre where there's a display looking at the impact plants have on our daily lives. There's also an underground exhibition area below the gardens where you'll find a Museum of Smuggling showing the ingenious lengths people have gone to in order to provide the local economy with a little extra tobacco and alcohol.

Yarmouth

Getting there Yarmouth is in the island's north-west corner on the A3054 and is linked to the mainland resort of Lymington via a car ferry **t** (0870) 582 7744.
Tourist office The Quay **t** (01983) 760015

Dinosaur hunting

The Isle of Wight is one of the best places in the entire country to go fossil-hunting. The southern cliffs of Brighstone and Brook Bays are particularly rich in dinosaur deposits. Not only are the rocks here of the right age to contain fossils (65–200 million years old) but they are also mainly made up of soft, easily eroded clay with the result that numerous new fossils are exposed by storms and high spring tides each year. In all, around 20 different species of dinosaur have been found here including Iguanodons (a 5m high herbivore), Polycanthuses (an armoured dinosaur), Brachiosauruses (one of the largest dinosaurs that ever lived) and the recently discovered Egyptyrannus Lengi, a fearsome meat-eater, a bit like a miniature T-Rex. Its name translates as 'Lengi's early tyrant' in honour of Gavin Lengi, the local fossil collector who uncovered it. Fossil hunts along the coast are organized by the Museum of Isle of Wight Geology (p.167) and the Dinosaur Farm Museum (p.170).

With a picturesque harbour filled with bobbing boats, this medieval port at the mouth of the River Yar makes a pleasant base for exploring the headline sights of the island's northwest tip – the Needles, Alum Bay et al. Its own sights are less well known but still worth checking out. There's the castle, which was the last to be built as part of Henry VIII's programme for improving the country's coastal defenses, though small, it's well preserved and can offer plenty of picnic spots. One mile west of the town, Fort Victoria Country Park, has 50 acres of woodland surrounding a 19th-century fort and leading down to a shingle beach. Within its confines, you'll find a planetarium, an aquarium and a maritime heritage centre plus a model railway (reckoned to be the largest in the country).

Alum Bay and The Needles

Getting there The Needles can be found right at the western tip of the island. Alum Bay is slightly east off the B3322. A ferry service links the nearby resort of Yarmouth (about 4 miles east) with Lymington in the New Forest t (0870) 582 7744

Cameras at the ready – this is probably the most photographed region of the entire island. Alum Bay, with its layers of multicoloured sand, is particularly photogenic. Its distinctive appearance is caused by the slow crumbling of the different rock strata that make up the cliff face and is seen to its best effect in wet weather when the shore becomes a riot of pinks, oranges and ochres.

Fancy a souvenir?

You can pick up that all-important souvenir – a small glass tube filled with coloured layers of sand – at the nearby Needles Park. This has a gentle seaside amusement park with crazy golf, carousels, glass-blowing and you can take a ride on the spectacular chairlift down to the beach, looking out on the way for the Needles, the row of chalky white pinnacles (with adjoining lighthouse) poking out of the sea that have become the emblem of the island itself. There are even better views from the Needles Old Battery just along the coast, a 19th-century sea fortress built 80m above sea-level. Walk through the 65m tunnel for the impressive views. Boat trips around the Needles are also available nearby.

Fort Victoria Country Park

Sconce Point, Westhill Lane, Norton
t (01983) 760860
Open Easter–Oct 10–6
Free (attractions charged individually)
Café, picnic areas, shop, disabled access, on-site parking

As well as walking along the coast and through the surrounding woodland, you can visit the Fort Victoria aquarium (£1.90), planetarium (£2) and Maritime Heritage Museum (£1).

Needles Old Battery

West High Down, Totland Bay **t** (01983) 754772
Open April–Oct Sun–Thurs 10.30–5 (daily during July and Aug, although, if the weather is at all bad, it's liable to close)
Adm Adult £2.50, child £1.25, family £6
Café, guided tours, disabled access

Needles Park

Alum Bay, Totland Bay **t** (01983) 752401
www.theneedles.co.uk
Open April–Nov 10–5 (later in summer)
Free (attractions charged individually)
Café, fast food, picnic areas, shop, mother and baby facilities, disabled access, on-site parking

Taste the results of traditional sweetmaking at the Sweet Factory and, if you can pull the kids away, watch the making of glass at the Alum Bay Glass Studio. On Thursday nights in August, the Park closes with an impressive fireworks display.

Other attractions

Amazon World

Watery Lane, Newchurch **t** (01983) 867122
Getting there It's 2 miles west of Sandown on the A3056 Newport Road
Open Daily 10–5.30
Adm Adult £4.95, child £3.60, under-3s **free**
Café, shop, picnic areas, disabled access

It's a sort of Amazonian taster with an array of rainforest creatures – including marmosets, toucans, flamingoes, tarantulas, terrapins and crocodiles – living in an authentic-looking jungle setting. Though fun (there are regular 'meet the animals' sessions), it's all presented from an environmental perspective with displays showing the ongoing damage that's being done to the real rainforest. Outside, there's an adventure playground (with a separate toddlers' area) and a small petting area.

Dinosaur Farm Museum

Military Road, near Brighstone **t** (01983) 740401
Open April–Sept Thurs and Sun 10–5 (July–Aug Tues and Fri), also Oct half-term
Adm Adult £2, child £1

Watch experts cleaning and repairing fossils and go for a guided dinosaur hunt on nearby Brighstone Bay. There's also a play area with 'educational' toys.

Isle of Wight Shipwreck Centre and Maritime Museum

Providence House, Sherbourne Street, Bembridge **t** (01983) 872223
Getting there It's on the island's eastern tip, 5 miles northeast of Sandown off the B3395
Open Mar–Oct 10–5
Adm Adult £2.35, child £1.35
Shop, disabled access, on-site parking

The museum tells the maritime history of the island with six galleries devoted to items salvaged from local wrecks and several model ships. The village of Bembridge itself is a quiet resort with lots of good walking in the nearby cliffs.

Isle of Wight Waxworks

High Street, Brading, Sandown **t** (01983) 407286
Getting there Brading is 3 miles north of Sandown on the A3055. It's also a station on the island's mainline railway which links the town with Ryde and Shanklin

Open Summer 10–10; Winter 10–5 (last adm 1hr before closing)
Adm Adult £4.75, child £3.25, under-5s **free**, family £15
Café, shop, mother and baby facilities, on-site parking

The history of the Isle of Wight is presented here as a series of garish waxwork scenes. It's not the most imaginative exhibition you're likely to see, but everything is presented in a lively way. There's the obligatory display of gruesome scenes 'The Chamber of Horrors' (where you are offered the rather dubious pleasure of 'photographing your own execution') as well as a collection of stuffed animals and birds.

Lilliput Doll and Toy Museum

High Street, Brading **t** (01983) 407231
Getting there Brading is 3 miles north of Sandown on the A3055. It's also a station on the island's mainline railway which links the town with Ryde and Shanklin
Open Summer 9.30–9.30; Winter 10–5
Adm Adult £1.45, child 95p
Shop, guided tours, disabled access

A private collection of over 2,000 toys and dolls from the last 2,000 years.

Yafford Watermill Farm Park

Yafford, Shorwell, Newport **t** (01983) 740610
Getting there Yafford is near the south coast between Brighstone and Shorwell on the B3399
Open 10–6 (or dusk if earlier)
Adm Adult £3.70, child £2.80, family £10
Café, picnic areas, shop, disabled access, mother and baby facilities, guided tours, on-site parking

This jolly farm is park home to numerous animals including goats, shetland ponies, Jacob sheep, pigs, rabbits, ducks, geese, turkeys, peacocks and pheasants. The most celebrated resident, however, is definitely Sophie the seal who lives in the millpond and can be seen feeding at 11.30, 2.30 and 3.30. There's also an adventure playground and, in summer, rides aboard a narrow-gauge railway are offered.

Cinemas

Cineworld

Coppins Bridge **t** (01983) 550800

11-screen multiplex with a bar, café and a games area.

Did you know...

The National Motor Museum at Beaulieu was founded by Lord Montagu, a motoring pioneer who as early as 1906, only 20 years after Daimler and Benz had invented the petrol-driven auto-mobile in Germany, was predicting that the car would 'replace nearly every other kind of trac-tion upon the surface of the earth'. Montagu had caught the motoring bug from his father who spoke with passion about the future of the car in both the House of Commons and the House of Lords. It was Montagu's father who was respon-sible for the laws which introduced registration plates, a move which led some to complain that motorists were being 'branded like convicts'.

Commodore

Star Street, Ryde **t** (01983) 565609

Medina Theatre

Newport **t** (01983) 527020

Theatres

Ryde Theatre

Lind Street, Ryde **t** (01983) 568099

Shanklin Theatre

Prospect Road, Shanklin **t** (01983) 868000

Winter Gardens

Pier Street, Ventnor **t** (01983) 855215

Activities

Offshore Sports

19 Orchardleigh Road, Shanklin, Isle of Wight
t (01983) 866269
Open Daily 9–6
Prices £9/day, £5/half-day (ID and £30 deposit required)
Bikes for adults and children, including tag-a-longs.

Medina Recreation Centre

Fairlee Road, Newport, Isle of Wight **t** (01983) 523767
Open Limited availability during term time but open all day on weekends and during school hols.
Adm Call in advance
Two swimming-pools including a toddlers' pool, waterslide, badminton, table-tennis, trampolining, a climbing wall and theatre/cinema venue.

SPECIAL TRIPS

Beaulieu

Beaulieu **t** (01590) 612345 **www**.beaulieu.uk
Getting there Beaulieu is in the New Forest about 6 miles south of Southampton on the B3054, B3055 and B3056 (J2 from the M27). The nearest train station is Brockenhurst, 6 miles west.
Open Daily 10–5, open until 6 during Easter
Adm Adult £8.75, child £6.25, family £28.50
Restaurant, gift shops, guided tours , some disabled access, adapted toilets

There are two sides to Beaulieu. A quiet serene side, as represented by the 16th-century Beaulieu Palace and its beautiful lakeside park; and the noisier, more exuberant side of its Motor Museum with its thousands of clanking, whirring exhibits.

A temple to all things mechanical, the museum houses exquisitely preserved cars representing the history of motoring from late 19th-century proto-types to ultra-modern speed machines. Priceless luxury cars, including a 1909 Rolls-Royce Silver Ghost and a 1962 E-Type Jaguar, sit alongside archetypal people-carriers: Volkswagen Beetles, Minis and, of course, the original people's car, the Ford Model T. The record-breakers of yesteryear are also here, including the 1927 Sunbeam 1000hp, the first car to break the 200mph barrier, and Donald Campbell's 1964 *Bluebird*, the first car to travel above 400mph.

Beaulieu has a good selection of less prestigious but no less loved models. These include the original Chitty Chitty Bang Bang (on which the car from the movie was based), which was built by Count Louis Zborowski to race at Brooklands, and the first £100 car – the Morris Minor of 1931. This diminutive two-seater was sold without bumpers, sported a 3 amp lighting set and managed an economical 50 miles to the gallon.

Elsewhere, you'll find an historic garage and an interactive gallery where children can unravel the mysteries of the internal combustion engine before sampling the museum's radio-controlled cars, mini bikes and hi-tech arcade simulators. A jaunty little monorail travels round the palace grounds at regular intervals.

The museum's showpiece is its 'Wheels' ride in which a motorized car trundles you past seven tableaux designed to tell the story of motoring in the 20th century.

AROUND AND ABOUT

Buckets and spades

Bournemouth

Getting there By road: Bournemouth is 100 miles from London via the A31 and the M3.
By train/coach: Trains from London run from Waterloo Station. Bournemouth's train station is about one mile east of the town centre (a frequent bus service runs from the station opposite). National Express run a regular coach service from London **Tourist office** Westover Road **t** (01202) 451700 **www.**bournemouth.co.uk

There are at least three sides to Bournemouth: a sleepy side (it is one of the country's most popular resorts with senior citizens); a lively side (its nightlife is second only to Brighton's on the south coast) and a family-friendly side – its beaches, parks and events attract hordes of family holiday-makers during the summer months. According to the tourist board it is 'clean, green and the place to be seen' and (whatever that might mean) it certainly has lots of places where kids can run about and play.

Apart from the beach itself, which is one of the cleanest and best maintained around, there are parks and gardens covering one-sixth of the town's area. At the Lower Gardens, just back from the seafront, you can take a ride in the Vistarama tethered balloon which ascends, somewhat jerkily, to a height of 500ft every 15 mins and, in summer, you can watch storytellers, illusionists and comedians, at the Pagoda, as part of the town's annual Festival of Fun. The festival also includes a free firework display at the end of the pier every Friday night, and there's a free Kids Entertain-tent and Game Zones on the beach.

The beach, which is patrolled by lifeguards, operates a Kidzone safety scheme, which splits the seafront into eight colour-coded sections (kids are issued with matching wristbands).

The town's best rainy day attractions are all clustered around the pier and are easily reached by one of the brightly coloured land trains that trundle regularly along the seafront. These include an IMAX 3-D cinema, the Wacky Warehouse kids' play area and the Oceanarium, a well-stocked sea life centre. The pier itself is cheerful and bustling and has a small amusement centre at the end which offers a bundle of fun including tea cup rides and radio-controlled cars.

Oceanarium
Pier Approach, West Beach **t** (01202) 311993
Open Daily 10–5, stays open later in the summer
Adm Adult £5.75, child £3.75
Café, gift shop, mother and baby facilities, disabled access

Vistarama
Lower Gardens **t** (01202) 399939
www.vistarama.co.uk
Operating times Daily 9am–dusk (summer 7.30am–10.30pm, weather permitting)
Adm After 9am: adult £9.95, child £5.50, family £24.95; before 9am: adult £7, child £4.50

Cinemas
ABC Film Centre
27 Westover Road **t** 0870 900 7694
Traditional 3-screen cinema.

Odeon
Westover Road **t** (01202) 551086/0870 50 50 007
Modern 6-screen cinema.

IMAX 3-D cinema
Bournemouth Pier **t** (01202) 553050

Theatres
Pavilion Theatre
Westover Road **t** (01202) 456456
Bournemouth's famous theatre comes complete with its own ballroom.

Pier Theatre
The Winter Gardens **t** (01202) 456456
Plenty of children's entertainment on here, mixed in with the struggling comedians and warbling crooners entertaining grandma.

Activities
Bournemouth International Centre Leisure Pool
Exeter Road, Bournemouth **t** (01202) 456580
Call in advance for details of times and prices
Leisure pool with giant slide and wave-making machine.

Littledown Centre
Chaseside, Bournemouth **t** (01202) 417600
Call in advance for details of times

Adm Adult £2.50, child £1.70, under-5s **free**
Café, on-site parking

Two swimming-pools with waterslides. Football, trampolining, basketball, badminton and crêche facilities also offered.

Christchurch

Getting there By road: Christchurch can be reached from London and the southeast via the M3 and the M27, and is linked to Southampton by the A35. By train/coach: Christchurch station has regular services from London Waterloo, Southampton, Poole, Bournemouth and Weymouth and there's a bus service from Bournemouth
Tourist office 23 High Street **t** (01202) 471780
www.resort-guide.co.uk/christchurch

The proud winner of a Britain in Bloom Award, Christchurch is a much more stately, sedate resort than neighbouring Bournemouth. It has six safe, sandy beaches, stretching across the sweep of Christchurch Bay, of which Avon Beach, with its deckchairs and pleasure rides, is probably the best. Just outside the town is the Alice in Wonderland Family Park which has swing boats, go-karts and an astro-slide, and is inhabited by various costumed characters from the Alice books.

Every Monday during the summer you can go for a guided tour with a difference when, at 11am, the town crier goes for a one-hour walkabout. Dressed in traditional costume and ringing his bell, he will point out (and shout about) all the local sights.

Alice in Wonderland Family Park
Merritown Lane **t** (01202) 483444
Open April–Sept daily 10–6
Adm £4
Restaurant, gift shop

Lulworth Cove
Getting there The cove is on the Dorset coast, 9 miles east of Weymouth off the B3070, which links to the A352

An almost perfect loop of sand overlooked by high, craggy cliffs, Lulworth is an understandably popular beauty spot and best appreciated outside high summer. There are good coastal walks to the west (to the east is army property) taking you past sheltered sandy bays and bizarre rock formations to Durdle Door, where a natural rock arch has been formed by the crashing sea. The Lulworth Cove Heritage Centre tells the story of the area's

geological formation and has an exhibition on smuggling.

Lulworth Cove Heritage Centre
Main Road, Lulworth Cove **t** (01929) 400587
Open Summer 10–6; winter 10–4
Free
Café, picnic areas, shop, guided tours, on-site parking

Poole

Getting there By road: Poole is on the South Devon coast next door to Bournemouth (the border is rather fuzzy and you can easily pass from one to the other without realizing it) and can be reached from London via the M3 and A31. By train: The train station is situated in the centre of the town and there are daily services from London
Tourist office 4 Poole High Street **t** (01202) 253253
www.poole.gov.uk/tourism

So close to Bournemouth as to be virtually the same town, the ancient seaport of Poole nevertheless has its own distinct character and a lively, continental feel to it with its alfresco restaurants. winding lanes and a bustling harbour (the largest natural harbour in Europe). Although the tourist board's claim that it is the 'St Tropez of the south coast' is somewhat exaggerated, its beaches, all five miles of them, are clean, sandy and safe. Indeed, the best, Sandbanks, has won no fewer than 13 European Blue Flags and has lifeguard coverage and trained beach staff. In the centre of town there's a pleasant park surrounding a 55-acre lake where you can hire rowboats, pedaloes and remote-controlled cars. There's also an indoor adventure playground (Gus Gorilla's Jungle Playground), a miniature railway and plenty of grassy lawns to run about on. Farmer Parmer's Farm Park is just 4 miles out of town (p.176).

Aquarium Complex
Hennings Wharf, The Quay **t** (01202) 686712
Open Daily 9.30–5.30
Adm Adult £5.25, child £4.75, under-2s **free**
Coffee shop, restaurant, shop

The complex contains an aquarium with sharks and piranhas, a serpentarium with rattle snakes and pythons, an insectarium with tarantulas and scorpions and a Crocodile Pool (crocodilarium?). There's also a small model-railway museum and a play area.

Brownsea Island

Poole Harbour, Poole **t** (01202) 707744
www.nationaltrust.org.uk
Getting there Regular daily ferries run to the island from Poole Quay, Sandbanks, Bournemouth Pier and Swanage
Open April–Sept daily 10–5 (open till 6 July and Aug)
Adm Landing **free**; adult £3.50, child £1.50, family £8.50
Café, mother and baby facilities, disabled access

This 500-acre nature reserve in the middle of Poole's natural harbour is home to a wide variety of wildlife, including butterflies, birds and the rare red squirrel, which was once common throughout the mainland but was driven almost to extinction by the introduction of the larger, grey squirrel. Guided walks are available in summer.

Poole Pottery

The Quay **t** (01202) 666200
www.poolepottery.co.uk
Open Daily 9–5.30 (Sun 10–5.30); school hols: Mon–Fri 9–8, Sat 9–5.30, Sun 10–5.30
Adm Factory tour: adult £2.50, child £1.50
Restaurant, tearoom, factory shop, disabled access

This is one of the town's biggest draws where you can watch skilled potters and glass-blowers while they work. There is a film on the history of pot-making (more interesting than you'd think) and, best of all, kids can try their hand at throwing a pot themselves in the 'Have a Go' area.

Waterfront Museum

Old High Street, Poole **t** (01202) 683138
Open Apr–Oct 10-5 Mon–Sat, noon–5 Sun; Nov–Mar 10–3 Mon–Sat, noon–3 Sun
Adm Adult £4, child £2.85, family £8–11.50

This fascinating maritime museum is really two museums in one. In part of it, Scalpen's Court, you can see where Cromwell's troops once stayed (there is even some soldier's graffiti round the fireplace). In the same building children will enjoy the reconstruction of a Victorian kitchen and a school room as well as the collection of antique toys and games. At the Waterfront Museum proper there are exhibits on the history of the area from Roman times to now – if you've never seen an Iron Age log boat then this is your chance.

Cinemas

Arts Centre

Kingland Road **t** (01202) 685222
Combined cinema and theatre.

UCI

Tower Park, Mannings Heath **t** 0870 010 2030
10-screen cinema with all the latest releases. Fight your way through the scrum to the Ben & Jerry's ice cream stand.

Theatres

Arts Centre

Kingland Road **t** (01202) 685222

Activities

Cool Cats Watersports Centre

Next to the Sandbanks Hotel, Sandbanks, Poole
t (01202) 701100 www.coolcatswatersports.com
Call in advance for details of times and prices
Catamaran sailing, windsurfing, kayaking, powerboating and bike hire.

Rockley Watersports

Rockley Point, Hamworthy, Poole **t** (01202) 677272
www.rockleywatersports.com
Call in advance for details of times and prices.
Courses in dinghy sailing, windsurfing and powerboating for all ages and abilities.

Splashdown

Tower Park Leisure Complex, Poole, Yarrow Road, Poole **t** (01202) 716000
Open Term time: Mon–Fri 2–9, Sat and Sun 10–7
School hols: Mon–Fri 10–9, Sat and Sun 10–7;
Aug Mon–Fri 9–7, Sat and Sun 9–7
Prices Call in advance
Restaurant, café, mother and baby facilities, disabled access, on-site parking

Housed in the largest commercial leisure centre in the UK, Splashdown boasts 11 full-on waterslides with names like Tennessee Twister and Louisiana Leap, as well as a paddling pool, a bubble bench and an interactive playzone (for very young children) and spa pools, saunas and an outdoor sun terrace (for adults). The centre also contains a 'Quasar 2000' laser battle-zone for 7–16 year olds, a 'Planet' Kidz for 3–12 year olds, as well as a 10-screen cinema, a Megabowl 30-lane bowling alley and lots of video games.

The New Forest

Getting there The New Forest occupies a vast swathe of countryside between Ringwood (to the west) and Southampton (to the east). Its major town is Lyndhurst on the A35 and A357

Tourist information Main car park, High Street, Lyndhurst **t** (023) 8028 2269

The New Forest represents the largest area of 'wild' vegetation in Britain south of the Scottish highlands: 145 square miles of light woodland, isolated ponds, deep forest and heath (in fact, despite its name, there's more heath than anything else) inhabited by numerous wild animals including deer (the forest owes its existence to William I's desire to preserve an area of habitat for the royal deer), badgers and the famous New Forest ponies, said to be descended from small Spanish horses captured from the Armada. If all the wild animals evade you, however, you can always check out some captive specimens at the New Forest Otter, Owl and Conservation Park **t** (023) 8029 2408 and Longdown Dairy Farm in Ashurst **t** (023) 8029 3326 or the New Forest Owl Sanctuary near Ringwood **t** (01425) 476487. At its heart the forest feels ancient and primordial, the last sprouting remains of a bygone age and, fittingly, the residents of the forest enjoy a range of centuries-old feudal rights including the right to cut peat in the forest (known as 'turbary' in the ancient local dialect), the right to collect firewood in the forest ('estover') and the right to let their pigs forage for acorns ('mast').

To get the best out of your visit, try and head away from the often heavily congested main roads – an estimated 10 million people visit the forest each year which works out at over 25,000 a day. Exploring the forest on horseback or by bike is probably your best bet; the forest boasts over 125 miles of car-free gravel pathways. Whatever your plans, however, you should first pay a call to the visitor centre at Lyndhurst, the capital of the forest, which can provide you with details of walks, guided tours, horse-riding centres, nature trails and campsites. The centre also has several excellent interactive displays (including a 'Feely Log', a 'Forest Hide' – lift the wooden panels to reveal the secret animal – and computer quizzes), a slide show theatre and a 25ft-long embroidery depicting the history of the region.

You might like to begin your exploration of the forest with a walk to the Rufus Stone, some three miles north of Lyndhurst, which marks the spot where William II (nicknamed 'Rufus' because of his reddish complexion), the son of William the Conqueror, was shot dead by an errant crossbow bolt while out hunting with the Royal party. It was, of course, an 'accident' although the man responsible, Sir William Tyrell, quickly fled to France while William's brother, Henry, who had accompanied him on the trip, ran equally quickly in the opposite direction to Winchester, where he was crowned king.

Activities

AA Bike Hire New Forest

Fern Glen, Gosport Lane, Lyndhurst **t** (023) 8028 3349

Getting there It is located near the tourist information centre on the edge of the coach park

Hires out mountain bikes, children's bikes, tandems and tag-a-longs from £6 a day.

Arniss Riding Stables

Sandy Balls Holiday Centre, Godshill, Fordingbridge **t** (01425) 654114 **www**.sandy-balls.co.uk

Horse-trekking in the New Forest for beginners and experienced riders.

Bagnum Riding Stables

Bagnum Lane, Ringwood **t** (01425) 476263 **www**.tmb.uk.com/bagnum

Lessons, pony club.

Burley Bike Hire

Village centre, Burley **t** (01425) 403584
Open Daily (except Wed)

Stocks adult bikes, child trailers (or 'bratmobiles' as it calls them), dog trailers ('mutmobiles') and tandems.

Burley-Villa School of Riding

B3058, nr New Milton **t** (01425) 610278

Pony- and horse-trekking.

New Forest Cycle Experience

Island Shop, 2–4 Brookley Road, Brockenhurst **t** (01590) 624202 **www**.cycleX.co.uk

Stocks adult bikes, children's bikes, tandems, tag-a-longs and child and dog trailers and can provide details of routes for all abilities through the forest.

Nature lovers

Farmer Palmer's Farm Park

Wareham Road, Organford, Poole **t** (01202) 622022
www.farmerpalmer.co.uk
Getting there The farm is off the A35, 4 miles from
Poole, heading towards Bere Regis
Open April–Sept 10–5.30; Oct–Mar open certain
weeks and weekends (call in advance)
Adm Adult £3.95, child £2.95, under-3s **free**,
family £12.90
Café, gift shop, guided tours, disabled access, on-site parking

This busy working dairy farm, just four miles
outside Poole, welcomes families throughout the
summer when there are lots of opportunities for
kids to get close to the animals. They can feed and
cuddle the lambs, goat kids and piglets, and groom
the ponies. There is also an undercover play area
and tractor rides.

Finkley Down Farm Park

Andover **t** (01264) 324141 Infoline **t** (01264) 352195
Getting there It's just northeast of Andover off the
A303 and A342
Open Mar–Oct daily 10–6
Adm Adult £4, child £3, under-2s **free**, family £13
*Refreshments, mother and baby facilities, disabled
access, on-site parking*

Good, solid working farm with animals and
poultry to pet and feed, a pets' corner, an adventure
playground and trampolines. Activities for children
are organized throughout the day.

Longdown Dairy Farm

Ashurst, near Southampton **t** (023) 8029 3326
www.longdowndairyfarm.co.uk
Getting there It's 5 miles southwest of
Southampton off the A35.
Open April–Oct daily 10–5
Adm Adult £4.30, child £3, under-2s **free**
Refreshments, gift shop

Much less developed and commercialized than
many of its competitors, Longdown, in the New
Forest, can nonetheless offer a wide range of farm
animals to look at and feed including pigs, sheep,
goats and cows. There may also be the chance to
watch the daily milking session from a viewing
gallery and if you come in spring you may be able
to see a calf being born.

Marwell Zoological Park

Colden Common **t** (01426) 943163
www.marwell.org.uk
Getting there It's 8 miles south of Winchester off
the B2177 (J12 from the M3)
Open Daily 10–6 (till 4 in winter)
Adm Adult £8, child £5, family £24
*Restaurant, café, gift shop, mother and baby room,
adapted toilets*

One of the country's leading conservation zoos
(its logo features the Oryx, one of the world's most
endangered species), the enclosures at Marwell
have been designed to imitate the animals' natural
environments as closely as possible. In particular,
look out for the leopards' enclosure where a collection of poles and platforms are used to replicate
the African tree tops – leopards spend much of
their time in trees and often drag their kills up into
the branches to prevent them being stolen by
other predators. All the headline beasts are here,
from lions, tigers and even black panthers to
zebras, giraffes and rhinos (including a baby rhino
born in 1999). Animal encounter sessions are organized in summer.

Moors Valley Country Park

Horton Road, Ashley Heath **t** (01425) 470721
www.bournemouth.co.uk
Getting there The park is 10 miles north of
Bournemouth
Open Daily dawn–dusk
Free
*Café, restaurant, shop, wheelchair access, on-site
parking*

This large country park is aimed very much at
families with a lake (with lakeside walks), a 400-
hectare swathe of forest (with a tree-top walkway,
a forest-play trail and nature trails), a miniature
steam railway and a play castle and sandworks for
toddlers. The visitor centre has bikes (including
tandems) for hire at £3.50 per 1.5hr + £25 deposit.

Paultons Park

Ower, Romsey **t** (023) 8081 4455
Getting there Ower is at the northern end of the
New Forest, west of Southampton, near the junc-
tion of the A31 and A36 (J2 from the M27). A bus
service runs from Southampton
Open Mar–Oct daily 10–6.30
Adm Adult £9.50, child £8.50, family £33
*Café, fast food, mother and baby facilities, some
disabled access, on-site parking*

Paultons is a bit like a mini Chessington with the same mix of rides and animals but done on a much smaller, gentler, kiddy-size scale. The park, which is spread out over 140 acres, contains areas of woodland and gardens (home to free-flying tropical birds including flamingoes) in addition to its rollercoasters, log flumes, bumper boats, go-karts, radio-controlled cars and animated dinosaurs. In truth, it's a little bit lightweight and perhaps best suited for very young children (there's a Tiny Tots Town and a small petting zoo) but it's a cheerful, welcoming place and more genuinely family-friendly that many of its larger, more overtly commercial competitors.

Look at this!

Milestones Living History Museum
Leisure Park, Churchill Way, Basingstoke
t (01256) 477766
Getting there It is just north of the M3 (J6)
Open Tues–Fri 10–5 Sat and Sun 10–6 (last adm 1 hr before closing)
Adm adult £5.95, child £2.95, under-5s free, family £14.90, concs £4.75
Café, shop, on-site parking

The recently opened Milestones museum, housed in a stunning glass structure in the town's famous Leisure Park (where you can also go ice skating and bowling), is an attempt to create an entire Victorian and 1930s replica town. Stroll along historic streets, tour historic factories and browse historic shops while staff dressed in period costume guide you through the exhibits. There are several designated kids' attractions including an interactive post office, a hands-on history section and a toy display where modern toys are compared with their historic counterparts.

Museum of Army Flying
Middle Wallop, Stockbridge **t** (01980) 674421
www.flying-museum.org.uk
Getting there It's on the A343 between Andover and Salisbury
Open Daily 10–5
Adm Adult £4.50, child £3, family £12.50
Café, gift shop, mother and baby facilities, guided tours, disabled facilities, on-site parking

Between Andover and Salisbury in the delightfully named Middle Wallop, this excellent museum is home to one of the country's largest collections of military flying machines – kites, gliders, planes, helicopters etc. – all displayed in a series of imaginative dioramas designed to illustrate the development of military flying from the First World War to the present day. For children, however, the highlight will undoubtedly be the Interactive Science Centre with its collection of hands-on flying exhibits (simulators, cockpits and the like) and the camera obscura which provides wonderful 'secret' views of the surrounding countryside.

Steam power

Watercress Line
Station Road, Alresford, nr Winchester
t (01962) 733810 **www**.watercressline.co.uk
Operating times Mar–Oct Sat and Sun and school hols; Nov–Feb Sun, eight trains a day
Fares Adult £8, child £5, family £24
Café, gift shop, mother and baby room

The name derives from the watercress beds which still grow in Alresford, the railway's headquarters and a picturesque Georgian town. From here, it's a 10-mile trip to Alresford from Alton passing through Ropley and Medstead and Marks, the highest station in southern England. Each of the four stops along the line recreate periods in the line's history from the Twenties through to the late Fifties. Even the station staff are kitted out in appropriate uniforms. Kids love the sight of these big children playing with their train sets and there is nothing quite so evocative as the 'toot' of the whistle and the hiss of steam to get young pulses racing. The journey to Alresford takes about half an hour and this little town is worth seeing if only for the quaint Georgian high street. The station has its own picnic area with a marquee provided if its wet. On the return journey try to make time for Ropely to see the locomotives being restored in the engine shed or, if the weather is nice, stop off at Four Marks for signposted woodland walks.

WILTSHIRE

Go West

SALISBURY

Getting there By road: Salisbury is 90 miles west of London on the A36. By train/coach: Trains run daily from London (Waterloo), Bath and Portsmouth. National Express coaches run daily from London, Bath and Portsmouth

Tourist information First Row **t** (01722) 334956 www.visitsalisbury.com

On the banks of the River Avon, Wiltshire's capital is an undeniably beautiful place with picturesque water meadows and a litter of old buildings, some dating back to the 13th century. It is also surprisingly small with most of its attractions grouped around its central Market Square (*see* below) and can easily be navigated on foot (*see* below for information on tours). The town's dominant feature is its magnificent cathedral with its famous spire (at 123m it is the highest in England), which can be seen for miles around. The main body of the cathedral was built during the 13th century (*c.* 1220–66) in a mere 38 years (38 years may not seem that quick but by medieval standards it was practically light speed; most cathedrals took well over 100 years to complete), while the spire was added early in the 14th century. As the original design did not include a spire, its addition caused major architectural problems. It weighs a mighty 6,400 tonnes and, if you look closely at the stone pillars supporting it, you can see that they have become bent under the enormous weight. The interior is dark and spooky with several interesting features to look out for, notably the sculpted tombs of medieval crusader heroes, the clock in the north aisle (built in 1386, this is the oldest continuously working clock in Europe) and the model of the cathedral in the north transept surrounded by miniature blacksmiths, carpenters and masons. Free guided tours of the cathedral and tower are offered twice daily.

Things to see

Medieval Hall
West Walk, Cathedral Close **t** (01722) 412472
Open April–Sept, performances run continuously from 11–5
Adm Adult £1.50, child £1, under-6s **free**
Refreshments, disabled access
Watch a 40-minute film on the history of Salisbury.

Old Sarum Castle
Castle Road **t** (01722) 335398
Open April–Oct daily 10–6; Nov–Mar daily 10–4
Adm Adult £2, child £1
Refreshments, gift shop, on-site parking
The original site of the town until it relocated in the 13th century, this large grassy corrugated mound two miles north of the city centre is scattered with ruins (a castle, a cathedral and a Bishop's Palace) and offers good views of the city and south Wiltshire countryside. An excellent picnic spot, there are family activities and events laid on at the castle throughout the summer including storytelling sessions, mask-making, iron age pottery, a medieval tournament and 'Jurassic Giants' when kids can help archaeologists reconstruct dinosaur skeletons.

Salisbury Cathedral
The Close, Salisbury **t** (01722) 555120
www.salisburycathedral.org.uk
Open June–Aug daily 7–8; Sept–May daily 7–6.30
Free (suggested donations: adults £3, family £6)
Coffee shop, souvenir shop, wheelchair access to ground floor only, on-site parking (£5 per car)
The cathedral's cloisters are the largest in the country and contain some wonderful bas-relief friezes depicting early Biblical stories as well as one of only four surviving copies of the *Magna Carta*. A brass rubbing centre opens in summer and there's a children's booklet 'Look at Salisbury Cathedral' available for a small charge.

Free guided tours of the cathedral and tower are given every day.

Salisbury and South Wiltshire Museum

The King's House, 65 The Close **t** (01722) 332151
Open Mon–Sat 10–5; July–Aug Sun 2–5
Adm Adult £3, child 75p
Café, gift shop, mother and baby facilities, disabled access

Award-winning museum with displays on Stonehenge, the Romans and Saxons, and a gruesome pre-NHS surgery. Includes a section on General Pitt Rivers, who excavated many of Wiltshire's sites, including Avebury.

Things to do

Shopping at the market

To see Salisbury at its best, visit on a Tuesday or a Saturday when the market is in full swing. Held in the medieval market square, its cheery bustle is a reminder that, despite its abundance of historic architecture, this is a real, living city and not, like so many other towns in this region, just a well-preserved tourist trap. Fruit, vegetables and clothes make up the bulk of the market's produce.

Walking tours

Guided tours leave from outside the tourist information centre twice daily, from May to September, and on Fridays there is a ghost tour.

Cinemas
Odeon
New Canal **t** (01722) 335924/0870 50 50 007
Major cinema close to the museums and cathedral.

Theatres
Arts Centre
Bedwin Street **t** (01722) 321744
Salisbury Playhouse
Malthouse Lane **t** (01722) 320333

Did you know...
That a market has been held on the same spot in Salisbury every week since 1361 (or well over 66,000 times – that's a lot of vegetables).

SPECIAL TRIPS

Avebury Stone Circle

Avebury, near Swindon
Getting there Avebury is about 10 miles south of Swindon and 22 miles east of Bath, off the A4361 and A4
Open Any reasonable time
Free
Cafés, restaurants, picnic areas, shops, parking outside village

The trouble with Stonehenge is that it has become so popular, you're no longer allowed to go right up to the stones. At Avebury, a slightly lesser-known ancient stone monument 19 miles to the north, you can get as close as you like, allowing you to appreciate fully just how big these great monoliths really are and what a feat of engineering it must have been for the ancient people to get them into position without the help of modern tools and technology. There are three circles, two inner ones and one large outer one, the outer one is so large it actually encircles the village and has been cut in to quarters (or sectors named northwest, northeast, southwest and southeast) by the two main roads running though it. Built some 3,500 years ago, there are obviously quite a lot of stones missing (many were used by villagers in the Middle Ages to build houses) although the northwest and southwest sectors are more or less complete. Children love following the circle around (careful crossing the roads), counting off the stones, noting the missing ones and, of course, clambering on top of some of the smaller ones. In fact, you should probably think of your day out at Avebury less as a visit to a historic site than a day spent meandering about in the open air, wandering through the trees on the outskirts of the village while the kids scamper over grassy lawns or roll down the defensive ditch that once surrounded the stones.

If you're particularly interested in ancient sites then the stretch of the A4 just south of Avebury, between Marlborough and Chippenham, will make for some fascinating driving taking you past chalk horses carved into the hillside and strange prehistoric burial mounds known as barrows. The most famous of these mounds can be found at West Kennet, just south of Avebury (it's about a three-quarters of a mile walk from the road, free entry).

The barrow, which was built around 4,000 years ago, is just over a 100m long and divided into several spooky, explorable chambers (bring a torch) which provided a final resting-place for around 50 people. The stones marking the entrance each weigh a mighty 7–10 tons and would have required hundreds of men to haul them into position.

Just north of the barrow is the great turfy flat-tened cone of Silbury Hill, the largest man-made mound in Europe (130ft high). It was built around 2,500 years ago and, as with many ancient sites, its precise purpose remains unknown.

Longleat

Warminster **t** (01985) 844400 Infoline: **t** 09068 884581 **www.**longleat.co.uk
Getting there It is situated on the A36, Warminster bypass. Follow the signs
Open April–Oct 11–6; Nov–Dec guided tours only 11–4 (opening times of attractions vary slightly)
Adm Passport Ticket valid for all Longleat attrac-tions if used by the end of the season
Café, restaurant, picnic areas, mother and baby facil-ities, guided tours, disabled access, on-site parking

The first private stately home to open its doors to the public, Longleat is still leading the way in terms of family entertainment with a range of attractions that put many of its more recent competitors to shame. Its grounds are home to one of the country's very best safari parks with lions, tigers (including a rare white tiger), monkeys (who climb over the visi-tors' cars and, if given half the chance, will happily remove your windscreen wipers), giraffes, rhinos, elephants and sea lions among its many residents. Families arriving without cars (or in a soft-top) can use the Safari Bus service (commentary provided) although there are a few sections of the park which can be tackled on foot. Walking past giraffes, llamas and zebras (although, thankfully, not lions), kids can pretend they are on a real safari out on the African plains. Don't miss taking a trip to see the gorillas on the island – children enjoy feeding the seals and sea lions while on the boat.

And if the kids become tired of the animals, there is lots more to keep them amused. See if they can find their way out of the maze (the largest hedge maze in the country, aerial views of which are often used as icons of the country itself), take them for a ride on the narrow-gauge railway or climb aboard the tethered balloon to see what the park looks like from an altitude of 400ft. There is also a collection of dolls' houses, an exhibition on devoted to the Timelord himself, Doctor Who, and a Postman Pat village. And if that wasn't enough, Longleat has an adventure castle, a King Arthur-themed mirror maze and a petting zoo.

Stonehenge

Amesbury, Salisbury **t** (01980) 624715
www.english-heritage.org.uk
Getting there Stonehenge is 2 miles west of Amesbury on the junction of the A303 and A344/A360. Salisbury train station is 9.5 miles away **t** (01722) 336855 for details of local buses
Open 16 Mar–31 May 9.30–6; 1 June–31 Aug 9–7; 1 Sept–15 Oct 9.30–6; 16 Oct–15 Mar 9.30–4
Adm Adult £4.20, child £2.20, family £10.60
Shop, refreshments, wheelchair access, on-site parking

One of the world's most famous and mysterious ancient monuments, Stonehenge has been astounding and baffling people in equal measure for centuries. Standing in the centre of Wiltshire's great Salisbury Plain, it consists of a huge outer ring of stones arranged in a series of trilithons (two upright stones with another stone laid as a lintel across the top), inside which are two concentric horseshoe arrangements of smaller stones and a central 'altar' stone. There's also another ring outside the main ring but only a few of these stones remain. The oldest stones, known as blue-stones, which make up the inner horseshoe, were transported here from the Welsh Coast some entrance fee does include an audio guide which will fill you in on the background history and the current state of scholarly debate regarding the stones' use. For the best views, however, you should come just after dawn when, in the swirling early morning mist, you can really get a sense of the stones' mystery and power – features which tend to get rather diluted when you're standing among hordes of snapping, chattering tourists.

4,000 years ago – presumably by sea, river and then, once on land, on wooden rollers (a round trip of some 240 miles) – a particularly impressive feat when you consider that each stone weighs around 4 tonnes. The larger outer stones were added around a thousand years later and were probably quarried less than 20 miles from the site. Such is their size, however (each weighs over 40 tonnes), that it has been estimated that it would have taken something like 600 people to move them into position.

The whole complex clearly had some sort of religious and/or mystical significance for whoever built it. The inner stones have been arranged so that they point towards the sun as it rises for the summer solstice on midsummer's day, although no one really knows why. Was it a temple for worshipping the sun, or something more sinister? In the 18th century certain scholars believed it had been a site of human sacrifice (at nearby Woodhenge, a similar, albeit organic ancient monument, the remains of a girl with axe wounds in her head was found in the centre of a circle of wooden posts) and they named one of the stones the 'Slaughter Stone', believing this may have been where the grizzly deeds took place. However, no evidence has been found linking Stonehenge with such practices. Others have claimed that Stonehenge may have had a more secular use and that its astronomical alignment was simply a means of measuring time. Whatever its purpose, it is still an impressive sight, indeed one of the must-see sights of the entire country. After the initial 'Cors!', however, you may find yourself feeling a little disappointed. The demands of conservation mean that you're no longer allowed to wander in among the stones and, in fact, have to stand quite a way back. And, while you're afforded good views, these are only marginally better (and a good deal more expensive) than the views from the A244. Still, the

AROUND AND ABOUT

Nature lovers

Cholderton Rare Breeds Farm

Amesbury Road, Cholderton, Salisbury **t** (01980) 629438 **www**.farm-animals.co.uk
Getting there The farm can be reached via the A303 from London and the A338 from Salisbury
Open April–Nov daily 10–6
Adm Adult £4.25, child £2.75, family £13
Café-restaurant, farm shop, mother and baby facilities, disabled access, on-site parking

If watching pigs running around a racecourse with teddy bear jockeys tied to their backs appeals, then Cholderton is just the place for you. Even if the pigs aren't running (races are only held during peak times, which usually means summer weekends), there's still plenty of farmyard fun to be had. The centre's function is twofold. Its main role, as home to British Animal Heritage, is to preserve traditional farm breeds for future generations, while its secondary role is to welcome and entertain families – it seems to perform both ably. Small children will love Rabbit World, which is home to over 50 breeds of rabbits (that's a lot of stroking), and there are goats, sheep and donkeys to meet, as well as a large, shaggy Shire horse. The centre also has a nature trail, picnic areas, a toddlers' play area, adventure playgrounds and it can offer tractor rides.

Farmer Giles Farmstead

Teffont, Salisbury **t** (01722) 716338
www.farmergiles.co.uk
Getting there From Salisbury take the A36 to Wilton and the A30 to Shaftesbury, then at Barford

St Martin take the B3089 towards Hindon and follow the brown signs at Teffont

Open April–Sept daily 10–6; Nov–Mar Sat and Sun 10–6

Adm Adult £3.95, child £2.85, family £13

'Old Barn' restaurant (traditional farm food), picnic areas, farm shop, guided tours, mother and baby facilities, disabled access, on-site parking

This has got pretty much everything you'd want from a day out at the farm – indoor and outdoor play areas, pigs, Shetland ponies, Shire horses, donkeys, sheep (with lambs to bottle-feed in early summer), chipmunks, a pets' corner, tractor rides (you get to sit in a trailer full of hay bales) and over 150 dairy cows. In the afternoon there is an opportunity to have a go at hand-milking the cows – not as easy as it looks.

Longleat

For further information *see p.180.*

Steam power

Steam – the Museum of the Great Western Railway

Kemble Drive, Swindon **t** (01793) 466627

www.steam-museum.org.uk

Getting there Leave the M4 at J16 and follow the brown tourist signs

Open Mon-Sat 10–5, Sun 11–5

Adm Adult £5.50 child £3.50, under-5s **free**, family £13.50

Café, disabled access, audio guide available

Recently renovated following a lottery grant, these old Swindon railway works (which are located next to a giant shopping centre), now house a huge museum of railway history. There are displays on the people who used to work and travel on the Great Western Railway and an exhibition on the great engineers such as Isambard Kingdom Brunel as well as a collection of vintage locomotives.

Visitors to the museum pass through a series of lively reconstructions where original equipment, video and interactive displays paint a portrait of what life was like for some of the 12,000 workforce employed by the GWR in its heyday before the First World War. You begin by walking past toiling clerks in the Office, bent over their desks. Then on to the

General Stores which supplied everything from pen nibs to railway sleepers. Next comes the Foundry where enough metal was produced to manufacture three locomotives a week before heading through the Machine Shop, the Carriage Body Shop and the Boiler Shop where the noise was once so great that employees were deaf at thirty. Finally, visitors are confronted by the product of all this combined effort – the express passenger locomotive *Caerphilly Castle* in ex-works condition with gleaming paint and brass.

The collection of memorabilia includes everything from tickets, posters and uniforms to engines and rolling stock. The mixture of video, footage and interactive displays, the touch-screen games and steam train simulator will all appeal to kids. Would-be boffins can see engines being repaired.

Steam firsts

In 1814 *The Times* became the first newspaper to be printed by steam power. It might seem pretty antiquated now but at the time it was state-of-the-art technology.

The British steamship, the *Sirius*, became the first vessel to cross the Atlantic solely under steam-power in 1838. With 49 passengers the *Sirius* had taken 18 days and 10 hours to complete the trip. When she arrived in New York Harbour the little 703-ton ship had only 15 tons of coal left in her bunkers. She'd made it, but only just!

The world's first successful submarine, designed by the Swedish engineer Nordenfelt, was first demonstrated in 1887. The steam-driven vessel had a surface speed of 9 knots and was also the first submarine to be armed with self-propelled torpedoes.

The world's first ever motor show was held in Paris in 1894. Among the exhibits at the Palais de l'Industriel on the Champs Élysées was a steam car and a steam tractor.

WHERE TO EAT

Bath

The Bear
6 –10 Wellsway **t** (01225) 425795
Open Mon–Sat 11–11, Sun 12–10.30, food served till 9.30pm, lounge restaurant closed 3–6pm
High chairs available

Traditional pub offering a huge 'Whole Hog' menu featuring roast lunches and curries as well as Chinese and vegetarian options. Kids, who are only allowed in the lounge restaurant, get a 'King Kranky' menu with colouring crayons and pads.

Beaujolais
5 Chapel Row, off Queen's Square **t** (01225) 423417
Open Mon–Sat 12–2.30 and 6–10, closed Sun

This is a very welcoming restaurant with a walled garden. The menu is predominantly French but staff are very accommodating to children's needs and the chef will happily rustle up a quick chicken and chips. Kids' portions and high chairs provided.
High chairs available, mother and baby room

Bella Pasta
13 Milsom Street **t** (01225) 462368
Open Mon–Wed 10–10, Thur–Sat 10–11, Sun 12–10
High chairs available

Cheery branch of the Italian pasta chain. Under 9s get their own menu.

Brown's
Orange Grove **t** (01225) 461199
Open Mon–Sat 11–11.30, Sun 12–11

Large branch of the ever family-friendly chain housed in the city's old police station, a stone's throw from the Baths, Abbey and Pump Room. Children get their own menu which they can colour in with the crayons provided and there are high chairs and mother and baby facilities. Diners wishing to smoke eat in what used to be the cells.

Café Cadbury
23 Union Street **t** (01225) 444030
Open Daily 8–6

A hybrid coffeehouse–chocolate shop, Café Cadbury aims to provide the best of both worlds – good café food and drinks, and vast supplies of quality chocolates. It's actually aimed at the adult Starbucks crowd with clean, minimalist décor and posters adorning the walls with words like 'refresh' and 'indulge' printed on them, but children are never averse to a few chocs.

Café René
Shires Yard **t** (01225) 447147
Open Daily 8–6
High chairs available

Situated in an 18th-century courtyard, the café serves filled French bread, sandwiches, salads, pastries and hot lunches. There's a children's menu (or, if your kids feel that is a bit beneath them, the kitchen are happy to adapt adult dishes to children's tastes), a full breakfast menu and seating inside and out.

Caffè Piazza
23 The Podium **t** (01225) 429299
Open Daily 8.30am–10.30pm

Offers a wide range of authentic Italian pasta and pizza dishes. Children's menu and high chairs available.

Sally Lunn's Old English Tea House
4 North Parade Passage **t** (01225) 461634
Open Mon–Sat 10–10, Sun 11–6

Not to be missed – enjoy a cream tea and a little historical sightseeing at the same time. The oldest house in Bath (it was built sometime towards the end of the 15th century), Sally Lunn's not only comprises an excellent tea shop (try the famous Sally Lunn Bun, still baked by hand according to her 1680 recipe), but also a museum where Sally's original kitchen can be seen and which kids can visit free of charge. There's a colour-in kids' menu and high chairs.

Around Bath

Waterwheel Grill
Old Mill Hotel, Tollbridge Road, Batheaston
t (01225) 858476
Open Mon–Sat 6–10.30, Sun 12 noon–3

Just outside town, the restaurant overlooks a picturesque stretch of the River Avon. It's quite upmarket but happy to welcome children, particularly on Sundays. There's a lovely garden running alongside the river (kids must be accompanied as

---

Sally Lunn Buns
Sally Lunn was supposedly a well-endowed lady who sold her buns on the streets of Bath. The buns are made of a rich dough rather like that of brioche. You can try them at Sally Lunn's Old English Tea House and Museum (*see* above), either for tea or with a savoury stuffing for dinner.

the river has no fencing) and a working water-wheel. Sunday lunch is £4.95 for children.

Beaulieu

Beaulieu Road Inn

Beaulieu Road, near Lyndhurst **t** (023) 8029 2342
Open Summer 11–11; Winter 11–3 and 6–11; food served 11.30–4 and 6–9.30

Country inn serving traditional and modern British cuisine (children's menu, vegetarian options and high chairs available) with a large garden with a play area and a paddock where there are ponies to stroke.

Monty's

Montaignè Arms Hotel, Beaulieu **t** (01590) 612324
Open Food served 12 noon–2.30 and 6–9.30

Upmarket pub-cum-brasserie where you can dine alfresco in summer or lounge by the log fire in winter. Children's menu and high chairs available.

Smithy Tea Rooms

Exbury Gardens, near Beaulieu **t** (023) 8089 8737
Open Daily 9–5

Home-made cakes and clotted cream teas in a picturesque location.

Bournemouth

Bistro 77

77 Southbourne Road, Southbourne
t (01202) 566660
Open Sun–Tues 12 noon–2, Wed–Sun 12 noon–10

Locally caught seafood (including lobster and crab) a speciality. Children's menu available.

Bourne's Restaurant

Sydney House Hotel, 6 West Cliff Road
t (01202) 555536
Open Coffee shop: daily 8–4; restaurant: Mon–Sat 6pm–10pm, closed Sun

Traditional English cuisine (roasts, steaks, meat pies) in the restaurant, and cream teas in the coffee shop. Children's menu and high chairs available.

Café Rouge

67–71 Seamoor Road, Westbourne **t** (01202) 757472
Open Mon–Sat 10am–11pm, Sun 10am–10.30pm

Family-friendly French restaurant chain offering a children's menu with crayons and stickers.

Chez Fred

10 Seamoor Road, Westbourne **t** (01202) 761023
Open Mon–Sat 11.30–2 and 5–10, Sun 5.30–10

Award-winning fish and chip restaurant. Kids get their own menu ('Fred's Sprat Pack Meals') and are given colouring books, pens and toys to keep them amused. Eat in or take away. High chairs available

Coriander

22 Richmond Hill **t** (01202) 552202
Open Mon–Thur, Sun noon–10.30, Fri & Sat noon–11

Kids are given crayons and paper at this friendly eaterie so they can have a go at producing colourful placemats. There are plenty of tasty Mexican dishes on the menu including nachos, dips and tortillas which are likely to appeal to kids, as are the sticky puddings.

The Salad Centre

667 Christchurch Road, Boscombe **t** (01202) 393673
Open Mon–Sat 11.30–4.30

More and more kids seem to be vegetarian these days so this should appeal with plenty of filling soups and home-made bread, lentil burgers and salads on the menu.

Uncle Sam's

148 Old Christchurch Road **t** (01202) 293355
Open Mon–Sat 12 noon–11.30pm, Sun 12 noon–10.30pm

Lively American-style diner serving up simple children's favourites including burgers, sausages, chicken nuggets, etc. High chairs available.

Isle of Wight

Blacksmiths Arms

Calbourne Road, Newport **t** (01983) 529263
Open Weekdays 11–3 and 6–11, weekends and Bank Hols 11–11

Award-winning, child-friendly pub which offers a children's menu, an indoor play area, a large garden and high chairs.

Bugle Inn

High Street, Brading, Sandown **t** (01983) 407359
Open Mon–Sat 11.30–3 and 6–11, Sun 12–3 and 7–10.30

Next door to the Isle of Wight Waxworks, the Bugle is very family-friendly and can offer a children's menu, an 'all you can eat' Sunday carvery, play equipment and nappy-changing facilities.

Caulkheads

Sandown **t** (01983) 403878
Open Mon–Sat 11.30–3 and 6–11, Sun 12–3 and 7–10.30

Large pub with an indoor kids play area and a large garden with play equipment.

Chequers

Nilton Road, Rookley **t** (01983) 840314
Open Mon–Sat 11.30–3 and 6–11, Sun 12–3 and 7–10.30

Aimed squarely at families, Chequers was once a customs and excise house and can now offer a large, no-smoking family room (children's menu available), an outdoor play area with a bouncy castle and a mother and baby room. 1999 winner of the UK Family Pub of the Year in the *Good Pub Guide*.

Crown Inn

Walkers Lane, Shorwell **t** (01983) 740293
Open Daily noon–2.30, 6–9.30

Family-friendly pub with high chairs and a children's menu which ventures beyond the usual beans and chips to include scampi and mini-portions of roast dinner. There's a stream at the end of the garden which is home to trout and quacking ducks.

The Hare and Hounds

Downende, Arreton **t** (01983) 523446
Open Mon–Sat 11.30–3 and 6–11, Sun 12–3 and 7–10.30

Pleasant, traditional country pub at the top of Arreton Downs, next to Robin Hill Country Park. It serves a full children's menu and the bar is reputedly made from the gibbet used to hang the notorious local murderer Michal Morey in 1736 — he was executed for killing his grandson, or as the local rhyme cheerily puts it:

Michal Morey is dead
For chopping off his grandson's head.
He is hung on Arreton Down
For rooks and ravens to peck down.

Horse and Groom

Main Road, Ningwood, Newport **t** (01983) 760672
Open Mon–Sat 11.30–3 and 6–11, Sun 12–3 and 7–10.30

This friendly West Wight pub is located three miles east of Yarmouth near Newtown Nature Reserve. Real ales and home-made meals (including vegetarian and children's options) are served and there are two beer gardens, one designed for families with a children's play area.

Spy Glass Inn

Esplanade, Ventor **t** (01983) 855338
Open May–Aug Mon–Sat 10.30–11pm; Sep–Apr Mon–Fri 10.30–3, 6.30–11

Fresh seafood, chips and good beer are on the menu. The pub overlooks Ventor's beach so parents can watch over their charges while they savour a drink.

Wight Mouse Inn and Clarendon Hotel

Newport Road, Chale **t** (01983) 730431
www.wightmouseinns.co.uk
Open Mon–Sat 11.30–3 and 6–11, Sun 12–3 and 7–10.30

Very child-friendly pub with three games rooms, an indoor play area 'Mouse World' and an outdoor play area with swings, climbing frames and, in summer, a bouncy castle. Food is served all day, seven days a week. There's a separate children's menu, plus a range of real ales and a selection of over 300 whiskies for parents.

Poole

Corkers Restaurant

1 High Street, The Quay **t** (01202) 681393
Open Mon–Sat Café bar: 8am–12 midnight, restaurant: 12 noon–10

Café bar and restaurant (with children's menu offered in both) overlooking the Quayside. High chairs available.

Salterns Restaurant

Salterns Hotel, 38 Salterns Road **t** (01202) 707321
Open Sun–Sat 7.30–9.30, 12 noon–2pm, 7–9.30

Attractive waterside restaurant offering al fresco dining, French-style cuisine and a continental atmosphere. Children's menu and high chairs available.

Sands Brasserie

Sandbanks Hotel, Shore Road **t** (01202) 707377
Open 7.30–9pm

Beachside brasserie with views across to Studland Bay. Children's menu (crayons on request) and light snacks available. Just in front is a kiosk selling snacks and ice creams.

Portsmouth

Charbar

25 The Boardwalk, Port Solent **t** (023) 9278 7978
Open Daily 12 noon–11pm

For something a little different – every table at Charbar comes fitted with a gas-fired barbecue on which you can cook the meat or seafood of your choice. Strict supervision is obviously necessary but kids absolutely love this. Free 'cocktails' for kids (fruit juices, milkshakes) are served 12 noon–6.

Children's menu (burgers, sausages and the like) and high chairs available.

Sallypot Tea Rooms

35 Broad Street, Old Portsmouth **t** (023) 9281 6265
Open Tues 12 noon–6, Wed–Sun 10–6

Housed in a 17th-century building on a narrow, cobbled street in Portsmouth's old quarter, this tearoom serves traditional fare, including home-made cakes, clotted cream scones and crumpets.

Shorties

8–9 Bellevue Terrace, Southsea **t** (023) 9283 1941
Open Mon–Thurs 6–11, Fri and Sat 6–12 midnight, Sun 6–10.30

Lively American-style diner serving burgers, spare ribs, fried chicken and steak with mini versions for children. High chairs provided.

Spice Island Inn

65 Broad Street, Old Portsmouth **t** (023) 9287 0543
Open Daily 12 noon–9

old-fashioned pub right on the waterfront so you can watch the ferries coming and going. It has an outdoor seating area (made of concrete, it is a bit dour to be honest) and a family room, serving traditional pub food, children's portions available.

Ye Olde Oyster House

291 Locksway Road, Milton **t** (01705) 727456
Open Daily 11-11

Good for the Docks and the *Mary Rose*, this family-friendly pub has a games room with pool and video machines. There is a pleasant beer garden and pub grub is served lunchtimes and evenings.

Salisbury

Bishops' Mill

7 The Maltings **t** (01722) 412127
Open Food served daily 11–6

Pleasant pub with a large garden overlooking the river where swans glide up and down. Cakes, pastries and traditional pub food are served to families during the day (they're flexible with portions), but this is much more adult-orientated at night.

Cross Keys Restaurant

Cross Keys Chequer, Queen Street **t** (01722) 320933
Open Mon–Sat 8.45–5.30, Sun 10–5

Set in a 14th-century listed building, this café-restaurant serves cakes and sandwiches as well as a full traditional English menu. Children's menu

and high chairs available. It's non-smoking throughout.

Debenhams

Blue Boar Row, Market Place **t** (01722) 333212
Open Mon–Fri 9–5, Sat 9–5.30

On the third floor of a 15th-century building, this Tudor-themed English restaurant, with waitress service, is supremely family-friendly offering light snacks and hearty English dishes. A full children's menu, free baby food, baby warmers for bottles, high chairs, cradle chairs and a baby-changing room are all laid on.

George and Dragon

85 Castle Street **t** (01722) 333942
Open Mon–Sat 11.30–2.30 and 6.30–9, Sun 12–2.30

Typical English village pub with a long lawned garden leading down to the River Avon.

Harlees Fish and Chips

11–13 Salt Lane **t** (01722) 411888
Open Mon–Sat 11.30–2.15 and 5–10

Multi-award-winning traditional fish and chip restaurant housed in a Grade II listed building. Chips are free for toddlers. Eat in or take away. High chairs available.

PizzaExpress

50 Blue Boar Row **t** (01722) 415191
Open Mon–Thur 12–11, Fri–Sun 12–11.30

Large 2-floor branch of the family-friendly pizza chain. There's no children's menu but they're flex-ible regarding pizza sizes. High chairs available.

Where to stay

06

The important thing is to find somewhere to stay that's family-friendly – not child-friendly, not parent-friendly, but family-friendly. It can be a difficult trick to pull off. Many hotels don't even bother trying but have instead simply imposed a blanket ban on all children under 12. Others go to the opposite extreme, putting so much emphasis on kiddy-friendliness that adults' needs are ignored.

The perfect family-friendly hotel should have all the facilities parents expect (large, well-equipped bedrooms, comfortable public rooms where they can relax, a babysitting service and crèche, and a decent restaurant serving cuisine beyond pizza or chips where they can enjoy an evening meal without the children), plus all the stuff kids need (high chairs, cots, suitable meal times, a supervised activity area filled with toys and games, a swimming pool and garden) but should, above all, display a welcoming attitude with staff prepared to go out of their way rather than merely tolerate children. Thankfully a fair few such hotels do exist.

Family-friendly hotel checklist

Do they offer:
▶ special family packages or discounts?
Do remember that British hotels tend to charge per person rather than a room rate, so cramming everyone into the same room doesn't always make sound economic sense. However, many hotels do allow children sharing their parents' room to stay free of charge.
▶ a choice of family rooms with 3 or more beds?
▶ rooms with interconnecting doors?
▶ a constantly monitored baby-listening service?
▶ access to whatever leisure facilities there might be? Nothing is guaranteed to put a dampner on a child's spirits more than being told they can't use the swimming-pool.
▶ cots and high chairs?
▶ children's meals? Are they healthy, served at a conveniently early time, in a family-friendly location, and if not, are children welcome in the restaurant?
▶ designated play areas for children? If there's an outdoor play area, is it safe and supervised?
▶ supplies of toys, books and, even better, computer games?
▶ a babysitting service?
▶ a crèche?
▶ organized activities for children?
▶ qualified child-care staff?

England hotel websites
www.theaa.co.uk/hotels (AA Hotel Guide)
www.s-h-systems.co.uk (UK Hotel and Guest House Directory)
www.britain.co.uk (Welcome to Britain)
www.hotels.uk.com
www.travel-uk.com
www.visitbritain.com
www.ukhotelsearch.com
www.smoothhound.co.uk

Hotel chains

Most chain hotels are aimed squarely at business clients, but that doesn't mean you should dismiss them out of hand. Many are keen to supplement their weekly business income with family trade at weekends and offer a range of competitive packages and deals for families, as well as activity programmes and children's menus in their restaurants. Babysitting, baby-listening, cots and high chairs often come as standard. True, the décor of many chains is a little generic and, of course, there's no guarantee that they will be offering a deal on the days you want to travel, but at least you can be sure that the rooms will be clean and well equipped and the service reliable. Large hotel chains may also have on-site leisure facilities and a swimming pool, which is a huge plus point for any family group. By relying on chains you may miss out on discovering a really good, individual hotel with a beauty and charm all of its own but, similarly, you will also avoid discovering that your supposedly 'well-appointed 3-star with sea view' is nothing of the sort.

All of the hotel chains listed below have a policy of welcoming families. The prices given are meant as a rough guide only and are based on two parents and two children sharing a room.

Best Western

www.bestwesternhotels.com
Price from £75 (prices do vary enormously, depending on the size and facilities of the hotel; this is by no means the minimum in all Best Western hotels)

The country's largest hotel group has properties in Aldeburgh, Bath, Brighton, Bournemouth, Bury St Edmunds, Cambridge, Chichester, Colchester, Eastbourne, Great Yarmouth, Hastings, Norwich,

Oxford, Poole, Portsmouth, Salisbury, Stratford-upon-Avon, Winchester, Windsor and Windermere.

Corus

t 0845 300 2000 **www.corushotels.com**
Price from £60

Operates 3-star hotels in Canterbury, Coventry and Oxford.

Under 16s stay free in their parents' room (1 adult per child) or at 50% in their own room. Under 6s eat free of charge, while children aged 6–15 pay a daily fixed price of £5 for breakfast and £10 for breakfast and dinner.

Queens Moat Houses

t 0646 213214 **www.moathousehotels.com**
Price from £120

Operates 3- and 4-star hotels (many with leisure facilities) in Bournemouth, Cambridge, Oxford, Stratford-upon-Avon, Winchester and Windsor.

Swallow

t 0845 600 4666 **www.swallowhotels.com**
Price from £99

Operates 3- and 4-star hotels (many with leisure facilities) in Bournemouth and Norwich.

Swallow Hotels were recently acquired by the Whitbread Hotel Company and are in the process of being rebranded as Marriott's.

Thistle

t (0800) 332244 **www.thistlehotels.com**
Price from £115

Operates 4-star hotels in Brighton and Stratford-upon-Avon.

Travel Inn

t 0870 242 8000 **www.travelinn.co.uk**
Price from £40.95

Operates budget hotels (usually with an adjoining family restaurant) in Colchester, Coventry, Hastings, Norwich, Oxford, Poole, Portsmouth, Salisbury, Southend-on-Sea and Whitstable.

Travelodge

t 0800 850950
Price from £45.95

Operates budget hotels (usually with an adjoining family restaurant) in Cambridge, Norwich and Oxford. One of their claims to fame is that you can always see the TV from the bathroom!

Luxury hotels

The terms 'luxury' and 'children' needn't be mutually exclusive. Until about 10 years ago, the idea of taking the kids to a top-notch hotel was a complete non-starter. 'An unnecessary intrusion' was how the majority of luxury hotels regarded the family trade; the sight of throngs of children running through their precious oak-panelled, marble-fireplaced, antique-laden interiors would, they felt, cause an immediate exodus of patrons.

That, however, was until Nigel Chapman opened the Woolley Grange in Bradford-on-Avon, a hotel dedicated to providing the best of both worlds – old-fashioned country-house opulence for parents and fun and games for the kids, with neither age group allowed to curtail the enjoyment of the other. Woolley Grange proved such a success that Chapman was soon able to open a further three 'Luxury Family Hotels' including the Old Bell in Malmesbury. They are all equipped with the same mix of elegant, restful public rooms and toy-filled playrooms, restaurants offering a full children's menu and child-free evening sittings, as well as a horde of facilities – such as tennis and swimming – that can be appreciated by both generations. All have enjoyed a similar level of success. Indeed, the template has proved so popular that it is now being copied by several other (formerly exclusively 'adult') luxury hotels.

Bed and breakfasts

A great british institution, the term 'bed and breakfast' (abbreviated to b&b) is used to describe a variety of usually quite cheap accommodation ranging from rooms in private houses and farms to large guesthouses that provide all the facilities of a hotel (minus a restaurant). Though more economical, most b&bs cannot offer a babysitting service or, indeed, any of the other services regularly provided by hotels that help to take the strain off parents while on holiday. There are, of course, a few notable exceptions but in the main the following list of recommended accommodation is made up almost exclusively of hotels. Should you wish to stay in a b&b, however, the following agencies can help you in your search.

Bed and Breakfast (GB) t (01491) 578803
Bed and Breakfast Nationwide t (01255) 831235
Discover Britain Holidays t (01905) 613 7464
Knights in Britain t (01747) 820574

RECOMMENDED ACCOMMODATION

The following are hotels which welcome children and provide facilities for families. That said, there is a great variation in the sorts of facilities that different hotels or guest houses can offer. Some of the hotels listed here go out of their way to welcome even young children or babies and can provide crèches and babysitting as standard. Others are only really suitable for older children. Prices are based on two adults and two children sharing a family room but are only meant as a rough guide. Hotel prices rise and fall with the season and many offer special deals.

DOWN SOUTH

Ashford

Eastwell Manor

Eastwell Park, Boughton Lees **t** (01233) 219955
www.eastwellmanor.co.uk
Price from £250

The hotel itself is grand and stately and set in 62 acres of grounds. The real draw for families will be the Victorian stable block, a minute's walk from the main house, which has been turned into 19, 1–3-bedroom cottage apartments, each with its own garden and garden furniture which can be hired on a self-catering basis. The hotel's facilities include a heated outdoor swimming-pool (which children can use for two 1-hour sessions a day), a croquet lawn, tennis courts and a putting green. There are two restaurants; one offers fine dining (largely adult-orientated) and the other is a more informal brasserie. In summer, the brasserie opens up onto a terrace, next to which is a collection of play equipment for children. A babysitting service is available.

Eastwell Manor is convenient for Canterbury (p.49), Whitstable (p.55) and Druidstone Wildlife Park (p.56).

Biddenden

Bishopsdale Oast

Biddenden **t** (01580) 291027
Price from £85

With the myriad delights of Eastbourne (p.42), Hastings (p.44) and Canterbury (p.49) all within easy reach, this converted oasthouse would make an ideal base from which to explore the delights of rural Kent.

There's a large garden (part of which supplies the produce you'll find on the table) with wild flowers and a pond. The rooms are comfy and of a reasonable size with exposed beams and modern amenities such as TV. The proprietors can cater for children of all ages. That said, they try to offer all their guests a peaceful break and past experience has led them to specify that children must be well-behaved.

Brighton

Adelaide

51 Regency Square **t** (01273) 205286
Price £84

One of Brighton's swankier hotels, the Adelaide is close to the seafront and Palace Pier, though it does not enjoy sea views. The family rooms are of a good size and breakfast in the dining room is a real treat.

Brighton Marina House Hotel

8 Charlotte Street **t** (01273) 605349
Price from £39

A very pleasant Victorian b&b by the sea. It's not super luxurious but it is very comfortable and will prove perfectly adequate for a short stay. Located in a quiet side street, parts of the hotel enjoy good sea views and there's a bright breakfast room where you can enjoy a 'full English' (vegan and vegetarian alternatives also available). Several of the bedrooms have been decorated according to a particular theme, so there's a Tudor Room, a Scandinavian Room and an Eastern 'Pavilion' Room. All of these have four-poster beds, as do the family rooms, which can incorporate up to two extra beds.

Dove

18 Regency Square **t** (01273) 779222
Price from £75

There are 9 comfortable rooms in this Regency house b&b, located in an historic seafront square. It can offer toys and games for the kids and a babysitting service.

Grand

King's Road **t** (01273) 321188
Price from £195

Perhaps the most famous hotel in Brighton, the mighty Grand was built in 1864 and contains over 200 luxuriously appointed ensuite rooms (70 family), a sauna, a solarium, a gym, a jacuzzi/spa and a heated indoor pool. It's located right on the seafront facing the Palace Pier (many of its rooms have sea views) and has an excellent restaurant.

Broadstairs
The Merriland Hotel
13 The Vale **t** (01843) 861064
Price £72

This child-friendly hotel has eight family-size rooms, baby-listening and children's portions in the restaurant. There's a comfortable lounge for the evenings, and a garden with an assortment of toys for younger kids. The owners claim to 'spoil children to death' when they visit.

Canterbury
Thanington Hotel
140 Wincheap **t** (01227) 453227 **www.thanington-hotel.co.uk**
Price £110

Probably the most child-friendly of Canterbury's hotels with two good-sized family rooms, a swimming-pool, a games room (with half-size snooker table, darts and board games) and a smallish garden. Opposite the hotel is a park with a playground and plenty of grassy lawns to run about on.

Ship Hotel
North Street **t** (01243) 778000 **www.shiphotel.com**
Price £125-£158

This hotel is convenient for the train station and has good size rooms than can accommodate families. Kids' menus and baby-listening available.

Chichester
Millstream Hotel
Bosham Lane **t** (01243) 573234 **www.millstream-hotel.co.uk**
Price £120

Situated four miles from Chichester in the pretty waterside village of Bosham, the Millstream Hotel has been converted from a row of early 18th-century cottages. A children's menu is available from 5.30-6 in the restaurant and the hotel also has a baby-listening service.

Dover
Wallett's Court Country House Hotel
Westcliffe **t** (01304) 852424
Price £130

Just three miles from Dover, this luxurious 17th-century manor house has five acres of grounds (look out for the treehouse) which gives kids plenty of space to range about. Provided they haven't been spirited away by the hotel's resident ghost, children can enjoy a high tea while parents relax elsewhere; or the whole family can eat together in the restaurant at an early sitting. Kids have access to the hotel's pool after 9am and then, following a short exclusion period, after 7 in the evening. The hotel's tennis court is also available. Just over a mile from the hotel is St Margaret's Bay, with a spartan swathe of beach, and home to the South Foreland Lighthouse. Built in Victorian times, it was designed to warn ships away from the Goodwin Sands, and in 1898 was the site of Marconi's first ship-to-shore experiments with radio.

Eastbourne
Grand
King Edward's Parade **t** (01825) 840216
Price from £100

A rather dignified (some might say staid) hotel that sums up the resort. At the western end of the seafront, this imposing Victorian behemoth can offer 20 large family rooms (out of 152), many with sea views, large public rooms adorned with flowers, indoor and outdoor pools (both heated) and a well-respected restaurant, the Mirabelle (children's portions available). The beach is only a short walk away.

Hastings
Beauport Park Hotel
Battle Road **t** (01424) 851222
Price from £150

A Georgian hotel occupying an idyllic setting in 33 acres of parkland just outside Hastings. You can choose to stay either in one of the two large family rooms in the hotel itself or in the Scandinavian-style lodges in the grounds which are perfect for families of up to five individuals. Sporting facilities include tennis courts, grass badminton court, boules and croquet pitches, and even a giant outdoor chess set, as well as large grassy lawns to run about on. The outdoor pool is heated and the riding school next door will happily arrange family treks. A children's menu is served in the award-winning garden restaurant.

Hastings is convenient for Battle Abbey (p.40), Bodiam Castle (p.40) and the Kent and East Sussex Railway (p.48).

Rye
Old Vicarage
66 Church Square **t** (01797) 222119
Price £86

A pretty little hotel, housed in a detached Georgian house, the Old Vicarage is full of character with exposed beams in the sitting room and dining room. Kids will enjoy the bedroom views across Rye's ancient rooftops.

White Vine House
High Street **t** (01797) 224748
Price £140

This large, ivy-clad Tudor townhouse is in the middle of Rye and has a spacious family-sized room, oak beams and stone fireplaces. The hotel only serves food at lunchtimes.

Whitstable
Fisherman's Huts
t (01227) 280280
Price £100-125

These 19th-century fisherman's huts can sleep up to four and open directly onto Whitstable's pebbly beach. Run by the nearby Hotel Continental, the wooden huts are sparsely furnished but comfortable. All are equipped with tea and coffee making facilities but have not been kitted out for self-catering. Open up the doors and windows to let in the sea breezes.

DUE NORTH

Bourton-on-the-Water
Old New Inn
High Street, **t** (01451) 820467
Price £112

The pretty village of Bourton-on-the-Water has a number of things to recommend it including a model village and a birdland park. The 17th-century Old New Inn has log fires in winter, a garden for the summer (complete with swings and a slide) and a fully-licensed restaurant. No baby-listening.

Great Milton
Le Manoir aux Quat' Saisons
Church Street **t** (01844) 278881 **www**.manoir.co.uk
Price from £300

For a truly stylish (not to say expensive) family holiday, you could try this terribly well-to-do 15th-century Oxfordshire manor house. Owned by renowned chef Raymond Blanc and set in 27 acres of parkland with lovely sculpture-adorned gardens, you could be forgiven for thinking that the hotel is strictly for adults only. However, they make a supreme effort to make little ones feel as comfortable as possible with games, toys and a special kids' menu in the excellent (as you'd expect, considering the provenance) restaurant.

The public rooms are typical country house affairs with fine furniture, deep-cushioned sofas, fresh flowers and open fires.

Great Milton is roughly 10 miles from the dreaming spires of Oxford (see p.74).

Maidenhead
Cliveden
Taplow **t** (01628) 668561 **www**.cliveden.co.uk
Price from £350

A posh treat – this is as luxurious as they come (Cliveden was once home to Nancy Astor, the first woman to sit in the House of Commons). Surrounded by a 375-acre National Trust-maintained estate, you approach along a grand, gravelled boulevard before entering one of the most aristocratic-looking hotels around, the sort of place you feel should still be hosting house parties and high society soirées. Indeed, considering just how swish its 39 bedrooms actually are (with maid-unpacking service and a butler's tray, for people who like that sort of thing) and just how lavish its public rooms (with their paintings, antiques and tapestries), it's surprising how family-friendly Cliveden actually is. Children are welcomed in the terrace restaurant during the day and in the conservatory restaurant at any time and there are wonderful gardens to explore, indoor and outdoor pools (both heated) and facilities for tennis, riding, and boating on the River Thames.

Cliveden is convenient for Windsor (p.77), Legoland (p.81) and Eton (p.78) to the south, and for Odds Farm Park (p.97) and Bekonscot model village (p.96) to the north.

Oxford
Parklands
100 Banbury Road **t** (01865) 554374
Price £98
   This comfortable hotel is fairly close to the centre and has a licensed restaurant and bar as well as a garden where kids can let off steam.

Stow-on-the-Wold
The Fosse Manor
Stow-on-the-Wold **t** (01451) 830354
www.fossemanor.co.uk
Price £118
   A mile south of Stow-on-the-Wold on the A429, the Fosse Manor is a secluded manor house surrounded by pretty gardens. Part of the garden is taken up by a play area which is kitted out with slides, swings and the rest.

Stratford-upon-Avon
Mallory Court
Harbury Lane, Bishop's Tachbrook, Leamington Spa **t** (01926) 330214
Price £475
   Large country house in its own grounds with plenty of space. Come winter and you can enjoy afternoon tea in front of a log fire. In the summer there is croquet on the lawn, an outdoor pool and a tennis court. With no baby-listening or high chairs, the hotel is not suitable for younger children.

The Swan's Nest
Bridgefoot **t** (0870) 400 8183
Price £128
   Of Stratfor's three Heritage Hotels, the Swan's Nest, on the banks of the river and just a few minutes from the town centre, is the most geared up for children, with decent sized family rooms and children's portions in the restaurant. There are no leisure facilities on site but a free pass to the local leisure centre (a couple of minutes walk away) can be obtained from reception. Baby-listening available.

Welcombe Hotel and Country Club
Warwick Road **t** (01789) 295 252
www.welcombe.co.uk
Price from £295
   Set in a Jacobean manor house overlooking 800 acres of landscaped parkland (some of which was once owned by Shakespeare himself), there are 64 ensuite rooms and a high quality restaurant which serves up a combined English–French menu. It adjoins a golf course and has a pool and floodlit tennis courts, babysitting and listening services. No children in the dining room after 7pm.
   As well as the delights of Stratford-upon-Avon, the Welcombe Hotel makes a convenient jumping off point to visit the Stratford Shire Horse Centre (p.93) which is 2 miles southeast and Warwick Castle (p.90) which is 10 miles northeast.

Warwick
Shrewley Pools Farm
Parish of Hasely, nr Warwick **t** (01926) 484315
Price £50 per adult plus £10 per child
   A working farm with plenty of animals to look at. The owners are experienced baby-handlers themselves and the farm reflects this with a good-sized garden and plenty of child-friendly facilities such as babysitting, assorted games and a comfy lounge where parents can relax while the children slumber upstairs.

Windsor
The Castle Hotel
High Street **t** (01753) 851011
Price £190 (includes free entry to Legoland)
   One of the Heritage Hotels group, the Castle Hotel has all the usual child-friendly facilities. Nearby amenities are good and include a local swimming pool (5 mins walk) and a park (2 mins walk). Being so close to Legoland, the hotel offers good value one- and two-night packages for 2 adults and 2 children which include free entry to the park.

EAST IS EAST

Aldeburgh
Brudenell Hotel
The Parade **t** (01728) 452071
Price £100–£140
   A 19th-century hotel with 47 reasonably-sized rooms (front rooms overlook the sea and back rooms have a view over the street of Aldeburgh and the marshes in the distance). There's no garden but the beach is just a few steps away. Comfortable lounge, baby-listening, plenty of high

chairs and a children's menu in the restaurant make this a good bet for a family break in Aldeburgh.

Wentworth Hotel

Wentworth Road **t** (01728) 452312
www.wentworthhotel.com
Price from £120

The Wentworth is not a dedicated family hotel per se, but it is very accommodating and can easily adapt any of its 31 bedrooms (some of which are located in Darfield House across the road) to the needs of a (small) family – the ones with ensuite annexes are perhaps the most suitable. The hotel occupies an idyllic location overlooking a famously unspoilt stretch of shingle coastline – the sort of place where fishing boats are still hauled onto the beach. High teas and half-portions for kids are served in the no-smoking restaurant. Minsmere Nature Reserve (p.142) is a short drive away.

Blakeney

Blakeney Hotel

Holt **t** (01263) 740797
www.blakeney-hotel.co.uk
Price from £140

With the North Norfolk Railway (p.141), the North Norfolk Shire Horse Centre (p.138), the Muckleburgh Collection (p.134) as well as the bird life and seals of Blakeney Point (p.137) all within easy reach, this award-winning 59 room (11 family) hotel overlooking a National Trust-owned harbour makes a perfect base for exploring the attractions of Norfolk's picturesque northern coast. The bedrooms are comfortable and user-friendly (many with good views out across the marshes to Blakeney Point) with bunk beds and cots available in the family rooms. There's also an indoor swimming-pool, a games room with table tennis and pool and a garden with a play area for kids to run about in. Children's high teas are served before dinner.

Cambridge

Arundel House

Chesterton Road **t** (01223) 367701
Price from £98

Set on the banks of the River Cam, this friendly terrace hotel overlooks Jesus Green and is only five minutes walk from the town centre. The hotel has its own small garden and there is plenty of nearby green space for kids to run around in. The restaurant has a separate children's menu and there is a comfortable bar and lounge.

Garden House Hotel

Granta Place, Mill Lane **t** (01223) 259988
Price from £180

As you might expect, the Garden House Hotel has its own private garden which overlooks the River Cam. Eight family-sized rooms and an indoor (unheated pool), as well as a riverside restaurant with children's menu make it reasonably child-friendly, although the hotel does not offer a baby-listening service.

Royal Cambridge

Trumpington Street **t** (01223) 351631
Price £130–£150

Just half a mile from the station, this Georgian hotel is in the heart of the city (the famous 'Backs' are only yards away). The hotel has its own bar/lounge, free parking out back and a restaurant with high chairs and a children's menu. Babysitting can be provided at £6 per hour.

Colchester

George

116 High Street **t** (01206) 578494
Price £136

Smack in the middle of the town, the George has good family-sized rooms as well as a fully-licensed restaurant with a children's menu. There's no pool or garden on site but a park and leisure centre are nearby. With no baby-listening service, the hotel is not ideal for parents travelling with toddlers or babies.

Great Yarmouth

Burlington Palm Court

North Drive **t** (01493) 844568
Price from £85

About half a mile from the pier, the Burlington Palm Court is a lumbering old place which sometimes fills up with coach parties. Despite this, the indoor pool, pool table and children's menu in the restaurant make it a reasonably family-friendly place to stay for a night or two.

Regency Lodge

Albert Square **t** (01493) 855070
www.meridianleisure.com
Price £75

Well situated for the beach, the Regency Lodge has five family-sized rooms, a heated indoor pool and its own garden. A small selection of board games are available from reception.

Ickworth

Ickworth House

Horringer, Bury St Edmunds **t** (01284) 735350
www.ickworthhotel.com
Price from £150

A new fifth member of the Luxury Family Hotels chain has opened (June 2002) at this grand East Anglian stately home. The National Trust, which manages the property, has granted the hotel group a 99-year lease on the east wing of the building. Expect all the facilities that have made the other four hotels in the chain such a success (*see* p.189), plus the chance to visit the stately home itself which is one of the most family-friendly around with grand gardens, a deer park, woodland walks, a family cycle trail, an adventure playground and quizzes and trails taking you around the house (for further information *see* p.143).

Nearby attractions to Ickworth House include West Stow Anglo Saxon Village (p.148) which is about 5 miles north and Cambridge (p.110) which is 30 or so miles to the west.

Norwich

Maid's Head Hotel

Tombland **t** (01603) 209955
Price £94

In the centre of Norwich, within sight of the cathedral, the Maid's Head Hotel is a characterful hotel with 7 family rooms. With no baby-listening facilities and only a small garden, the hotel is not ideal for parents travelling with younger children but, given its location and good value for money (children under 15 stay free), it may be suitable for an overnight stay.

Norwich Sports Village

Drayton High Road, Hellesdon **t** (01603) 788898
www.norwichsportsvillage.com
Price from £75

About 10 minutes drive from the centre of Norwich, this complex has its own aqua park (complete with white water rapids and 550ft-long flume as well as a toddler pool), two restaurants and a 3-storey play area for the under 10s (with ball pool, slides and its own restaurant). Two additional restaurants and an assortment of reasonably-priced family-sized rooms (equipped with SKY TV), tennis, badminton and squash courts, make this a good base from which to explore Norwich.

Southwold

The Crown

90 High Street **t** (01502) 722275
Price from £107

Pleasant hotel with two family rooms and a thriving restaurant (*see* p.152). The staff tend to go home early so baby-listening is not a realistic possiblity but the rooms are comfortable and the service friendly. A kids' high tea is served between 5 and 7.30pm.

Swaffham

Strattons

Ash Close, **t** (01760) 723845
www.strattons-hotel.co.uk
Price from £90

Strattons is small but perfectly formed with just 6 individually decorated rooms, each with their own distinct theme (Venetian, Victorian, Tuscan, Sea, Palladian and Red) housed in a Queen Anne-style villa. There are lots of toys and games and a pleasant garden where children can play with the hotel's numerous resident cats.

A stay in this pleasant little hotel could happily be combined with a day trip to the historic town of Norwich (p.126) which is some 15 miles to the east.

GO WEST

Bath

Paradise House

88 Holloway **t** (01225) 317723
Price £120

A stiff(ish) walk up the hill from the town centre, but worth it if only for the splendid views over the city. The hotel has two family-sized rooms and a nice garden with a croquet lawn and a space set aside for boules. With no restaurant or baby-listening, the hotel is only suitable for parents with older children.

Royal Crescent

16 Royal Crescent **t** (01225) 339401
Price from £190

The Royal Crescent is slap bang in the middle of the famous Royal Crescent, one of Bath's main tourist attractions and one of the country's finest examples of Georgian architecture. Indeed, considering its location, it's surprisingly child-friendly with 8 large family rooms (all with CD and video players), a supply of toys, a spacious garden, an indoor pool, an outdoor plunge pool and a river launch. The hotel even has its own hot air balloon and will happily arrange flights.

Tasburgh House Hotel
Warminster Road t (01225) 425096
Price £115

Half a mile from the City centre on the A36, the Tasburgh House Hotel sits in seven acres of gardens and meadow park which run along the Kennet & Avon canal. Bags of room for a gentle game of kick-about or frisbee. With three en-suite family rooms and a children's 'gourmet' menu available in the conservatory ('parents allowed provided they are well behaved') the hotel is reasonably child-friendly, though there is no baby-listening service on offer.

Beaulieu
Beaulieu Hotel
Beaulieu Road t (023) 8029 3344
Price £120–£140

A country house hotel mid-way between Lyndhurst and Beaulieu. Try and get a room with views across the open forest which is virtually on the hotel's doorstep. The Beaulieu has one family-sized room and another room which has its own lounge (£20 supplement). Baby-listening can be provided. The restaurant is pretty good and has a children's menu and a couple of high chairs. Indoor pool.

Bournemouth
Anglo Swiss Hotel
Gervis Rd t (01202) 554794
Price £75

Two miles from the station, the Anglo Swiss is surrounded by trees on the picturesque East Cliff, and is only a short stroll from the town centre and sea front. There's a good mix of bedrooms, including some chalet rooms which are ideal for families. Other facilities include baby-listening and a leisure complex, which claims to have the biggest private indoor pool in Bournemouth. Special

weekend rates for families are particularly good value (a family of four with two children under 12 can stay here for the weekend for as little as £124).

Chine
Boscombe Spa Road t (01202) 396234
Price from £115

Run by the same people as the Sandbanks in Poole, the Chine is equally family-friendly with easy access to the beach and pier along pine-scented footpaths. Set in its own gardens with good sea views, it can offer 13 large family rooms (out of 69), a very good restaurant serving a hybrid French–English menu (children's menu available), indoor and outdoor heated pools, a croquet lawn, a putting green, a sauna, a solarium and indoor and outdoor children's play areas.

Highcliff Marriot Hotel
105 St Michael's Road t (01202) 557 702
Price £120–£170

Cliff top hotel with panoramic sea views across the bay. Close to the town centre and beach. The hotel has a number of 'junior suites' which can accommodate up to two adults and three children. These large rooms (some of which have sea views) come equipped with a separate seating area and SKY TV (ideal for bumper-to-bumper cartoons). There are ample leisure facilities including outdoor and indoor pools, a floodlit tennis court, mini golf and a games room (open during the holidays). The hotel doesn't have baby-listening but has a contact with a reliable babysitting firm (£5 per hour), should parents fancy a night on the town.

Laguna Hotel
Suffolk Road South, Westcliff t (01202) 767022
Price from £25

Cheap and cheerful but perfectly serviceable seaside bed and breakfast just back from the seafront. Families are well catered for with a couple of large family rooms, a heated indoor swimming-pool, a games room with pool and table tennis, indoor and outdoor play areas and a baby-listening service. High chairs are available in the dining room.

Bradford-on-Avon
Woolley Grange
t (01225) 864705 **www.woolleygrange.com**
and **www.luxury-family-hotels.co.uk**
Price From £180

The Woolley Grange is the flagship establishment of the 'Luxury Family Hotels' group who have spent the past 10 years proving that it's possible to combine the facilities of top-notch hotel accommodation with a genuinely family-centric attitude. In other words, the Woolley Grange offers the best of both worlds – lots of entertainment for the children and an elegant, restful space for parents. The bedrooms are cosy and snug, with all the facilities a family would expect and yet elegant and refined. The public rooms are quite charming, with fresh flowers, a smattering of antiques and log fires in winter. Children are supremely well catered for with a variety of facilities aimed at different age groups. The huge 'Woolley Bears' den in the old stable block is filled with toys and games and is open 10–6 every day for 7s and under while 8s and over are steered towards the 'Hen House', where there's television, videos, Nintendo and board games.

Outside, there are facilities for badminton and croquet as well as a swimming-pool (unheated) and 14 acres of grounds for children to play in.

There are also separate eating arrangements to suit the different generations. Children can eat in the crèche without their parents in tow at a time that suits them (i.e. early), while parents can relax, alone, in the evening in the award-winning restaurant. Alternatively, if you prefer, the whole family can join up for a meal in the Victorian conservatory.

The only downside to your stay will be the price. Expect to pay something in the region of £380 for a weekend for a family of 4.

If you and the kids can drag yourselves away from the myriad delights of the hotel, Bath (p.156) is about 10 miles west.

Brockenhurst
Watersplash
The Rise **t** (01590) 622344
Price from £75

In the heart of the New Forest, within easy reach of Beaulieu and Paultons Park theme park, the Watersplash makes a good, solid base for a family break. The house is Victorian (though much-altered over the past 100 years) and has been in the same family for over 50 years. There are six large family rooms at the top of the house with sloping ceilings and views out over the leafy garden where you'll find a heated pool with a terrace and picnic area. There's also an outdoor children's play area, an indoor games room with toys and board games and a baby-listening service. Early high teas for children are served in the restaurant overlooking the garden. High chairs available.

Calcot
Calcot Manor
Near Tetbury **t** (01666) 890391
www.calcotmanor.com
Price £180

A great base for exploring the western end of the Cotswolds, the very grand Calcot Manor – log fires in the lounge, a smattering of antiques, that sort of thing – was originally a Cistercian abbey and still has a few remaining 14th-century features. There are 9 family rooms, including a few two-bedroom suites in the Granary Barn (baby-listening service available), a children's 'Playzone' staffed by nannies and filled with games, toys and computer games, a small outdoor swimming-pool, 2 tennis courts and an outdoor play area with bikes and climbing equipment. Older children are welcome in the evening in the hotel restaurant, which is very smart and opens on to a conservatory, while high teas are served for younger children at around 5.30pm in the 'Playzone'.

Calcot Manor is convenient for Bath (p.156) which is roughly 15 miles away.

Isle of Wight
Biskra Beach
17 St Thomas Street, Ryde **t** (01983) 567913
www.biskra-hotel.com
Price from £120

Right on the seafront with good views out over the Solent, the Biskra has recently been refurbished and now boasts a stark, modern-looking interior, all clean lines and minimalist décor. In fact, it looks more like a trendy Saturday night hangout than a typical family hotel. Nonetheless, it is very child-friendly with a children's games room, children's meals in the restaurant, a baby-monitoring service and an outdoor hot tub. There are 14 rooms (some with sea views) of which 2 are designated family rooms, as well as 2 self-catering apartments with lawned gardens running down to the beach. Extra cots can be provided free of charge.

Clarendon Hotel and Wight Mouse Inn

Chale, Ventnor **t** (01983) 730431
www.wightmouseinns.co.uk
Price from £60

The Clarendon Hotel is a pleasant, family bed and breakfast housed in a 17th-century former coaching inn. Situated on the southwest slopes of of St Catherine's Down, it overlooks Chale Bay and the Needles. There are 9 large family rooms, a good restaurant (early teas and high chairs available), a sun lounge and a friendly, welcoming atmosphere – particularly in the adjacent Wight Mouse pub which is very child-friendly with 3 games rooms, an indoor play area 'Mouse World' and an outdoor play area with swings, climbing frames and, in summer, a bouncy castle. There are reductions for children sharing their parents' room (under 3s stay free) and the hotel will happily organize activities such as horse-riding, para-gliding and fossil hunting. Baby-listening service available.

Old Park Hotel

St Lawrence, Ventnor **t** (01983) 852583
Price from £60

The island's most southerly hotel is a large Victorian house (with a modern wing) and pleasant gardens filled with subtropical greenery. There are several family suites (with master bedroom and separate children's room), an indoor swimming-pool, a large, supervised soft play area as well as a self-catering cottage and apartment in the grounds. It's a 10-minute walk to the nearest rockpool-lined beach.

Ryde Castle Hotel

Esplanade, Ryde **t** (01983) 563755
Price £115

Recently refurbished, Ryde Castle Hotel is a distinctive and majestic Victorian building just minutes from Ryde's beach. Both the hotel's restaurant and bar can provide children's portions and the kids have a chance to let off steam in the play area which has a sand pit and various toys. Baby-listening is available.

Seaview Hotel

High Street, Seaview, **t** (01983) 612711
www.seaviewhotel.co.uk
Price from £90

The Seaview is a real gem of a hotel! Its public rooms adorned with nautical pictures, it is the quintessential seaside hotel – clean, cosy, comfortable and just a short walk from the rock pools and sand of Priory Bay. The 16 bedrooms do vary in size and there's only one family room, but even the smaller ones are comfortable and well appointed (all have been kitted out exclusively from John Lewis) and some have sea views. Under 12s sharing their parents' room stay at a reduced price. A children's menu is available in both hotel restaurants which are smart but informal (one is non-smoking) and early high teas are served for younger children. Both specialize in locally caught seafood. Better-than-average lighter (and not so light) bar food is also on offer. The hotel has a small studio apartment at the back though this is not really suitable for families. It can also offer self-catering accommodation in an 18th-century fisherman's cottage and arrange sailing lessons.

Lyndhurst

Lyndhurst Park Hotel

High St **t** (023) 8028 3923
Price £105

On the outskirts of the historic capital of the New Forest and close to Beaulieu, this Georgian mansion is set within three acres of garden and surrounded by 90,000 acres of open forest (home to free-roaming ponies). It's a large place with a choice of bars, lounges and restaurants as well as an outdoor swimming pool, indoor games room (with table tennis, snooker and darts), a sauna and a tennis court.

Malmesbury

The Old Bell

Abbey Row **t** (01666) 822344
www.oldbellhotel.com
and **www.**luxury-family-hotels.co.uk
Price £180–90

Another of Nigel Chapman's now famous 'Luxury Family Hotels', this ivy-covered coaching inn is in the centre of Malmesbury (next to the Abbey). All the goodies are here in abundance. It has a paddling pool, an outdoor play area, a games room, complete with computer consoles, and the obligatory, supervised 'den' full of games and toys. The house itself is a Grade I listed building and retains many of its original features (it claims to be England's oldest hotel, along with around 20 other establishments around the country), while the bedrooms are decorated in a variety of styles ranging from antique Edwardian (in the main house), to modernist Japanese (in the old Coach house). Children sharing their parents' room stay free of charge. Baby-listening service available.

Painswick
Painswick Hotel
Kemps Lane t (01452) 812160
www.painswickhotel.com
Price from £110

The Painswick Hotel is an 18th-century white-washed mansion in the heart of a beautiful Cotswold village (home to over a hundred listed buildings). It has 19 rather grand rooms including two large family-sized rooms. Several have good views of the valley. The public rooms are deco-rated with antiques and fine furniture and there is the odd individual touch (can you spot the model battleship in the library?). There's also a lovely garden for youngsters to romp about in. It's much more child-friendly than it looks from the outside with friendly staff and a welcoming lack of pomposity.

In the village, pay a visit to the church of St Mary, the grounds of which have been planted with 99 yew trees (according to local legend, the devil will steal away the 100th yew should it ever be planted) and the Rococo Gardens, laid out in the 1740s with a maze and a nature trail, which should keep kids happy for an afternoon.

Nearby child-friendly attractions are thin on the ground but for a relaxing weekend away, enjoying the simple pleasures of life, the hotel is hard to beat.

Petersfield
Mizzards Farm
Rogate, Petersfield t (01730) 821656
Price from £125

Close to Portsmouth and Chichester, Mizzard's Farm is an upmarket b&b with two acres of garden with a river running through it, a swimming pool, croquet lawn and an 8ft-square game of outdoor chess. There are no family-sized rooms but well-behaved children over eight can be accommodated in one of the two smaller bedrooms.

Poole
Sandbanks
15 Banks Road t (01202) 707377
www.sandbanks.co.uk
Price from £130

Sandbanks may be a functional, purpose-built, typically seasidey hotel, but what it lacks in beauty, it more than makes up for in family-friendliness and can offer lovely views out over Poole Bay and the yacht harbour. Thirty of its hundred-plus rooms have been set aside for family use and there's a soft-play room, an outdoor playground and children's entertainers are laid on during the school holidays. Kids even get their own 'Wipe Clean' food bar serving up dishes of gloopy favourites (and are also welcome in the main restaurant). The hotel has access to a blue flag beach where you'll find a pirate ship play area.

Portsmouth
Innlodge Hotel
Burrfields Road t (023) 9265 0510
Price from £59

Comfortable but rather faceless, the Innlodge is located on the outskirts of the city and can offer 73 ensuite rooms (10 family), a decent restaurant (children's menu and high chairs available) and indoor and outdoor children's play areas.

Keppel's Head Hotel
The Hard t (023) 9283 3231
Price £75

Just 50 yards from Portsmouth's station, the Keppel's Head Hotel, built in 1803, overlooks the harbour and the masts of the historic tall ships. There's no children's menu as such in the restaurant but the chef (who claims to lock all children in the basement if they're bad) is happy to produce half-portions. Bar, baby-listening and a friendly welcome.

Salisbury & Stonehenge
Howard's House Hotel
Teffont Evias t (01722) 716392
Price from £160

About 10 miles out of Salisbury, this friendly Michelin three-star hotel manages to combine an informal air with top-notch facilities. There's a large garden with croquet, a variety of board games and a flexible approach to children's fickle dietary requirements.

Southampton
Busketts Lawn Hotel
174 Woodlands Road, Woodlands **t** (023) 8029 2272
Price from £70

Simple, informal hotel on the edge of the New Forest within easy reach of Southampton. Its 14 ensuite rooms (3 family) are attractively furnished and there's a heated outdoor pool, a garden, a croquet lawn and a no-smoking restaurant.

West Lulworth
Cromwell House Hotel
Lulworth Cove **t** (01929) 400253
Price from £70

The century-old Cromwell occupies an idyllic location overlooking Lulworth Cove. The best views are probably from the heated outdoor swimming-pool which is set high above the building so as to catch the maximum amount of sunshine. Furnished in classic country house style with a bright, cheerful décor, it has 14 rooms, of which 3 are suitable for families (one has a four-poster bed). Cream teas are served in the dining room where, in the evening, you can tuck into crabs and lobsters caught by local fishermen.

Westonbirt
Hare and Hounds
Near Tetbury **t** (01666) 880233
Price from £93

A pleasant, welcoming choice housed in a former farmhouse near the Westonbirt Arboretum (with adjoining coach house), the Hare and Hounds, with its 31 large bedrooms (3 family), makes a good base for touring the western half of the Cotswolds. There are 10 acres of gardens with wide grassy lawns to run about on, a family-friendly, non-smoking restaurant and facilities for pool, table tennis, tennis and croquet.

Nearby attractions include the city of Bath (p.156) which is roughly 15 miles further south.

OTHER OPTIONS

Youth Hostels

Hostels are probably not the first thing you consider when looking for suitable family accommodation, conjuring up, as they do, images of backpackers, meagre facilities and endless 'cuppa soup' meals. Hostels, however, have changed. Many now actively seek out family groups and have installed the amenities necessary to attract them, offering family rooms with 4–6 bunks (with duvets and bedside lamps), central heating, carpets and, in some cases, even ensuite facilities. Similarly, many of the rules which in the past made staying at a hostel akin to staying at a particularly draconian army camp have now been relaxed. The rule of 'one night and you're out' no longer applies; lights can now stay on till the heady hour of 11.30pm (sometimes even later) and, best of all, families are even exempt from participating in the chores and tasks which used to be such a fundamental part of the hostelling experience. Furthermore, unlike individual travellers, families are allowed to stay inside the hostel during the day if they want. At meal times, you have the option of going self-catering or eating from the hostel menu – some of which are very impressive with children's menus offered.

Some hostels have also begun organizing activities and outings for families. The North Norfolk Youth Hostel, for instance, arranges visits to the local Shire horse centre and steam railway.

With prices as competitive as they come – a night for a family of four (self-catering) can cost as little as £35 – it's no wonder that families are now the fastest growing sector of the hostel market. The Youth Hostel Association has reported year on year growth for family bookings over the past half decade.

It is worth bearing in mind that, although many hostels have changed for the better, there are still a few that adhere to the old-fashioned template (single-sex dormitories, etc.) and certainly aren't suitable for families, especially with young children. Also, do be aware that in high season family rooms will be at a premium, so book in advance.

Annual family membership of the YHA costs £24 (£12 for a single-parent family) which entitles you to stay in youth hostels not just in Britain but all over the world.

YHA t (01433) 620235 **www.yha.org.uk**
Can provide a list of family-friendly hostels in England.

Self-catering

For a stay of even two nights, it can be worth considering the self-catering option which can provide a cheaper and much more flexible alternative to hotel accommodation. Not only will a flat or a cottage provide you with more living space (not to mention a good deal more independence), it will also give you a chance to become familiar with the local community. Again, there are important questions that need to be asked before you book in order to find out whether a potential property is truly child-friendly:

▶ How far is your accommodation from the nearest shops, supermarket, restaurants, bus stop and launderette? A 20-minute walk may be fine for an adult but is far less manageable with a baby and toddler in tow.

▶ How many bedrooms does the property have? The term 'sleeps 6' can be ambiguous. You cannot assume 'sleeps 6' means your accommodation will have three bedrooms. You may be expected to convert the sofa in your living room into a bed.

▶ Is there a phone for emergencies?

▶ Are cots supplied and, if so, is there an additional charge for them?

▶ Are the children's rooms fitted with bunk beds and, if so, do these have safety rails?

▶ Is use of gas and electricity included in the rent?

▶ Is cleaning included in the rent and, if so, how often is the property cleaned?

▶ Are there high chairs, games, toys, beach equipment, a washing machine, stereo, TV and video?

▶ Will you need to bring a can opener, corkscrew, cups or a sharp knife? If in doubt, ask for a full inventory.

▶ Is the garden or pool fenced off and are there any nearby ponds, streams or other potential hazards?

▶ Is it safe for children to play unsupervised in the garden?

▶ Can babysitting be arranged locally?

Types of property

Cottage holidays are something of an institution in England and there are a vast number of agencies offering you the chance to settle into an idyllically situated, ivy-clad country house for a weekend of relaxing and exploring. If you really want to splash out, you can even choose to stay in an historic

Farms

One of the most popular choices in recent years has been the farm-based holiday where visitors are invited to participate in the farmyard tasks – collecting eggs, sprinkling corn, helping with the milking, etc. At certain times of the year you may even be able to watch (and possibly even participate in) the birth of the baby animals.

Farmers, for their part, under pressure from the horrors of BSE and, more recently, the foot and mouth crises, are grateful for the extra revenue this kind of trade provides and many are becoming increasingly welcome to children. Most will not be able to provide self-catering for a stay of only two nights but many offer B&B (prices start from around £23 per person/£10 per child under 14).

Cartwheel
t 0870 241 1098 www.cartwheel.org

A consortium of over 200 farm-based holidays including bed and breakfasts and campsites.

The Farm Bureau
t (024) 7669 6909
www.webscape.co.uk/farmaccom

This co-operative of accommodation-offering farms has also produced a booklet 'Stay on a Farm' which has over 1,200 farms, big and small, spread out across the country (for other guides see below).

Farm and Cottage Holidays
t (01237) 479698 www.farmcott.co.uk
West country properties.

Norfolk and Suffolk Farm Holiday Group
t (01359) 231013 www.farmstayanglia.co.uk
Represents over 60 properties on working farms.

Books and guides
Self-Catering Holiday Homes £9.99
Stillwell's Independent Holiday Cottages £2.95

home – a 15th-century manor house, a Gothic tower or an old lighthouse perhaps (although this is not recommended for families with very young children). The Landmark Trust and National Trust both have a large number of specially adapted historic homes on their books. Some of these are available for short (two night) stays.

Self-catering agencies
Barclay International Group t (020) 7495 2986
Globe Apartments t (020) 7935 9512
www.globeapt.demon.co.uk

Cottages

Most of the websites below have sophisticated search engines, allowing you to specify the area, the number of nights you want to stay and even whether your cottage should have a pool!

Blakes t 08700 708090
www.blakes-cottages.co.uk
Over 2,000 bargain properties in the UK.
Classic Cottages t (01326) 555555
www.classic-cottages.co.uk
Cottages in the Southwest from £150 per week.
Country Holidays t 08700 725725
www.country-holidays.co.uk
Over 3,000 properties.
English Country Cottages t (08700) 781 100
www.english-country-cottages.co.uk
Good bookings service and well-trained staff.
Helpful Holidays t (01647) 433593
www.helpfulholidays.com
Cottage properties in the Southwest, including several with heated indoor swimming-pools.
Hoseasons t (01502) 501515
www.hoseasons.co.uk
Over 1,000 properties throughout the country.
Norfolk Country Cottages t (01603) 871872
www.norfolkcottages.co.uk)
Good range of cottages in the Norfolk area.
Rural Retreats t (01386) 701177
www.ruralretreats.co.uk
Luxury cottages throughout the country.
Toad Hall Cottages t (01548) 853089
www.toadhallcottages.com
Cottages throughout the Southwest from £225 per week. Includes Eeyore Cottage in South Devon where the real Christopher Robin once lived.

Cottage websites
Cottages Direct **www.cottages.direct.com**
Premier Cottages Direct
www.premiercottages.co.uk
Recommended Cottage Holidays
www.recommended-cottages.co.uk
UK Holiday Cottages Online **www.oas.co.uk**

Historic houses
Landmark Trust **t (01628) 825925**
www.landmarktrust.co.uk
National Trust **t (020) 7222 9251**
www.nationaltrust.org.uk

Camping & caravans

These days staying in a tent or caravan does not have to mean roughing it. Most organized campsites tend to keep privations to a minimum and are often equipped with toilets, shower blocks, shops and entertainment, making them ideal for families.

In fact, some campsites are more like canvas hotels, with even the bothersome task of pitching the tent taken off your hands. Several sites have luxury tents which come pre-pitched and ready for use. These can be huge apartment-style things (think Bedouin chief's desert palace) divided into separate rooms by zipped partitions. Most have all mod cons and some even have their own separate toilet tent. Sites such as this can usually rent you a caravan as an alternative and usually give a great deal of thought to families, often providing organized children's activities, babysitting and baby-equipment rental.

Contacts
British Tourist Authority t (020) 8846 9000
Provides a list of camping and caravan parks.
Camping and Caravan Club t (024) 7669 4995
www.campingandcaravanningclub.co.uk

Websites
Cades **www.cades.co.uk**
Canvas Holidays **www.canvas.co.uk**
Eurocamp **www.eurocamp.co.uk**
Keycamp **www.keycamp.co.uk**

Books and guides
AA Caravan and Camping Guide – Britain and Ireland £8.99
British Tourist Authority Caravan and Camping Parks £5.99
Cades Camping, Touring and Motor Campsite Guide £4.99

Camping and caravanning checklist:
► Is it possible to book a pitch away from the road and (if camping) in the shade?
► Does the site have shower and toilet facilities?
► Does the site have a children's play area?
► Can the site provide a babysitting service?

Practicalities A-Z

07

By rail

In the main, Britain's railways provide a decent service, despite the high prices and the myriad problems which privatisation has brought in its wake. All the major cities and towns in this guide are linked by fast services which still represent one of the most efficient ways of moving around the country. Phone National Rail Enquiries, **t** (0845) 748 4950 for train times and ticket prices. Let the operator know if you want to reserve your tickets with a credit card (they will give you a separate number to ring). Alternatively, visit the rail travel centres at any of London mainline stations for help with timetables and ticket booking.

Safety note

There are two types of train currently in operation. Do be careful if you find yourself travelling on one of the older models with hinged, slamming doors. Not only is it possible to open the door while the train is moving but the windows open low enough for a determined child to be able to stick its head out.

By coach

National Express **t** (0870) 580 8080 offers services to every major town and city in the country. All coaches leave from Victoria Coach Station which is on Buckingham Road, a short walk from Victoria rail and tube stations. Though efficient and cheap, they are fairly slow compared to trains but for journeys of only an hour or so they can prove an efficient and cheap alternative. For details of local city and town buses, you should contact the relevant tourist authority.

Sightseeing bus discounts

The Guide Friday company offers sightseeing tours in open-top double decker buses with either live or recorded commentary in the following towns included in this guide: Bath, Cambridge, Dover, Hastings, Norwich, Oxford, Portsmouth, Stratford-upon-Avon and Windsor. You can buy a book of four discounted tickets for £20 from: Guide Friday Ltd, Civic Hall, 14 Rother Street, Stratford-upon-Avon, Warwickshire CV37 **t** (01789) 294466.

Times and distances from London

	Miles	By train	By coach/car
Bath	118	1hr 11min	2hr 10min
Brighton	51	51min	1hr 45min
Cambridge	61	52min	1hr 50min
Canterbury	56	1hr 22min	1hr 45min
Chichester	60	1hr 45min	1hr 35min
Colchester	70	45min	1hr 15min
Dover	80	1hr 45min	2hr 30min
Norwich	115	1hr 35min	2hr 40min
Oxford	57	48min	1hr 40min
Portsmouth	70	1hr 21min	2hr 05min
Rye	62	1hr 40min	1hr 45min
Salisbury	84	1hr 18min	2hr 40min
Stratford/Avon	92	2hr 12min	2hr 45min
Winchester	70	1hr	1hr 45min
Windsor	20	50min	1hr

By car

If you plan to move around a lot during your weekend break, especially in more rural areas, then motoring is the only feasible option. Car hire prices are competitive (though still expensive) and England's roads are among the safest in Europe. Be aware that most major towns and cities do not lend themselves easily to motoring. Pedestrianized areas, incomprehensible one-way systems and draconian parking regulations are just some of the hazards. Many large towns and cities, such as Bath or Brighton, are best explored on foot or using public transport. These often operate park and ride schemes which allow you to leave your car a little way out of the city and hop onto a bus.

If you are new to this country, remember to drive on the left. Remember, too, that using carseats and wearing seatbelts front and back is compulsory in Britain.

Car rental firms

All rental companies require that the person driving be over 21 (more usually over 23) and that they have held their licence for over a year. Child seats should be available on request.

Bring a valid driving licence with you.

You don't need to carry your driving papers with you when driving but, if stopped, you will usually be asked to present them at a police station within five days.

Car rental firms in the UK

Alamo **t** (020) 7408 1255
Avis **t** 0990 900500
Europcar **t** 08457 222525
Hertz **t** 0990 996699
National **t** (01895) 233300
Thrifty **t** 0990 168238

Tourist information

Almost every town in this guide has its own tourist office. You can save a great deal of time and trouble by visiting these as soon as you arrive. Tourist offices generally offer a friendly welcome and can provide you with information on the local area. Many can also arrange overnight accommodation as part of their book-a-bed-ahead (BABA) scheme. Opening hours are typically Mon–Fri 9–5 for smaller offices with big city branches often staying open over the weekend. Before you leave London, why not visit the new British Visitor Centre which has guidebooks, leaflets and travel advice. You can book rail and coach tickets from here, reserve accommodation and change money. There's even a bookshop.

British Visitor Centre, 1 Lower Regent Street, Piccadilly Circus, SW1; open Mon–Fri 9–6.30, Sat and Sun 10–4 **t** (020) 8846 9000

Other sources of information

The number of resources for families living in the south east is constantly growing. Magazines are a good source of information. Besides the usual glossy parenting magazines, two of the best are
Families Southeast (monthly) **t** (020) 8699 7240
Regional-based parenting magazine.
Family Travel (quarterly) **t** (020) 7272 7441
Quarterly subscription with information and advice on family holidays (domestic and international).

The internet is a good source of information although there is inevitably a lot of junk on the world wide web and you can easily find yourself wasting a good hour without finding out very much. Two of the most reliable sites are
www. family-travel.co.uk
www.kidsnet.co.uk

Alternatively, the main British daily broadsheets – the *Guardian*, *The Times* et al. – produce travel supplements (as do their Sunday equivalents). Family-orientated features are often carried during the school holidays.

Making your escape

London is the country's main transport hub and has no fewer than eight mainline rail terminal which serve all the major regions.

Head for the following stations to make your escape from the capital to the destinations listed in this guide. Some towns and cities, such as Cambridge and Portsmouth, are served by more than one station, though journey times differ. When this occurs, only the fastest route has been listed.

Charing Cross, The Strand WC2
Battle (*see* p.40)
Canterbury (*see* p.49)
Dover (*see* p.52)
Hastings (*see* p.44)
Rye (change at Ashford) (*see* p.36)
King's Cross, Euston Road N1
Cambridge (fast service) (*see* p.110)
Liverpool Street, Liverpool Street EC2
Cambridge (*see* p.110)
Colchester (*see* p.118)
Norwich (*see* p.126)
Paddington, Praed Street W2
Bath (*see* p.156)
Oxford (*see* p.74)
Stratford-upon-Avon (*see* p.85)
Warwick (*see* p.90)
Victoria, Terminus Place SW1
Brighton (*see* p.32)
Broadstairs (*see* p.54)
Canterbury (*see* p.49)
Chichester (*see* p.35)
Eastbourne (*see* p.42)
Margate (*see* p.53)
Ramsgate (*see* p.54)
Whitstable (*see* p.55)
Waterloo, York Road SE1
Bournemouth (*see* p.172)
Portsmouth (*see* p.161)
Salisbury (*see* p.178)
Windsor (*see* p.77)

PRACTICALITIES A–Z

Discount passes

There are a variety of discount passes available giving you free or reduced entry to many of the attractions close to London. Two of the best are

English Heritage membership

English Heritage Membership Department
PO Box 1BB, London W1A **t** (020) 7973 3400
Prices Adults £28 each or £46 for 2, under 16s £12, 16–21 £17, family £49.50, single-parent family £29

Gives you free entry for a year to all English Heritage properties including Dover Castle, Hasting's Castle, Osborne House and Stonehenge. As an added bonus, members get half-price admission to more than a hundred historic sites in Scotland, Wales and the Isle of Man (free after your first year of membership) and also receive a guide to English Heritage properties and quarterly editions of *Heritage Today*, the organization's magazine.

National Trust Membership

National Trust Membership Department
PO Box 39, Bromley, Kent BR1 **t** (020) 8315 1111
www.nationaltrust.org.uk
Prices Adults £30, under 26s £15, family (2 adults, 2 under 18s) £57, single-parent family £43

Gives you free entry for a one year period to all National Trust properties (including Scotland).

Food

The importance of the family market to the restaurant industry has become increasingly apparent in recent years with many eateries now offering specialized children's menus, highchairs and activity packs. Some restaurants have even set Sunday aside as a special 'Family' day when children's entertainment, in the form of puppet shows, face painting and magic demonstrations, is laid on.

England's huge, multifarious ethnic population has bred a great culinary diversity. Whatever your tastes, be it for Italian pasta, Turkish kebabs, Mexican chilli, Spanish tapas or Japanese noodles, you'll probably find somewhere serving it up. Not all British culinary expertize is imported. Although as a nation Britain has never hit great gastronomic heights, its traditional cuisine has many devotees. Pubs, in particular, are good sources of sturdy traditional English fare – Shepherd's Pie, Toad-in-the-Hole – and many have become increas-

ingly child-friendly in recent years offering designated family rooms, play areas and full children's menus.

Across the regions, with the steady rise of food chains, you are likely to find less variety than you might have 50 years ago. That said, there are still specialities to look out for. Kent, for instance, is known as the 'garden of England' and is particularly good for apples; look out for home-cooked apple pies made with local produce. And then, of course, there's fish and chips, which in most seaside towns will be superior to the fare served further inland. The university cities of Oxford and Cambridge are rich pickings for tea rooms (students obviously like cake) as are the pretty Cotswold towns where quaint tea shops line the high streets, serving cream teas and irresistible cakes. Then there are more specific delicacies. If you're in Bath, try a Bath Bun at Sally Lunn's Old English Tea House (p.183), the oldest house in Bath. If you're in Whitstable, make room for a plate of oysters at Pearson's Crab and Oyster House (p.70), as the little town is famous for them.

Medical matters

Visitors from the European Union, Iceland, Liechtenstein and Norway can claim free or reduced cost medical treatment under the auspices of Britain's National Health Service, so long as they carry with them the appropriate validated form. In the EU, this is the E111 form which covers families with dependent children up to the age of 16 (or 19, if in full-time education). The only things you will be expected to pay for are medical prescriptions (currently £5.95 a pop, these are dispensed at chemists, see below) and visits to the optician or dentist – although these are free to children, senior citizens and the unemployed.

Visitors from other countries should take out an appropriate level of medical insurance.

In an emergency

If you or a member of your family requires urgent medical treatment, you should call an ambulance by dialling 999 or 112.

Chemists

Most high streets have a dispensing chemist where you must go to buy any medicine prescribed to you by a doctor. In Britain, only a limited range of drugs can be dispensed without a doctor's prescription. Chemists will also often stock a selection of basic medical and cosmetic products such as cough mixture, plasters (band aids), bandages, nappies and hairspray. Your local police station can provide a list of late-opening chemists. *See* below for a list of useful telephone numbers and addresses.

Action for Sick Children t (020) 7833 2041 provides advice to help parents get the best possible health care for their children

The Health Education Authority Hotline
t 0800 555777, freephone advisory number
Medical Advisory Service for Travellers Abroad
t 0891 224100
St John's Ambulance Supplies t (020) 7278 7888, provides baby and toddler first-aid guides

Money and banks

The currency in Britain is the pound sterling (written £) which is divided into 100 pence (written p). There are 8 coin denominations: 1p, 2p, 5p, 20p, 50p, £1 and £2 (all issued by the Royal Mint) and 4 note denominations: £5, £10, £20 and £50 – the last is the most easily forged and you'll find that a number of shops and restaurants refuse to accept £50 notes in any circumstances. Most shops and restaurants accept the big name credit and debit cards: Visa, Delta, Mastercard, American Express, Barclaycard, Diners Club, Switch.

The biggest high street banks are Barclays, NatWest, HSBC and Lloyds. Most have automatic cash dispensers which can be used 24 hours a day and will often dispense money on foreign bank cards, although you will usually have to pay a hefty commission for the privilege. All banks are open from 9.30 to 3.30 although many are open later (till around 5pm) and some even open on Saturday mornings.

National holidays

Britain's national holidays are always arranged to fall on a Monday – Christmas, New Year's Day and Good Friday excepted. Shops and services tend to operate according to their Sunday template and banks are always closed. The full holiday list is

New Year's Day
Good Friday
Easter Monday
May Day (first Monday in May)
Spring Bank Holiday (last Monday in May)
Summer Bank Holiday (last Monday in August)
Christmas Day

Boxing Day (plus December 27 if either Christmas or Boxing Day fall on a weekend)

One-parent families

There are various organizations offering advice and support for single parents travelling with children:

Gingerbread, 16–17 Clerkenwell Close, EC1R
t (020) 7336 8183
The National Council for One Parent Families
255 Kentish Town Road, NW5 **t** (020) 7428 5400
One Parent Family Holidays t (01465) 821288
Women's Travel Advisory Bureau t (01386) 701082

Opening hours

The traditional opening times for shops and offices are 9–5.30 although these days, especially in cities and large towns, many shops observe a more continental-style day, 10–7 perhaps, and have one nominated day, usually Wednesday or Thursday, on which they stay open until 8 or 9. Sunday opening, most commonly between 12 noon and 5, has also become the norm in towns in recent years. Opening hours tend to be a little more restricted in rural areas where shops often have one nominated day (usually Wednesday) when they close early at around 1pm. Britain's pubs and restaurants observe very strict licensing laws – no alcohol can be served outside the period 11am–11pm. Motorway service stations stay open 24 hours a day.

Post offices

t 08457 223344 **www**.royalmail.com
You can buy stamps, post parcels and pay bills in post offices Mon–Fri 9–5.30 and Sat 9–12 noon, although there's no need to go to one to send a postcard. Newsagents sell stamps – the cost of sending a letter or postcard first class to anywhere in the UK or Europe is 27p; to America 44p – and post boxes, painted a distinctive red, are common.

Carrying money around with you
Pickpocketing is common in the big cities, especially in busy shopping areas. Use a money belt fastened around your waist under a tucked-in shirt or T-shirt. Otherwise, always keep wallets in your trouser pockets and hold purses and bags close to your body with the flap facing towards you and the strap over your shoulder.

There are usually four collections a day Mon–Sat, the last at 6pm, and one at 12 noon on Sunday.

Safety

In the event of an emergency you can call the Police/Fire Brigade/Ambulance on 999 or 112

You are at no greater risk on England's streets than you are in any other western country. England has its fair share of lawlessness but muggings and armed crime are, thankfully, still relatively uncommon. As you remain vigilant, and take sensible precautions with your valuables, you should be able to enjoy a largely trouble-free holiday.

Service stations

Three companies, Granada, Roadchef and Welcome Break, control 68 of the country's 74 service stations. They offer toilets, petrol and a chance to get off the road. Beside that, food prices are high and the quality, generally, is awful. A recent *Which?* report concluded that, of the bunch, Welcome Break offered the better food.

Special needs

There are a number of specialist tour operators in Britain which cater for the needs of physically disabled travellers – the Association of Independent Tour Operators **t** (020) 8607 9080 can provide a list, as can RADAR (Royal Association for Disability and Rehabilitation) **t** (020) 7250 3222 which also publishes its own guides to holidays and travel.

Telephones

Most modern pay phones accept coins (any denomination from 10p up) and phone cards (available in denominations of £1, £2, £5, £10 and £20 from any newsagent or post office) although some are either/or. Some booths let you pay by swiping a credit card. International calls are cheapest in the evening after 6pm and on weekends.

Useful numbers

Emergency (Police, Fire Brigade, Ambulance) **999** or **112**
Operator **100**
Directory enquiries **192**
International operator **155**
International directory enquiries **153**

International dialling codes

United States and Canada **00 1**
Ireland **00 353**
France **00 33**
Italy **00 39**
Germany **00 49**
Australia **00 61**
New Zealand **00 64**

Time

Britain or, more exactly, London is the official home of time. The prime meridian, the line of 0° longitude, runs through the quiet southeast London borough of Greenwich and, since 1884, Greenwich Mean Time (GMT) has been the standard against which all other times are set. GMT is usually one hour ahead of western Europe. In summer, however, the country switches to British Summer Time (BST) which is one hour ahead of GMT. Britain is 5 hours ahead of New York, 8 hours ahead of San Francisco and 10 hours behind Tokyo and Sydney.

In everyday conversation, the majority of people will use the 12 hour clock – 9am, 3pm – but printed event times and transport timetables are often given using the 24hr clock.

Tipping

10–15 per cent is the usual rate in restaurants, taxis and hairdressers. You are not obliged to tip, however, especially if the service was unsatisfactory. You would not normally tip a bartender in a pub. Restaurants sometimes add a service charge of 10–15 per cent which should be shown on the menu. Tipping staff, such as chambermaids and porters, is discretionary.

Toilets

The whereabouts of the nearest toilet is perhaps the single most important piece of information a parent can know. Public loos are most commonly found in train and bus stations (where you may be expected to pay a small fee, usually 20p), motorway service stations, large department stores as well as some fast food outlets (notably McDonald's and Burger King). Pubs and restaurants, however, will often only let you use their facilities (even in an emergency) if you're going to buy something. Street toilets are now an increasingly rare sight. The type you are most likely to come across are free-standing automatic toilets known, in local parlance, as 'super loos' but, be warned, your 20p entitles you to precisely 15 minutes' use of the facilities after which the door will swoosh open revealing you (in whatever stage of undress) to the street.

Best for...

King of the castles

Sandy shores

Park life

On the rails

Toast of the coasters

Also available from Cadogan Guides

Italy

Italy
Italy: The Bay of Naples and Southern Italy
Italy: Lombardy and the Italian Lakes
Italy: Tuscany, Umbria and the Marches
Italy: Tuscany
Italy: Umbria
Italy: Northeast Italy
Italy: Italian Riviera
Italy: Bologna and Emilia Romagna
Italy: Rome and the Heart of Italy
Sardinia
Sicily
Rome, Florence, Venice
Florence, Siena, Pisa & Lucca
Venice

Spain

Spain
Spain: Andalucía
Spain: Northern Spain
Spain: Bilbao and the Basque Lands
Granada, Seville, Cordoba
Madrid, Barcelona, Seville

Greece

Greece: The Peloponnese
Greek Islands
Greek Islands By Air
Corfu & the Ionian Islands
Mykonos, Santorini & the Cyclades
Rhodes & the Dodecanese
Crete

France

France
France: Dordogne & the Lot
France: Gascony & the Pyrenees
France: Brittany
France: Loire
France: The South of France
France: Provence
France: Côte d'Azur
Corsica
Short Breaks in Northern France

The UK and Ireland

London–Amsterdam
London–Edinburgh
London–Paris
London–Brussels

Scotland
Scotland: Highlands and Islands
Edinburgh

Ireland
Ireland: Southwest Ireland
Ireland: Northern Ireland

Other Europe

Portugal
Portugal: The Algarve
Madeira & Porto Santo

Malta
Germany: Bavaria
Holland

The City Guide Series

Amsterdam
Brussels
Paris
Rome
Barcelona
Madrid
London
Florence
Prague
Bruges
Sydney

Cadogan Guides are available from good bookshops, or via **Grantham Book Services**, Isaac Newton Way, Alma Park Industrial Estate, Grantham NG31 9SD, **t** (01476) 541 080, **f** (01476) 541 061; and **The Globe Pequot Press**, 246 Goose Lane, PO Box 480, Guilford, Connecticut 06437–0480, **t** (800) 458 4500/**f** (203) 458 4500, **t** (203) 458 4603.

take the kids
Short breaks touring atlas

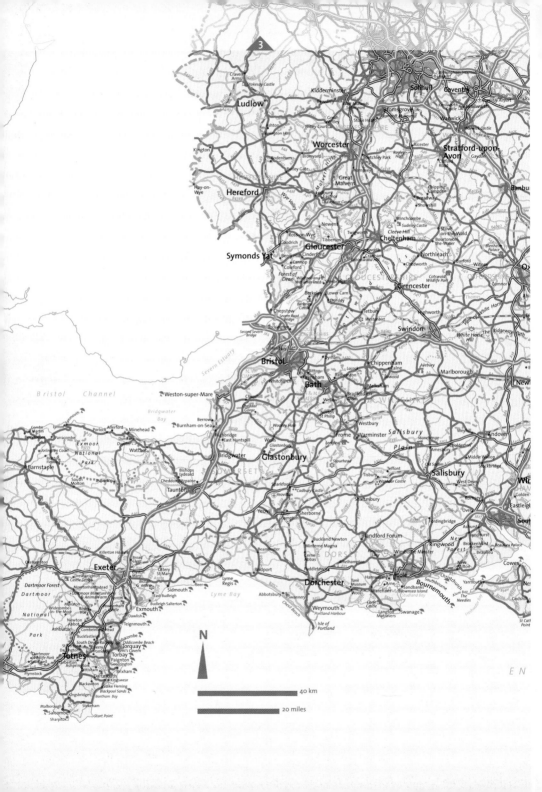

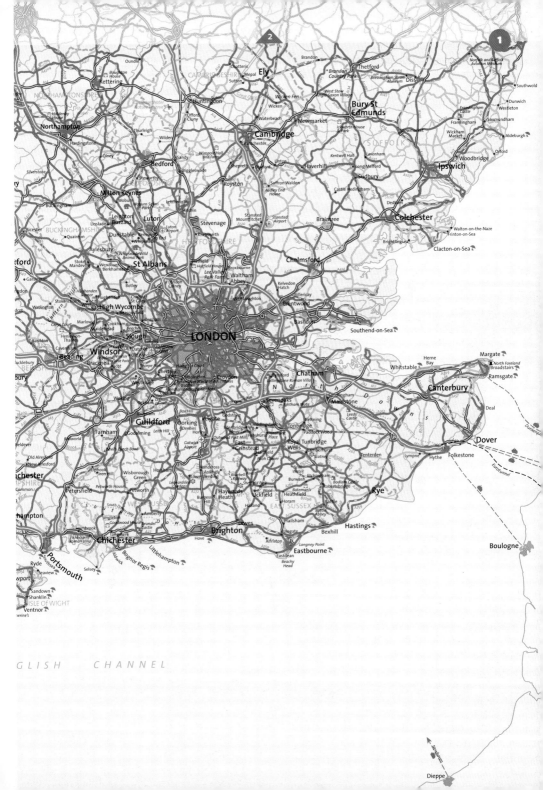

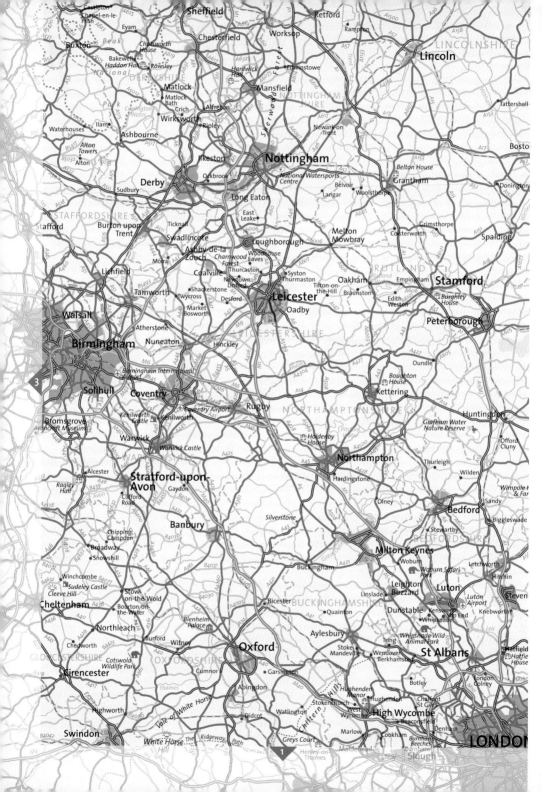

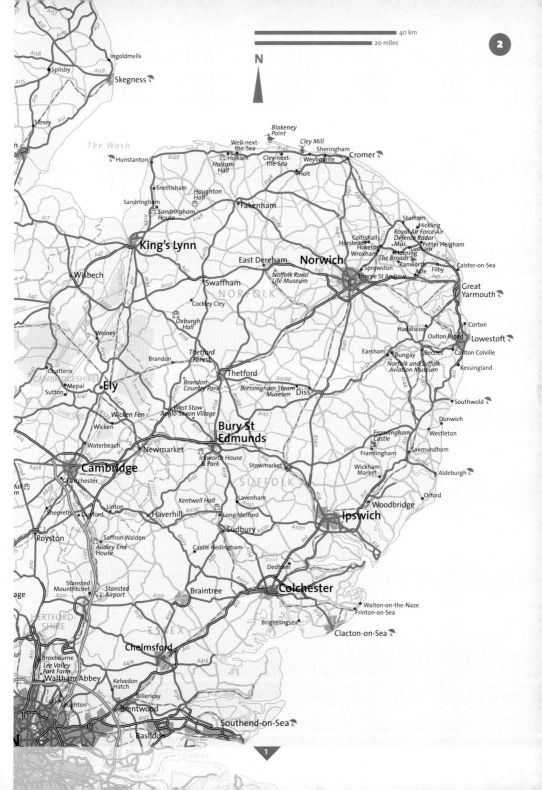

40 km
20 miles

N

A158   Ingoldmells

Spilsby   A158

A155   Skegness

A16

Sibsey   A52

A17

The Wash

Hunstanton   A149   Well-next-the-Sea   *Blakeney Point*   Cley Mill

Holkham   *Holkham Hall*   Cley-next-the-Sea   Sheringham   Weybourne   Cromer

Snettisham   *Houghton Hall*   Holt

Sandringham   *Sandringham House*   A148   Fakenham

A17

Wisbech   King's Lynn   A47

East Dereham   *Nolfolk Rural Life Museum*   Stalham   Hickling

Swaffham   Coltishall   *Royal Air Force Air Defence Radar Mus.*   Ludham   Potter Heigham

A1122   Horstead   Hoveton   Horning

NORFOLK   Wroxton   *The Broads*

Cockley Cley   Norwich   Sprowston   Ranworth   Acle   Filby   Caister-on-Sea

Oxburgh Hall   Thorpe St Andrew

Welney   Great Yarmouth

Chatteris   CAMBRIDGESHIRE   Brandon   *Thetford Forest*   Haddiscoe   Corton

Mepal   Ely   *Brandon Country Park*   Thetford   A1066   Earsham   Oulton Broad   Lowestoft

Sutton   A142   *Bressingham Steam Museum*   Diss   Bungay   Beccles   Carlton Colville

Wicken Fen   *West Stow Anglo-Saxon Village*   *Norfolk and Suffolk Aviation Museum*   Kessingland

Wicken   Southwold

Waterbeach   Newmarket   Bury St Edmunds   Dunwich   Westleton

Cambridge   *Ickworth House & Park*   *Framlingham Castle*   Saxmundham

Grantchester   Stowmarket   Framlingham   Aldeburgh

SUFFOLK   Wickham Market

Shepreth   Linton   Duxford   *Kentwell Hall*   Lavenham   Orford

Royston   Haverhill   Long Melford   Woodbridge

Saffron Walden   Sudbury   Ipswich

Audley End House   Castle Hedingham

Stansted Mountfitchet   Stansted Airport   Dedham

HERTFORD-SHIRE   Braintree   Colchester   Walton-on-the-Naze

ESSEX   Frinton-on-Sea

Broxbourne   *Lee Valley Park Farm*   Brightlingsea   Clacton-on-Sea

Waltham Abbey   Kelvedon Hatch   Chelmsford

Loughton   Billericay   Brentwood   Southend-on-Sea

Basildon

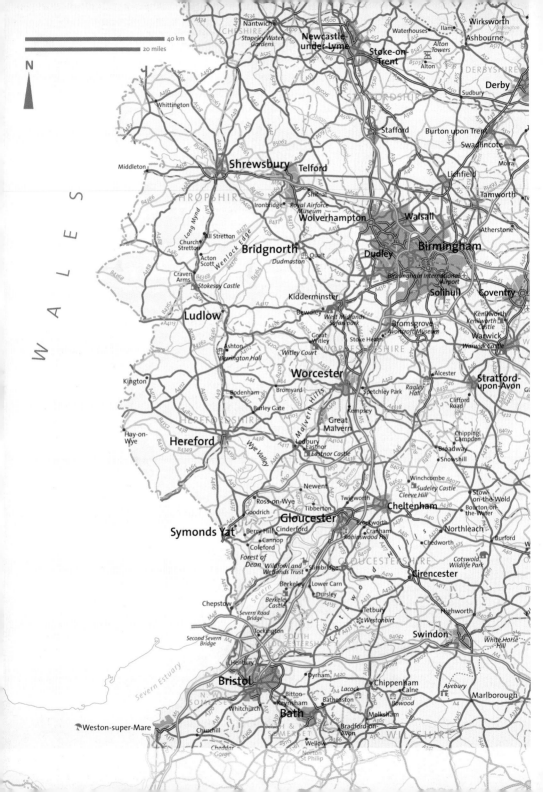

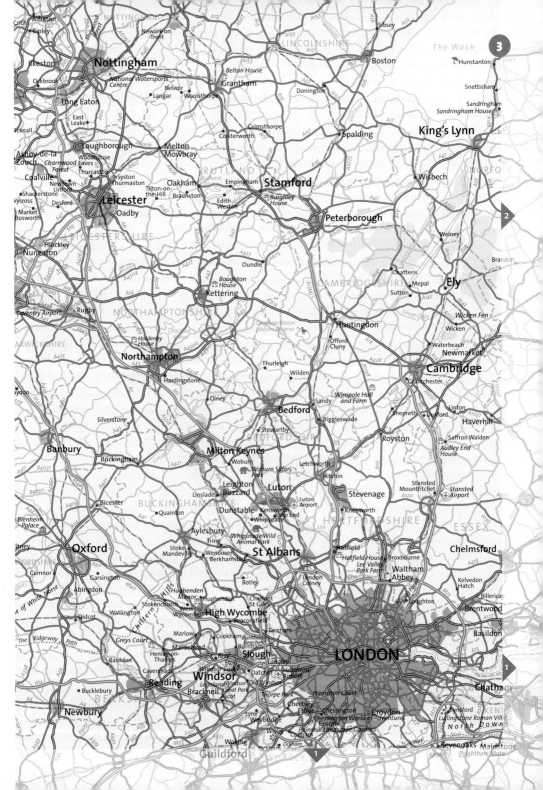

take the kids series

▶ the first series of its kind for parents
▶ lots of family holiday ideas, top tips and themes
▶ expert advice on health, safety and budgets
▶ what to do in an emergency
▶ stress-busting games and stories for bored kids

titles 2003

▶ South of France
▶ Southern Spain

also available

▶ London
▶ England
▶ Paris And Disneyland® Resort Paris
▶ Travelling

Further information
Cadogan Guides
Network House
1 Ariel Way
London
W12 7SL
t (020) 8600 3550
f (020) 8600 3599
e info@cadoganguides.com
www.cadoganguides.com

Distribution
Grantham Book Services Ltd
Isaac Newton Way
Alma Park Industial Estate
Grantham
NG31 9SD
t (01476) 541080
f (01476) 541061